Statutes in Court

Statutes in Court

The History and Theory of Statutory Interpretation

William D. Popkin

Duke University Press

Durham & London 1999

© 1999 Duke University Press
All rights reserved
Printed in the United States of America on acid-free paper ∞
Designed by Rebecca Filene
Typeset in Sabon by Tseng Information Systems, Inc.
Library of Congress Cataloging-in-Publication Data
appear on the last printed page of this book.

To my wife, Prema

Contents

Preface

My interest in statutory interpretation goes back a long way, to my years in law school and especially to my tax teacher, Ernest Brown. I cannot tell if he would approve of any of my conclusions, but he is responsible for my lifelong fascination with how statutory meaning is determined and I thank him for that.

I also want to express my appreciation to my students and colleagues over the years, who have been a constant source of questions and information. They greatly enriched my thinking. Special thanks go to my colleagues, Dan Conkle and Bruce Markell, who read and commented on earlier drafts of this book.

Introduction

It must come as a surprise to nonlawyers that statutory interpretation has had to claw its way into the legal consciousness of American scholars.[1] The explanation is simple: we are a common law country. Just as European authors find it difficult to fit case law into a world of statutory codes, so we have trouble fitting statutes into a common law system. It also has not helped that the great common law lawyer Justice Benjamin Cardozo warned that "no man can make [statutory construction] interesting."[2]

But signs of a change are at hand. The last twenty-five years have seen an explosion of interest in the field of statutory interpretation.[3] We now have a well-developed understanding of what law and economics and literary criticism can contribute to determining statutory meaning. We also have a much better understanding of what we mean by the raw material of statutory interpretation—text, legislative intent, legislative history, etc.—on which to build a sophisticated analysis of how judges determine the meaning of statutes. Moreover, authors in specific substantive fields of law are growing more aware of statutory interpretation as a discipline and are integrating its insights into studies of particular statutes, the way common law analysis has always infiltrated into specific fields of substantive common law.

However, something of a crisis looms. As the pragmatists warn us, no single perspective provides the appropriate lens for addressing all interpretive issues. And this reality has led to concern that, without a key to interpretive analysis, the effort to develop theories of statutory interpretation must fail or at least lack rigor. But the need for analytical rigor has never paralyzed common law decision-making and should not concern those who seek to fit statutes into a common law world. What is missing in the current literature is a sense of historical perspective—of the way statutory interpretation has evolved—that can help us understand how statutes fit into our law without insisting on more rigor than is appropriate to the task. These pages attempt to provide that perspective.

This book is dominated by one major idea and one major thesis—both informed by a historical perspective. The major idea is to adopt the second of two rival views of law that influence the role of the judge in statutory interpretation. The first view adopts an "airtight compartment" conception of legislating and judging. It allocates the lawmaking function exclusively to legislatures, with judges accorded only a minimal role. In its extreme form, this is an impossible view to maintain in a country with a common law tradition. But in a modified form it holds a respectable position in allocating lawmaking responsibility exclusively to legislatures when the area of the law is created by or preempted by legislation, and allowing a judicial lawmaking role only in areas of common law purposely left open by legislation or delegated by legislatures to judges.

The second view of the interaction of legislating and judging is that law is an overarching concept (what Guido Calabresi calls a legal landscape or broader fabric of law) into which all specific sources of law must fit—whether statutes or common law. In either case, judges play a discretionary lawmaking role in working out that fit. It is not easy in modern times, after a long period of judicial arrogance and the twentieth-century Legal Realist critique of "political" judging, to sustain this view. The modern challenge is to defend that discretionary judicial role drained of judicial arrogance.

The major thesis of this book is that the best perspective for understanding the discretionary judicial role is an understanding of "ordinary judging," whereby judges indulge a modest competence to contribute to good government. In the context of statutory interpretation, this competence resides in helping to fit statutes into their past and future—their temporal dimension. This approach rejects legitimacy as the preferred way to understand the judicial role. Although questions of legitimacy loom large at critical junctures in any country's legal history—such as the American Revolutionary-Constitutional period (1776 through 1789) and the New Deal—the rhetoric of legitimacy provides an inadequate understanding of what judicial institutions are expected to do. More mundane questions of institutional competence have always played a greater role in determining what courts can do than questions of legitimacy; such mundane questions have, in fact, been the dominant historical force in shaping judgments about judicial behavior. Indeed, the only thing new about the emphasis on institutional competence in the Legal Process approach to lawmaking, which achieved its final formulation in the late 1950s, was its emphasis on the competence of twentieth-century institutions (that is, agencies and legislatures), not on its adoption of a competence perspective on lawmaking in general and judging in particular. This conclusion does not simplify matters. Plenty of opportunities arise to dispute who is competent to make certain decisions and what counts as competent or incompetent decision-making. But the competence perspective is where the debate should focus.

Ordinary judging also supplies what is missing in contemporary pragmatism. It shares with modern pragmatism the rejection of strong foundationalism—the disposition to ground the judicial role in statutory interpretation on a special role for the court in protecting fundamental rights, in making up for deficiencies in the legislative process, and in helping to reveal the dynamic evolutionary aspects of statutory meaning. But it does not yield to the tendency in modern pragmatism to go to the other extreme—lapsing into a description of what judges do. No one has struggled more subtly or creatively with these issues than William Eskridge, but even his work shows signs of a swing from a more or less strong foundationalism (in the form of dynamic evolutionary interpretation[4] and an emphasis on fundamental values)[5] to a descriptive pragmatism (in the form of a model of interpretive criteria used by courts).[6] Ordinary judging provides a weak foundationalist justification for an affirmative judicial role in statutory interpretation without lapsing into either strong foundationalism or descriptive pragmatism.

The book is divided into two parts. Part I provides the historical perspective, and Part II explains ordinary judging. The four chapters of Part I trace the history of statutory interpretation up to about 1960. Chapter 1 examines English history through the eighteenth century to observe the early dominance of common law courts over legislation well into the period when legislative sovereignty ostensibly provided the standard of legitimate lawmaking. This was a period of "equitable interpretation," which allowed courts to limit or extend statutes to implement the spirit of the law. The singular brief quotation that captures the view of English judges about judging and legislating is from Lord Mansfield, written in the eighteenth century: "[t]he common law . . . works itself pure by rules drawn from the fountain of justice," and "*for this reason* [it is] superior to an act of parliament" (emphasis added).[7]

Chapter 2 looks at the American experience, beginning around the time of the Revolution. For a brief period, legitimacy seemed to dominate competence as the critical issue in working out the relationship of legislating and judging, and, indeed, it never completely disappeared from the American scene. But with the advent of the United States in 1789, legitimacy recedes as the dominant framework for understanding the relationship of legislation to judging.

Chapter 3 turns to the nineteenth century. Initially, we encounter a period of cooperation between legislature and courts, though the potential for rivalry based on appeals to popular sovereignty remained close to the surface. The middle to end of the nineteenth century witnessed a resurgence of judicial claims to lawmaking competence (based on a "science" of the common law), which could not help but take the form of hostility to an increasingly robust legislature. This hostility most famously took the form of early twentieth-century decisions establishing constitutional limits on legislation that interfered with common law rights, but it also led to interpreting statutes to prevent them from overriding the common law.

Chapter 4 discusses the decades up to about 1960, when the growing sense of legislative competence made judicial claims to lawmaking superiority impossible to sustain, and the interaction between legislation and judging took the form of a collaborative relationship under the umbrella of purposivist interpretation. Purposivism charged courts with the responsibility of sympathetically elaborating legislative purpose—a kind of extensive equitable interpretation. Many observers viewed purposive interpretation as requiring a creative judicial role—though for some this risk was to be avoided, for others it was a normal feature of judging. But as long as there was faith in legislation as the product of "reasonable persons pursuing reasonable purposes reasonably" (the 1958 Legal Process formulation), creative judging and legislating formed a defensible collaborative partnership.

Part II deals with the modern period and a decline of confidence in legislating, which had significant effects on interpretive theory. From both Right and Left, the image of legislation took a beating. From the Right, no purpose was worth elaborating or promoting. From the Left, a cultural bias prevented certain voices from being heard in the legislative forum. This inability to be heard had two consequences for statutory interpretation. First, there was a retreat to textualism—giving judges as little to do as possible (chapter 5). Second, efforts were made to give judges something to do, either robustly through Republicanism, or with as much restraint as possible through the use of traditional substantive canons of interpretation (chapter 6).

None of these modern efforts seemed entirely satisfactory, however. They were too extreme in their affirmative and negative claims about legislating and judging. This shortcoming led to a retreat to pragmatism, although just what constitutes a pragmatic theory of statutory interpretation has not always been clear. Chapter 7 is my effort to provide such a theory. It emphasizes "ordinary judging" as the interpretive theory that gives judges something (but not too much) to do and that fits best with our legal traditions. Ordinary judging rests on the view that judges can reasonably lay a modest claim to lawmaking competence, helping the legislature implement good government by fitting statutes into their past and their future (their temporal dimension). In addition, ordinary judging comes as close as anything can to being an inevitable aspect of judging because through the application of a text to facts the judge is forced to think about how the text fits into its past and its future. Finally, once the judge accepts the responsibility to engage in ordinary judging, he or she must make judgments about substantive values and comparative institutional competence. Yet no foundational theory explains what those judgments should be, nor does it provide the justification for ordinary judging in the first place. Substantive and institutional judgments follow *from* ordinary judging; they do not justify it in the first place.

The audience for this book should consist of those who are concerned with conscientious judging. It assumes what may not necessarily be the case: that a judge should (and probably wants to) develop and articulate a coherent approach to statutory interpretation. Some judges undoubtedly question that assumption for one or more of the following reasons. Developing a theory of interpretation may seem too daunting. Substantive considerations may dominate decision-making to such a degree that the rhetoric of statutory interpretation is only a peripheral and manipulated byproduct of opinion-writing. The pressures of time and the need for collegial agreement deprive opinions of the coherence required by any interpretive theory; this incoherence of judicial opinions may even be a positive virtue, paying deference to the multiple plausible theories of statutory interpretation, refusing to insist on any one theory.

This dose of realism about statutory interpretation and judicial opinion-writing serves an important function. It reminds us that a theory of interpretation cannot account for everything a judge does when determining statutory meaning or writing an opinion. But sometimes theory matters, and I suspect that many judges who strive for conscientious statutory interpretation are hampered by the lack of a framework in which to fit their approach and a well-understood common vocabulary to explain what they do. In any event, this book is aimed at those for whom these issues are a serious concern, whether they be judges or those who look critically at judging.

Part I

The Evolution of Statutory Interpretation:

English Antecedents and United States Experience

Our thinking about statutory interpretation is the product of a long period of evolution from earliest English practice to the modern period. This part of the book traces that evolution to about 1960, just before the disintegration of faith in *both* legislating and judging that characterizes the modern debate about statutory interpretation.

Two references in the title are more than casual introductory terms. First, the "experience" of judging has never been as extreme as the rhetoric used to explain the judicial role in statutory interpretation. The rhetoric tends to emphasize questions of legitimacy, kept in reserve to respond in moments of political crisis. But the day-to-day task of ordinary judging proceeds in the light of more mundane considerations, allocating decision-making among different institutions on the basis of lawmaking competence rather than lawmaking legitimacy. We can understand statutory interpretation much better by building our sense of the judicial role upward from the experience of ordinary judging rather than dwelling obsessively on questions of legitimacy.

Second, our experience has been of an "evolution" of ideas, not a revolution. Although the American Revolutionary and Constitutional periods reshaped the inherited English tradition, this restructuring was done with nothing like the upheaval experienced on the Continent as a result of the French Revolution. As a consequence, no clear picture of the judicial role in statutory interpretation emerges from the period from 1776 until 1789. Instead, the process of evolutionary change in approaches to statutory interpretation continued after the Revolution, incorporating the impact of ideas about popular sovereignty. That evolutionary process has continued to this day.

Chapter 1 presents the English tradition through the end of the eighteenth century. Chapter 2 recounts how the American experience reworked the inherited tradition from 1776 until 1789. Chapter 3 explains how that tradition evolved in the nineteenth century when the experience of increased reliance on legislation and the efforts at accommodating the interaction between statutes and the common law produced both collaboration and, eventually, conflict between judges and legislatures. Chapter 4 explains how the twentieth century witnessed the search to overcome this conflict through purposive interpretation. These chapters provide the groundwork for understanding the crisis in modern statutory interpretation, which arises from the collapse of the foundations on which nineteenth-century and twentieth-century approaches to statutory interpretation rested.

1 English History

Early Tradition

By the time of the American Revolution, England had a long tradition of statutory interpretation. Just how much of this tradition entered into the American bloodstream will be explored in chapter 2, but there is no doubt that previous English approaches influenced legal thought in this country. We therefore begin with a review of how the English bench and bar conceptualized the judge's interpretive role. The story is familiar in its broad outline, but we need to mine it for those features that continue to shape our thinking about statutory interpretation.[1]

The most obvious point is that statutory interpretation could not exist until legislatures developed a sense of separation from judging. Until that sense was achieved, nothing was "out there" to interpret. Separation occurred gradually from the thirteenth to seventeenth centuries. Initially, in the thirteenth century, Parliament was a shifting group of powerful people summoned and discharged by the king. Parliament's job included agreeing to pay taxes (it did not legislate taxes so much as assent to requests for money), dealing with matters of state (often foreign affairs), responding to petitions (what we would call private legislation), and passing some general rules (often prompted by petitions). Parliament was not so much a body as an occasion at which people met to parley or speak with the king as they saw fit. As Thorne notes: "Who could then say what a statute was, or be certain that any particular document was a statute? Who could say, even, what the actual words of any acknowledged statute really were?"

In this environment, English judges simply did the best they could to decide cases with whatever materials were available, including whatever Parliament had done. A shared sense of a common enterprise between Parliament and the courts, based on the common training and political experience of judges and legislators, reflected this blurring of institutional authority. Judge Hengham could, with reason and authority, tell counsel in 1305: "Do not gloss the statute; we understand it better than you, for we made it."[2]

During the following centuries, Parliament gradually separated itself from judging, acquiring the attributes of a modern lawmaking institution. By the middle of the seventeenth century, it had successfully asserted the right to determine its members' qualifications, to impeach officials, and to avoid arrest. Parliament's developing affirmative sense of lawmaking authority was evidenced by general legislation, publishing sessions laws, writing preambles for statutes, initiating legislation, keeping journals (the House of Lords beginning in 1509; the House of Commons in 1547), and conducting business by formal internal procedures. Finally, Parliament established its right to convene and remain in session without depending on the king's pleasure.

Parliament's growing sense of institutional competence was eventually accompanied by the acquisition of sovereignty at the end of the seventeenth century. In response to the Stuart monarchy's claim to sovereignty in the early seventeenth century, Parliament asserted its rights—eventually initiating a civil war in 1642, disposing of Charles I in 1649 (by beheading), and setting up a nonmonarchical commonwealth from 1649 until 1660. The Interregnum even witnessed that traditional harbinger of legislative lawmaking potency—a serious political movement for codification of the entire law (including common law).[3] Thereafter, England restored the monarchy, but further conflict with the Crown resulted in the Glorious Revolution of 1688, which established the principle of parliamentary sovereignty.

These changes in Parliament's organization and legal authority had some effect on the relationship of legislation to judging, including statutory interpretation—or at least it had an effect on the rhetoric used to explain how judges interpreted legislation. It would be premature, however, to view the institutional separation of Parliament from judges by the end of the seventeenth century against a background of modern separation of powers doctrine in the sense of separate institutional roles for the judicial and legislative branches. Throughout this period *the* serious rival to Parliament was the Crown, not the courts. Parliament *and* the courts both appealed to the common law in their battles with the Crown, and the common law was viewed as Parliament's source of privilege and authority. Despite the fact that Parliament was obviously making law, the idea persisted, long after the reality was otherwise, that it was only declaring what customary common law had been.

Moreover, the shared sense of common enterprise of which Judge Hengham spoke in the early fourteenth century never completely left English judges. They continued to share membership with legislators in a close-knit ruling elite and to serve as both judges and legislators, sometimes simultaneously. Even the judges' practice of claiming privileged knowledge of what the statute meant because they drafted the legislation had not died out entirely in the late seventeenth century.[4] And the House of Lords did not clearly relinquish its power to make legal decisions to a specialized group of Law Lords until the 1800s.[5]

In sum, both Parliament and courts in theory were under the law, and, for the most part, judges continued to view themselves as the senior partners in the collaborative effort to identify what that law was.

Equitable Interpretation

THEORY

There was, however, enough separation between the English Parliament and the English courts for judges to require a theory of statutory interpretation that would still preserve the dominant judicial role. That theory was known as "equitable interpretation." Judges came to think of statutes as *both* letter and spirit; and the "spirit" was referred to as the "equity of the statute." "Equity" had two meanings: (1) the statute's objective and (2) substantive background considerations, usually derived from the common law. Courts could limit or expand the statute beyond what the letter appeared to say to implement "equity" in either sense of the term. Thorne argues that judges were more likely to limit than to extend statutes, reflecting their jealous attachment to the common law that was threatened by legislation, but no sign of that distinction is given in the best-known explanation of equitable interpretation in the late sixteenth century, Plowden's *Commentaries*.

Plowden appended commentaries to his reports of decided cases, and his comments reporting the 1574 case of Eyston v. Studd dwelt at length on statutory interpretation.[6] The clear message is that something underlying the text is the "real" law—what he calls the "soul of the law." "[O]ur law (like all others) consists of two parts, viz. of body and soul, the letter of the law is the body of the law, and the sense and reason of the law is the soul of the law . . . ." Consequently, Plowden says, you may know the letter, but not the sense, "for sometimes the sense is more confined and contracted than the letter, and sometimes it is more large and extensive." It is "equity" which "enlarges or diminishes the letter according to its discretion. . . . And this correction of the general words is much used in the law of England. . . ."

Moreover, the soul of the law is what the judge *should* seek when interpreting a statute. Plowden analogizes law to a nut that has a shell (the letter) and a kernel (the sense), and "the fruit and profit of the nut lies in the kernel, and not in the shell [and] the fruit and profit of the law consists in the sense more than in the letter." Furthermore, "if there is any defect in the law, it should be reformed by equity, which is no part of the law, but a moral virtue which corrects the law."

Plowden describes the judge as someone who carries on a conversation with the hypothetical lawmaker, an image that we will see revived in Judge Learned Hand's twentieth-century writings about statutory interpretation: "[I]n order to form a right judgment when the letter of a statute is restrained, and when enlarged, by equity, it is a good way, when you peruse a statute, to suppose that the law-maker is present, and that you have asked him the question you want to know touching the equity, then you must give yourself such an answer as you imagine he would have done, if he had been present."

Several important observations should be made about Plowden's approach which invite historical comparison to later approaches to statutory interpretation. First, he does not shy away from the word "discretion" to describe judging. Second, statutes are not their texts. Third, equitable interpretation is good: it is a "moral virtue" that "corrects" the law.

Fourth, and most important, judges have an unself-conscious sense of their legal competence, which is apparent in the following quotation from another lesser-known observation by Plowden. Although this short quotation appears to pay judicial deference to the intent of absent legislative drafters (to their "minds"), it affirms that it is judicial "sage"-like "talent" that is required to perform the task of construing legislative words when legislators are (inevitably) "dispersed":

> For words, which are no other than the *verberation of the air* (emphasis added), do not constitute the statute, but are only the image of it, and the life of the statute rests in the minds of the expositors of the words, that is, the makers of the statutes. And if they are dispersed, so that their minds cannot be known, then those who may approach nearest to their minds shall construe the words, and these are the sages of the law whose talents are exercised in the study of such matters.[7]

Plowden is not alone in emphasizing sagelike judicial competence. Another sixteenth-century treatise on statutory interpretation, written by Lord Chancellor (Sir Christopher) Hatton, first notes that legislators are not available to explain the statute they passed, and then describes judicial power in these terms: "For the sages of the law . . . have the interpretation in their hands, and their authority no man taketh in hand to control: wherefore their power is very great, and high, and we seek their interpretation as oracles from their mouthes."[8]

PRACTICE

To our modern ears, attuned to separation of powers concerns, the judicial claim to sagelike oracular wisdom is too arrogant, but that may be an anachronistic judgment. Although sixteenth-century judges evinced a confidence in their abilities that we would find excessive, they operated in a very different legal environment. Neither statutes nor legislatures were anything like what they are today. Statutes were understood to provide partial rather than comprehensive solutions. And legislatures were engaged in a shared responsibility to determine the law along with judges. Nothing like a modern doctrine of separation of powers deprived judges of the power to fit statutes into the law, and it would be inaccurate to label judges arrogant when they made the attempt.

At least some of the examples used by commentators to illustrate equitable interpretation suggest that judicial "sages" were engaged in a relatively modest task. Plowden's examples reveal an innocent judicial objective of helping the legislature achieve its more or less obvious goal. His first two examples limit the reach of the criminal law: a statute defines a crime in general language, but the court exempts infants and people of unsound mind from the letter; and a statute defines as an accessory to a crime anyone who gives food to the criminal, but the court interprets the law to excuse the wife who feeds her husband. These are commonsensical exceptions, providing relief from the overbreadth of general language, and implementing traditional common law rules about criminal responsibility and spousal relationships.

Moreover, Plowden was not adopting any special rule to limit the reach of *criminal* statutes (known today as the rule of lenity). In his comments to Eyston v. Studd, he rejects any special rule for penal laws, stating: "[E]quity knows no difference between penal laws and others, for the intent, (which is the only thing regarded by equity . . .) ought to be followed and taken for law, as well in penal laws as in others." The actual judicial practice of the time regarding penal statutes is unclear. Thorne suggests that penal statutes could not be extended by equity, but they could be limited (e.g., "park" cannot be extended to include "forest").[9] But Hatton states that some penal statutes can be extended by equity when they remedy a great mischief; however, equitable extension is improper if the law inflicts "grevious punishments" unless "the words may bear an equity itself" (as when murder of a "master" also applies to murder of a "mistress").[10]

Other examples from Plowden reveal an unself-conscious judicial effort to help the legislature achieve its goals—by expanding as well as limiting the text. (1) A statute aimed at preventing jailers from extorting money from inmates was interpreted not to apply to a traditional award of money to pay for certain services performed by the jailer; (2) a requirement that the sheriff retain and not sell goods from a shipwreck, so that ownership could be determined later, did not apply to perishables; (3) "executors" includes administrators; and (4) the phrase "life or for years" also applied to a transaction of only one year.[11]

Many of Hatton's examples of equitable interpretation were also similarly unremarkable. A statute that prohibited giving alms to a beggar was interpreted as not applying if the beggar would die before reaching another town where relief might be afforded; a law prohibiting breaking out of prison would not apply if the prison was on fire; executors included administrators; and a statute applying to "officers" was limited to the king's officers, based on what the statutory preface said about the scope of the statute.[12]

Some examples of equitable interpretation will not, however, strike us as unremarkable exercises of judicial power. A likely illustration is the most famous statutory interpretation case from the sixteenth century—Heydon's Case (1584). The court was faced with a statute that listed transfers of specific types of property which could not be used to avoid Henry VIII's seizure of church property. The statute failed to list a "copyhold" interest, however, and transfers of this type of interest were being used to evade the law. The court extended the statute to cover copyholds.

The report of the opinion contains a statement about how to interpret statutes. After listing three interpretive criteria—the prior common law, the mischief for which it failed to provide, and the legislative remedy—the court invoked the "true reason of the remedy," arguing that "the office of all the judges is always to make such construction as shall suppress the mischief and advance the remedy, and to suppress subtle inventions and evasions for continuance of the mischief. . . ." Reliance on the "true reason of the remedy" is another version of "equity," allowing the judge to rely on the spirit rather than the letter of the law. And it is this bold claim to implement the "reason of the remedy" that might strike us as an excessive assertion of judicial power.

Thorne suggests that we should be cautious in characterizing Heydon's Case as an example of bold judging. In his view, it was little more than the judge engaging in equitable interpretation to help the legislature out by allowing for "the strict, literal meaning of a statute [to] be extended, but only *slightly* extended" (emphasis added). Samuel Thorne makes this point in part to disagree with a claim by James Landis that the twentieth-century interpretive practice of relying on legislative purpose—where the court exercises judgment about whether the statute's purposes should be enthusiastically embraced—had a secure foundation in Heydon's Case.[13] Because other cases undermine Thorne's claim, it would be unproductive for us to try to decide whether Heydon's Case is only a "slight" extension or whether it foreshadowed modern purposivist interpretation (explained in chapter 4).

For example, Thorne cites the case of applying a law dealing with the "death of a husband" to a case of a dissolved marriage,[14] which (despite Thorne's characterization) can hardly be viewed as a slight extension. Moreover, other examples of sixteenth-century statutory interpretation are similar to modern purposivism, where the court "liberally" interprets a statute. An example from the turn of the seventeenth century is the case law that grew up around a statute protecting creditors from the debtor's efforts to frustrate debt collection by property transfers. In Twyne's Case,[15] the court dealt with an exception in a statute that otherwise voided transfers in fraud of creditors. The exception allowed "*bona fide*" transfers, but the court construed this exception not to apply to any transfers in which the debtor retained possession of the transferred property. "[B]ecause fraud and deceit abound in these days more than in former times, . . . all statutes made against fraud should be liberally and beneficially expounded to suppress the fraud."

The point we can properly take from Thorne's observations is that these extensions and liberal interpretations, although they may strike us as examples of bold judging, were second nature to judges in helping the legislature to make law. Whatever their relation to modern purposivism, such extensions and interpretations were almost certainly unproblematic in the context of sixteenth-century legislating and judging when statutes were considered partial and tentative solutions for general problems.

Not everyone would agree with this characterization of judging as a more or less innocent effort to help legislatures make law. One observer described judging in this early period as a "process [that] has occasionally been carried to such an unwarrantable extent as to justify the expression of driving a coach and four through Acts of Parliament."[16] The setting in which this judging was most likely to occur was one in which a statute threatened to override the common law. A typical comment invoked the canon of statutory construction that "all acts which restrain the common law ought themselves to be restrained by exposition." [17] Hatton's sixteenth-century work explicitly affirmed that statutes which "derogate" the common law should be strictly construed.

If such bolder acts of judging in fact occurred, they undoubtedly sprung from what a judge in 1616 referred to as "that liberty and authority which judges have over laws, *especially over statute laws*, according to reason and best convenience, to mould them to the truest and best use" (emphasis added).[18] The reference to "convenience" sounds innocent enough, but it marked out a range of judicial power that was widely expansive. By the nineteenth century, some judges adopted a more restrained role by drawing a line between the merely "convenient," which was not their province, and "fundamental" values, which courts continued to enforce. But expressions of a more modest judicial role lay in the future. In the meantime, the concern with "best convenience" allowed judges to be relatively aggressive in working out the relationship of statutes to the law, perhaps departing from what Parliament might have intended.

But there is still reason to be cautious in assuming that claims of judicial authority to deal with statutes—especially their interaction with the common law—were as hostile to legislation as they sound to modern ears. We view earlier practice through a lens that has been distorted by the late nineteenth-century hostility to legislation (discussed in chapter 3), which led courts to strike down some statutes that changed the common law as unconstitutional or, in the same spirit, to narrow the more or less obvious scope of statutes by arguably "spurious" interpretation. Some of these acts probably occurred in sixteenth- and seventeenth-century England, but many instances of "strict" interpretation were probably not so hostile.

Better-known examples of judging, which allegedly illustrate full-bodied judicial hostility to statutes, may be better understood as a more innocent effort to work out the relationship of legislation to the law at a time when statutes were admittedly incomplete and poorly drafted or were simply aged and lacking in legislative repair. The first example is the Statute of Uses, enacted in 1535. This law prevented property owners from engaging in conveyancing techniques that would deprive the king of feudal claims to revenues, something we would recognize today as a statute designed to prevent tax avoidance. According to Sir William Holdsworth, some commentators consider courts responsible for the statute's failure to achieve its purpose; but (Holdsworth also notes) any failure occurred only after the feudal rights protected by the statute had become obsolete a century after the law was passed.[19] We may think that 1535 and 1635 are close in time, but that astigmatism comes from viewing events through the wrong end of the temporal telescope. A hundred years is a long time for a statute to survive intact, and judges who undermine a century-old statute are hardly guilty of driving a coach and four through the legislation.

The second example is the Statute of Frauds, a 1677 law designed to reduce fraudulent claims about the formation and contents of a contract. This statute was not received warmly by many judges. Arthur Corbin states that the statute was "amputated and bandaged" by the courts, which did "bold constructive work, carving out exceptions and making limitations," because the statute ran "counter to the habits and practices of mankind."[20] But, as Holdsworth explains,[21] sensible reasons often were behind this judicial reaction. The statute's bad drafting was in part the result of the undeveloped shape of contract law at the time. Moreover, some of the less hospitable judges sat in courts of "equity," which had different procedures from courts of "law," and the procedures in equity courts made statutory protection from fraud less essential. Finally, some of the more hostile judicial reactions came more than a century later, when the statute was of a ripe age, from the pen of Lord Mansfield, whose tendency to make judgments as though he were sitting in a court of equity was well known.

One last illustration of judging from this period might seem to mark out an exceedingly bold judicial role in dealing with statutes, threatening to undermine legislation. Judges claimed the power to interpret statutes to prevent interference with "common right or reason," or what we might call fundamental rights. The most famous example was Dr. Bonham's Case (1610), where Lord Coke stated: "[I]t appears in our books that in many cases the common law will controul acts of parliament and sometimes adjudge them to be utterly void: for when an act of parliament is against common right or reason, or repugnant, or impossible to be performed, the common law will controul it and adjudge such Act to be void."[22] This statement often has been taken to assert a power of judicial review to strike down statutes, an obviously bold claim to judicial review that might also imply broad interpretive powers to protect fundamental rights. Thorne argues that something much less dramatic was going on in Bonham's Case. The specific issue was whether a doctor could be fined for the unlicensed practice of medicine. The occasion for the statement about the statute violating "common right or reason" was that doctors acted as judges to determine whether the fine should be imposed, and—since the doctors would derive some benefit from the fine—this action violated the principle that no person should decide a case in which he could benefit.[23] According to Thorne, application of this principle fell comfortably within the judge's traditional power to interpret a statute to avoid "absurd" results, which was nothing more than an example of judicial power to work out the relationship of statutes to the broader law, of which both statute law and common law were a part.[24]

This more limited reading of Bonham's Case fits well with what we know about Lord Edward Coke's views of judging and Parliament. Coke's professional life was concerned with opposing both the common law and Parliament to the Crown, not with opposing Parliament.[25] While speaker of the House of Commons, he worked to preserve parliamentary privilege against the Crown. Later, as a member of Parliament, he urged adoption of the Petition of Right, which protected common law rights from the exercise of the Crown's prerogative. And his famous statement about the law being *artificial* reason, known to judges, was directed against King James's claim to know *natural* reason, which could prove a rival to judicial authority.[26] (Coke also told the king that the king was protected by the law.[27] Other judges—perhaps influenced by the fact that judges at this time did not have tenure, but served at the pleasure of the Crown, affirmed the contrary—that "rex is lex" rather than "lex is rex.")[28]

The judge's privileged access to artificial reason certainly reflected judicial self-confidence in the ability to identify law. But, in support of Thorne's view, it made little sense that this power was invoked in *conflict* with Parliament. The English experience of linking Parliament *to* law,[29] and therefore to judging, was very different from the European experience, which ripened in the French Revolution, of opposing the legislature to judge-made law. If Coke was claiming the extraordinary power to declare statutes void, we might have expected some parliamentary objection, but none occurred. Interpreting a text to prevent overriding a strong common law principle protecting "common right or reason" simply prevented the unthinkable (the "absurd") rather than confronting Parliament with a rival claim of judicial power.

In sum, the judicial role in statutory interpretation was broad and undifferentiated. It extended and limited statutes to help out the legislature and to preserve the common law, both when the issues were matters of mere convenience and when they were fundamental. If the common law turned out to have a special pride of place, courts could hardly be faulted for reaching this conclusion because it was true. Judges not only viewed the common law as the predominant and preeminent source of law, but statutes were understood in terms of their relationship to that law—either declaratory of the common law, remedying a defect in the common law, or, in some cases, in derogation of the common law. Judges retained immense flexibility in deciding how to deal with statutes by deciding which of these categories to apply. A "remedial" statute would be extended; a statute in derogation of the common law would be limited to its text or limited further through a narrowing construction. A "declaratory" statute—one found to declare the common law—would be interpreted so that it did not override prior common law.[30]

The categories in which judges thought—extending and limiting statutes, matters of convenience and fundamental concerns, the common law and legislation—lacked the sharp edges they developed later with the advent of separation of powers as a realistic description of both constitutional theory and institutional practice. In this early period, judges simply worked out the relationship of statutes to the broader fabric of the law. They judged with an unself-conscious self-confidence, whether they were interpreting statutes or expounding the common law. These words from Matthew Hale, one of the most distinguished lawyers and judges writing in the mid-seventeenth century, capture this spirit best: "As to exposition of Acts of Parliament and written laws certainly he that hath been educated in the study of the law hath a great advantage over those that have been otherwise exercised. . . ."[31]

Eighteenth Century

By the eighteenth century the increasing sense of parliamentary lawmaking authority, symbolized by the affirmation of parliamentary sovereignty in 1688 and evidenced by the increased quantity of legislation, led to a perceptible shift in the rhetoric if not the practice of statutory interpretation. For example, a 1742 opinion stated: "When the words of an Act are doubtful and uncertain, it is proper to inquire what was the intent of the Legislature: but it is very dangerous for Judges to launch out too far in searching into the intent of the Legislature, when they have expressed themselves in plain and clear words."[32] And a 1785 opinion denies judges the power to extend a statute to cover a *casus omissus*[33]—that is, the power to engage in extensive equitable interpretation, such as extending the list of property in Heydon's Case to include copyholds.

BLACKSTONE

The leading English author about law in the eighteenth century was, of course, Sir William Blackstone, and a quick reading of what he had to say about legislation and statutory interpretation in his *Commentaries on the Laws of England* seems to support a decline of both equitable interpretation and judicial self-confidence in statutory interpretation. But we need to spend some time with

Blackstone to understand why this is an incomplete and inaccurate picture of his views.

On first reading, the statutory text appears preeminent: "The fairest and most rational method to interpret the will of the legislator, is by exploring his intentions at the time when the law was made, by *signs* the most natural and probable."[34] Blackstone then proceeds to make statements that a modern textualist might find congenial. He lists the most natural signs of statutory meaning as "the words, the context, the subject matter, the effects and consequence, or the spirit and reason of the law," and he argues for a sequential interpretive process. Words are, first of all, "to be understood in their usual and most known signification; not so much regarding the propriety of grammar, as their general and popular use"—in other words, common or colloquial understanding. The interpreter then moves beyond the words *only* when they "happen to be still dubious." The next step is to look at "context," which is defined in a way that suggests looking only at the surrounding text (Blackstone refers to the preamble of the statute). Next he looks to subject matter, the example of which sounds to a modern observer like the kind of linguistic context that is properly understood as part of determining the meaning of words in the first place. His example is a statute forbidding "all ecclesiastical persons to purchase *provisions* at Rome." Blackstone says: "it might seem to prohibit the buying of grain and other victual; but when we consider that the statute was made to repress the usurpations of the papal fee, and that the nominations to benefices by the pope were called *provisions,* we shall see that the restraint is intended to be laid upon such provisions only." A commonsense reading of the surrounding statutory text would certainly inform the interpreter what the word "provisions" means. In other words, armed (as we are) with a more subtle modern understanding of language theory, it is hard to deny that Blackstone's list of interpretive material is dominated by textualist criteria.

Blackstone moves on to other interpretive criteria only after these indicators of textual meaning fail. He considers "the effects and consequence" (though narrowly), looking to see if the words bear "a very absurd signification, if literally understood," in which case "we must a little deviate from the received sense of them." The illustration is the famous example of "the Bolognian law, mentioned by Puffendorf, which enacted 'that whoever drew blood in the streets should be punished with the utmost severity,'" and "was held after long debate not to extend to the surgeon, who opened the vein of a person that fell down in the street with a fit." Avoiding "absurdity" through statutory interpretation calls for a relatively modest judicial role (as we will see in discussing the Golden Rule), one that is accepted even by modern textualists who would reduce judging to a minimum.

At the end of this chain of interpretive criteria, Blackstone gets to equitable interpretation. He states that "lastly, the most universal and effectual way of discovering the true meaning of a law, when the words are dubious, is by considering the reason and spirit of it; or the cause which moved the legislator to enact it. For when this reason ceases, the law itself ought likewise to cease with it." He refers to

> this method of interpreting laws . . . [as] *Equity;* which is . . . "the correction of that, wherein the law (by reason of its universality) is deficient." For since in laws all cases cannot be foreseen or expressed, it is necessary, that when the general decrees of the law come to be applied to particular cases, there should be somewhere a power vested of defining those circumstances, which (had they been foreseen) the legislator himself would have expressed.

Although Blackstone praises "equity" as "the most universal and effectual way of discovering the true meaning of a law," he is clear about priorities. He unequivocally states that law should prevail over equity:

> [T]he liberty of considering all cases in an equitable light must not be indulged too far, lest thereby we destroy all law, and leave the decision of every question entirely in the breast of the judge. And law, without equity, though hard and disagreeable, is much more desirable for the public good, than equity without law: which would make every judge a legislator, and introduce infinite confusion; as there would then be almost as many different rules of action laid down in our courts, as there are differences of capacity and sentiment in the human mind.

Blackstone later rejects the view that a court could void an Act of Parliament against common right or reason. He affirms legislative sovereignty—"if the parliament will positively enact a thing to be done which is unreasonable, I know of no power that can control it"—and he gives the principle of Bonham's Case a decidedly textualist reading: "But where some collateral matter arises out of the *general* words, and happens to be unreasonable; there the judges are in decency to conclude that this consequence was not foreseen by the parliament, and therefore they are at liberty to expound the statute by equity, and only [to that extent] disregard it" (emphasis added).[35] Blackstone gives as an example a statute authorizing a judge to hear *all* types of cases, which should be interpreted to exclude a case in which the judge is a party.

Thus, the specific holding in Bonham's Case (that no judge should decide a case in which he could benefit) is reduced simply to interpreting a generally worded statute to exclude unreasonable specific applications, a more textualist and less bold claim to judicial power than many observers associate with Coke's early seventeenth-century decision.

This reading of Blackstone as more of a textualist than an advocate of equitable interpretation presents a puzzle. It fits very badly with what we know about how Blackstone and his contemporaries viewed legislation. The increase in eighteenth-century legislation met with a barrage of commentary about its shortcomings on competence grounds; statutes were badly drafted and they contained mistakes and inconsistencies.[36] The sheer size of the statute book came in for considerable comment (Coke had complained about the "confusion introduced by ill-judging and unlearned legislators," but the number of statutes had grown tenfold during the eighteenth century).[37] James Oldham states that "more statutes of a regulatory nature were passed than is commonly supposed," but that the subject matter was "narrow and disconnected" and the "relationship of enactments to preexisting statutes on the same subject was frequently indeterminate."[38]

The objections to legislation were also more substantively based, contrasting statutes unfavorably with the common law. Blackstone complained of the "mischiefs . . . from inconsiderate alterations in our laws," most of which he traced to "innovations that have been made in [the common law] by acts of parliament."[39] He referred to the imperfection of "statute laws where [legislators] have not the foundation of the common law to build on";[40] and to the way in which the "regular edifice" of the common law had been "swollen, shrunk, curtailed, enlarged, altered and mangled by various and contradictory statutes."[41] And one reason that Blackstone wrote his commentaries was to remedy the "defective education of our senators" and to make "the penners of our modern statutes . . . better informed . . . in the knowledge of the common law";[42] by contrast, the common law was the "perfection of reason."[43] Not coincidentally, his work would help maintain the legal status quo against the power of Parliament, which was growing ever more attuned to the interests of an increasingly powerful middle class.[44]

William Murray, Lord Mansfield, perhaps the most famous eighteenth-century judge, was of the same view. His famous statement that "[t]he common law . . . works itself pure by rules drawn from the fountain of justice" concluded with the observation that the common law "is for this reason superior to an act of parliament."[45]

LEGISLATIVE SOVEREIGNTY AND JUDGING

Reconciling these negative views of legislation with Blackstone's apparent deference to the statutory text and his affirmation of legislative sovereignty is not easy for modern observers, influenced as we are by contemporary debates about legitimacy. The answer probably lies in the eighteenth-century understanding of law and legislative sovereignty. The complexity of attitudes toward parliamentary sovereignty at this time is obviously signaled by the fact that Coke, whose views are so often cited as a precursor of judicial review, also embraced the concept of a Parliament with "transcendent and absolute" power.[46]

Legislative sovereignty can work its way into a legal system in several ways. First, all law is (formally) legislative. This view was associated with Jeremy Bentham,[47] who wrote at the end of the eighteenth century and the beginning of the nineteenth. He argued that law was a command—an act of will—and the common law did not fit that definition because it was both unclear in content and issued by multiple judicial sources. But his, obviously, was not the eighteenth-century view.

Second, legislative sovereignty might permit the judge to be resourceful in developing the common law but subservient regarding statute law. Undoubtedly, the seeds of that view were planted during the eighteenth century, but it is unlikely that it describes either the theory or practice of judicial interaction with legislation at that time. Indeed, at least some of the criticism of eighteenth-century equitable interpretation rested on a concern that only *some* judges should have a broad interpretive power—specifically, those sitting in courts of equity—as opposed to judges in courts of law (an obsolete distinction in current practice).[48]

Third, the legislature might be sovereign in the sense of having the first and last word, but judges still would have significant discretion to work things out in between. This in-between role seems to best capture the theory and reality of eighteenth-century judging. As David Lieberman notes, the courts' attitude toward parliamentary lawmaking was not "fully disclosed in . . . formal doctrines of constitutional sovereignty."[49] Courts undoubtedly paid greater heed to what Parliament did (especially the text) in light of the growing importance of legislation, but judges still played an important role in working out how the statute fit into the legal system. Charles Haines suggests this middle ground:

[T]here were instances in which the courts interpreting the common law changed the meaning of statutes, refused to give them the effect intended, or to apply a rule . . . until [the legislature issued] an unmistakable mandate, which the courts reluctantly at times conceded it was their duty to obey. Short of such mandates clearly and unequivocally expressed there was a wide realm in which the courts applied the basic principles of reason of the common law and were seldom interfered with by either the king or Parliament.[50]

This middle ground is developed more fully by Gerald Postema in his discussion of the views of the influential mid-seventeenth-century English judge and lawyer, Matthew Hale.[51] Hale argues that changes in the law occur both from changes in the common law and by Acts of Parliament, but statutes have no impact on the law until they gain community acceptance—that is, until they are incorporated into the common law. Postema argues that this perspective accommodates legislative sovereignty on the theory that "[w]ithout finding a place in [the common law], legislation can only be a matter of isolated rules having no *general* impact on the law beyond the narrow application of the statutory language . . . ." In this respect, legislation is like a judicial opinion, which (Blackstone affirmed) is only "evidence" of the law, and that, if later found to be "manifestly absurd or unjust," it was not "bad law," but was "not law" in the first place.[52]

This conception of law—as existing independent of its statement by either judges or legislatures (as a "brooding omnipresence," in Holmes's phrase)— is the key to understanding how Parliament can be sovereign and yet how judges retain considerable power in determining the meaning of a statute. In this view, both judicial pronouncements and statutes are examples of the law striving to provide an answer—whether that answer is thought to reside in the ancient traditions of pre-Norman England or in the adaptation of the law to contemporary conditions. In either case, the judge must question the meaning of earlier statements about what the law is (whether they appear in cases or statutes) as they decide the case at hand. The principle that the law stands outside its particular pronouncements allows legislative sovereignty and judicial discretion in statutory interpretation to coexist.

To the modern ear, the argument that sovereignty can be judicially qualified in this manner may sound sophistic. Sovereignty is sovereignty, and that is that. But the eighteenth-century understanding of sovereignty meant primarily legislative ascendance over the Crown, not judicial passivity. In seventeenth-century England the Crown had claimed sovereignty. Faced with this monarchical claim, it was only natural that Parliament would make a claim rival to the Crown's—that is, a claim to sovereignty. And, after the Glorious

Revolution of 1688, legislative sovereignty was in fact primarily asserted in dealings with the Crown in what we would consider constitutional legislation about the powers of government institutions. Typical examples were statutes limiting the power of the Crown set forth in the Bill of Rights of 1689, the Toleration Act of 1689 protecting Protestant dissenters, and the Act of Settlement establishing judicial tenure independent of the Crown (1701).[53] The age of legislation as *the* dominant source of law, for which parliamentary sovereignty was a necessary but not sufficient condition, lay in the future. Until that reality developed, abstract notions of sovereignty could not relegate the "equity of the statute" approach to the historical dust bin. As Richard Posner puts it: "Blackstone emphasized the role of courts in making law because, when he wrote, most law in England was judge-made. But he did not neglect the role of legislation. . . . [He] assigned a limited role to statutory law: its proper office was to resolve conflicts between common law precedents and otherwise to supplement and patch common law doctrine."[54] And, as Hans Baade states: parliamentary sovereignty "was . . . more apparent than real, for the common law reigned supreme. . . ."[55] Perhaps the most telling observation is by John Reid: that eighteenth-century lawyers were not taught that Parliament was sovereign.[56]

Commentators on Blackstone certainly failed to see in him a deferential view of the judge's role in statutory interpretation. The leading critic of judging and the common law was Jeremy Bentham, who criticizes Blackstone's invocation of "reason and spirit" in statutory interpretation because it would prevent the judge from deferring to the historical legislature. Bentham viewed Blackstone's reference to "unreasonable" law in his discussion of Bonham's Case as authorizing too much judicial discretion because the standard was not "fixed and certain." Apparently, whatever Blackstone said, Bentham anticipated that Blackstone-trained lawyers would exercise equitable interpretation (through applying "reason and spirit"). In Bentham's view, "[t]he question . . . is whose opinion shall be the standard? that of the Legislature, or that of the Judge? or of him whose office is to *make* his Will be the law, or of him whose office is no other than to find out that Will and carry it into effect?" Bentham feared that the judicial "license of interpretation" was just "another branch of customary" (that is, common) law that should be rejected.

Bentham almost certainly perceived judicial practice correctly, even if a perceptible change was taking place in judicial rhetoric. With the rise of parliamentary sovereignty, it became harder to refer to "equitable interpretation." This development probably suited those common law judges who were hostile to the expanding role of legislation and therefore wary of *extensive* equitable interpretation. The court could say that Parliament was sovereign as far as it had spoken, that courts had limited powers, and that therefore the statute could not be extended since courts could do nothing about an omitted case (a *casus omissus*). But when the statute impinged on the common law (that is, legislation was in derogation of the common law), the courts could narrowly interpret the statute by appealing to the canon of interpretation that such statutes should be narrowly construed.

If we approach our reading of Blackstone's *Commentaries* skeptical of claims that he favors judicial deference to legislative commands rather than judicial discretion, we can find support from several sources. First, Blackstone's discussion of words, context, subject matter, etc., appeared in a section entitled "Of the Nature of Laws in General."[57] When in a later section he comes to the discussion "Of the Laws of England,"[58] he presents "rules to be observed with regard to the construction of statutes" that paint a very different picture of the judicial role. Now he sets forth substantive canons that guide the judge: "Penal statutes must be strictly construed." "Statutes against frauds are to be liberally and beneficially expounded." "[I]t is the business of the judges so to construe the act, as to suppress the mischief and advance the remedy." The contrast between Laws in General and Laws of England may parallel that between legislative sovereignty *in the abstract* and statutory interpretation *in practice*. Both the priority of language and parliamentary sovereignty were abstract propositions of post-1688 legal theory, but the actual practice of interpreting the "Laws of England" had to take account of the substantive values enforceable by common law courts in light of which both legislatures and judges operated.

Second, Blackstone's emphasis on "formal" doctrine may also be attributable to the fact that he was writing not only for lawyers but also for a non-legally trained audience, whose expectations regarding eighteenth-century doctrine would include parliamentary sovereignty.[59]

Third, Blackstone's concern about equitable interpretation is grounded more in the risk of uncertain law (he refers to "infinite confusion") than in the illegitimacy of the judicial role. Certainty in the law was a major theme for Blackstone, as evidenced by his disagreement with Mansfield's view[60] that an ancient rule for the construction of deeds (known as Shelley's Case) could be overcome and thereby rendered uncertain in application by proof of what the drafter actually intended.[61]

Fourth, both Blackstone and Mansfield used similar language in speaking of the relationship of judges to statutes *and* common law decisions, suggesting that judges played an equally constructive role in working statutes and judicial opinions into the law. For example, here is what Mansfield says about following prior common law precedents: "Inconvenience, Injustice and many Absurditys must follow if the letter of a general rule was to govern cases not within the reason and therefore exceptions are implied from time to time. . . ."[62] This language, though discussing the common law, is similar to that used to explain how judges interpret statutes; the reference to "cases not within the reason" of the common law harks back to Heydon's Case and Plowden's *Commentaries* about equitable interpretation as well as to a time when words like "inconvenience" and "absurdity" were commonly used to explain the judicial role in statutory interpretation.

Similarly, Blackstone urges the practice of following case law precedent unless the result was "flatly absurd or unjust";[63] this is similar to the language he uses regarding statutory interpretation, which should avoid "absurd consequences" by equitable construction.[64] And, in speaking of statutory interpretation, Blackstone invokes the principle that "when [the] reason ceases, the law itself ought likewise to cease,"[65] which is a traditional canon applicable to judicial application of common law precedents. Finally, Blackstone uses the same standard for deciding whether a later statute displaces prior common or statute law. "[T]he common law gives place to the statute; and an old statute gives place to a new one,"[66] based on the principle that later law prevails, and subject to the qualification that the later statute must be explicit or negative by implication.

A more aggressive judicial practice of statutory interpretation, in contrast to Blackstone's theory, which sounds more deferential, was probably attributable to a shared sense of institutional enterprise between the judiciary and legislature. The point is not the familiar one that judges shared a substantive political agenda with legislators based on their common social and political background, a reality that in any event had begun to dissipate in the eighteenth century with the increasing representation of commercial classes in Parliament. Nor is it the point that judges could sometimes claim a privileged knowledge of the legislature's specific substantive intent, based on participation in drafting legislation. The more fundamental point is that the shared institutional background of judges and lawyer-trained legislators—derived from their membership and training in the Inns of Court and, in many instances, service as both judges and members of Parliament—had the effect of increasing the judge's sense of institutional competence in working out the law, regardless of substantive impact. Judges simply thought of themselves as politically savvy.

The Inns of Court provided a close-knit training ground for lawyers from whose ranks all of the judges and many legislators were chosen. One commentator refers to the Inns of Court as "political clubs,"[67] and another refers to the "peculiar combination of camaraderie and competitiveness [that] made its groupings social first and professional second."[68] The shared sense of institutional enterprise thrived in the "small world of [eighteenth-century] national politics,"[69] in which "[t]he courts held the central position because they combined . . . the judicial and legislative functions of the government," including the development of new legal codes, at a time when "Parliament was unable or unwilling to perform this function. . . ."[70]

Even more telling was the fact that judges, especially at the higher levels, were usually members of Parliament at some point in their careers. Judges were not forbidden from sitting in the House of Commons until 1873,[71] and the Law Lords did not become specialist judges until the nineteenth century. The eighteenth-century judicial establishment was not simply a small elite, though they were certainly that—only seventeen such judges were on the bench in 1727,[72] 68 percent of whom went to Oxford or Cambridge from 1727 through 1760,[73] and all but 96 percent of whom attended three of the Inns of Court.[74] They also served in the legislature. From 1727 through 1760, 57 percent sat in Parliament; from 1760 until 1790, this number leveled at 50 percent; the figures are even higher for the middle and highest levels of the bench.[75] Both Blackstone and Mansfield were judges *and* legislators. Blackstone was a member of Parliament from 1761 to 1770, before becoming a judge from 1770 to 1780.[76] And Mansfield became solicitor general and member of the House of Commons in 1742, attorney general in 1754, and later served as chief justice of the King's Bench from 1756 until 1788, during which period (as a member of the House of Lords) he continued the practice he had begun as solicitor general and attorney general of drafting legislation.[77]

In sum, eighteenth-century legal practice took only halting steps toward abandoning equitable interpretation in practice, whatever the rhetoric. Indeed, other commentators imparted a different rhetorical emphasis to statutory interpretation than Blackstone, affirming the dominance of equitable interpretation. For example, the "Statute" heading in the 1762 edition of Giles Jacob's *Dictionary* (first published in 1729) contains language that sounds much more like Plowden's view of equitable interpretation than Blackstone's: "Statutes consist of two parts, the words, and the sense; and 'tis the office of an expositor, to put such a sense upon the words of the statute, as is agreeable to equity and right reason: equity must necessarily take place in the exposition of statutes . . . ."[78]

Despite the textualist rhetoric and emphasis on legislative sovereignty, courts continued to fit statutes (and common law precedent) into the broader legal system, though there was undoubtedly a growing awareness that performing this role was a more vulnerable pursuit than in the past. Statutes, like the common law, had to be continually worked into the law by the judges, even if the theoretical foundations for this judicial role were threatened by the rise of parliamentary sovereignty.

2 The United States: From the Revolution
to the Founding

Revolutionary Perspectives

American legal thought at the time of the Revolution differed from its English antecedents in two important respects that were important for the relationship between legislatures and judges. First, legislative sovereignty was more than an abstract theory of lawmaking (as it was in eighteenth-century England); it was experienced firsthand as an expression of popular will, separate from judging. Second, that experience established a link between the people and legislatures, which had a robust sense of lawmaking competence that Parliament lacked. In the politics of 1776, legislatures (and juries) were the voice of the people. Indeed, with the exception of Massachusetts (where the state constitution was submitted to the people for ratification in both 1778 and 1780), *legislatures* adopted state constitutions in the Revolutionary period.

Not only were legislatures an affirmative source of creative lawmaking, but judges were suspect. The Declaration of Independence lists among its complaints that the king "made judges dependent on his will, for the tenure of their offices, and the amount and payment of their salaries." (Colonial judges did not enjoy tenure during good behavior, as had English judges since the Act of Settlement of 1701.)[1] Equity judges exercised discretion without juries. And the common law, especially in its more technical manifestations, was a foreign import ill-suited to the needs of the new republic, which was free of the trappings of a feudal and aristocratic society. As Associate Justice John Dudley in New Hampshire said somewhat later (he served from 1785-97) in charging a jury—"do justice between the parties; not by any quirks o' the law out of Coke or Blackstone—books that I never read and never will—but by common sense . . . between man and man."[2]

The constitutions in the newly independent states overcame judicial power in a variety of ways. Most legislatures either shared in or completely controlled the appointment of judges, and they further confined judges through a power of removal from office and control of their salaries.[3] The equity power of courts was often limited or eliminated, and juries were empowered to decide the *law*, not just the facts.[4] Only English common law suited to conditions in the new states was adopted by the new constitutions,[5] and, in any event, it was expected that the subtleties of English common law would be replaced by legislation (many state constitutions explicitly stated that the adopted common law could be altered by statute). Even codification of the common law seemed a distinct possibility.[6]

Legislatures not only attempted to control judges, but they also passed laws that we would describe as adjudication. Some of these acts were familiar practice in the eighteenth century when most legislation was in the nature of private laws, such as granting corporate charters and divorces to specific people and providing individual legal relief (often from debts). But, in many instances, legislation directly impinged on judging by retroactively overriding judicial decisions and granting new trials.[7]

Not surprisingly, judicial interpretation was a concern; a widespread belief developed that " 'meaning' became virtually dependent on interpreters."[8] Gordon Wood quotes one author in 1777 as saying that "no axiom is more dangerous than that the spirit of the law ought to be considered, and not the letter."[9] Morton Horwitz argues that, for the colonists, judicial discretion in statutory interpretation was considered more dangerous than common law adjudication.[10]

Thomas Jefferson was typical in his opposition to judicial discretion (the judge must "be a mere machine")[11] and in his support of legislation. He disliked what had happened to the common law, which he viewed as a Saxon creation ending with the Magna Carta and thereafter corrupted by Norman lawyers.[12] He objected to the "honeyed Mansfieldism" of Blackstone, which he associated with excessive judicial discretion, and he was concerned about the effect of Blackstone's *Commentaries* on young law students.[13] He preferred *legislative* protection of citizens' rights rather than relying on a common law birthright enforced by courts; and he favored juries, even in courts of equity.[14]

Ambivalence Toward Judging

This focus on revolutionary perspectives, however, does not begin to capture the ambivalence in the public's attitude toward the relationship between judges and legislatures that evolved during the period from 1776 to 1789. Even in 1776, popular and legislative sovereignty did not exactly equate, as evidenced by some objections to the early legislatures' writing state constitutions because they were not elected as constitutional conventions and did not (with the exception of Massachusetts) submit their constitutional drafts for popular approval. More fundamentally, the experience with legislation during the Revolutionary period produced a reaction against legislatures, at least in the formation of the federal Constitution. Legislative competence was called into question.

The proliferation of statutes turned out to increase rather than decrease judicial discretion.[15] Even Jefferson, an early proponent of expansive legislative power and always a critic of judicial lawmaking, came to fear legislative encroachment on individual rights; he characterized the mixture of legislative, executive, and judicial functions in legislative hands as "despotic government."[16] Substantively, legislation alarmed many people by threatening creditors' rights. And special legislation providing equitable relief from judicial judgments seemed to usurp the judicial function.[17]

This swing of the pendulum away from confidence in legislatures had implications for judging. By the 1780s, many people viewed legislatures as a threat equal to what judicial power had been a decade earlier. In Massachusetts, popular movements often closed the courts, even before Shays's Rebellion in 1786–87.[18] Some state decisions, relying on Coke's statement that statutes might be void, developed doctrines of judicial review to strike down legislation.[19] And some judges asserted a link to popular sovereignty by claiming to speak for the people through constitutional decisions and through the common law, which was viewed as custom sanctioned by popular acceptance.[20] Finally, the idea that judges had legal expertise probably persisted through the influence of Blackstone and Hale, even though muted during the 1776–89 period.

This partial and cautious rehabilitation of judging relied on a readily available English tradition. For many, the common law retained a mystic attraction as a source of rights, enforceable by courts. The Continental Congress in 1774 had emphasized that the "colonies [were] entitled to the common law of England,"[21] and common law principles were embodied in many early state constitutions adopting declarations of rights and in the federal Constitution's incorporation of a Bill of Rights (whose first eight articles included traditional common law rights enjoyed by Englishmen).

A more general point is that the American Revolution was not the French Revolution. The French Revolution adopted measures to subjugate the judiciary, some of which resembled those adopted in the American colonies, such as election of judges for short terms.[22] Like many American states, the French also retreated soon after the Revolution to appointment rather than election of judges.[23] But the French dichotomy between legislating and judging persisted with an intensity foreign to the American tradition, which never completely lost contact with the notion that both legislation and judge-made law were derived from a common source. French courts were even required to address questions of interpretive doubt to the legislature,[24] reflecting the ideology that courts lacked any lawmaking discretion.

A more important indication of the difference between French and American judges is the history of judicial opinions in each country. After the French Revolution, French judges were required to publish their opinions to demonstrate their subservience to governing legislation.[25] In the United States, publication often served the very different function of helping to justify the court's independent judgment.[26] In France, judicial opinions were brief to a fault and anonymous. In the United States a different practice prevailed. Though short by modern standards, early nineteenth-century judicial opinions contained lengthy reasoning to justify the exercise of judicial discretion. And the American judge usually signed the opinion, indicating acceptance of individual responsibility rather than assuming the guise of faceless anonymity associated with a compliant institution.[27] The American practice of unanimous opinions (which usually prevailed in the early nineteenth century) also had a different significance from the rigid insistence on unanimous opinions in the French system. Judicial unanimity in France confirmed an image of nondiscretionary judging. But the unanimity that usually characterized American opinions was a shift toward greater judicial authority and away from the English practice of each judge issuing an opinion, which had diluted the power of individual judges.

The distinctive American emphasis on popular sovereignty and the developing ambivalence toward legislating and judging is well known, but it is unclear what implications it has for this book's specific concern—statutory interpretation. Our inquiry is complicated by the fact that statutory interpretation was simply not a major focus of attention when the federal and state constitutions were being constructed. First, judging itself was not the major concern. Much more important were issues of the legislature's composition (one or two houses) and representation, the selection of the executive, and the executive veto. Second, when judging was an issue, the primary focus was not on interpretation but on *control* of judges—through (1) selection (appointment by the legislature or executive or some combination thereof); (2) conditions of removal (tenure during good behavior vs. terms of years; impeachment for wrongdoing; removal at the request of a majority or two-thirds of the legislature, with or without the governor's consent); and (3) control of salary (should judicial salary, while the judge was in office, be immune from increase or decrease). Third, when interpretation was discussed, it focused primarily on the U.S. Constitution.

Consequently, if we are to learn much about statutory interpretation from what happened between 1776 and 1789, we must construct a sense of judicial role from those features of the constitutional structure that dealt with the legislative-judicial relationship, and not from any specific provisions dealing with statutory interpretation.

Constitutional Structures and the Role of Judges

Early constitutions contain two sets of provisions from which we might construct a sense of judicial role: (1) appointment and postappointment control of judges; and (2) provisions regarding separation of powers. My own conclusion is that the evidence is hopelessly, perhaps purposefully, ambiguous regarding the role of judges and statutory interpretation.

Preliminarily, two objections can be made to our paying much attention to evidence of original constitutional intent about statutory interpretation. First, much of the concern in the 1776–89 period was about *limiting* legislation.[28] The focus was on liberty *from* government and rested on a negative original-sin, self-aggrandizing image of human nature. It is unclear what we should do with these eighteenth-century perspectives in the contemporary era, where we place much greater reliance on government and a more optimistic and humanistic view of human nature.

Second, the perspective on judging differed slightly at the state and federal levels. State constitutions favored more legislative control over judges, and the U.S. Constitution tilted more toward judicial independence. To the extent that evidence of legislative-judicial relationships sheds any light on the judicial role in statutory interpretation, the material on state constitutions may not be dispositive regarding the role of federal courts, especially in the modern period when federal legislation is so significant.

Nonetheless, it is hard to suppress the view that the original constitutional understanding has at least some relevance for the contemporary judicial role. We therefore should turn to an examination of what the evidence from state and federal constitutions suggests. (That evidence is explained in the following text and summarized for state constitutions in an appendix to this chapter.)

State and federal constitutional provisions about appointment and post-appointment control of judges were very different. The dominant state constitutional pattern was appointment either by the legislature or by a governor and council,[29] both of whom were chosen by the legislature. In only three states were judicial appointments made by a governor who was popularly elected and then only with participation by a council elected by the legislature. And, in one state, appointment of judges was by a popularly elected council, but the president (that is, the governor) joined in the appointment process, and the president was chosen by the legislature and the council.

The overall pattern regarding state judicial appointments is clearly one of legislative control over judges. Postappointment control in state constitutions presents a different picture. In most states, judges held office during good behavior, tempered by a power of (1) impeachment by the legislature for misconduct; and (2) in some cases, removal upon the address of the legislature (not limited to impeachment grounds), sometimes with the consent of the governor and/or the council. As for judicial payment, constitutions often stated that salaries should be fixed, adequate, and/or permanent. We lack evidence, however, about how the power of removal and control over salary was actually exercised, though it is clear that state impeachment of judges was a realistic threat,[30] and salary control was sometimes exercised despite the state constitution's protections.[31]

By contrast, the federal constitutional structure was unambiguously in favor of judicial independence. The post-Revolutionary reaction against legislative dominance over judging was clear. Federal judges were appointed by the president with the advice and consent of the Senate. Judges had tenure during good behavior; removal was only possible through impeachment by the House and conviction by the Senate; and salaries could not be reduced.

Drawing inferences about statutory interpretation from this constitutional material is difficult. First, what does the amount of legislative control over judges suggest? One view is that greater legislative control characteristic of the early state constitutions is an expression of hostility toward judicial lawmaking. Few can doubt that the drafters of state constitutional provisions controlling the appointment, removal, and salary of judges shared the view that judicial discretion was a serious danger to the republican principles of popular sovereignty that underlay the Revolution. But after popular legislative control over judges was established, it is not clear that judicial discretion was meant to be completely eliminated. Legislative control, especially the appointment and impeachment process, may have been a method of accommodating the inevitability of some judicial discretion rather than eliminating it.

Assertions of judicial independence from legislative control characteristic of the U.S. Constitution carry the same ambiguity. Judicial independence might be taken to mean enthusiasm for judicial discretion, but it did not necessarily carry that meaning. Judicial independence might instead be intended to reduce legislative interference with *specific* judicial decisions, without implying anything about an affirmative creative lawmaking role for independent judges.

Second, it is not only difficult to draw inferences about the judicial role from constitutional provisions about legislative control and judicial independence, but evidence also is present in the constitutional materials of *both* legislative control and judicial independence. State constitutions provided for tight control over appointments, but they were extremely cautious about postappointment control. The federal constitution allowed for postappointment impeachment, which was expected to be a realistic check on judges in this early period, but otherwise it gave judges life tenure and salary protection.

SEPARATION OF POWERS

Perhaps the right place to look for inferences about judicial power is not in the specifics of the legislative-judicial relationship but in provisions about separation of powers. But that, too, proves disappointing. Only a minority of constitutions adopted separation of powers provisions, and the significance of separation of powers for judging is unclear.

Only six states explicitly adopted such provisions,[32] the most famous of which is in the 1780 Massachusetts constitution: "In the government of this commonwealth, the legislative department shall never exercise the executive and judicial powers, or either of them; the executive shall never exercise the legislative and judicial powers, or either of them; the judicial shall never exercise the legislative and executive powers, or either of them; to the end it may be a government of laws, and not of men."[33] The 1784 New Hampshire constitution, which copied the Massachusetts constitution in many respects, was more modest, requiring only so much separation of powers "as is consistent" with the "fabric of the constitution."[34]

Four other explicit separation of powers provisions were adopted in the

1776–89 constitutions. North Carolina and Maryland stated in their declarations of rights that the legislative, executive, and judicial powers "ought" to be separate; Virginia and Georgia specified in their constitutions that the departments exercising these powers "shall" be "separate and distinct." [35]

There was no explicit separation of powers clause in the federal Constitution, which is striking, considering the confidence that modern observers exhibit regarding both the existence of separation of powers in our governmental system and its meaning. James Madison proposed amending the Constitution to provide that the three departments of government would not exercise the powers vested in the other departments;[36] the amendment passed the House but not the Senate.[37]

The more fundamental problem with drawing inferences about the judicial role (especially statutory interpretation) from separation of powers is not that explicit provisions appear in only a minority of constitutions but that the meaning of separation of powers is unclear. There were at least three relevant views of separation of powers,[38] and none of them has clear implications for statutory interpretation.

MEANING 1: "AIRTIGHT COMPARTMENT"

Under one view of separation of powers—that of airtight compartments—legislatures legislate and courts do not; they only judge. This perspective is often associated with Alexander Hamilton's observations in *Federalist* 78, where he contrasted legislatures and judges by asserting that legislatures had "will," but judges had "merely judgment." [39] Even if we accept the "airtight compartment" view, however, it leaves us with unanswered questions: Does judging include *some* element of what we would today call lawmaking? What did "judgment" mean in the late eighteenth century? Both the inherited English legal tradition and some American efforts to give voice to popular sovereignty suggest that judicial judgment was anything but passive, containing significant elements of creative lawmaking potential. After all, Hamilton in *Federalist* 78 also referred to "judicial discretion." [40]

It is not easy for us to grasp what judicial judgment meant at that time, in part because lawyers and judges in the late eighteenth century would never have used the term "lawmaking" to describe what they did. The dominant image was one of "discovering" the law. But two aspects to the process of "discovery" in the inherited legal tradition suggest that judgment included elements of discretion that we would comfortably label as lawmaking, even though we would not equate it with an exercise of legislative will.

First, there were two different traditions about discovering the law.[41] One tradition required what Coke had called "artificial reason," possessed by those with the expertise gained from legal training. Coke preached the view that there actually *was* a common law in the English past that was out there to be discovered by judges. Although it is obvious from studies of Coke's decisions that his discoveries of ancient law involved a lot of creative judgment, the "discovery" myth did not acknowledge what we would call lawmaking discretion.

But a second and equally influential view of the common law and judging was that inherited from Matthew Hale, an author well-known to American lawyers in the late eighteenth century,[42] whose view of the common law was markedly different from Coke's. His image of the common law is captured by a vivid metaphor that compares the evolution of the common law to "the Argonauts Ship[, which] was the same when it returned home, as it was when it went out, tho' in the long Voyage it had successive Amendments, and scarce came back with any of its former Materials."[43] In this view, the common law, though connected to the past, changed. The judges' expertise involved some element of choice, as each judge helped the law adapt to current needs. A similar adaptive view derived from Henry Home, Lord Kames, a Scottish judge and philosopher, also well-known to American lawyers in the late eighteenth century.[44] Kames wrote extensively about the judicial role in law reform, arguing that "[m]atters of law . . . are ripened . . . by warmth of debate at the bar and coolness of judgment on the bench," and law had to "keep pace with historical development and social change."[45]

Second, both Blackstone and Hale had an image of the judicial role that fit comfortably with the idea that judicial judgment had some creative part to play in effecting legal change. As noted, Blackstone explicitly affirmed that judicial opinion was only evidence of law[46] (although, admittedly, he had a strong commitment to judicial precedent, absent a showing that the decisions were "manifestly absurd or unjust");[47] Hale, for his part, envisioned judgments becoming part of the law only when they were incorporated into custom by popular acceptance.

In addition to conceptions of judicial judgment inherited from English legal thought, a distinctly American point of view was associated with the Scottish "common sense" philosophy current during the period we are examining; this philosophy influenced such diverse thinkers as the Anti-Federalist Thomas Jefferson[48] and the Federalist James Wilson.[49] The general idea was that people had a common sense that enabled them to make right judgments, although possibly self-interest and poor education might cloud this mental faculty.[50] Lord Kames devoted the final chapter of his *Elements of Criticism* to "disproving the 'dangerous' maxim 'There is no disputing about taste'"; he argued instead that people had standards of taste, based on a "sense or conviction of a common nature."[51] Wilson agreed, rejecting the idea that it is "fruitless to dispute concerning matters of taste"; "Nothing . . . can be farther from the truth."[52] The underlying assumption, as Jefferson put it, was that "[t]he moral sense is as much a part of our constitution as that of feeling, seeing, or hearing; . . . [and] every human mind feels pleasure in doing good to another."[53]

Thomas Reid's Common Sense philosophy closely associated common sense with judgment: "[S]ense, in its most common, and therefore its most proper meaning, signifies judgment"; "common sense . . . mean[s] common judgment"; "in common language, sense always implies judgment."[54] And, contrary to David Hume, Reid argued that the moral sense is not feeling without judging, but a sentiment that consists of "*judgment accompanied with feeling*" (emphasis in original); "the moral sense . . . is the power of judging in morals."[55] If judgment were a matter of feeling, Reid asserted, the judge would instead be called a "feeler."[56]

The implications of "common sense" philosophy for the institution of judging were varied. For many, commonsense philosophy did not favor common law lawyers and judges, but instead it supported decision-making by legislatures and juries. These observers suggested that the common law embodied old artificial language and artificial reason, which no longer had the virtues that Coke attributed to it. Jefferson, Thomas Paine, and others expected (or at least hoped) that the meaning of a new, simpler language would be accessible to the common sense and popular sentiments of a newly independent people, in whom Paine saw "the simple voice of nature and reason."[57] The political goal was to achieve freedom from " 'the Bastille of a word' and replace a language of artifice with a language of nature."[58] Consequently, new legislative codes would be written in simple, natural language appropriate to a free people and accessible to their common sense. And the jury would provide a strong link to popular common sense (recall the New Hampshire Judge Dudley's charge to the jury that they rely on "common sense").

But others relied on common sense to construct an affirmative role for judges. Hamilton referred to the "common sense" of the judicial rules of legal interpretation.[59] Wilson relied on the common sense of *both* judges and juries to determine the law,[60] arguing (as Shannon Stimson notes) that the "reasoned and discursive 'common sense' judgment of the people was vested in [the Supreme Court]. . . ."[61] The distinctly American variation on common sense philosophy, as it relates to judging, was to transform the cramped English idea of discretionary judgment into a more robust conception of common sense judgment that could claim a link to the people, from whom all power in the new Republic arose. Put somewhat differently, common sense would replace artificial reason in the judicial mind-set.

This effort to explain how people understood judicial judgment in the late eighteenth century would have struck some as overly ambitious. Madison honestly captured that uncertainty, in *Federalist* 37 when he wrote:

> The faculties of the mind itself have never yet been distinguished and defined, with satisfactory precision, by all the efforts of the most acute and metaphysical philosophers. Sense, perception, *judgment*, desire, volition, memory, imagination, are found to be separated, by such delicate shades and minute gradations, that their boundaries have eluded the most subtle investigations, and remain a pregnant source of ingenious disquisition and controversy. (emphasis added)[62]

This honest admission of the difficulty of defining judgment reinforces the notion that no clear sense existed of what judgment entailed. Nor was Madison alone in noting this problem; Thomas Reid stated: "There are . . . no words in language more liable to ambiguity than those by which we express the operations of the mind. . . ."[63]

In sum, two different traditions gave content to the idea of a "separate" power of judicial judgment: (1) an inherited English tradition of judging that expected judicial discretion in the process of discovering and applying the law; and (2) an American conception of "common sense" that was accessible to judges as well as to others. The relevance of these traditions for American judging and statutory interpretation was controversial, but that is exactly the point. No single view of judging predominated.

MEANING 2: CHECKS AND BALANCES

Even if we fully understood what the "airtight compartment" approach to separation of powers meant for judging during the period from 1776 until 1789, another conception of separation of powers must not be overlooked. Checks and balances—in which governmental power is shared and each department checks the other—was at least as important as the compartmentalizing of the legislative and judicial functions. Indeed, it should be plain from the discussion of legislative control over judging that the airtight compartment view of separation of powers yielded in practice to checks and balances.

Madison in *Federalist* 47 makes the point that Separation of Powers only precludes one branch from having the *whole* power of another branch. (An example would be a legislature's complete control of the judiciary through appointment and postappointment control.) It is quite another matter, Madison argued, if one branch has a "partial agency in" or some control over the activities of another branch, what we would call checks and balances—for example, when the executive can veto a statute.

In the context of judging, the legislature had *some* judicial power—for example, through impeachment and removal of judges. Conversely, judges could control the legislature through judicial review of statutes to assure that those statutes were constitutional.[64] In New York, judges even played a direct role in the political and legislative process through the Council of Revision,[65] which had the power to veto legislation when laws were "inconsistent with the spirit of the constitution, or with the public good."[66]

As for statutory interpretation, Hamilton argued in *Federalist* 78 that it provided a check on the legislature, stating: "[T]he independence of the judges may be an essential safeguard against the effects of occasional ill-humours in the society," not just when there are "infractions of the constitution," but also when there is "injury of the private rights of particular classes of citizens, by unjust and partial laws"; the "firmness of the judicial magistracy is of vast importance in mitigating the severity, and confining the operation of such laws."[67]

We might infer that the *federal* constitutional structure rejected a judicial check on legislation because proposals for a federal Council of Revision were rejected. The question is especially important for contemporary debates about judging because those objecting to too much judicial lawmaking often rely on the fact that federal judges do *not* sit as a Council of Revision.[68] But the arguments about whether judges should participate on such a council do not imply diminished judicial discretion through judicial review and statutory interpretation.

Some of the reasons for the defeat of the council in the federal Constitution were prudential: judges who passed on proposed legislation might be biased when the law came up later for judicial review; and political involvement by judges might damage their judicial reputation and make their other work more difficult. The more fundamental objection was the "airtight compartment" version of separation of powers—that is, the Council of Revision would give judges a legislative power. Elbridge Gerry was the council's foremost opponent on separation of powers grounds, stating: "It was quite foreign from the nature of [the judicial] office to make them judges of the policy of public measures."[69]

But none of the major protagonists saw a link between a political role for judges on a Council of Revision and more selective opportunities for judicial discretion through judicial review and statutory interpretation. Gerry, who opposed judges serving on a council, did *not* oppose judicial review of statutes for unconstitutionality. And Madison favored the Council of Revision, in part because it would *preclude* judicial review in regard to unconstitutionality.[70]

MEANING 3: MULTIPLE OFFICEHOLDING

A further complication in deciding what separation of powers meant for judging is that for some people, perhaps most, it meant a prohibition of multiple officeholding, not a separation of governmental functions.[71] For example, when Essex County rejected the proposed 1778 Massachusetts constitution, a major point was that the "three powers [of government] ought to be in different hands"; and "[i]f the legislative and judicial powers are united, the maker of the law will also interpret it. . . ."[72]

In other words, judicial interpretation is objectionable when the legislative and the judicial are merged. Similarly, objections in Essex County to "artful [judicial] constructions" was *not* a free-floating concern about judicial interpretation but was explicitly tied to the problem of united executive and judicial powers. The objectors stated: "Should the executive and judicial powers be united, the subject would then have no permanent security of his person and property. The executive power would interpret the laws and bend them to his will; as he is the judge and may leap over them by artful construction, and gratify, with impunity, the most rapacious passions." Notice also that the text of the Massachusetts provision, which is often thought to be the strongest statement of separation of powers, is best read as concerned with separation of officeholding and checks and balances, not separation of government functions. It states that the purpose of separation is the preservation of a government of laws, not men, which is best achieved by keeping offices in separate hands so that each branch can effectively check the other (a view shared by Blackstone).[73]

One argument against inferring that separation of powers was primarily concerned with preventing multiple officeholding is the existence of *explicit* provisions in many state constitutions from 1776 until 1789 against judges holding political office.[74] Such provisions would be unnecessary if separation of powers already precluded this result. But the vaguely worded "separation" clauses may have been legally unenforceable, requiring something more specific to prohibit multiple officeholding. Three of the six constitutional provisions requiring separation of powers (noted earlier) stated that powers "ought to be" separate, and three say they "shall" be. As Akhil Amar notes, such provisions were not generally enforceable in eighteenth-century England and might not have created legal rights in the early state constitutions.[75] Marshall argued that the Virginia declaration of rights had moral but not legal force.[76] Consequently, explicit prohibitions of multiple officeholding shed no light on what the vague constitutional attachment to separation of powers principles implies.

THE UNCERTAIN CONSTITUTIONAL LEGACY

The period from the Revolution to the ratification of the U.S. Constitution put to rest any casual acceptance of judges as "sages" capable of identifying the law into which legislation and common law must fit. Although periods have occurred in which efforts were made to revive this level of commitment to judging, ideas about popular sovereignty and legislative competence were here to stay, making judicial confidence harder to sustain. But it would be a mistake to assume that the pendulum had swung to the other extreme—that is, in favor of legislation to the exclusion of a significant role for the judiciary. The American Revolutionary experience made legislative dominance a real possibility rather than just a technical matter of sovereignty (as was true in eighteenth-century England), but it did not end the uncertainty about how legislating and judging should interact. The rules about legislative appointment and postappointment control of judges and about separation of powers contained within them an ambiguity about, rather than a resolution of, the judicial role.

The ambiguity of the evidence about the judicial role is consistent with the historical reality that state and federal constitution-builders were intensely pragmatic, not concerned with whether the governments they created fit some theoretically consistent mold. Indeed, the need to attract widespread support led them to compromises that avoided a rigid constitutional model. They rejected the extremes of monarchical and legislative sovereignty, but they were never entirely clear what they created in between. All that was clear was that the boundaries within which judges operated, as determined by the reality of popular sovereignty and legislative competence, were narrower than those set by the formal principle of parliamentary sovereignty in England. The central idea of the constitutions written from 1776 through 1789 was that there is no obvious message about judicial lawmaking power, especially regarding statutory interpretation. As Governeur Morris stated (chairman of the Committee on Style at the Constitutional Convention) regarding the federal Constitution: "I believed [the Constitution] to be as clear as our language would permit; *excepting* . . . a part of what relates to the judiciary" (emphasis added).[77] Consequently, considerable room remained for future generations to work out the inherited English legal tradition suitable for the legal environment in which they operated.

Judicial Practice of Statutory Interpretation

The ambivalence and controversy about judging also are apparent in what little evidence we have from judicial practice during the 1776–89 period. The discussion in chapter 1 suggested that the inherited English tradition leaned toward an undifferentiated exercise of judicial power to determine the law. Lines that we might draw today were either not set down by early English judges or were only beginning to be established in the eighteenth century. Statutes were extended *and* limited; extension included adding to statutory lists *and* the liberal interpretation of statutes dealing with selected subject matter. Limitation of statutes included both restraining coverage suggested by overly broad texts to help the legislature achieve an imperfectly thought-out scheme *and* the narrow interpretation of statutes in derogation of the common law or common right, which sometimes did and did not implement likely legislative intent. Courts did these things both to prevent absurdity and injustice (fundamental values) *and* to avoid inconvenient results. Even statutes and common law were not so clearly differentiated; both were conceived of as evidence of a broader legal landscape. During all of these changes, judges acted more or less unself-consciously in performing their judicial role.

The American experience destroyed the ability of judges to be unself-conscious about their lawmaking role, and tremendous pressure was put on the failure to differentiate among the different elements of that role. We have seen that eighteenth-century English judges became more skeptical of list extension and began to draw lines between the text and equity of the statute as legislation became a more prominent (and, technically, sovereign) source of law. How much greater must the pressure have been on American judges to be selective in the way that they aggressively interacted with legislation in light of the reality of popular sovereignty and a growing sense of legislative competence. Indeed, sporadic indications were clear of a differentiation among the possible judicial roles in some of the evidence we have of judicial practice from 1776 until 1789.

A lot of the controversy over the judicial role regarding statutes during the 1776–89 period concerned review to strike down legislation.[78] Even before courts relied on the Constitution as superior law (which was Hamilton's argument for judicial review in *Federalist* 78), they often relied on Coke's decision in Bonham's Case for the proposition that a statute in violation of common right or natural law was void (whatever Bonham's Case might have meant in England). This was a common practice before adoption of written constitutions, as Jefferson's "Reports of Cases" suggests.[79] But it also persisted in both federal and state courts even after adoption of written constitutions, most famously by Justice Samuel Chase in Calder v. Bull ("vital principles . . . will determine and over-rule an apparent and flagrant abuse of legislative power"; an "act . . . contrary to the great first principles of the social compact cannot be considered a rightful exercise of legislative authority").[80]

But judges did not limit their aggressive interaction with statutes to judicial review. They also injected substantive values into the process of statutory interpretation. Somewhere between Coke's voiding of statutes for violation of common right and absolute parliamentary sovereignty lay a middle way in eighteenth-century England whereby courts "changed the meaning of statutes, refused to give them the effect intended, or to apply a rule . . . until the [legislature issued] an unmistakable mandate, which the courts reluctantly at times conceded it was their duty to obey."[81] We are so accustomed to observing that American constitutional theory (which justified judicial review of legislation) was a sharp departure from English eighteenth-century constitutional *theory* (which affirmed parliamentary sovereignty) that we overlook the similarity in *practice* between clear statement rules in statutory interpretation and judicial review. The effect of the two practices is certainly different—judicial review can be overturned only by constitutional amendment, and statutory interpretation remands an issue for legislative reexamination—but the historical practices were more closely linked than we often allow. Both were methods for judges to raise doubts about legislation, as Hamilton suggested when he spoke in *Federalist* 78 about judicial review for unconstitutionality *and* the prevention of injustice through statutory interpretation.

Some evidence is clear from judicial practice that courts did *not* always distinguish sharply between judicial review and statutory interpretation. For example, in the 1789 case of Ham v. M'Claws, the South Carolina court relied, indifferently, on both judicial review to preserve principles of common right (reminiscent of Bonham's Case) and statutory interpretation to protect such principles. The court stated:

> statutes passed against the plain and obvious principles of common right, and common reason, are absolutely null and void. . . . [W]e would not do the legislature who passed this act, so much injustice, as to sit here and say that it was their intention to make a forfeiture of property. . . . We are, therefore, bound to give such a construction to this [act] as will be consistent with justice, and the dictates of natural reason, though contrary to the strict letter of the law. . . .[82]

But in one well-known decision the court *did* distinguish between judicial review and statutory interpretation. In the 1784 New York case of Rutgers v. Waddingdon, the court acknowledged legislative supremacy, denying a judicial power to strike down a statute as unconstitutional, but it still interpreted the statute narrowly to preserve the common law. The case involved a suit against a British subject who entered and used the property of a New York resident who had fled the invading British troops. The question was whether the British defendant could defend his action by relying on the law of nations, which was part of the substantive common law, or whether a statute abrogated this defense. The court adopted an "equitable interpretation" approach to preserve the common law defense (urged upon the court by Alexander Hamilton for the defendant), stressing the substantively laden judicial role envisioned by Plowden in fitting statutes into the broader fabric of the law: "In order, [Plowden] says, to form a right judgment whether a case be within the equity of a statute, it is a good way to suppose the law maker present, and that you asked him the question — did you intend to comprehend this case? Then you must give yourself such answer as you imagine, he *being an upright and reasonable man,* would have given" (emphasis in original).[83] The court held that "unreasonable" results arising from "general words" regarding some "collateral matter" are presumed "not foreseen by the Legislature" and are not included in the statute by "expound[ing] the statute by equity. . . . [T]his is the language of Blackstone in his celebrated commentaries, and this is the practice of the courts of justice, from which we have copied our jurisprudence. . . ."[84]

The decision created a great stir in New York, leading to calls in the state assembly for replacement of the judicial official (which did not pass) because the court, in effect, had engaged in legislation, altering rather than declaring law.[85] It is unclear, however, what interpretive approach would have prevailed on appeal. Perhaps because of that uncertainty, the case was settled by compromise before an appeal was perfected.[86]

The decision in Rutgers v. Waddingdon, although it differentiated between judicial review and statutory interpretation, did not distinguish between judicial protection of fundamental and other values through statutory interpretation. Other courts, however, may have made that distinction. One interesting feature of the South Carolina case mentioned earlier is its concern with protecting "common right" and "justice." Although the decision did *not* differentiate sharply between judicial review and statutory interpretation, its reference to "common right" and "justice" hinted at a distinction between judicial protection of fundamental values and a less aggressive judicial role when less important values were at stake. When we look at his statutory interpretation opinions in chapter 3, we will see that Chief Justice Marshall adopted this distinction in explaining the judge's interpretive role.

If we extend our examination of statutory interpretation to the 1790s (including cases cited by William N. Eskridge Jr. in a recent study),[87] we find the same ambivalence and controversy about the judicial role as before. Several opinions by President Pendleton of the Virginia Court of Appeals are illustrative. In Watson & Hartshorne v. Alexander,[88] he affirmed that the "safest and surest guide is to pursue the words of the law," but in Johnson v. Buffington,[89] he refused a narrowing construction because it was not "consistent with the justice of the case, and the intention of the legislature," and in Warder v. Arell,[90] he relied on both the "spirit, as well as the just exposition of the words of the law."

Two New Jersey cases illustrate the persistence of the judge's traditional concern with interpreting legislation to prevent "inconvenience." In Executors of Barrecliff v. Administrator of Griscom, the judge relied on both the "designs and intentions of the legislature, so far as they are to be gathered from the expressions which they have employed," and a concern about "serious inconveniences."[91] In Woodbridge v. Amboy, the court did "not consider [itself] bound by the strictly grammatical construction of the words of the act," adding that it would "not hesitate to adopt a construction which the words will clearly warrant, free from those inconveniences which must flow from any other interpretation."[92]

Finally, a 1795 Pennsylvania decision demonstrates the difference between at least some late-eighteenth-century judges and modern textualists. For the modern textualist, numbers in a statutory text present the strongest case for a literal reading. Judge Easterbrook emphasizes this point when he insists that a statutory provision exempting a specific dollar amount of debtor property from seizure by a creditor should not be adjusted for inflation.[93] By contrast, the Pennsylvania decision interpreted a 1729 statute protecting debtors' apparel, bedding, and tools of the trade in the amount of "five pounds" as "not . . . controlled by the *enhanced prices* of those articles (emphasis added)." [94] Consequently, the statutory term "five pounds" did not mean five pounds, but was increased to account for price inflation.

The Debate Over Constitutional Interpretation

Although our primary concern is with statutory interpretation, for two reasons we also should look at the debates and practice regarding constitutional interpretation during and after the ratification period. First, the disputes over constitutional interpretation shed some light on how interpretive issues were analyzed at that time, even though their relevance for statutory interpretation is unclear. Second, the practice of constitutional interpretation provides us with some information about how at least one document was interpreted and, if we take Marshall's approach as paradigmatic, is a precursor of modern purposive statutory interpretation. Most examples of statutory interpretation in the previous discussion limited the statute's reach, a not unsurprising result given judicial suspicion of legislation. But Marshall had no intention of limiting the powers granted by the U.S. Constitution. His expansive interpretation of the Constitution is easily recognized by a modern observer as similar to the kind of purposivism that eventually dominated twentieth-century approaches to statutory interpretation.

Opponents of ratifying the Constitution (known as Anti-Federalists) expressed fear that federal judges would apply Blackstone's interpretive approach to constitutional interpretation to enhance the Federalist's political agenda of expanding the power of the national government. Whatever anyone else thought Blackstone meant, one opponent (writing under the pseudonym of Brutus) believed that he favored "equitable interpretation." Explicitly citing Blackstone as the source of interpretive method, Brutus states: "By [equity the judges] are empowered, to explain the constitution according to the reasoning spirit of it, without being confined to the words or letter." [95] And: "[T]his [Supreme] court will be authorized to decide upon the meaning of the constitution, . . . not only according to the natural and obvious meaning of the words, but also according to the spirit and intention of it." [96] Because the constitutional preamble referred to a "more perfect union," reliance on the "spirit and reason" of the Constitution would tend toward enhancing the power of the general government in accordance with Federalist views. [97] In sum, the Supreme Court was vested with a "power of giving an *equitable* construction to the constitution" (emphasis in original) [98] and that power would be exercised to extend the powers given by the Constitution to the federal government.

Brutus had nothing to worry about if the Anti-Federalist substantive view of the constitutional spirit prevailed, resulting in strict construction of federal power. If the Constitution was a compact among states—if that was its spirit—the general government's powers would be narrowly construed—that is, subjected to a limiting equitable interpretation. Justice Chase, in an early Supreme Court case, adopted this substantive view of the Constitution's spirit to decide that the ex post facto clause applied only to criminal laws and not to civil state legislation. "It appears to me a self-evident proposition, that the several State Legislatures retain all the powers of legislation, delegated to them by the State Constitutions; which are not expressly taken away by the Constitution of the United States." [99] And in 1803, George Tucker's comments on Blackstone's *Commentaries* argued for a narrow reading of the central government's constitutional powers so as to preserve the rights of the people and to avoid destroying the states by implication. [100] But Brutus did have a lot to worry about. He accurately feared equitable construction by Federalist judges, which would embrace an expansive substantive view of the Constitution that would aggrandize federal power.

Brutus wrote his comments on constitutional interpretation between January 31 and March 30, 1788. Hamilton responded to Brutus in *Federalist*s 78–84, the first of which appeared on May 28, 1788. Essentially, Hamilton said not to worry; judicial interpretation was no threat. He denied that judges had the interpretive freedom that Brutus feared. But he was at best disingenuous. Hamilton knew full well that judges had interpretive potential that could pose a threat to Anti-Federalist values.

Most of Hamilton's remarks dealt with the issue of judicial review of potentially unconstitutional legislation. But he also commented on "equitable" interpretation, presenting what we would recognize as a nondenial denial. "[T]here is not a syllable in the plan which *directly* empowers the national courts to construe the laws according to the spirit of the constitution . . ." (emphasis in original). [101]

Other efforts could be made to soften the potential impact of judicial interpretive discretion. If Brutus could invoke Blackstone against the Federalists, Hamilton could invoke the rhetoric of "common sense," which had often been associated with Anti-Federalist advocates of state legislative power. But Hamilton turned common sense to his own uses, tying it to judicial interpretive practice. In *Federalist* 83: "The rules of legal interpretation are rules of *common sense*, adopted by the courts in the construction of the laws" (emphasis in original);[102] they arose from "the nature and reason of the thing."[103]

Hamilton realized, of course, that interpretive rules were hard to defend as commonsensical. Many were technical and artificial. Anticipating such an argument, Hamilton responded that technical interpretive rules were out of place when interpreting the Constitution, an area where courts would rely on the "natural and obvious sense of its provisions,"[104] though (by implication) they were appropriate for statutory interpretation. (In other words, artificial reason and the more technical features of the inherited English tradition of statutory interpretation might persist for determining the meaning of statutes, but not for the Constitution.) Hamilton makes this point regarding the interpretive maxim which asserts that express statements imply a negative (*expressio unius est exclusio alterius*). Anti-Federalist opponents of the Constitution argued that the provision for juries in criminal cases might preclude jury requirements in civil trials. Potential application of the technical *expressio* maxim was enough of a threat that the Ninth Amendment was adopted, stating that "[t]he enumeration in the Constitution, of certain rights, shall not be construed to deny or disparage others retained by the people."[105]

Hamilton's soothing references to "common sense" could not mollify the Anti-Federalists. The judge's reliance on common sense carried within it the seeds of interpretive discretion that could be no less unsettling than reliance on "equity." Indeed, the approaches could seem quite similar. The meaning accessible to common sense required understanding the sentiments underlying language in much the same way that the soul of a text might determine its meaning. "[R]eal meaning lay in the speaker's feelings and intentions and not in the words themselves," and common sense overcame "the problematic gulf between intention and statement. . . ."[106] Common sense therefore required the judge to be attuned to proper sentiments to make the right interpretive inference, and the Anti-Federalists could hardly be expected to conclude that Federalist judges were properly in tune. One critic of the Federalist Chief Justice Marshall's expansive interpretation of federal legislative power stated that the choice was between "common sense," which addresses understanding, and responding to "prejudice and self-interest."[107] Obviously, one person's common sense could be another's prejudice. Common sense and equitable interpretation might both be subject to abuse.

Indeed, Hamilton's confidential opinion to President George Washington on the constitutionality of a national bank was much more forthright about the reality of judicial interpretation than the *Federalist Papers*. He made all the arguments that Brutus had anticipated. Liberality is a *formal* judicial principle of federal constitutional interpretation (which is a call for "equitable inter-pretation"). In response to Attorney General Edmund Randolph's argument to "construe[] with greater strictness" a federal rather than a state constitu-tion, Hamilton stated that the "reason of the rule" was otherwise.[108] And in his notes for a response to the attorney general's opinion on a national bank, Hamilton observed: "There is a real difference between the rule of interpre-tation, applied to a law and a constitution. The one comprises a summary of matter, for the detail of which numberless Laws will be necessary; the other is the very detail. The one is therefore to be construed with a discreet liberality; the other with a closer adherence to the literal meaning."[109] (This distinc-tion between constitutional and statutory interpretation recurs in Marshall's opinions, discussed in chapter 3.)[110]

But liberality was not just a formal interpretive principle, allowing the judge to implement the document's "equity" or spirit. The *substantive* spirit of the Constitution that the judge should implement was, in Hamilton's view, also "liberal," referring now to the substantive principle of expansive government power: "[T]he powers contained in a constitution of government, especially those which concern the general administration of the affairs of a country . . . ought to be construed liberally. . . ."[111]

Early judicial decisions interpreting the Constitution also reflect the ten-sion apparent in the debate between Brutus and Hamilton about whether the Constitution should be interpreted "equitably." The best-known statement with which Brutus would have agreed is by Justice Samuel Chase in Priest-man v. United States.[112] Chase stated that no rule of construction "can be more dangerous, than that, which distinguishing between the intent and the words of the legislature, declares, that a case not within the meaning of a statute, according to the opinion of the judges, shall not be embraced in the operation of the statute, although it is clearly within the words: or, vice versa, that a case within the meaning, though not within the words, shall be em-braced"; and he implied a contrast between British and American courts—"For my part, however, sitting in an American Court, I shall always deem it a duty to conform to the expressions of the legislature, to the letter of the statute, when free from ambiguity and doubt; without indulging a specula-tion, either upon the impolicy or the hardship of the law."

A good example of the Hamiltonian approach is from Justice James Wil-son's 1793 decision in Chisholm v. Georgia.[113] Wilson, more than any of the Founders, emphasized that the people were sovereign *and* that the courts, as well as the legislature, spoke for the people. Not only was the Constitution a product of "We the People," but (for Wilson) the common law itself was the embodiment of custom, which derived support from popular consent.

The Federalist Justice Wilson was under none of Hamilton's compunctions about describing judicial power. Wilson believed, almost reverentially,[114] in the common sense of the common law.[115] The people's common sense, embodied in custom, underlay development of the common law and provided the link between judge-made law and popular government that was essential in the new Republic. Common law, custom, and consent of the governed were not incompatible. Judges, far from being antidemocratic, were the voice of the people (subject, of course, to correction). Judges, more than representative legislatures, could directly implement the common sense conceptions of the common law to which the people had assented. Indeed, judicial review was one way — perhaps the best way — for the people's voice to be heard.[116]

When Wilson applied his commonsense approach, he confirmed the Anti-Federalist's fear that, in the hands of a Federalist judge, there was not much difference between equity and common sense. In Chisholm v. Georgia,[117] Wilson wrote an opinion affirming that states were not immune from lawsuits in federal courts. (Hamilton had assured readers of the *Federalist Papers* to the contrary, that immunity from suit without consent was "the general sense, and the general practice of mankind.")[118] Wilson's opinion is structured first as a discussion of general jurisprudence ("I am, first, to examine this question by the principles of general jurisprudence"), to which he appends an explicit encomium to the Common Sense philosopher Thomas Reid.[119] He then proceeds to a discussion of the laws and practice of different states. Finally, he gets to the Constitution, or, more specifically to what he calls "the general texture of the Constitution of the United States."[120] That texture is "to form an union more perfect" and to "form themselves into a nation for national purposes."[121] He asks rhetorically: "Is it congruous, that, with regard to such purposes, any man or body of men, any person natural or artificial, should be permitted to claim successfully an entire exemption from the jurisdiction of the national Government? Would not such claims, crowned with success, be repugnant to our very existence as a nation?"[122] The text is not so much corrected (to use Plowden's phrase) by Wilson's vision of the Constitution's texture as it is imbued with it, an approach that will become readily familiar when we encounter twentieth-century purposive interpretation.[123]

It is symptomatic of the difficulty which early American courts faced in claiming judicial discretion that Wilson's understanding of the Constitution's underlying purpose was not shared by those on whose behalf he claimed to speak. It did not take long (1798) for the people to correct Wilson by passing the Eleventh Amendment, preserving state sovereign immunity in federal court.

In sum, the period from the Revolution to ratification of the Constitution included intense but unresolved debates about judging from which it is difficult to derive any clear message about the judicial role in statutory interpretation. The force with which popular sovereignty shaped American legal thinking precluded any simplistic incorporation of the inherited English tradition, but popular sovereignty was also unable to marginalize that tradition, at least after the fading of revolutionary fervor. Future generations in the nineteenth and twentieth centuries have continued to work out the relationship of judging to legislation within a broad and indeterminate constitutional heritage.

Appendix A
State Constitutional Provisions: Appointment and Postappointment Control of Judges

Table A.1 Appointment Power

State	Constitution adopted	Appointment provision
New Jersey[a]	1776	Legislature
North Carolina	1776	Legislature
Virginia	1776	Legislature
Delaware[b]	1776	Legislature and President, chosen by legislature
South Carolina[c]	1776	Legislature
	1778	Legislature
Maryland	1776	Governor, chosen by legislature; and council, chosen by legislature
Massachusetts	1780	Governor, chosen by people; and council, chosen by legislature
New Hampshire	1784	President, chosen by people; and council, chosen by legislature
New York[a]	1777	Governor, chosen by people; and council, chosen by legislature

Table A.1 Appointment Power *continued*

State	Constitution adopted	Appointment provision
Pennsylvania	1776	President, chosen by legislature and council; and council, chosen by people
Georgia[d]	1777/1789	Legislature
Connecticut[d]	1784 statute	Legislature
Rhode Island[d]	pre-1776 charter	Legislature

SOURCE: Unless otherwise specified, the material in this table is based on *The Federal and State Constitutions, Colonial Charters, and Other Organic Laws of the United States,* part 1, 960 (Benjamin Poore, 2d ed., 1878).

[a] In two states the highest court of appeal included legislators; in New Jersey the court of appeal consisted of the governor and the legislative council (senate); in New York the Court of Errors consisted of senators and judges.

[b] The highest court of appeals for Delaware consisted of the president and six judges, three elected by each legislative branch.

[c] In both the 1776 and 1778 Constitutions, the chancery court comprised an executive official and a privy council, consisting of legislators elected by the legislature, until the legislature provided otherwise.

[d] The information for Georgia, Connecticut, and Rhode Island is derived from Evan Haynes, *The Selection and Tenure of Judges,* 105, 108, 127–28 (1944) (hereafter Haynes). The Georgia 1777 and 1789 constitutions are unclear. Connecticut's 1776 constitution adopted its 1662 charter. Rhode Island operated under its 1663 charter.

Table A.2 Postappointment Control

State (year of constitution)	Term (good behavior or term of years)	Removal (impeachment; legislative address)	Salary
New Jersey (1776)	7/5 years	Impeach only	no provision
North Carolina (1776)	Good behavior	Impeach only	adequate
Virginia (1776)	Good behavior	Impeach only	fixed, adequate

Table A.2   Postappointment Control *continued*

State (year of constitution)	Term (good behavior or term of years)	Removal (impeachment; legislative address)	Salary
Delaware (1776)	Good behavior	Impeach; and by address of legislature	adequate, fixed
South Carolina (1776)	Good behavior	no impeachment provision; by address of legislatures	established by act
(1778)	Good behavior	Impeach; and by address of legislature	adequate, fixed
Maryland (1776)	Good behavior	no impeach provision,[a] remove by governor on address by 2/3 of legislature	liberal, not profuse; secured
Massachusetts (1780)	Good behavior	Impeach; and by governor and council, on address of legislature	established by law; permanent
New Hampshire (1784)	Good behavior	Impeach; and by governor and council, on address of legislature	established by law; permanent
New York (1777)	Good behavior	Impeach only	no provision
Pennsylvania (1776)	7 years	Impeach; and by address of legislature for "misbehavior"	fixed
Georgia (1789)[b]	3 years	Impeach	no increase/ decrease

SOURCE: Unless otherwise specified, the material in this table is based on *The Federal and State Constitutions, Colonial Charters, and Other Organic Laws of the United States*, Part 1, 960 (Benjamin Poore, 2d ed., 1878).

The chart provides no information on Connecticut and Rhode Island, which continued to be governed by their pre-Revolutionary charters.

ª Judges could be removed if convicted in a court of law.

ᵇ The 1777 Georgia constitution is uncertain regarding tenure, but judges probably served at the pleasure of the legislature. Haynes, 108. The state constitution provided that every "officer . . . shall be liable to be called to account by the [legislature]." There was no provision about salaries.

3 The United States: Nineteenth Century

With a constitutional structure more or less in place—at least at the federal level (state constitutions were amended with some frequency)—courts and legislatures at the start of the nineteenth century turned to the task of making law and of continuing to develop the theory and practice of statutory interpretation. The dominant reality, with important implications for statutory interpretation, was an increasing reliance on statutes; at the same time, the practicing bar was reluctant to accept legislation as a significant source of law.

Initially, the task of creating law was shared by courts and legislatures, as Morton Horwitz has explained for courts,[1] and, more recently, William Novak for legislation.[2] Lawyers generally remained skeptical of legislation, though in the first half of the century this took the form more of benign neglect than active hostility. But the legislative/judicial lawmaking partnership dissolved around the middle of the century as courts (supported by the bar) set themselves actively against legal change, whether judicial or legislative (except for the change needed to make the Constitution an effective bulwark against legal innovation).

This evolution in the relationship of legislatures and courts is now well understood, and it is not my purpose to retell the story but to explain its significance for the evolution of statutory interpretation. This chapter begins with a brief comment on the expanding importance of nineteenth-century legislation and the related phenomenon of increased commentary on statutory interpretation. Despite what lawyers may have thought about statutes, they indirectly acknowledged their importance by writing and buying treatises that explained how courts interpreted legislation.

We next look at the pre-Civil War material, first at the commentators, and then at what judges actually did. The commentary reveals a gradual shift toward criticism of the disrespect shown by bench and bar toward legislation, concentrating their attack on "equitable interpretation" and attempting to alter the traditional view that judges had a relative advantage in lawmaking competence over legislatures. The picture we get of pre-Civil War judging is, however, more complicated than might be suggested by reading the commentators. First, judges were not as disrespectful of statutes as many of the commentators indicated. Second, federal statutory interpretation (at least as represented by John Marshall) was different from state statutory interpretation, probably for good institutional reasons related to the role of the federal government in the first half of the nineteenth century.[3]

We then examine the changes that began around the Civil War and persisted thereafter, which set judges against legislation. A shift in the legal culture occurred during this period, separating law from the people, which intensified hostility toward legislation by the bench and bar. We are familiar with this hostility when it took the form of courts declaring statutes unconstitutional, but judges also evinced antagonism toward legislation through statutory interpretation, primarily by aggressive application of the canon that statutes in derogation of the common law be narrowly construed. But, once again, the actual practice of judging was (I argue) less hostile than is suggested by discussions about statutory interpretation and the use of the derogation canon.

The tendency for actual judging to be less extreme in its approach to statutory interpretation than was portrayed by nineteenth-century commentators is important to the book's thesis (developed in chapter 7) that ordinary judging is a relatively mundane activity concerned with judicial competence. The aspect of judicial competence that most concerned judges who invoked the derogation canon was working out the interaction of statutes with their past—more specifically, with prior common law. This view is in contrast to the more recent concern with judicial competence in helping statutes adjust to their future ("dynamic statutory interpretation") and with working out the interaction of statutes with prior legislation (discussed in chapter 7, below).

Importance of Statutes in the Nineteenth Century

Statutes were important in the United States during the nineteenth century. From Independence on, a considerable amount of legislation *and* evolution of the common law occurred, especially at the state level. William Novak's 1991 study argues persuasively against the popular view that pre-Civil War statutes were only distributional, not regulatory.[4] Novak's review of legislative activity emphasizes these areas of activity: numerous private bills authorized specific corporations to construct public works, such as canals and bridges; the shift from private legislation to general laws (for example, regarding incorporation, divorce, and adoption); the exercise of the police power to protect against fire and health hazards beyond what was traditionally a common law violation; control of banking and bankruptcy; some reform-minded statutes, such as those creating mechanic's liens and the Married Women's Property Acts. In addition, most states "revised" their statutes in the sense of updating, correcting, and (in some cases) making significant changes, placing all legislation in a statutory code.

After the Civil War, federal legislation became important. Civil rights laws were passed to implement the Civil War amendments to the Constitution in 1866, 1871, and 1875. The first modern regulatory agency—the Interstate Commerce Commission—was created in 1877; the Sherman Antitrust Law was adopted in 1890, and the first peacetime income tax (on corporations) was adopted in 1894. But despite this federal legislation, the country had not come to the point of accepting a federal power to spend for the "general welfare." President James Madison's veto of federal canal and road building in 1817,[5] and President Franklin Pierce's veto of a bill to help the indigent insane in 1854[6] were still thought of throughout the nineteenth century as implementing a sound view of the role of the federal government.

Perhaps a more fundamental sign of the growing importance of federal legislation was the groundwork laid by the first codification in 1874[7] and Congress's replacement of the informal process of recording legislative debates through financial support to private publishers with direct supervision of the *Congressional Record* through the Government Printing Office in 1873.[8] These two steps signaled Congress's effort to improve the quality of legislation and were part of a continuing and general trend toward imposing structure on the law, which had began with the treatise tradition in the middle third of the nineteenth century and continued with the spread of national law schools and the development of the West Digest system in the last third of the century.

Nonetheless, nineteenth-century legislative activity at both federal and state levels still lacked the broad programmatic and reformist themes of modern twentieth-century legislation. Certainly, no one would confuse nineteenth-century statutes with the Constitution, which was infused with a spirit that guided its interpretation. Indeed, the almost religious introductory language to the Constitution—"ordain and establish"—differed markedly from the more mundane "be it enacted," with which statutes began.[9] The dominant view (at least among most lawyers in the first half of the century) was that legislation primarily patched up the common law, which continued to dominate the law. Francis Hilliard stated that most statutes did "not in general . . . alter or abrogate the principles of the common law."[10] Joseph Story said that a "man may live a century, and feel (comparatively speaking) but in few instances the operation of statutes, either as to his rights or duties; but the common law surrounds him, on every side, like the atmosphere which he breathes";[11] and, the Revised Statutes "[do] not provide for one case in a thousand, perhaps not for one in a hundred thousand, which is of daily occurrence and activity."[12] Certainly, many lawyers did not consider statutes very important. David Hoffman's *A Course of Legal Study* referred to the "casual and desultory" acquaintance of lawyers with statutes.[13] One observer analogized lawyers' ignorance of legislation to a corn merchant who knows nothing about cultivation.[14]

By the end of the nineteenth century the greatest enthusiasm about legislation that voices in the legal establishment could muster was to hope for improvement in a legislative process that they viewed with disdain. In an opening address before the American Social Science Association, Yale law professor Francis Wayland asked: "How can we rescue legislation from merited contempt? How can we relieve our courts from the intolerable burden of construing enactments which are an insult to common sense . . . ?"[15] Typical of the nineteenth century, Wayland looked for help from experts through appointment of apolitical commissioners to study and recommend changes,[16] a practice that began with the formation in 1892 of the National Conference of Commissioners on Uniform State Laws, sponsored by the American Bar Association.[17]

Although acceptance of nineteenth-century legislation by bench and bar was grudging, the obvious reality was the increasing importance of statutes. A growing number of published commentaries dealt with statutory interpretation and were eventually devoted to that subject alone. Initially, statutory interpretation did not attract nearly as much attention as the Constitution had in the late eighteenth century and early nineteenth century. Tucker's notes to his 1803 edition of Blackstone's *Commentaries* contained a few comments on constitutional interpretation, but it said nothing about statutory interpretation.[18] Former New York Chancellor James Kent's 1826 *Commentaries* devoted one lecture to statutes and their interpretation.[19] U.S. Supreme Court Justice Joseph Story wrote a major work about the Constitution—*Commentaries on the Constitution*—and contributed a piece on statutes and statutory interpretation to the *Encyclopedia Americana* in 1831.[20] Francis Lieber's 1839 book on hermeneutics discussed statutory interpretation as part of a general essay on the interpretation of written documents.[21]

As the century progressed, the literature on statutory interpretation increased. E. Fitch Smith's 1848 *Commentaries* dealt with statutes first, observing that no American work had been published on the construction of statutes and rejecting advice that the issue was "too trivial."[22] And Theodore Sedgwick, a moderate Republican,[23] wrote a treatise in 1857 after retiring from his New York law practice, giving far more consideration to statutes than to the Constitution.[24]

Separate treatises on statutes appeared after the Civil War. Several were English treatises with notes and comments by American authors: Platt Potter, a New York judge, published an 1871 edition of Sir Fortunatus Dwarris's English treatise on statutes, with comments appropriate to the U.S. system;[25] John Pomeroy, a law professor, published an 1874 edition of Sedgwick's 1857 *Treatise*, with numerous updated notes about statutory interpretation, and G. A. Endlich, a Pennsylvania judge, published an 1888 American edition of Sir Peter Maxwell's English treatise on interpretation.[26]

American-authored treatises on statutory interpretation also appeared. Joel Bishop, a lawyer who gave up practice to write books for the last forty or more years of his life, published his commentaries on statutory interpretation in 1882.[27] In 1891, J. G. Sutherland's *Statutes and Statutory Construction* appeared.[28] And in 1896, West Publishing Company brought out Henry Black's *Construction and Interpretation of the Laws*.[29] In addition, Thomas Cooley's 1872 *Commentaries on Blackstone*, unlike St. George Tucker's 1803 edition, discussed statutory interpretation.[30]

These treatises, especially those written after the Civil War, seemed to fill a widespread need among the practicing bar for material on statutory interpretation. Consistent with the spirit of the late nineteenth century, Bishop argued that interpretation law could be reduced to organized rules and that "statutory interpretation [was] governed as absolutely by rules as anything else in the law."[31] Sutherland's 1891 treatise states that, unlike contracts and other private documents, "law for the construction of *Written Laws*" is not as "well defined"; "[w]hen it is considered how many legislative bodies there are," it is important that "principles [be] generalized, with a view to maintaining the domain of the law as a science. . . ."[32] Black stated that his work followed "the general plan of the Hornbook Series . . . after the manner of a code, expressed in brief black-letter paragraphs. . . ."[33]

More significantly, no one had to defend writing about statutory interpretation, as Smith had done. Bishop probably spoke for all treatise writers in stating that "[i]n practical importance, there is no legal subject which approaches this."[34] Still, even at this late date in 1891, Sutherland admitted that "[s]tatutes are but a small part of our jurisprudence."[35]

Pre–Civil War Commentaries and Judges

The growing impact of statutes on legal change meant that statutory inter-pretation had to be taken seriously, a fact reflected among pre–Civil War commentators in the evolution from a suspicion of legislatures and praise for judicial competence and the priority of judge-made law to a reversal of roles—toward a growing awareness of legislative competence, judicial short-comings, and the importance of legislation. From James Kent's praise of the common law (1826) to Theodore Sedgwick's suspicion of judicial competence and confidence in legislative competence (1857), there was a demonstrable shift away from taking judicial lawmaking discretion and equitable interpre-tation for granted.

When we look at what judges did, however, the picture is more complex. Chief Justice Marshall, whom I take as the example of federal statutory inter-pretation, reacted against the traditional judicial dominance over legislation but staked out a special judicial interpretive role in protecting fundamen-tal values. At the state level—especially for Chief Justice Lemuel Shaw in Massachusetts—statutory interpretation did not clearly differentiate between fundamental values and matters of mere inconvenience. State judges, more so than Marshall, appeared willing to incorporate the English legal tradition of trying to help the legislature reach a sensible result in all types of cases, but without the judicial arrogance or priority of judge-made law which was part of that tradition.

COMMENTATORS

The evolution among pre–Civil War commentators begins with Chancellor James Kent (1826), whose praise for the common law and the relative advan-tages of judging over legislating is captured in his observation (quoting Lord Chancellor John Wilmot) that the common law is a "nursing father," but a "statute is like a tyrant." [36] Thereafter, commentators moved perceptibly away from Kent's point of view. Joseph Story (1831) was less enthusiastic about the common law and more cautious about the judicial role in statutory interpre-tation. Francis Lieber (1839) warned against equitable interpretation (what he called "construction" as opposed to "interpretation"), though he would have preserved an important judicial role in statutory interpretation when fundamental values were at stake. E. Fitch Smith (1848) was unequivocal in opposing equitable interpretation, as was Sedgwick (1857). Sedgwick's views are the most well-developed, explicitly based on his affirmative view of the growing competence of the legislature and the incompetence of judges.

James Kent

James Kent was the earliest of the commentators and the most committed to the common law—to judicial over legislative competence. He had been a Federalist state legislator from 1790 until 1793 and was identified with defense of established property rights and opposition to universal suffrage; he and Hamilton were close political friends. Kent became a New York judge in 1798 and was chancellor of the equity court system from 1814 until 1823, when he was forced to retire at age sixty under a state constitutional provision.

Kent's statutory interpretation opinions are unself-conscious in their willingness to use equitable interpretation or not, as the judge sees fit. More often, he restrained the reach of a statute that did not adopt the common law and avoided extensive equitable interpretation.[37] Occasionally, he gave legislation an expansive interpretation, even allowing for government intrusion on private property. But he did so grudgingly and apologetically. In one case, where the intrusion occurred to allow completion of canal construction, he stated that "[s]tatutes made for the public good . . . are to receive a very liberal construction, and to be expounded in such a manner, as that they may, as far as possible, attain the end."[38] But he noted that the entry onto private property was carefully circumscribed to protect the owners from unnecessary damage and avoided a broader taking of the entire property that would have required government compensation. "The rule is, that [statutes made for the public good] are to be so construed . . . always to advance the public interest, *doing as little damage as possible to the private interest*" (emphasis added).

In his 1826 *Commentaries,* Kent explains why there should be a strong judicial role in statutory interpretation. He calls attention not only to the "imperfection of human language" (echoing James Madison), but also to the "want of technical skill in the [legislative] makers of the law."[39] He affirms that the "common law [is] the perfection of reason."[40] No wonder he believed that "[s]tatutes are . . . to be construed in reference to the principles of the common law, for it is not to be presumed the legislature intended to make any innovation upon the common law, further than the case absolutely required."[41] And in a letter to Edward Livingston, the codifier of Louisiana law, he states: "I think . . . Lord Mansfield, or Burke . . . possessed ten times as much practical good sense and sound wisdom as . . . Jeremy Bentham"; he concludes by telling Livingston that he (Kent) "lag[s] so far behind the spirit of the age" but justifies it on the ground that he "ha[s] spent the best years of my life in administering the old common law of the land . . . *with all its imperfections on its head*" (emphasis in the original).[42]

Nonetheless, Kent does not sound as extreme as the English common law lawyers and judges before the eighteenth century. He affirms that the "true meaning of the statute is generally and properly to be sought from the body of the act itself" (the reference to "body" shows how far from Plowden we have come).[43] And Kent's reference to "practical good sense and sound wisdom," while leaving no doubt about his faith in judges, does not revert to the rhetoric of sagelike artificial reason.

Joseph Story

Joseph Story, a Republican legislator in Massachusetts beginning in 1805, also served in the U.S. Congress until his appointment to the U.S. Supreme Court in 1811, where he served until 1845. His commitment to the Republican Party was not single-minded, however. (Jefferson called him a pseudo-Republican.) His biographer suggests that his Republican affiliation had much to do with following his father's political attachments. Eventually, Story became disillusioned with party politics in general, shifting his allegiance to the science of law rather than the art of politics.[44]

Story's few judicial opinions commenting on statutory interpretation reveal a modestly aggressive interpreter. For example, he affirmed the importance of legislative intent, derived from the "natural interpretation of the words," but with a cautious eye on "inconveniences" that might be caused by an interpretation;[45] he appealed to the canon that statutes in derogation of the common law should be narrowly construed;[46] and he believed that the decision whether to adopt a strict or a liberal interpretation was a question of common law doctrine that the judge must decide.[47] But his judicial comments about statutory interpretation are too few and unreflective to support much generalization.[48]

As a commentator, Story presented his views on statutes and statutory interpretation in an article written in 1831 for the *Encyclopedia Americana*, edited by his friend Francis Lieber. Story's view of legislation was more positive and his view of the common law less favorable than Kent's. The problem with statutes, he believed, was not anything inherent about language or the legislature's lack of technical skill, but it stemmed from their unadaptability to change—the Aristotelian justification for a judicial role in statutory interpretation. Speaking of statutes, Story asked rhetorically: "But is it possible to foresee, or to provide beforehand, for all . . . cases?"[49]

As for the common law, Story was not as reverential as Kent. Not that Story failed to place immense faith in the common law. He clearly viewed it as the dominant source of law ("[a] man may live a century, and feel . . . but in few instances the operation of statutes . . . ; but the common law [is] like the atmosphere which he breathes"); and legislation, though coextensive with sovereignty, "is in fact employed, if not universally, at least generally, in mere acts of amendment and supplement to the existing laws and institutions. Its office is ordinarily not so much to create systems of laws, as to supply defects, and cure mischiefs in the systems already existing."[50]

Story also viewed the common law as a dynamic engine of lawmaking, not a static tradition (noting that "a great portion of English common law is of modern growth"). He, like Kent, advocated revisiting the Supreme Court's decision in Hudson & Goodwin, which held that there was no federal common law of crimes.[51] And he authored Swift v. Tyson, upholding a federal commercial common law.[52] But Story also admitted that the common law could become atrophied, "quite as unyielding as any code can be,"[53] and that legislative enactment is needed to modify the common law.[54] The last part of his article was devoted to a defense of moderate codification efforts. He also served on the committee to codify the Massachusetts law. The common thread in Story's view of the law is change, primarily through the common law, but through legislation where appropriate.

When he dealt explicitly with statutory interpretation, Story tracked William Blackstone's discussion[55] without citation and without any creative gloss, perhaps because he did not think the subject of great importance. He affirmed that the "intention of the legislature is to be followed," but it should be "gathered from the words, the context, the subject matter, the effects and consequences, and the spirit or reason of the law." He then explained what he meant in Blackstonian language—words are understood in their "ordinary and natural sense"; "context" consists of "other passages and sentences"; a consideration of "effects and consequences" can prevent "absurd" results but not if "the legislature has clearly expressed [a contrary] will." "The reason and spirit of the law are also regarded; but this is always in subordination to the words, and not to control the natural and fair interpretation of them. In short, the spirit and the reason are derived principally from examining the whole text, and not a single passage. . . ."

There was a place—but a modest place—for "equity." In Story's view, "extreme" cases can be excluded from the "generality of the words [by] contraction or extension" pursuant to "equity," which he associated with construing words in "their mildest, and not in their harshest sense, it being open to adopt either."

Story's explanation for how the common law interacts with legislation was consistent with a subtle shift away from Kent's extreme enthusiasm for the common law. Story said that "[i]n all cases of a *doubtful* nature, the common law will prevail, and the statute not be construed to repeal it" (emphasis added). This assertion contrasted with Kent's view that "[s]tatutes are . . . to be construed in reference to the principles of the common law, for it is not to be presumed the legislature intended to make any innovation upon the common law, further than the case absolutely required."[56] Moreover, Story's observation that the common law should prevail was followed immediately by an example: "Hence, where a remedy is given by statute . . . , it is not construed to extend so as to alter the common law in other cases." In other words, statutes supplement the common law, and the interpreter should not extend the statutory remedy by negative implication to reject common law remedies. This falls well short of hostility to statutes, in the sense of narrowly construing legislation when the text seems to change common law rules. It is the sort of accommodation between new statutory remedies and the old common law that often made good sense.

Francis Lieber

Francis Lieber's 1839 book, *Legal and Political Hermeneutics,* did not focus explicitly on statutes but dealt with the entire range of legal and political texts. He was a complex thinker whose German background is apparent in the formal categorical structures he imparted to his views, but who wedded this tendency to American common sense.[57] He spent most of his academic life as a professor of history and political economy at South Carolina College (1835–56), but he moved to Columbia University in 1856, and from 1865 until his death in 1872 he was one of two law professors at Columbia Law School.[58]

Lieber's formalism was best exemplified by his distinction between interpretation and construction and for the related view that interpretation precedes construction.[59] In making this distinction, he appeared to warn against equitable interpretation, committing to the text and expressing suspicion of judicial "construction" that takes judges beyond the interpretation of textual meaning (construction is "dangerous" if it goes "beyond the absolute sense of the text").[60] And, in his occasional use of the phrase "genuine" interpretation,[61] he foreshadowed Roscoe Pound's 1907 distinction between genuine and spurious interpretation (discussed in chapter 4).[62] But Lieber also had a strong pragmatic streak, appealing to "[c]ommon sense and good faith [as] the leading stars of all genuine interpretation."[63]

More importantly, Lieber's attitude toward "construction" is ambivalent.

He defined it in familiar "equity of the statute" language, though he stressed the role of the text in identifying the spirit of the law: it is "the drawing of conclusions respecting subjects, that lie beyond the direct expression of the text, from elements known from and given in the text—conclusions which are in the spirit, though not within the letter of the text."[64] Despite his concern that construction is "dangerous," he believed that it was "unavoidable."[65] And he acknowledged the difficulty of confining the occasions for construction of statutes. Despite his view that "nothing is so favorable to that great essential of all civil liberty—the protection of individual rights, as close interpretation and construction,"[66] he advocated a liberal construction to prevent the flogging of a Christian Native Indian in the British Army.[67] "[T]here are considerations, which ought to induce us to abandon interpretation . . . ; especially not to slaughter justice, the sovereign object of laws, to the law itself, the means of obtaining it."[68]

Construction was also linked to the need to adapt statutes to change because "[m]en who use words . . . cannot foresee all possible complex cases. . . ."[69] Consequently, the older the text, the freer the construction.[70] Moreover, judicial adaptation of statutes to change by construction was more important when "the subject to which the text relates [is] of . . . elementary, vital, and absorbing importance to society . . ."; in that case, "every other interest, or consideration, must yield; so that in construing the difficult parts of the text, we are obliged to regulate our decision rather by the meaning which the words would now have, considering things and circumstances as they now exist, than by the known meaning which the utterer attached to them, considering the then relations."[71]

Lieber's suspicion of judicial construction of statutes continues the nineteenth-century trend away from Kent's preference for judge-made law over legislation, but his belief in the inevitability of construction (especially regarding matters of "justice" and "elementary importance") places him in the nineteenth-century tradition of statutory interpretation, which we will later observe in Chief Justice Marshall's opinions—that is, nervous about extreme cases of equitable interpretation but intent on retaining a significant interpretive role for the judge where fundamental values are at stake.

E. Fitch Smith

E. Fitch Smith's 1848 treatise on statutory and constitutional interpretation abandons all caution in criticizing equitable interpretation. His book is primarily a compendium of what other authors had said, without expressing a point of view. However, in a chapter that seems to come closest to expressing his own position ("Of Legislative and Judicial Interpretation"), he strongly denounces equitable interpretation.

More than any other pre–Civil War commentator, Smith emphasizes concerns of legitimacy over competence in warning against equitable interpretation. He agrees with this statement from the dissent in Mayor v. Lord (a case to be discussed): "Where the legislature have used words of plain and definite import, it would be dangerous to put upon them a construction which would amount to holding that the legislature did not mean what they had clearly expressed."[72] Smith also quotes Dwarris's warning that "judges are not to be encouraged to direct their conduct 'by the crooked cord of discretion, but by the golden metwand [measuring rod] of the law.' "[73] Otherwise, "equitable construction [will] usurp legislative authority." And he favorably cites Supreme Court Justice Chase's views in the Priestman case,[74] objecting to equitable construction because it "assumed a legislative power" and stating that no rule of construction "can be more dangerous than that which distinguishes between the intent and the words of the legislature, which declares that a case not within the meaning of the statute, according to the opinion of the judges, shall not be embraced within the operation of it, although it is clearly within the words; and vice versa, that a case within the meaning, though not within the words, shall be embraced."[75]

These views lead Smith to ask rhetorically whether "courts [are] to proceed upon established principles—to be governed by fixed rules; or, exercising a liberal discretion, to have recourse, in doubtful cases, to natural principles,—to aid and to moderate the law according to equitable considerations,—to include in their deliberations those cases and circumstances, which the legislator himself would have expressed, had he foreseen them?"[76] His answer is that it is "the duty of the judges, in a land jealous of its liberties, to give effect to the expressed sense, of words, of the law . . . ;" "[t]he duty of the judge is to adhere to the legal text, as his sole guide."[77]

Theodore Sedgwick

Like Smith, Theodore Sedgwick in his 1857 treatise provides the reader with an extensive range of material about different approaches to interpretation, but his own views are clear. He leaves no doubt that he opposes equitable interpretation. He describes *both* "liberal and strict construction" as an example of the "judicial function . . . blended with and lost in the legislative attributes."[78] Consequently, "if [the] intention is expressed in a manner devoid of contradiction and ambiguity, there is no room for interpretation or construction, and the judiciary are not at liberty, on consideration of policy or hardship, to depart from the words of the statute. . . ."[79] These views are consistent with Sedgwick's advocacy of Republican principles, which included suspicion of judges, although his was a moderate Republicanism, opposing the election of judges.[80]

Although some of Sedgwick's arguments dwell on legitimacy—he is opposed to blending the legislative and judicial functions, and, like Smith, he cites favorably both Justice Samuel Chase in the Priestman case and the dissent in Mayor of New York v. Lord[81]—his opposition to equitable interpretation is based primarily on the comparative lawmaking competence of legislatures and judges. Just as Blackstone's concern about legislative *in*competence shaped Blackstone's views of what judges could do to help out the legislature, Sedgwick believed that the improving quality of legislation altered the judge's interpretive role. Sedgwick felt nothing like Kent's suspicion of the legislature's abilities. Equitable interpretation is obsolete because "the legislator has now time to frame his statute in simple and intelligible language."[82] Sedgwick sounds especially modern in worrying about the practical impact of equitable interpretation in encouraging "unbounded [legislative] carelessness."[83]

Equally as important as legislative competence was judicial incompetence. Sedgwick held that, compared to an earlier time, the judge's ability to know what the legislature wanted was much reduced. He emphasizes the weakening of the strong link between judges and legislators, which was an apt description of English judges but (he argues) was no longer true of the American judiciary.[84]

> It may very well be that, in the condition of English jurisprudence in former times, when laws were few and rarely passed, when the business of legislation was confined to a small and select class, to which practically the judiciary belonged, when the legislative and judicial bodies sat in the same place, and, indeed, in the same building,—in such a state of things, it may well be that the judiciary might suppose themselves to possess, that they might indeed really possess, a considerable personal knowledge of the legislative intent, and that they might come almost to consider themselves as a co-ordinate body with the Legislature.

Striking a note that will sound familiar to modern students of legislation, Sedgwick argues that "where the business of legislation has become multifarious and enormous, and especially in this country where the judiciary is so completely separated from the Legislature, it must be untrue in fact that they can have any personal knowledge sufficient really to instruct them as to the legislative intention; and if untrue in fact, any general theory or loose idea of this kind must be dangerous in practice."[85]

Whether U.S. judges had in fact lost that intimate knowledge of statutes which helped to support a bold interpretive approach is, however, far from clear. The briefest sampling of biographical reviews of nineteenth-century state judges reveals their political connections. Of the seven best-known state judges (as characterized by Willard Hurst)[86]—James Kent (New York), Lemuel Shaw (Massachusetts), John Gibson (Pennsylvania), Isaac Blackford (Indiana), Thomas Ruffin (North Carolina), Charles Doe (New Hampshire), and Thomas Cooley (Michigan)—all of them, except for Doe and Cooley, served in the legislature;[87] Doe was, however, very politically active before becoming a judge,[88] and Cooley was elected to the state supreme court and later served as chair of the Interstate Commerce Commission.[89] Of the approximately seventy judges of the Ohio supreme court who served in the nineteenth century, about fifty had held an elected office—governor, state or federal legislature, or prosecutor.[90] Of the ten Indiana supreme court justices serving on the "old court"—that is, before the 1851 constitution—at least eight had served in the legislature.[91] And, as Hurst notes, election of judges generally meant selection by party leaders, thereby further assuring that judges would bring a political caste of mind to the bench. The judges' background undoubtedly encouraged them to think of themselves as politically savvy.

Of special concern to Sedgwick was the narrow interpretation of statutes in derogation of common law, a type of equitable construction.[92] Sedgwick traces this approach to Coke's now-obsolete view that the common law was perfect. ("It is difficult, if not impossible, now to understand this enthusiastic loyalty to a body of law, the most peculiar features of which the activity of the present generation has been largely occupied in uprooting and destroying.")[93]

Sedgwick's dominant theme, however, is pragmatic. He refused to dwell on some of the old chestnuts of statutory interpretation—such as whether a law which prohibits striking a father applies when the son shakes his father out of a fit: "These and similar discussions have amused the fancy and exhausted the arguments of text writers. I cannot, however, consider them of much value for the student of jurisprudence . . .;" "[w]hat is required . . . is not formal rules, or nice terminology, or ingenious classification; but that thorough intellectual training, that complete education of the mind, which lead it to a correct result, wholly independent of rules, and, indeed, almost unconscious of the process by which the end is attained;" and he argues that "[o]urs is eminently a practical science. It is only by an intimate acquaintance with its application to the affairs of life, as they actually occur, that we can acquire that sagacity requisite to decide new and doubtful cases."[94]

The unmistakable shift among the commentators toward criticism of equitable interpretation might suggest that the inherited English legal tradition of judges working with the legislature to develop the law had been abandoned, but that would be misleading. Two variations on that tradition survived. First, at the federal level (in Chief Justice Marshall's opinions), statutory interpretation concentrated on protecting fundamental values, rejecting the aggressive judicial role that English judges had taken in matters of mere inconvenience. Second, at the state level, judges continued to engage in equitable interpretation, but without the arrogance that had characterized a good deal of English judging. We look first at Marshall's opinions to illustrate federal judging, and then at state judges (especially Chief Justice Lemuel Shaw in Massachusetts).

FEDERAL STATUTORY INTERPRETATION: CHIEF JUSTICE JOHN MARSHALL

John Marshall wrote opinions both as a circuit court judge and as a Supreme Court justice (from 1801 to 1835). He was a Federalist committed to a belief in inalienable presocial rights and in an independent judiciary whose role was to protect those rights through constitutional and statutory interpretation.[95] He carved out a role for judges in statutory interpretation that cut back on the bolder versions of equitable interpretation, but with an important exception; where fundamental values were at stake, statutes would not be interpreted to impair such values, absent a clear statement in the legislation.[96] Marshall therefore built on that strand in the inherited English tradition which focused on protection of fundamental values through statutory interpretation. I would hazard the guess that Marshall's retreat was mainly tactical, rather than a commitment to a theory of judging, and was attributable to his desire to preserve a strong federal judicial role in constitutional interpretation in an era of minimal federal legislation. The significance of his views for modern statutory interpretation is therefore limited, now that federal legislation is an accepted and pervasive part of the law.

Statutory interpretation. Marshall's opinions emphasize that statutory interpretation had evolved away from the more extreme versions of equitable interpretation, noting that the practice of going "far beyond the words" in "the construction of ancient statutes" has "in modern times . . . been a good deal restrained."[97] This viewpoint leads him to emphasize the statutory text.[98]

Thus: the "law is the best expositor of itself";[99] "[m]en use a language calculated to express the idea they mean to convey;[100] "intention [of the legislature] is to be searched for in the words . . .";[101] "[b]y the spirit of the law, I understand, the intention of the legislature, to be collected from the general language of the act, the scope of its provisions, and the objects to be attained."[102]

Marshall's most famous statutory interpretation decision is United States v. Fisher.[103] It contains a quote about statutory interpretation that can drastically mislead when taken out of context: "Where the mind labours to discover the design of the legislature, it seizes every thing from which aid can be derived. . . ."[104] But the immediate setting for this statement is Marshall's use of the act's title, which (he says) "claims a degree of notice, and will have its due share of consideration," but cannot "controul plain words in the body of the statute"; and, "[w]here the intent is plain, nothing is left to construction."[105]

The core of Marshall's view of statutory interpretation appears later in the same opinion. His approach was to distinguish between fundamental principles, on the one hand, and political regulation and inconvenience, on the other, leaving political regulation to the legislature. "Where rights are infringed, where fundamental principles are overthrown, where the general system of the laws is departed from, the legislative intention must be expressed with irresistible clearness to induce a court of justice to suppose a design to effect such objects."[106] Marshall here sounds a lot like Alexander Hamilton, whose only comment on statutory interpretation in the *Federalist Papers* asserts a power to *limit* statutes through interpretation to prevent injustice.[107] However, Marshall advocates a different, more textual approach when less than fundamental values are at stake.

> But where only a political regulation is made, which is *inconvenient* [emphasis added], if the intention of the legislature be expressed in terms which are sufficiently intelligible to leave no doubt in the mind when the words are taken in their ordinary sense, it would be going a great way to say that a constrained interpretation must be put upon them, to avoid an inconvenience which ought to have been contemplated in the legislature when the act was passed, and which, in their opinion, was probably overbalanced by the particular advantages it was calculated to produce.

In matters of political regulation, "[i]t is for the legislature to appreciate them. They are not of such magnitude as to induce an opinion that the legislature could not intend to expose the citizens of the United States to them, when words are used which manifest that intent."

Marshall's focus on the "fundamental" reflected one important aspect of the legal culture that the United States inherited from England at the time of the Founding. English statutory interpretation had always been concerned with fundamental values, as Coke's decision in Bonham's Case illustrated. But this was not the only, or even the dominant, element in equitable interpretation. Equitable interpretation was not limited to fundamental concerns but had been broadly conceived in the inherited tradition as the way for courts to make sense of how statutes fit into the law.

However, the American experience put significant pressure on the inherited English tradition. As Gordon Wood argues, *the* significant break with English legal theory was to highlight not merely the existence of fundamental law as opposed to ordinary law but also the court's role in enforcing it.[108] This break led to the adoption of a Constitution that embodied fundamental values and judicial review to enforce them. But it also created a serious problem for statutory interpretation in a society equally intent on giving legislatures (at least state legislatures) a dynamic lawmaking role, not just technical sovereignty. One way to reconcile these two objectives was to bifurcate law into fundamental values, for which courts continued to have a special responsibility, and the inconvenient, which was left to the legislature. This commitment to fundamental values drew on what William Nelson identifies as a shared consensus about fundamentals,[109] which *we* may consider naïve and even manipulative, especially when it coexists with a revulsion (as Marshall put it) to a "wild and enthusiastic" democracy.[110] But the dichotomy between the fundamental and merely inconvenient was an operative principle for many judges, and Marshall's approach to statutory interpretation implemented that view.

We can recognize Marshall's reliance on fundamental values in statutory interpretation as an approach that eventually matured in the nineteenth century into what became known as the Golden Rule.[111] The Golden Rule deferred to the text unless it produced "absurd" (or unjust) results, in which case the text was limited to prevent those consequences. The best-known formulation of the Golden Rule is from the English case of Becke v. Smith: "It is a very useful rule, in the construction of a statute, to adhere to the ordinary meaning of the words used . . . unless that is at variance with the intention of the legislature, to be collected from the statute itself, or leads to any manifest absurdity or repugnance, in which case the language may be varied or modified, so as to avoid such inconvenience, but no further." [112]

Some formulations of the Golden Rule were much broader, however, and were hard to distinguish from traditional equitable interpretation. For example, "an inconsistency, or an absurdity or *inconvenience* so great as to convince the Court that the intention could not have been to use [words] in their ordinary signification . . ." (emphasis added) will permit judges to attribute a "less proper" meaning to statutory language.[113] The "inconvenience" standard can draw judges into a bolder role in statutory interpretation than the narrower concern with "absurdity," and it is, of course, hard to draw a line between the fundamental and inconvenient. Indeed, Marshall would have been the first to admit that it is difficult to sort out what a judge is actually doing based on generalities. He notes that there is "no difference of opinion" about "abstract principles" of statutory interpretation, but "in the application of those principles . . . the difference discovers itself." [114] We should not be surprised therefore to find that property ownership was one value that Marshall considered fundamental. "There are certainly few cases in which . . . freedom of construction can be justified. If any act will justify it, it is the act for regulating conveyances." [115] And the statutory "absurdity" from which the English court recoiled in Becke v. Smith was the imposition of statutory liability without fault, which was symptomatic of the propensity to equate fundamental values with the common law (where fault was required for liability) that became so common in the second half of the nineteenth century.

Comparison to constitutional interpretation. Marshall's constitutional interpretation opinions contrast with his statutory interpretation decisions. He was firmly committed (when necessary) to an equitable interpretation approach that *expanded* the constitutional text, where the text was capable of bearing that meaning. In this respect, Marshall's approach to constitutional interpretation anticipates twentieth-century purposivism, with its sympathetic elaboration of values implicit in the document.

Marshall was, however, more circumspect than James Wilson, probably because he was determined as chief justice to expand the Court's influence and therefore not anxious to be seen taking controversial interpretive approaches. His opinions do not reveal a single-minded commitment to the kind of equitable interpretation that Wilson embraced in Chisholm v. Georgia,[116] which relied primarily on a sense of the underlying spirit of the document. Marshall was, consequently, readily willing to rely on the language of the constitutional text, even on the kind of technical interpretive maxims that Hamilton had rejected for a constitution. For example, in Marbury v. Madison,[117] Marshall supported his view that Congress could not add to the constitutional list of original jurisdiction of the Supreme Court with an appeal to the common law maxim of interpretation that "[a]ffirmative words are often, in their operation, negative of other objects than those affirmed; and in this case, a negative or exclusive sense must be given to them or they have no operation at all." [118] (This was the maxim that Hamilton had rejected for constitutional interpretation.)

Marshall was also willing to affirm a textual approach *when* the result rejected a "spirit" that would *limit* federal power. In Gibbons v. Ogden,[119] he relied primarily on the text to conclude that a federal statute exercising power to "regulate commerce" prevented the states from parallel regulation. Because the constitutional language appeared to give Congress the power to supersede state regulation, Marshall stuck to the text and rejected a strict constructionist "spirit."[120]

> This instrument contains an enumeration of powers expressly granted by the people to their government. It has been said, that these powers ought to be construed strictly. . . . What do [they] mean, by a strict construction? If they contend only against that enlarged construction, which would extend words beyond their natural and obvious import, we might question the application of the term, but should not controvert the principle.

In other words, sticking to the text is not strict *limiting* construction; it only avoids extensive equitable interpretation. Moreover, Marshall acknowledges and rejects another meaning of strict construction—that of limiting equitable interpretation.

> If they contend for that narrow construction which, in support of some theory not to be found in the constitution, would deny to the government those powers which the words of the grant, as usually understood, import, and which are consistent with the general views and objects of the instrument. . . . then we cannot perceive the propriety of this strict construction, nor adopt it as the rule by which the constitution is to be expounded.

With language on his side, Marshall sees little need to argue about underlying principles. He relies on the words "in their natural sense" and on the assumption that the framers "intended what they have said."

His opinion in McCulloch v. Maryland,[121] upholding the constitutionality of the national bank, is often cited to support an equitable interpretation approach to constitutional interpretation, based on his statement that "it is a *constitution* we are expounding" (emphasis in original),[122] and elements of the opinion certainly support this view. The quotation about expounding the Constitution is preceded by statements about the principles of national government[123]—the fact that the Constitution emanated from the people and was not the act of sovereign states. But the same passage which affirms that it is a constitution we are expounding also contrasts "the prolixity of a legal code" —that is, a statute—with the language of this constitution, whose "nature . . . requires, that only its great outlines should be marked. . . ."[124] Thus, the text itself might require resort to the underlying reason of the rule, rather than the underlying spirit being the driving force behind the interpretation of the document. When Marshall goes on to explain that the Constitution was "intended to endure for ages to come," [125] he could well have meant only that this required *legislative* flexibility (an expansive federal legislative power), not that the courts had an aggressive equitable power of interpretation.[126]

At this point, Marshall's constitutional opinions reveal at most only a cautious tilt toward equitable interpretation. But he commits to a full-bodied embrace of a broad power of judicial construction in the second of two opinions dealing with the federal Constitution's Impairment of Contract clause, which asserts that "no State shall pass any law impairing the obligation of contracts." When forced to choose, Marshall favors extensive equitable interpretation, bringing an underlying sense of the document to the task of determining its meaning.

The first case, Sturges v. Crowninshield,[127] held that a state unconstitutionally impairs a prior contract when it attempts to discharge an insolvent debtor from his obligation. The state argued that this was not the specific mischief that concerned the Constitution's authors. Marshall responds to this argument with the textualist-oriented Golden Rule, an interpretive approach that favored the security of contracts in this case. He favors sticking to the text—except, of course, if the results would be absurd, or (as he puts it) "monstrous." The argument had been made that

> although all legislative acts which discharge the obligation of a contract without performance, are within the very words of the constitution, yet an insolvent act, containing this principle, is not within its spirit, because such acts have been passed by Colonial and State Legislatures from the first settlement of the country, and because we know from the history of the times that the mind of the Convention was directed to other laws which were fraudulent in their character, which enabled the debtor to escape from his obligation, and yet hold his property, not to this, which is beneficial in its operation.

He rejected this effort to limit the text to accord with the historical mischief at which the document was aimed:

> Before discussing this argument, it may not be improper to premise that, although the spirit of an instrument, especially of a constitution, is to be respected not less than its letter, yet the spirit is to be collected chiefly from its words. It would be dangerous in the extreme to infer from extrinsic circum-

stances, that a case for which the words of an instrument expressly provide, shall be exempted from its operation. . . . [I]f, in any case, the plain meaning of a provision, not contradicted by any other provision in the same instrument, is to be disregarded, because we believe the framers of that instrument could not intend what they say, it must be one in which the absurdity and injustice of applying the provision to the case, would be so monstrous, that all mankind would, without hesitation, unite in rejecting the application.

Although the historical mischief addressed by the constitutional provision prohibiting impairment of contracts was not insolvency laws, "[n]o court can be justified in restricting such comprehensive words to a particular mischief to which no allusion is made."

And then came Ogden v. Saunders.[128] In this case, a state bankruptcy law operated on a contract entered into *after* the statute's passage. The majority of the Court held that state law unconstitutionally impaired a contract only if it operated on *preexisting* contracts. Marshall dissented.[129] He starts with a textual argument—what else could he do after his stirring claim that the constitutional text controlled when the debt arose *prior* to the state law. But his argument is weak. He notes that the "impairment" clause appeared along with other prohibitions, some of which affected events *after* adoption of state legislation. But, as the majority noted, the "family" of prohibitions with which the impairment clause was associated was concerned primarily with retroactive laws—including a prohibition on ex post facto laws.[130]

In fact, Marshall's heart is not in the textualist argument. What drives his opinion is his deep commitment to a view of contracts, society, and the state of nature, much as Wilson's view of government and sovereign immunity shaped his decision in Chisholm v. Georgia. Marshall rejects the view that "contract is the mere creature of society, and derives all its obligation from human legislation"; contract law instead imposes "pre-existing intrinsic obligation[s] which human law enforces," "anterior to, and independent of society," "natural rights, brought with man into society, . . . not given by human legislation." Marshall invokes the "state of nature, [where] individuals may contract, their contracts are obligatory, and force may rightfully be employed to coerce the party who has broken his engagement."

Marshall also looks back to the time of the Founding to describe the mischief at which the constitutional provision was aimed. He makes the familiar interpretive move of describing the mischief at a higher level of generality than the specifics that occupied the Framers and describes the mischief as state exercise of a "power [to] chang[e] the relative situation of debtor and creditor. . . ." Moreover, this mischief was serious stuff, requiring (he might have said) an expansive equitable interpretation of the constitutional text to prohibit state interference.

> The mischief had become so great, so alarming, as not only to impair commercial intercourse, and threaten the existence of credit, but to sap the morals of the people, and destroy the sanctity of private faith. To guard against the continuance of the evil was an object of deep interest with all the truly wise, as well as the virtuous, of this great community, and was one of the important benefits expected from a reform of the government.

Marshall's embrace of equitable interpretation of the Constitution permitted him to infuse the text with meaning, which took shape in accordance with the substantive principle of guarding against a mischievous threat to commercial intercourse and to the extension of credit.

In sum, by drawing a distinction between the "fundamental" and "inconvenient," Marshall's approach to interpretation differentiated among components of equitable interpretation that the English tradition had merged. This position enabled him to preserve an aggressive but selective role for judges in protecting fundamental values, limiting the reach of statutes, and expanding constitutional purposes. It was a judicial role that implemented Marshall's philosophy of government and, by not making broader claims for judicial authority, insulated the federal judiciary from too much criticism.

STATE STATUTORY INTERPRETATION

Focusing on federal courts provides a distorted picture of nineteenth-century statutory interpretation. The federal government had only limited governmental powers, and it was not until the twentieth century that federal legislation began to dominate much of our law. Most statutes were passed by state legislatures, and it is to state statutory interpretation that we should look to learn more about the evolution of interpretive theory and practice.

State judicial practice in general

From reading the commentators we might form one of two opposite impressions: either that equitable interpretation was in complete decline (Sedgwick), except, perhaps, for protecting fundamental values (Lieber), or that it continued to be rampant in its most extreme form in which the judge paid little attention to what the legislature said (Smith). Neither impression would be accurate.

Was equitable interpretation in complete decline? Sedgwick claims that his opposition to equitable interpretation accurately reflects judicial practice. He says that "the judges themselves set limits to the powers they had arrogated; and abandoning all pretensions of a right to exercise any control over legislation, to correct its errors or supply its deficiencies, they confined their power of construction to admitted cases of doubt. Such is now the settled doctrine both in England and in this country." [131]

But the wish was father to the thought. Sedgwick admits that "[t]he notion of a restricted or an enlarged construction has been introduced and practiced upon rather with reference to the kind or class of laws to which the statute in question belonged than to the clearness or ambiguity of the letter of the enactment." [132] And a book review of Sedgwick's work suggests that his opposition to equitable interpretation was not uniformly reflected in judicial practice.[133] The reviewer takes Sedgwick to task specifically for his incorrect characterization of a decision by Justice Shaw that applied a statutory prohibition on sales of liquor even when the liquor was for a medicinal purpose. Sedgwick had emphasized the textualist aspects of Shaw's opinion. "The decisive answer is, that the Legislature has made no such exception [for medicinal liquor]. If the law is more restricted in its present form than the Legislature intended, it must be regulated by legislative action." [134] But, the reviewer notes, Shaw had in fact defended his textualist reading of the statute *because* it made policy sense— because an exception for medicinal alcohol could encourage avoidance of the statute's objectives.[135] Shaw had not passively deferred to the statutory text; he had instead taken account of how well the interpretation implemented statutory policy, which is the way of traditional equitable interpretation.

It is also clear from E. Fitch Smith's text that he is criticizing, not describing, judicial practice. He acknowledges that "able judges" have had to "correct abuses and introduc[e] improvements," and he blames this judicial practice on the "supineness" of the legislature and on "the want of a proper understanding at what point interpretation ought to end, and legislation should begin." [136]

Although it may be unclear just how bold early nineteenth-century judges were when interpreting statutes, the suggestion that equitable interpretation had vanished seems overdrawn and tendentious.

Did traditional "extreme" equitable interpretation survive? Perhaps equitable interpretation not only failed to vanish but actually persisted in extreme form, with judges implacably hostile to legislation and distorting the meaning of statutes. Smith, for example, accused the court in the New York case of Mayor v. Lord of "put[ting] upon [the words] a construction which would amount to holding that the legislature did not mean what they had clearly expressed," and of engaging in "equitable construction [which will] usurp legislative authority." In fact, Mayor v. Lord itself and a related case suggest that a much less extreme form of equitable interpretation survived, one that tilted rather than overrode the text.

On December 16, 1835, New York City experienced a devastating fire. Because of bitter cold, the water used to fight fires froze and, as had been a common practice, the mayor ordered many buildings to be blown up to keep the fire from spreading.[137] This gave rise to *statutory* claims for compensation under state law, resulting in two cases that interpreted the statute—one in 1837 in which both lower and appellate courts provided compensation, and one in 1840 that denied compensation.[138] The opinions in both cases contained expositions of interpretive philosophy about equitable interpretation.

The 1837 case involved a claim for compensation by a tenant who owned goods lost in the destroyed building (a department store); the 1840 case concerned a claim for loss of goods owned by someone who was *neither* owner nor tenant of the destroyed building but whose goods were there when the fire occurred. The statutory text (sec. 81) permitted the city to "pull down or destroy . . ." a building to prevent the spread of fire, but it imposed an obligation on the city to "assess the damages which the owners of such building, and *all persons having any estate or interest therein,* have respectively sustained by the pulling down or destroying thereof . . ." (emphasis added). The statute also provided a procedure to assess the amount of loss that would be paid "in full satisfaction of all demands . . . by reason of the pulling down or destroying such building. . . ." Sec. 83 specified that the "sum assessed . . . for any building so pulled down or destroyed" shall be defrayed by the city.

In the 1837 case, in which the appellate court awarded compensation to the tenant by a vote of 16 to 6, the court's interpretive credo stated: "Among [the] fixed principles, or rules for the interpretation and construction of statutes, which have been adopted in this country and in England, is that of construing the statute by equity, so as to produce neither injustice nor absurdity, where the language of the statute is such as to admit of different interpretations or constructions. . . ." The court, referring to this set of principles as a "system of legal hermeneutics," neatly combines the language of "equity" and the Golden Rule (injustice or absurdity) with a bow to the text, "where the language . . . admit[s] of different interpretations." The court argued that "natural equity"—meaning the constitutional principle that private property shall not be taken for public use without just compensation—could be considered to resolve doubts about meaning.

The dissenting judge in the lower court had argued that the majority had been too cavalier with the text. He rejected equitable construction, arguing that "we are not at liberty to act upon the supposed intention of the legislature," and that it was usually "dangerous" to "go beyond the letter, for the purpose of carrying into effect the intent of the law-maker"; "[w]e are not at liberty to act upon the supposed intention of the legislature. . . ." The appellate court dissenters approved of equitable interpretation only when the words were "doubtful."

In the 1840 case, the tenant of a destroyed building sought compensation for goods that, although in his possession, were owned by others who had no "estate or interest" in the building. By a vote of 15 to 3, the court held *against* compensation. One judge made general statements that were as hostile to equitable interpretation as the prior majority opinion was generous: the "experience of later years ha[d] taught courts the danger of excess in bold interpretation, according to the presumed intent and against the plain language of acts." Interestingly, the opinion still acknowledged a possible judicial role in going beyond the text (reminiscent of the Golden Rule and Marshall's approach), "where there is some acknowledged rule of justice or right wholly independent of the statute, and to which its provisions fail to give full effect . . . ," but the opinion denied that power "when a statute rests upon legislative discretion alone, or judgment upon public policy. . . ."

Several points are worth noting about these cases. First, the rhetoric is more extreme than the decisions warrant, at least in my reading of the statutory text. In the 1837 case, the text seemed doubtful enough to justify consideration of additional interpretive factors to compensate the tenant for lost property. The dissent emphasized the reference in sec. 83 to the "sum assessed . . . for any building so pulled down or destroyed," but (as the majority explicitly noted) sec. 81 contained broader language regarding damages "sustained by the pulling down or destroying" of the building. This case was not one in which the court paid little attention to statutory language, unlike many older decisions applying equitable interpretation.

Second, the impassioned rhetoric about equitable interpretation in both cases may have reflected the judges' divergent views of their judicial role. The deciding appellate court was the Court of Errors in New York, which included both the chancellor *and* senators. Its 1837 decision contains two opinions, one by the chancellor favoring equitable interpretation, and one by Senator Samuel Edwards speaking against equitable interpretation. The 1840 case reports three decisions by senators, some of which contain language opposing equitable interpretation. The New York chancellor was a more traditional judge who might be expected to favor judicial discretion, and the senators most likely reflected the "popular" point of view, favoring public control over judges and less judicial discretion.

Third, the real dispute was probably about which values the court should consider when interpreting the statute. This was a period of intense conflict over the respective rights of private property and public claims on private property for the public good. The older common law view had required people to commit their property to the community for the common good without compensation [139] (one judge in the 1840 case stated that there was "no reason of justice why that large portion of the city wholly out of hazard should" pay for the loss). But a rival and increasingly weighty view contended that private property owners had a strong claim to compensation whenever their property was committed to the public good. This view may have led the majority in the 1837 case to tilt the statutory text in favor of a statutory purpose with which the judges were in strong sympathy (one judge who favored compensation in the 1837 case saw the "equity and justice" in providing compensation). Indeed, these values may have struck the judges as "fundamental"—the protection of private property rights—which further deprives the case of significance as an example of the survival of a strong version of the inherited English practice of equitable interpretation.

State judicial practice: Chief Justice Lemuel Shaw
and commonsense interpretation

This sketchy look at some nineteenth-century cases suggests that equitable interpretation neither died out nor persisted in extreme form. It is possible that it survived primarily in one of its differentiated forms—specifically, to protect fundamental values (the Golden Rule), as illustrated at the federal level by Marshall. But I suspect that many state judges were comfortable with a more undifferentiated approach to statutory interpretation (typical of the inherited English tradition), which fit statutes into the broader fabric of the law, but an approach tempered by a greater acceptance of legislation and reduced confidence in judging than in the English tradition. This state interpretive practice would be consistent with a tendency for state courts to accept a more politically active role than federal courts, as evidenced by the many state constitutions which provided that advisory judicial opinions could be given to other branches of the government.[140]

I do not mean that judicial concerns about legitimate judging completely evaporated. Among the embers of Revolutionary enthusiasm, one can still come across legitimacy arguments both denying a judicial role in statutory interpretation regarding matters of mere inconvenience and rejecting a broad equitable interpretation power. For example, in a 1798 Delaware case [141] the judge was reluctant to expand a statute: "Inconveniences may arise, but they will not warrant the court to apply the law to a case not within it. Our powers are judicial, not legislative." In fact, the statute in the case was in derogation of the common law, and the judge could have said just as easily that he would not on that account expansively interpret the law. Instead, he appealed to a notion of separation of powers to deny judicial discretion to expand the statute's coverage. [142]

But state judges often avoided the rhetoric of legitimacy and instead helped out the legislature in the common venture of making sensible law. At least that is the approach of Massachusetts Chief Justice Lemuel Shaw, who served in that position from 1830 to 1860. [143] In selecting Shaw for more thorough scrutiny, I am aware that he (or any judge, for that matter) may not be typical. Shaw's atypicality as a "great" judge [144] should not, however, detain us. His greatness lay in his common law decisions, and he was not likely on that account to be unrepresentative in the mid-nineteenth century of the general attitude of common law judges toward interpreting statutes.

Shaw has been described as more concerned with "common sense" than with being a "legal technician" and as preferring "arguments based on what he called 'the plain dictates of natural justice.' " [145] Another observer, writing soon after Shaw's death, characterized him as someone who "insist[s] upon grasping the principles involved, and wheeling the case into line." [146] Perhaps this proclivity had something to do with the fact that he had done three stints in the state legislature (1811–15, 1820–22, and 1829–30), [147] lending to his judicial temper a sense of shared judicial-legislative enterprise. He was certainly different in temperament from Kent and Story, both of whom were scholars and law professors, as well as judges and legislators, during their careers. Shaw seemed to fit in with Sedgwick's more pragmatic approach much better than with the developing formalistic science of American law, suggesting that Sedgwick's observation about judges having lost a sense of personal knowledge of legislative intent may be overstated.

Shaw shared with many nineteenth-century judges a skepticism about legislation. Although "[i]n the multitude of legislators, . . . there is much learning, prudence, and experience," there is also "a great deal of ignorance, vanity, and pretension," he wrote, and "it is not always easy to distinguish between a restless impatience of things as they are, a wanton love of innovation, and a sincere and ardent zeal for improvement." [148] This wariness toward legislation sometimes led Shaw to be cautious about interpreting "positive" law (that is, statutes) to make dramatic changes: "[A] wide departure from established rules of law, founded in considerations of public policy, and depending solely upon provisions of positive law . . . is, therefore, to be construed strictly, and not extended beyond the limits to which it is plainly carried by such provisions of statute."[149]

And, like Marshall, he would limit a statute which "disturb[ed] the fundamental principles of right."[150] One issue that Shaw obviously viewed as "fundamental" was his notion that juries should not decide questions of law. He interpreted a statute that sought to make juries the judge of the law as simply "a declaratory act, making no substantial change in the law regulating the relative rights and functions of the court and the jury. . . ."[151] The statute had, however, stated the contrary: "In all trials for criminal offenses, it shall be the duty of the jury . . . to decide at their discretion . . . both the fact and the law. . . ."[152] As the dissent noted: "Legislation is usually resorted to, not to reaffirm existing laws or decisions of the court, but to correct some supposed defect or omission in former statutes, or to introduce some change in the law as administered and declared by the court."[153]

But Shaw was certainly no blind devotee of the old common law, which he spent much of his judicial life revising and updating.[154] Whatever suspicions he had about legislation were balanced by a realistic view of the common law. He considered placing exclusive reliance on "a system of artificial and technical rules, having very little regard to principle" to be a "partial and erroneous" view of the law.[155] And he would not construe a statute narrowly just because it was in derogation of the common law. In response to an argument "that this statute disturbs the symmetry of the common law," he observed that "[a]ll statutes are intended to modify the common law to affect remedies. . . ."[156] He approved of some statutory changes in the common law, such as changing the "established and inflexible rule of the common law, that . . . lands [acquired after making a will] will not pass by devise. . . ."[157]

The most interesting aspect of Shaw's approach to statutory interpretation was not his occasional willingness to limit statutes that made dramatic changes or impinged on fundamental values, but his nondoctrinaire approach to statutory interpretation. He avoided extreme statements about whether interpretation depended on text, statutory purpose, or equity, and he did his best to fit statutes into the legal system, relying on whatever helped him figure out their meaning.

Perhaps as a state rather than a federal judge Shaw had fewer of Marshall's doubts about the judge's power of statutory interpretation. He also acted in an environment of frequently changing statutes written against a common law background, which was a much more complex statutory world than Marshall encountered in early nineteenth-century federal legislation. In that setting, Shaw *really* did "seize every thing from which aid c[ould] be derived" to interpret statutes.

Shaw's statutory interpretation opinions often appeal to *both* the text and the spirit or reason underlying the statute (or, analogously, to statutory purpose, policy, or intent), without distinguishing between the weights attributable to these criteria. Some samples: "within the letter of the present statute, and . . . equally within its spirit and purpose";[158] "certainly not within the words of the statute, and . . . not within its reason";[159] "nothing in the terms, and nothing in the object or purpose of the statute";[160] "nothing in the terms or the spirit of the statute."[161] Given Shaw's concern about the "reason" and "spirit" of legislation, it is not surprising to find him supporting equitable interpretation with none of the anxiety that afflicted many nineteenth-century commentators. Sometimes he even sounds like Plowden:

> [I]t is well established, that in the construction of remedial statutes, cases not within the letter of the statute, are taken to be within its spirit and equity, upon a reasonable certainty arising from a consideration of the statute and of every part and clause of it, and from the obvious end and purpose to be accomplished by it, that it was so intended by the legislature: and also that a case may come within the letter, which shall not be judicially construed to be within the act, because it is alike manifest, to a reasonable certainty, that it was not so intended by the makers of the act.[162]

Moreover, Shaw would also rely on fundamental principles to *extend* a statute's remedial purpose. "This construction appears to us to be entirely reasonable and necessary. It is a remedial act, intended to carry into execution that most equitable provision of the constitution. . . ."[163] The provision awarded compensation when private property was taken for public use, implementing the same values that were embraced in the 1837 New York case of Mayor v. Lord (discussed above).

The effort to figure out what the legislature was trying to do also led Shaw to the "whole act" over "literal" meaning."[164] Moreover, the "whole text" extended beyond the specific statute to include related legislation: "[w]ere this a new act of legislation," one meaning might be inferred, but it is a revision and "some light may be thrown on the subject by considering the course of legislation";[165] it is "necessary to examine the other parts of the revised statutes, and the earlier laws, indicating the course of policy . . . upon the subject of taxation."[166]

Shaw's determination to understand what the legislature was trying to do even led him to rely on legislative history in the form of materials generated by the legislative process. The conventional wisdom is that legislative history, in the sense of materials written during the legislative process, did not begin to gain judicial acceptance as a source of statutory meaning until the end of the nineteenth century.[167] But Shaw's opinions suggest otherwise. He was comfortable citing reports of commissioners who drafted the revised laws for codification into a state statutory code. Most of his references to this legislative history were to a statute's drafting history[168] — that is, changes made in the text of drafts as they work their way to final legislative passage. But some of his references are to statements in commissioners' reports about legislative goals, analogous to modern legislative history found in committee reports.[169]

I am not suggesting that Shaw was disrespectful of the statutory text. His opinions contain statements deferential to statutory language and that lean away from relying on equity, spirit, and reason. He argues that the "inconvenience" of an interpretation is relevant only when language is "doubtful"; there is no construction in cases "where the terms are plain and explicit." [170] And, like Marshall, he says that "[a] statute is no doubt to be construed according to the intent of the legislature; but it is the intent gathered from the words of the enactment. . . ." [171] However, the dominant pattern in his statutory interpretation opinions is a pragmatic "every thing from which aid can be derived" approach to the text, purpose, and equity of the law. In this regard, he followed Sedgwick's advice (noted earlier) that "[o]urs is eminently a practical science. It is only by an intimate acquaintance with its application to the affairs of life, as they actually occur, that we can acquire that sagacity requisite to decide new and doubtful cases." [172]

The Midcentury Shift in the Legal Culture: Law vs. The People

The debate about the judicial role in statutory interpretation began to take on a sharper edge somewhere around the middle of the nineteenth century, as judges and the bar reasserted the preeminence of judge-made law. The defining shift in the legal culture that brought about this change was a split between the law and the people.[173]

To appreciate what happened, we must look back again to the period from 1776 until 1789. In this earlier period, faith in an ideal that the people and the law shared a common objective had resulted in part from what William Nelson describes as "the early nineteenth century [view of] 'the people' as a politically homogenous and cohesive body possessing common political goals and aspirations, not as a congeries of factions and interest groups, each having its own set of goals and aspirations." [174] This faith also is implicit in the observation in *Federalist* 51 that, if it were not for the fact that judicial independence was necessary, "all appointments," including judicial, "should be drawn from . . . the people." [175]

Intense disputes took place, to be sure, about *who* would best implement this ideal of a link between the law and the people. Some placed more confidence in the legislature as the people's voice, though skeptics suspected that the legislature would destroy liberties protected by law. Jefferson, for example, relied heavily on the jury as the popular voice of the law.[176] And Wilson linked the law to popular consent by conceiving of judicial opinions as expressions of custom embodied in the common law.[177] Indeed, even the Bill of Rights (which we consider the quintessential assertion of protection of legal rights from popular dominance) was meant to assure majoritarian participation in preserving justice, most notably through the important role it provided for juries.[178] But whichever institution was relied on, its authority rested on a supposed link between the law and the people.

That link disintegrated in the middle and later decades of the nineteenth century, no doubt because more and more of "the people" exercised their right to vote.[179] The "people" became less and less an abstraction and more and more a numerical reality. Earlier confidence in the "people" had always been tinged by the qualification that only educated people deserved that confidence. But as long as the "masses" were not an effective political force, the tension between the law and the people could be contained.

This tension could not, however, endure the strains of real democracy. We can symbolically date the growing split between the law and the people to the inauguration of President Andrew Jackson in 1829, where masses of people were invited to attend the White House reception, resulting in danger to life and limb and destruction of property; Justice Story was prompted to observe that "the reign of king 'Mob' seemed triumphant." [180] With the extensive exercise of the franchise and real democracy, the dissolution of politics into factions and the threat *to* law *from* the people (as some viewed it) seemed assured. At best, law and the people were tenuously linked by the superior expertise of those trained in the law to discern the principles that a more educated people would adopt. But the gap in training was so great that, for all practical purposes, the law was separate from those on whose behalf the legal experts claimed to speak. This separation is best symbolized by the changing role of that quintessential voice of the people—the jury—which, in the beginning of the nineteenth century, determined both the law and the facts, but by 1900 had only the more limited task of deciding the facts.[181]

The dominant perception that supported a separation of the law from the people was that law was a science accessible to legal experts. The rhetorical appeal of a "science" of law had been apparent since the eighteenth century, when Blackstone developed (in Daniel Boorstin's phrase) the "mysterious science of the law." [182] By that time, science had seized the popular imagination, and Blackstone set out to do for law what Isaac Newton had done for physics. But the eighteenth-century Blackstone had to be cautious. Science, with its confidence in human capacity, could destabilize the principles on which law was based; hence, the need for some mystery—what Boorstin refers to as the "mysterious clarity of the law." [183] By the nineteenth century, however, a more humanistic American culture was confident of its legal science without the mystery or fear of its destabilizing effect. Lawyers were convinced that a science of the law could discern, organize, and explain the principles on which the law was based, a process that yielded numerous treatises that proved self-fulfilling.[184] Some attenuated link to the "people" persisted in the claim that "scientific inquiry" was the best way to measure "true popular will," but direct resort to expressions of popular opinion would be unavailing, because such opinion was "unreasoning," "uninformed and unscientific." [185]

This faith in the expertise of the scientifically trained lawyer reached its apex in the last third of the nineteenth century, when it was institutionalized in law schools and bar associations. Beginning in the 1870s with Christopher Columbus Langdell at Harvard Law School, law was taught as a science whose principles were derived from cases, just as the natural sciences derived principles from data.[186] Whether or not this was good science or a good analogy is irrelevant; it enhanced the image of law as an autonomous neutral body of principles accessible to experts. Moreover, if law was a science, what could be more natural than for legally trained experts to band together in associations, which is what happened in the 1870s? The first organized modern-day bar association was the Association of the Bar of the City of New York, formed in 1870; others followed during the decade (e.g., Chicago, Cincinnati, Iowa, Boston, New York State), including the American Bar Association in 1878.[187]

The impact of the nineteenth-century split between the law and the people was apparent not only in the role of the jury changing from both law-finder and fact-finder to fact-finder alone, but also in how lawyers reacted to two other significant events, which are discussed in the remainder of this section: the popular election of judges and the codification of substantive common law.

POPULAR ELECTION OF JUDGES

State constitutions, unlike the federal Constitution, were often amended in the nineteenth century. The most significant result of this process was the democratizing of the electoral process, both in law and practice. Most property qualifications were eliminated (as long as the voter was male and white). Thus, in 1800, three states had universal manhood suffrage; but, by 1828, liberal though not universal suffrage existed in all but two of the original thirteen states. And, in contrast with the original state constitutions, only two of which had been ratified by the people, between 1830 and 1850 all but two had been approved at the polls.[188]

The movement toward democracy did not directly affect judges until around midcentury.[189] While Mississippi was the first state (in 1832) to elect all judges,[190] it was only when New York State did the same in its 1846 constitution that the movement spread rapidly. Within ten years thereafter, fifteen of the twenty-nine states in existence in 1846 provided for popular election of judges; and all states entering the Union after 1846 made that provision.[191]

On first impression, we might think that electing judges would bind the law more closely to the people, but instead the opposite occurred. First, direct election of judges did not mean that people had faith in popularly elected legislatures. Mid-nineteenth-century legislatures often passed legislation that favored only a few economically powerful interests and that undermined state credit by excessive borrowing. This situation led to state constitutional prohibitions of "special legislation" and of practices that threatened to bankrupt state government.[192] The 1846 New York constitution not only provided for election of judges, but it also limited legislative power as a reaction to legislative "abuses." [193] The lack of any connection between popular election of judges and faith in legislatures is apparent in the statistic that thirteen of the twenty states that changed to popular election of at least some judges in the mid-nineteenth century switched away from *legislative* selection (the others shifted from selection by the governor with consent of the legislative branch).[194] Although the contrast between direct expressions of popular will and faith in the legislature would not be *clearly* demarcated until the late nineteenth and early twentieth centuries (when the Populist and Progressive movements led to initiatives and referendums to bypass and impose checks on legislative lawmaking), neither did the election of judges in the mid-nineteenth century establish a closer connection between law passed by popularly elected legislatures and judging. Whether elected or not, judges drew on suspicion of legislatures to justify a more aggressive lawmaking role during the second half of the nineteenth century, perhaps responding to a complaint that they were *too* subservient to legislatures.[195]

Second, popular election not only did not link judges to the popularly elected legislature, but it also did not dampen their independent sense of legal expertise. If anything, popular election helped to advance an equal and opposite reaction among the bench and the bar, which were intent on proving that judges (whether or not elected) owed a prior allegiance to the "law"; such allegiance was accessible only to experts trained in its scientific principles. Indeed, I would guess that popular election made judges even more anxious to protect themselves from public criticism by claiming that unpopular decisions were required by the "law"—the "law made me do it" defense.

The evolution of New York's constitutional provisions dealing with elected judges and their selection suggests how the process adapted itself to a split between the law and the people.[196] The 1846 constitution embodied democratic principles, providing that the justices of the court of appeals (the highest court in the state) and the state supreme court (the highest court of original jurisdiction) would be elected for eight-year terms. Four of the eight members of the court of appeals were elected to eight-year terms, with the first four judges to serve for two, four, six, and eight years, respectively, so that eventually one judge would be elected every two years. The other four court of appeals judges would be chosen from state supreme court judges with the shortest terms to serve. This provision made it almost impossible for the court of appeals to develop a sense of independent collegial cohesion.

However, in 1867–68 a new constitutional convention initiated an amendment that resulted in the court of appeals consisting of seven members elected for concurrently running fourteen-year terms. This change "was a sharp turning away from the 1846 Convention's policy, based on a conviction that the court and public would benefit by short, staggered terms for judges calling for frequent public review of individual judicial performance." Consequently, the court became a collegial body, more confident of its legal pronouncements and capable of working out the science of the law. Moreover, although the election process was technically partisan, political parties relied on the growing influence of the organized bar (the New York City and New York State Bar Associations) to take the elections out of electoral politics. One commentator states that "in the vast majority of cases, the nomination of the incumbents of the office of judge . . . has been nomination by the profession."[197]

This development did not mean that political issues were always unimportant in electing judges. When the New York court of appeals in 1911 held that the workers' compensation law was unconstitutional because it provided for no-fault liability[198] rather than liability based on negligence, the chief justice's support of this decision contributed to his defeat for reelection.[199] The response of the political parties and the bar, however, was to circle the wagons and agree to take the election of the chief justice out of politics. (Instead, the senior associate justice would be backed by both parties for promotion to chief judge, a practice which was nonetheless sometimes honored in the breach rather than the observance.)[200]

CODIFICATION

The shift in the legal culture toward a split between the law and the people was also evident in the defeat of efforts during the nineteenth century to codify the common law into statutory form. Proposals for codification have always contained a tension between a commitment to the people vs. the law. One version of codification sought to replace all law, including common law, with statutes, often idealized as a simpler uncomplicated nontechnical version of the law accessible to the people. Alternatively, the "legal-professional" version of codification was the consolidation of statute law, with *some* changes to weed out obsolete statutes and (perhaps) *some* legislation of common law principles. These two approaches arose from entirely different images of legislation. Proposals to replace all law with a statutory code placed their faith in legislation and the common sense of the people. The consolidators had a sharply different view; they were disturbed by the chaos and uncertainty in the statute books and wanted to employ legal expertise to bring some order to the law by placing statutes in a well-organized code.

Both codification themes were present in English legal history. Early codification efforts, advanced by Francis Bacon in the late 1500s and early 1600s, sought consolidation of statute law to overcome uncertainty in the growing body of legislation.[201] His goal was not legal change (except to weed out obsolete statutes), and it certainly was not replacement of the common law with a code (even though James I might have preferred to codify the entire common law).[202] Bacon advocated a *digest* of the common law to provide certainty,[203] which differed from statutory codification in the same way that modern restatements differ from legislative replacement of the common law.

More radical proposals to codify the common law had some early English adherents, associated with the Revolutionary period from 1640 to 1660,[204] which supports the notion that real legislative codification generally accompanies political revolution. The hope was that simple codes adopted by a popularly elected legislature would replace the common law. But it was not until Jeremy Bentham in the late eighteenth and early nineteenth centuries that a strong English voice could be heard for replacing the common law with a statutory code.[205]

In the United States, the Revolution spawned some pressure for legislative replacement of the common law, and the issue was constantly debated in the first half of the nineteenth century; Gordon, for example, refers to an "obsession" with codification among legal commentators from 1820 to 1850.[206] Nearly every issue of the periodical *American Jurist* at this time contained some discussion of codification. Indeed, codification was much more prominent in the literature about legislation than statutory interpretation. But the debate paid little attention to Bentham's proposals to codify the common law and focused instead on the more professionally oriented efforts to consolidate the statute books. Indeed, as Robert Gordon explains, real codification never stood much of a chance.[207] Bentham was viewed as too radical, and, despite his offers to assist American governments in codifying the law,[208] his approach and certainly his mantle were generally spurned.[209]

The commonly used term for the more moderate U.S. version of codification was "revision" of the law. This process implied something more than a simple mechanical compiling of statutes, and it often included some changes in the common law, but it fell far short of codifying the entire common law. Codification in the sense of "revision" of state statutes was widespread in the first half of the nineteenth century.[210] Even Story participated in the revision process, serving as chair of the Massachusetts Commission on the Codification of the Common Law and as sole author of its report.[211] But more drastic codification of the common law was discouraged in part by the authoring of treatises that organized the common law and helped to undermine the argument that statutory codification was necessary. In the first half of the nineteenth century, Kent and Story wrote law treatises that made claims of legal expertise plausible in a country where a dearth of law reports and organized legal doctrine had prevailed.[212] It also was rumored that Daniel Webster urged Shaw's appointment to the bench because Shaw's ability to explain the common law would dampen enthusiasm for codification.[213]

For our purposes—concerned principally with shifts in nineteenth-century legal culture—the interesting events in the disputes over codification occurred in midcentury and thereafter when a more realistic opportunity occurred to codify all law, not just revise the statute book. The signal event was the 1846 New York State constitution, known as the People's Constitution.[214] In addition to providing for elected judges, it established two commissions, one to look into codifying procedural law, the other to examine substantive law.[215] David Dudley Field, the prime mover behind these efforts, eventually served on both commissions.[216]

Some part of the procedure code was adopted in New York in 1848,[217] although adoption did not guarantee a hospitable response from the legal profession. Field attributed this reaction to an inherent tendency of lawyers to resist change; he observed that at least one judge had simply disregarded the statutory provision in the procedure code which rejected the canon that statutes in derogation of the common law be narrowly construed.[218] Nonetheless, the procedure code achieved widespread national acceptance.

The same success did not await the proposed substantive codes. The fact that two New York laws created commissions to codify substantive law — the first law was repealed and revived only in 1857[219] — suggests that enthusiasm for codifying substantive law did not match enthusiasm for a procedural code. New York never adopted the substantive codes (although the civil code passed one or both houses on several occasions),[220] and the codes enjoyed success only in some Western states.[221]

Nonetheless, the debate about codification continued well into the second half of the nineteenth century, and the arguments reflected the split between the law and the people. Not surprisingly, many common law lawyers were vocal in opposing common law codification. Their arguments against codification were based on grounds of legislative incompetence, denying the ability of the people's representatives to make good law, and on the judge's competence to make better law than the legislature. The legislature was considered unresponsive to change (compared to the case-by-case adjustments of the common law), and statutory texts were considered unable to capture the complexities of specific cases (echoing James Madison's comments about the imperfection of language).[222] These "competence" arguments were most clearly articulated in the work of James Carter, a lawyer who chaired a New York City Bar Association Committee that opposed codification.[223] He attacked codification on the following grounds: a code will not make law predictable if it is written in general terms; it will be arbitrary and inflexible if written in specific terms; and, in any event, novel situations will undermine the utility of the statutory language.[224] Others, including American Bar Association presidents, were outspoken in referring to legislative evils and the imperfection of statute law.[225]

Carter's affirmative case for judicial competence in making common law merged arguments based on scientific legal expertise and the judge's ability to adapt custom to new situations.[226] As for custom, Carter stated: "Human nature is not likely to undergo a radical change, and, therefore, that to which we give the name of Law always has been, still is, and will forever continue to be Custom." [227] Custom (as James Wilson had urged in the late eighteenth century) *could* provide a link between the people and the law developed by judges, and it also could appeal to the pragmatic and Burkean strain in American legal thought. But an appeal to legal science was also part of Carter's argument. He asked, rhetorically, whether the "growth, development and improvement of the law" should "remain under the guidance of men selected by the people on account of their special qualifications for the work" or "be transferred to a numerous legislative body, disqualified by the nature of their duties for the discharge of this supreme function?" [228]

Not all lawyers viewed codification as clumsy legislative efforts to make law. But they reduced the codification debate to an intra-professional dispute over whether a legislative code or the common law was the best way to implement legal science. In late nineteenth-century California, for example, the need for scientific ordering of the law was a relatively more important argument favoring legislative codification than in the East, where the battle was about the relative advantages of legislation over judge-made law.[229] Eventually, the "science" argument led not to codification, but to professionally sponsored alternatives. In 1892 the organized bar helped to form the quasi-public National Conference of Commissioners on Uniform State Laws,[230] which took on the task of drafting uniform laws and offering them to state legislatures for passage. And in 1923 the American Law Institute was formed by leading practitioners, judges, and academics with the purpose of "promot[ing] the clarification and simplification of the law and its better adaptation to social needs, to secure the better administration of justice, and to encourage and carry on scholarly and scientific legal work." [231] The institute's primary task was drafting restatements of the common law, which would obviate the need for legislative codes.

The idea of law as a science even permeated treatises on statutory interpretation. The contrast between Sedgwick's 1857 "practical science" and the late nineteenth-century commentators is striking. As noted, Bishop argued that interpretation law could be reduced to organized rules and that "statutory interpretation [was] governed as absolutely by rules as anything else in the law." [232] J. G. Sutherland's 1891 treatise states that, it is important that "principles [of interpretation be] generalized, with a view to maintaining the domain of the law as a science. . . ." [233] And Henry Black stated that his 1896 work followed "the general plan of the Hornbook Series . . . after the manner of a code, expressed in brief black-letter paragraphs. . . ." [234]

Post–Civil War: Narrow Interpretation of Statutes
in Derogation of Common Law

In a period of increasing pressure for legislative change, attempts to revive the older common law lawyers' image of legal expertise capable of discovering common law principles was bound to produce serious political conflict. This development was most dramatic in constitutional law, which evolved to read common law property and contract rights into the due process clause to strike down legislation. But statutory interpretation was also infused with a similar animus—through the doctrine that statutes in derogation of the common law should be narrowly construed (the derogation canon).

It is easy to make the case that judicial hostility toward legislation and a preference for the preexisting common law overstepped the boundaries of legitimate judging by relying on the "derogation" canon. Indeed, Roscoe Pound made that argument in his 1907 article, "Spurious Interpretation,"[235] discussed in chapter 4. This perspective on judging rests on an examination of what judges wrote in a variety of decisions involving traditional property rights and family values and what commentators said about this judicial practice. But I will argue that a difference between the rhetoric of judging and what judges actually did weakens any argument that courts were illegitimately usurping legislative authority. In my view, many if not most of the judicial decisions provided examples of ordinary legitimate judging, whereby judges exercised their competence to help fit statutes into their temporal setting by integrating them with prior law. An extensive review of these cases is therefore important for understanding the centrality of the temporal dimension for ordinary judging in statutory interpretation, a theme I return to in chapter 7.

THE RHETORIC

For rhetorical enthusiasm about the common law in preference to statutes, it would be hard to rival the following statement in an 1894 Minnesota case.[236] The court there quoted Coke's laudatory observations: "The wisdom of the judges and sages of the law has always suppressed new and subtle inventions in derogation of the common law"; it then added some praiseworthy comments of its own: "The principles of the common law were founded upon practical reasons, and not upon a theoretical logical system; and usually, when these principles have been departed from, the evil consequences of the departure have developed what these reasons were."

Another case warned against the evils of attaching property in violation of rights "sacred" at common law when the issue was whether one who extended credit without knowledge of a fraudulent statement by the defendant could use the statutory remedy of prejudgment attachment, which allowed a creditor to obtain jurisdiction and helped to assure collectability of any later judgment. The court quoted favorably from a well-known treatise:

> [Attachment] amounts to the involuntary dispossession of the owner prior to any adjudication to determine the rights of the parties. It violates every principle of proprietary right held sacred by the common law. It is, to some extent, equivalent to execution in advance of trial and judgment. Property is taken, under legal process, at the instance of one without even a claim of title from the possession of another whose title is unquestioned. . . .[237]

The court linked its objections to attachment to both broad and narrow versions of the Golden Rule, stating: "The *inconvenience* and *injustice* resulting from any other construction is so manifest as to bear strongly upon the intention of the legislature, for a statute should be so construed, when the language will permit, as to make it practicable, just, and reasonably convenient" (emphasis added).

Similar encomiums to the common law are found in cases involving traditional family values, which interpreted the Married Women's Property Acts. These acts altered the common law by giving wives certain rights in the ownership and management of their property, free of their husband's control, that they had lacked at common law. In one case,[238] the court refused to interpret the law generously in the wife's favor, stating that "[i]t is impossible that a woman can use and enjoy her property as fully and separately after marriage as before"; "[t]he husband is still the head of the family." Consequently, the court would "presume that no innovation on the old law was intended further than was absolutely required."

If we look at what commentators said about statutory interpretation after the Civil War, we also might get the impression that courts overstepped the boundaries of legitimate judging. There was a continuation of the pre–Civil War pattern that we observed in Smith and Sedgwick—opposing equitable interpretation[239]—but with special emphasis on rejecting any special rule narrowly interpreting statutes in derogation of the common law. Thomas Cooley's 1872 *Commentaries on Blackstone* was the exception in speaking favorably of the derogation canon: "But where the new statute does not in terms repeal the old law, the two will stand together so far as effect can be given to both. . . . A statute which makes an innovation on the established principles of the common law must be strictly construed."[240] But other commentators were critical of the preference for the common law, while usually acknowledging its prevalence in judicial opinions.

The criticism is clear. Pomeroy's 1874 edition of Theodore Sedgwick contains a long note criticizing the narrow interpretation of statutes in derogation of the common law.[241] G. A. Endlich's Maxwell is critical of a narrowing interpretation to preserve common law: prior law of any kind, whether statute or common law, should not be implicitly repealed, but the common law deserved no special protection.[242] Joel Bishop[243] and Henry Black[244] argue that the relationship of both prior common and statute law to a later statute is the same; there is a general rule against implied repeals in both situations, but there is nothing special about prior common law.

However, the commentators also leave no doubt that they are criticizing what the courts were doing in preferring common law. Pomeroy gives citations to this practice in many jurisdictions.[245] Endlich notes, despite his own preference, that it is easier to alter statute law than common law.[246] Sutherland, in a descriptive mode, states that "in all doubtful matters, and when the statute is in general terms, it is subject to the principles of the common law. . . ."[247] And Platt Potter's Dwarris affirms that "our courts, federal and state," hold that there should be no "innovation upon the common law, further than the case absolutely required," citing James Kent's eulogy of the common law as the perfection of reason.[248]

A few hints can be detected among the commentators that the narrow interpretation of statutes in derogation of common law might make sense if it protected important rights, after the fashion of the Golden Rule and Chief Justice Marshall. Sutherland states that "statutes in derogation of [common law], and especially of *common right,* are strictly construed, and will not be extended by construction beyond their natural import" (emphasis added).[249] And Endlich suggests a somewhat greater concern to preserve the prior common law from statutory innovation when that prior law protects personal and property rights, with the qualification that this is true only "so far as that rule has any legitimate force or application."[250] But the general tone of late nineteenth-century commentary opposed judicial hostility toward legislation through invocation of the derogation canon.

JUDICIAL PRACTICE

If we take this judicial rhetoric and the commentators' reactions at face value, we would get an unbalanced picture of statutory interpretation. To be sure, judges were favorably inclined toward preserving the common law, but it is misleading to generalize to the conclusion that what they did was judicial usurpation of legitimate lawmaking power—a violation of the separation of powers. In many instances their decisions were well within legitimate interpretive boundaries, even if we would consider them wrongheaded, looking back on the nineteenth century from a twentieth-century, drenched-in-statutes, legislative-reform-minded perspective. Courts were certainly proponents of common law; at times, they were even hostile to statutes. But the statutes themselves often left room for interpretation that could accommodate survival of the common law.

For example, the actual 1894 Minnesota decision where the judge invoked Coke's praise of the common law was hardly unreasonable. The case dealt with a statute making a telegraph company that fails to transmit or deliver a message within a reasonable time "liable in a civil action at the suit of the party injured for all actual damages sustained by reason of such"[251] failure. All the decision concluded was that the statute did not authorize a recovery for *mental* suffering.

The substantive conclusion is not only sensible, but the decision does not support the view that courts displayed the kind of hostility to legislation that the quotation from Coke implies. First, the court was not entirely rigid in following the common law, noting that the cause of action concerned a contract violation and that the scope of damages in tort actions might be different. Second, the rhetoric was a reaction to an upstart Texas decision;[252] the court noted that "[i]t is somewhat remarkable that, although telegraphy has now been in use for over 50 years, it never seems to have occurred to any court, or, so far as we can discover, to any lawyer, that damages were recoverable for mental suffering resulting from neglect to transmit or deliver a telegram until it was so held in 1881 by the [Texas supreme court], citing in support of the doctrine only actions in tort for physical injuries."[253] Third, the court's language opposing innovation was hostile to change not only by statute but also in the *common law*.[254] All legal change was suspect at this time, as evidenced by the House of Lords' decision in 1898 that judicial precedent could not be overruled, a view that survived in England until 1966.[255]

Of course, one decision does not create a pattern. In the rest of this chapter, we need to look more closely at a larger body of judicial opinions to see just how hostile judges were toward legislation and how close they came to the boundary of legitimate judicial behavior. I conclude that even in the heyday of judicial hostility to statutes, a lot of what judges did to preserve the common law from legislative change operated well within the boundaries of legitimate statutory interpretation, asking the legislature just how far it meant to go in changing prior law.

To support this thesis, I present examples of statutory interpretation dealing with property rights (prejudgment attachment and mechanic's liens), tort liability (wrongful death acts), and relationships between husbands and wives (Married Women's Property Acts).

Although I am concerned primarily with understanding how the derogation canon was applied to limit legislation and what that implies about interpretive theory, we should remember that this period was not one of single-minded judicial hostility to statutes. Some cases rejected the derogation canon altogether, often invoking the countercanon—that the legislation was remedial (the "remedial" canon)—urging a liberal interpretation of the statute. Although some appeals to the remedial canon had the effect of protecting property interests,[256] which were more conventionally protected by the derogation canon, the remedial canon was sometimes invoked to override common law values.

Moreover, *some* judges refused to be drawn into the interpretive sparring that accompanied citations to the derogation canon or the rival principle that remedial statutes should be liberally construed. For example: "Laws of this . . . kind have been held by some courts to be remedial, and therefore to be liberally construed. By others they have been construed strictly as in derogation of the common law. The true principle sustained by the sounder reason, in our judgment, is that they should be construed neither liberally nor strictly, but reasonably, so as to carry out the clear purpose and policy for which they are enacted."[257]

In order to evaluate this material on statutory interpretation and the derogation canon, it is important to keep in mind the variety of ways that courts could accommodate statutes to the preexisting common law. Whether that accommodation exceeded legitimate interpretive boundaries is impossible to describe without our having some sense of what barriers the statute presented to the court's efforts. My point is that the statute was often relatively malleable from the perspective of interpretive theory and that therefore the courts were, in many instances, not acting illegitimately.

First, recall Chief Justice Marshall's distinction between two meanings of "strict" construction. One meaning insisted on sticking to the letter of the law, not varying from the text to achieve some underlying purpose. Another meaning narrowed the text. The line between the two is not always easy to draw because it requires knowing what the text means before indulging a presumption about survival of the common law; yet in many cases it is a clear enough line to draw. The distinction is important for our purposes because the specter of judicial usurpation of lawmaking authority is more pronounced when judges limited the text than when courts simply refused to vary from the statutory letter. Many cases invoking the derogation canon did so only to insist on the letter of the statute rather than narrow the statutory language.

Second, many statutory texts when impartially examined were uncertain in meaning. Tilting in favor of the common law in such cases could hardly be labeled a violation of separation of powers, revealing a judicial hostility to statutes that denied them their proper place in the legal system, even if one concludes that the judicial decision was wrong.

Third, even some cases that rewrote the statutory text, narrowing the statute's coverage to prevent a result in derogation of the common law, were defensible. The purpose of a statute was not always clear enough to conclude that something more than a *partial* repeal of the common law had been achieved by the legislature. Courts might have reasonably concluded that the statute had begun the task of altering the common law, but it had not completely rejected all of the policies embodied in the traditional common law.

The material in this section has a lot of dry technical law talk, and I have put as much of it as I could in footnotes. I would not burden the reader with an elaboration of so many cases but for the fact that getting some sense of real judging as opposed to that conveyed in the rhetoric of debates is central to understanding the history of statutory interpretation and the lessons it holds for us today. Nothing like a complete survey of cases is attempted. I have put myself at the mercy of the on-line database sources, specifically Westlaw, which I searched for all state cases before 1900 in which "derogation" and "common law" appeared in the same sentence. I also examined the cases cited by J. G. Sutherland in his second 1904 edition.

ATTACHMENT

Statutory authority for prejudgment attachment was in derogation of common law. This attachment remedy was generally used when debtors were outside the jurisdiction or likely to abscond. Although courts interpreting these statutes often invoked the derogation canon,[258] the cases provide little support for the thesis that judges overstepped the boundaries of legitimate statutory interpretation. The judges usually insisted on the letter of the law, or else the meaning of the text was uncertain.

For example, one case expressed concern about the severity of attachment without adequate procedures, but all it held was that the person seeking attachment had failed to comply with the statute's requirement that he state the grounds of his claim.[259] The case insisted on the letter of the law and refused to excuse a procedural failure. (Other cases insisting on the letter of procedural law to protect property rights, which involved statutes other than attachment legislation, are presented in a footnote.)[260]

We should be suspicious of claims that a court was *merely* insisting on the letter of the law. Modern textualism implies that such an approach is passive, but in a period when extensive equitable interpretation was still plausible, sticking to the letter of the law was an affirmative judicial act. In the appropriate case, judges would excuse procedural lapses, often by invoking the "remedial" canon. For example, a Colorado case[261] dealt with a "survival" statute, which allowed specified parties to enforce claims of a decedent. Survival statutes altered the common law in what the court called a "remedial" fashion "in aid of the common law, not in derogation thereof." The court, after noting that most states treat these laws as remedial, adopted a liberal construction of a rule that the action be brought within one year; it treated commencement of the suit during that period against the *wrong* defendant under advice of counsel as adequate compliance with the law.

Still, it would be incorrect to equate the judicial role in refusing to relax the letter of the law with narrowing judicial construction. Several centuries of criticism of how judges interpreted statutes had elevated the text to a position of prominence that it previously lacked, and the decision to stick to the text, though discretionary in some respects, was (by the late nineteenth century) less bold an act of statutory interpretation than narrowing the statutory language.

Judges invoking the derogation canon not only stuck to the statutory letter but also relied on the common law when the text was unclear, as they did in a case[262] protecting a nonfraudulent partner from prejudgment attachment based on a partner's fraud. The statute allowed attachment when the defendant "fraudulently contracted the debt or incurred the obligation respecting which the suit is brought." It also stated: "When two or more persons are jointly indebted as . . . partners, . . . the attachment may be issued against the separate or joint estates or property of such joint debtors or any of them, and the same proceedings shall be had as hereinbefore prescribed." To my reading, this statute left open whether a nonfraudulent partner was subject to attachment, permitting the court some space to incorporate concerns derived from the common law to protect property rights.[263]

A case mentioned earlier, which had characterized attachment as "involuntary dispossession," also dealt with a statute whose text was unclear.[264] The text authorized attachment "where, for the purpose of procuring credit . . . defendant has made a false statement in writing . . . as to his financial responsibility. . . ." But the person seeking attachment was *not* the person who relied on the false statement, and the text hardly forced a reading that allowed attachment for someone who was not the object of the defendant's purposeful fraud. The court (reasonably, if not inevitably) invoked policy concerns to preclude extending the attachment remedy beyond the person who was injured by the fraud, arguing that "[i]t would be an anomaly in commercial law to permit a wrongful act, that injured no one, to disrupt a man's business by allowing any creditor to seize his property at any time . . . ," and, consequently, that "[i]t is unreasonable to suppose that the legislature intended that a single false statement should follow a man through life, and expose his property to attack by his creditors at any time they chose. This would virtually withdraw from his property for all time the safeguards which protect the property of all other persons. It would be perpetual outlawry applied to his property, and would tend not only to drive him out of business, but to expel him from the state."

The defense of the judge's interpretive role in attachment cases does not depend solely on the argument that the statute provided some room for preserving the common law. The claim that late nineteenth-century judges were unreasonably hostile to statutes also has a substantive aspect, namely, that courts were unwilling to accept the forward movement in the law imparted by reform legislation. This argument is important though difficult to evaluate because it blames courts for being insufficiently enthusiastic about the future. Moreover, it is hard to conclude that insensitivity to the future is illegitimate judging; judges play an important role in *both* preserving the past and anticipating the future. But, in any event, the attachment cases are a poor example of a judicial failure to yield to the future trend of the law. Modern constitutional due process law is highly solicitous of defendants whose assets are attached.[265]

MECHANIC'S LIENS

Statutory mechanic's liens provide a security interest (a lien) in real estate (land and buildings) for those who worked to improve the property. Their original purpose was to encourage the construction industry. By one account, the first such law was in Maryland, passed at the urging of Jefferson and Madison to encourage building in the nation's capital.[266]

These statutes were eventually adopted in all states in the nineteenth century and were in derogation of the common law. Their impact was not entirely sanguine. Depending on the details, the property owner could be exposed to the risk of double payment if he paid the contractor and was then forced again to pay the workers; and sale of real estate might be impaired if buyers could be exposed to unknown liens.[267]

The mixed policy implications of mechanic's lien laws contrasted with attachment statutes, whose impairment of the common law was uniformly viewed as having negative results. It is therefore not surprising to find a variety of judicial approaches to interpreting mechanic's lien laws, some advocating a liberal reading of these "remedial" statutes and some a narrowing construction.[268] Often, a court would argue for a strict reading of the statutory provisions that determined eligibility for the lien and, once eligibility was established, a liberal reading of other provisions.[269]

However, enough narrow construction, particularly in early cases, led to statutory amendments that liberalized coverage in response to restrictive judicial decisions.[270] This leads us to ask the same question that we asked about the attachment cases: was narrow construction of mechanic's lien statutes beyond the boundaries of legitimate interpretation? We look at cases in three areas: who is entitled to the lien? have formal procedural requirements for the lien been met? and who is subject to the lien?

Many cases defined the person entitled to the lien so that only those who did manual labor were eligible—where the statute referred to a "laborer" or the like. Although appealing to the derogation canon, the courts limited the law sensibly (if not necessarily) to those people whom the legislature intended to benefit. For example, an Oregon case[271] observed that the statute's "provisions are intended to secure to a laborer or employe[e] the benefit of his wages when his employer's property has been levied upon by virtue of any judicial process. A proper definition of the terms 'laborer,' 'employe[e],' and 'wages' becomes necessary, to correctly interpret the act." The court goes on to define the text to fit the statutory goal, "favor[ing] those who earned their money by the sweat of their own brows, not those who were mere contractors to have the work done, and whose compensation was the profit they would realize on the transaction."

To the same effect is a Michigan case,[272] where the court relied on the derogation canon to prevent contractors as opposed to laborers from benefiting from the mechanic's lien law. "To admit such claimants to an equal footing with those of the ordinary wage earner would have the effect to defeat the purpose of the enactment. This statute is in derogation of the common-law rights of the parties. . . . [N]or do we think it possible, in a case like the present, to separate the profits of the contract from the value of the services, and to give a lien for the personal services of the claimant."

Certainly, no hostility was showed toward statutes in the way these cases defined those eligible for mechanic's liens.[273] Modern mechanic's liens statutes often address the textual uncertainty of older law by precisely specifying whether contractors as well as laborers are entitled to the lien.

Other cases forced those seeking mechanic's liens to comply with the procedural letter of the law to obtain the lien, as was true in many of the attachment cases. In an Illinois case,[274] the court referred to the derogation canon, but only to insist that statutory notice be given to the property owner. And, in a Pennsylvania case denying the lien, the claimant failed to comply with the formal requirements for filing statements that identified the property against which the lien was filed.[275]

In some cases, the text was insufficiently clear, and the court opted for an interpretation denying the lien. For example, when the statutory text was uncertain about whether to require personal service on the owner, the court insisted on such service, invoking the derogation canon in the interest of providing adequate notice to the property owner.[276]

Some cases holding the claimant to a high procedural standard display a somewhat greater hostility to mechanic's lien legislation than the discussion so far implies. In these cases, the court's refusal to excuse formal lapses in statutory requirements occurred even when the lapses did not produce any harm, suggesting an unwillingness to respond sympathetically to statutory policy favoring the person possessing the lien. For example, in an Illinois case,[277] failure to meet technical formal requirements entitling the owner to notice of the times when material was furnished or labor performed was fatal to the lien, even though the owner "knew the times when the brick was furnished, and could suffer no damage by the error in the claim of lien. . . ." The court stated: "The lien claimed must exist, if at all, by reason of the appellant's compliance with the provisions of the statute, and neither the knowledge nor the ignorance of appellees of the facts can affect the vital inquiry, — has appellant so complied with the statute as to entitle it to a lien?"[278]

Some cases "narrowly" construed mechanic's lien laws to assure that only the proper persons were subjected to the statutory lien. For example, an Illinois statute stated that a lien could be imposed against "the owner of any lot or piece of land." The work was done for the *tenant*, not for the owner, and, when the tenant failed to pay rent, the land reverted to the owner of the property. The court observed that "[t]he statute which gives a mechanic a lien is in derogation of the common law, and must receive a strict construction. It will not be applied by the court to cases which do not fall within its provisions."[279] But the case only refused to give the lien against the owner of property for repair work contracted for by the tenant, which was far from a hostile reading of the text.[280]

These mechanic's lien cases describe statutes that often are capable of absorbing an interpretation denying the lien and preserving the common law. From the perspective of the interpretive process, the decisions are therefore reasonable, if not inevitable. It is more difficult to sustain the view that the courts were substantively attuned to the future evolution of statutory policy, especially in decisions refusing to allow the lien when procedural lapses were harmless. The intensity of the judge's backward-looking perspective is clearly evident in two cases that contain language typical of nineteenth-century judicial hostility to statutes. They argue that the mechanic's lien law provides "a privilege enjoyed by one class of the community above that of all others";[281] and that "[s]uch special class legislation [is] in derogation of the common law, and in some respects against the common right. . . ."[282] A common nineteenth-century way of indicating hostility toward statutes was to label them class legislation, raising the specter of socialist revolution and class warfare whenever a law had a redistributionist impact.[283] This judicial perspective anchored the law in the past and resolutely set itself against the future.

WRONGFUL DEATH STATUTES

A wrongful death statute provides a cause of action for losses (such as loss of support) suffered as a result of the death of certain relatives. The common law, based on an uncommonly recent 1808 heritage,[284] did not provide recovery for such losses. The British changed their common law by statute in 1848 and U.S. legislatures followed suit, but many courts insisted that the statutes were in derogation of common law.[285]

This insistence is illustrated by late nineteenth-century decisions dealing with whether a lawsuit could be instituted for *both* wrongful death to compensate surviving relatives and a "survival" action that allowed a lawsuit for causes of action that decedents would have had if they had not died. For example, a Michigan opinion[286] invoked the derogation canon to prevent a claim for the same injury under both statutes: "While the act relates to a remedy, it is, nevertheless, in derogation of the common law, because it gives a right of action where none existed at common law; and so it should be strictly construed." This decision flew in the face of the statutory texts authorizing both causes of action, and without justification. The problem that worried the judges was the risk of double recovery for the same damages, but the law could easily have been interpreted so that both causes of action would coexist without damage duplication. A survival statute could allow recovery for the decedent's losses, and wrongful death statutes allow recovery for losses suffered by the decedent's relatives.

It may be plausible to argue that this Michigan decision demonstrates a hostility toward wrongful death statutes that overstepped the boundaries of legitimate judging. But it is far from clear that nineteenth-century judicial opinions in wrongful death cases usually had this impact. As was noted by the majority and dissent in the earlier case,[287] judicial decisions in some states allowed both survival and wrongful death causes of action to proceed. And, in other cases, courts that leaned away from favoring wrongful death plaintiffs were dealing with unclear statutory texts.[288]

MARRIED WOMEN'S PROPERTY ACTS

Married Women's Property Acts (MWPAs) gave property rights to wives free of their husbands' control and in derogation of the common law. Early versions of these acts prevented husbands from committing a wife's property to his creditors, but they often added (or were amended to add) a provision stating that the wife could deal with her own property as though she were unmarried.[289] A typical provision stated that the wife's property would not be subject to the disposal of her husband, or be liable for his debts, and that the property would continue as her sole and separate property, as if she were a single female, and, further, that any married female could take by inheritance, or by gift, grant, devise, or bequest and hold the property to her sole and separate use, and convey and devise in the same manner as if she were unmarried.[290]

These statutes were too much for many judges to take, and they invoked the derogation canon to limit their scope, but we need to ask again just how hostile these decisions were to the statutory scheme. The critical issues concerned the apparent declaration in the MWPAs that the wife could deal with her property as though she were unmarried. One group of cases dealt with the wife's business relationships with the husband; recognition often was refused to property transactions incident to those relationships. This narrow interpretation's rationale was that the MWPAs protected the wife's property, and, if she were allowed to deal with her husband, she would, as a practical matter, be exposed to the kind of dominance by her husband that the law was supposed to eliminate.

An example of a narrow interpretation is a Washington, D.C., case preventing the wife from being her husband's business partner.[291] The court rejected the "suggestion, that, unless she can become his partner, she will not be wholly free . . . ," observing that allowing her to become her husband's partner

> will place her and her property within touch of the very dangers which it is sought in the first place to withdraw her from. Her improvident husband, by the most ordinary persuasion . . . could, in spite of her, unless she assumed a hostility which would endanger the continuance of the marriage relation, waste and dissipate her entire estate, and thus the very purpose which it seems to us stands out the most clearly in the act in question, *i.e.,* to secure her protection in the management and enjoyment of her estate, would be defeated.

(The court cited similar decisions in other states, including Maine, Michigan, New York, and Indiana.) The court's doubts about the wife's ability to take care of own business affairs were sufficiently great [292] to overcome a provision in the state law that the "rule of common law that statutes in derogation thereof are to be strictly construed has no application to this chapter [but] . . . shall be liberally construed with a view to effect its object." A similar paternalism appears in other cases holding that the wife could not sign her husband's note to lend him her credit. [293]

These decisions, no doubt, strike us as hostile to the legislative purpose of recognizing the wife's independent capacity to deal with her property. In modern terms, the issue was whether the statutes should be interpreted to continue, paternalistically, to protect her from her husband, even though the statutory text seemed to give her powers similar to a male property owner in dealing with others. We would have little trouble today deciding that the wife could take care of herself in dealing with her husband, although the modern decision upholding exclusion of women from being drafted into the armed services suggests that such paternalism is far from obsolete. [294] But the failure to anticipate the future is, as I argued earlier, not the same thing as illegitimate judging. The common law contained a variety of rules that made the wife dependent on her husband and denied her complete independence, and it is unclear just how far the legislature went in changing the old law. It is certainly not uncommon for statutes to take small steps in changing the law, and a court is not necessarily stretching the boundaries of legitimate judicial practice by asking how far the legislature intended to go. [295]

Other cases were more ready to recognize the wife's ability to take care of herself in commercial relations with her husband. For example, the highest court in New York reversed a lower court decision and allowed a wife to be a surety for her husband, even though she would not directly benefit from her husband's loan.[296] And a Colorado decision spoke eloquently about "allowing [the wife] to control, handle, and dispose of her individual property, and deal with her husband in all that pertains to it, as well as with others, as if she were feme sole." [297] But we should not conclude that the rhetoric in the Colorado case was necessarily an effective declaration of commercial independence for wives. All the case did was to allow the husband to deal with his wife as an independent party by preferring her as a creditor; no rights of the wife in dealing with her own property were involved.[298]

Perhaps courts were not clearly wrong in narrowing the text of MWPAs when husbands and wives dealt with each other. But it is harder to defend other decisions in which the court limited the wife's ability to deal with her own property with outside parties as though she were unmarried, free of her husband's control. An example is the refusal to interpret MWPAs to eliminate the husband's common law property right known as "curtesy." (Curtesy gave the husband a life interest in his wife's property upon her death if there were surviving children born during marriage.) [299] In a New York case [300] the statute provided that the wife's property [301] "shall not be subject to the disposal of her (future) husband, nor be liable for his debts, and shall continue her sole and separate property, as if she were a single female"; and "that any married female may take by inheritance, or by gift, grant, devise or bequest, . . . and hold to her sole and separate use, and convey and devise . . . , in the same manner, and *with like effect,* as if she was unmarried, and the same shall not be subject to the disposal of her husband, nor liable for his debts" (emphasis in original).

The judge held that the statute gave the wife a lifetime power to dispose of and use property during the marriage and to protect her property from her husband's disposition and his creditors, but did not allow her to eliminate the husband's tenancy by the curtesy in property by will, if she had not conveyed the property during her lifetime. The judge was hostile toward the statute, characterizing as "simply absurd" its statement that a married woman shall own property as if she were single: "What principle of public policy or political economy would have induced the legislature to take away" the husband's curtesy rights? [302]

To the same effect is a Pennsylvania case [303] where the statute stated that property acquired by a married woman "shall be owned, used, and enjoyed by her as her own separate property," and that "the said property shall not be subject to levy and execution for the debts of her husband, . . ." The court rewrote the text so that the "and" at the beginning of the second clause said "and therefore" or "so that," limiting the statutory protection to seizure for the husband's debts. The husband's curtesy interest therefore survived. Otherwise, the statute "is hardly consistent with the plain common sense of the law." The court "presume[s] that no innovation on the old law was intended further than was absolutely required." The rest of the opinion praises the traditional husband-centered family: "It is impossible that a woman can use and enjoy her property as fully and separately after marriage as before"; "[t]he husband is still the head of the family."

It might be a mistake, however, to exaggerate the extent to which the decisions preserving the husband's curtesy interest were hostile to MWPA legislation. All that these decisions did was to preserve a right in the husband when a child of the marriage survived the wife's death. In at least one state—New Jersey—the legislature explicitly affirmed prior judicial interpretations of the MWPA that the statute did not deprive the husband of his curtesy interest.[304]

And, as usual, not all judges were so favorable to the husband's curtesy interest or hostile to MWPA statutes. Some characterized the MWPAs as remedial, with no particular preference for survival of the prior common law. One example is Judge Platt Potter in New York, who refused to narrow what he thought was the plain import of the MWPA's statutory text: "Is the glory of the ancient common law so dazzling, that the learning of the present day, and all the attempted reforms upon the system to meet the wants of the age, are to be regarded as dangerous experiments?"[305]

I do not mean that all judicial decisions adopting a strict construction of MWPAs could be as readily defended as I have suggested above. Some did not involve dealings between husband and wife or curtesy interests, and I find it hard to characterize them as legitimate exercises of interpretive power. They simply preserved the husband's right to control the wife's property notwithstanding broad statutory language giving her the right to deal with her property as though she were unmarried. The Pennsylvania case preserving the husband's curtesy interest also held that the wife was not free to invest funds without her husband's consent. And in a Maryland case,[306] where the statute stated that "any married woman may become seized or possessed of any property . . . in her own name and as of her own property," the court held that this statute was passed to effectuate the state constitutional provision protecting a wife's property from her husband's debts and this purpose limited the statutory text. Consequently, the law did "not operate to change the rights of property acquired by marriage, so as to deprive the husband of all his marital rights secured to him by the common law." Therefore, the wife (who had left her husband) could not force the husband to provide her with support out of the income from the property in his possession which had come to him from her by virtue of the marriage. "When people understand that they *must* live together . . . , they learn to soften . . . that yoke which they know they cannot shake off; they become good husbands and good wives . . ." (emphasis in original).

These "hostile" decisions interpreting MWPAS certainly resonate with a common late-nineteenth-century theme: the refusal to accord full economic rights to women. One example is the unwillingness to change the traditional common law rule denying women the right to become members of the bar.[307] Statutes allowing a "person" (or similar wording) to be a member of the bar were held not to apply to women, often emphasizing her common law disability to practice law as a reason for this interpretation. The Wisconsin court went relatively far in stating: "We cannot but think the common law wise in excluding women from the profession of the law. . . . The law of nature destines and qualifies the female sex for the bearing and nurture . . . of our race and for the custody of the homes of the world and their maintenance in love and honor." [308] These decisions were by no means unanimous, however. Some states affirmed that the common law *allowed* women to practice law,[309] and many state legislatures so provided by statute.[310]

Conclusion

This review of nineteenth-century decisions preserving the common law against statutory change suggests that judges were clearly suspicious of the policies underlying legislation.[311] The argument that this proclivity was usually illegitimate judging (Roscoe Pound called it "spurious") is much more difficult to sustain. In many cases, the courts simply refused to depart from the letter of the law or to tilt an uncertain text in the direction of overriding the common law. Even when they narrowed the text, they sometimes did so to make good sense of the statute.[312] In some of these cases a court more in tune with the future of legislative reform might have been less protective of the common law, but in many instances the court was sensible (if not uncontroversial) in questioning the legislature about how far it wanted to go in changing the common law. The argument that judges act illegitimately when they query the legislature about how much of the past they want to discard is much more difficult to sustain than opponents of late nineteenth-century judging admit.

The strongest conclusion we can reach about nineteenth-century statutory interpretation is that courts resisted the view that statutes and the policies they embodied deserved to be enthusiastically incorporated into the law, but that history does not mean that the results violated legitimate norms of judicial practice. Expansive interpretation of legislative purposes may have been the wave of the future in the twentieth century, but courts which did not anticipate that wave were not thereby acting improperly. Both approaches—expansive and restrictive interpretation—are legitimate examples of ordinary judging within a wide range of possible decisions, however wrongheaded we might think the judge is.

4 From 1900 to the 1960s:

Purposive Interpretation

The nineteenth century received the undifferentiated English tradition of statutory interpretation and broke it down into its components, distinguishing between the protection of fundamental values and matters of mere inconvenience (the Golden Rule and Chief Justice John Marshall) and between the practice of limiting the reach of statutes through the "derogation" canon (which was favored), and, less often, extensive liberal interpretation of remedial statutes. Twentieth-century purposivism also differentiated the judicial role, but with a different emphasis. The dominant practice was to extend statutes to achieve their purpose (whether involving fundamental values or matters of inconvenience) rather than to limit statutes to preserve the common law.

In tracing the development of twentieth-century purposivism, we first look briefly at the importance of legislation, which eventually forced courts to be more sympathetic toward statutes than they had been during the previous century. Second, we look at early twentieth-century images of the legislative process, which predate purposivism but which were prerequisites to its development—the growing faith in a science of legislation and in the reliability of legislative history as a source of information about what legislatures were doing. Third, we examine the views of two transitional figures whose writings about statutory interpretation bridge the gap to modern purposivism—one a commentator (Roscoe Pound) and the other a judge (Oliver Wendell Holmes, Jr.). Finally, we look at how modern purposivism was practiced by judges—both in its more cautious version (Judges Learned Hand and Felix Frankfurter) and in its more full-bodied version—and at how modern purposivism was explained by commentators (the Legal Realists and the Hart & Sacks Legal Process materials).

Importance of Statutes in the Twentieth Century

Twentieth-century legislation at both the state and federal levels had a vitality and scope that earlier legislation lacked. It often replaced the common law and created whole new bodies of statute law. Federal regulatory statutes established the Food and Drug Commission (1906),[1] the Federal Reserve Board (1913),[2] and the Federal Trade Commission (1914).[3] Workers' compensation replaced much of tort law regarding employer and employee relationships, both at the state level (beginning in the first decade of the twentieth century)[4] and at the federal level for federal employees (1916)[5] and for longshoremen (1927).[6] Some purely redistributionist state statutes appeared, such as state mothers' pensions acts in the 1910s.[7] The federal income tax (1913)[8] also had a redistributionist populist tinge, despite rates that strike us as ridiculously low. And all of these statutes came before the New Deal explosion of regulatory and redistributionist legislation.

State and federal legislative reforms continued to meet with judicial hostility. Statutes interfering with common law rights were struck down as unconstitutional, and state courts narrowly interpreted statutes in derogation of the common law. New York State even held its workers' compensation law unconstitutional because it eliminated the common law requirement of fault as a basis of liability.[9] But there were signs of a change.

Nineteenth-century commentators had criticized judicial hostility to statutes and, occasionally, advanced an expansive twentieth-century image of legislation to describe how statutes fit into the broader legal fabric, with obvious implications for statutory interpretation. Joel Bishop in 1882, for example, describes a "new statutory provision [as] cast into a body of written and unwritten laws, . . . not altogether unlike a drop of coloring matter to a pail of water"; the color "[n]ot so fully, yet to a considerable extent, . . . changes the hue of the whole body; and how far and where it works the change can be seen only by him who comprehends the relations of the parts, and discerns how each particle acts upon and governs and is governed by the others."[10] But, except for generalized references to increased legislative competence and some appealing imagery, the commentators' critique lacked an affirmative defense of legislation. By contrast, those favoring the narrow interpretation of statutes in derogation of common law had a well-developed theory and affirmative image of the common law as custom, sanctified by long usage and popular consent, and as a science, accessible to legal expertise, both of which gave courts the confidence to limit the reach of legislation.

In the early twentieth century, commentators corrected that imbalance. They explained that legislation was good because it was becoming a science, capable of dealing with the kinds of change to which the slow-moving common law could not adjust. Even the U.S. Supreme Court, though routinely hostile to social welfare legislation, affirmed the constitutionality of laws that could be grounded in apparently scientific empirical data, the classic example of which is the decision upholding state statutes that limited working hours for women.[11] Moreover, not only was legislation more scientific, but the "science" of the common law was revealed to be riddled with political choices, giving legislation a comparative advantage as a source of law.

Eventually, as the century progressed, faith in legislation was associated with an affirmative image of democracy. This development served to heal the split between the law and the people, but it also made reliance on legal expertise as a source of judicial discretion obsolete. Now, with law affirmatively associated with popular will, the judicial role in statutory interpretation could not be justified as an appeal to custom or legal science, but only as a way of implementing popular will, embodied in legislative purpose.

Enthusiasm for democratic principles had been evident before, but such approval was continuously controversial. Throughout the nineteenth century it was always respectable to object to too much democracy, playing on fears of the mob and anarchy, as well as of legislative incompetence. Even Roscoe Pound's famous 1906 speech on the causes of popular dissatisfaction with the law referred to the "crude and unorganized character of American Legislation," even though he tilted toward legislation by contrasting the "individualist spirit of the common law and the collectivist spirit of the present age" and arguing that the "supremacy of law" was concerned not just with the individual but with the "whole people." [12] But, as Morton Horwitz explains,[13] the twentieth century eventually witnessed the widespread acceptance of democracy as a political principle, rejecting the earlier negative "tyranny-of-the-majority" image. Democratic principles were widely embraced, for example, in the amendments to the U.S. Constitution which provided that the U.S. Senate should be popularly elected (1913) and that women could vote (1920).[14]

Not all images of legislation were positive, but the remedy was in the direction of "more," rather than less, democracy. The Populist and Progressive movements at the end of the nineteenth century and the beginning of the twentieth century had considerable success in reviving the old idea of *direct* democracy.[15] The dominant idea behind direct democracy was to bypass special interest obstacles to popular reform legislation and to check the legislature's proclivity to favor narrow-interest groups. Politically, these movements were concentrated in a farmer-labor coalition opposed to big business, and they had their major successes in the West and South. Between 1898 and 1918, eighteen states adopted initiatives (which allowed voters to adopt legislation) and referendums (which allowed voters to approve of legislation passed by the legislature); four states adopted referendums only; and one state adopted only the initiative. All but four of these states were in the West or South.[16]

Between 1908 and 1933, twelve states also provided for recall of elected state officials, with seven of these recall provisions including judges. All but two of the recall states were in the West or South.[17] The issue of judicial recall was so contentious that Arizona's request for admission to the Union was denied because its constitution contained such a provision. Admission was granted only when judicial recall was removed, after which Arizona adopted judicial recall on its own.[18] The Progressive Party, led by Theodore Roosevelt, even favored recall of specific judicial decisions by popular vote, as follows: "That when an Act . . . is held unconstitutional under the State Constitution, by the courts, the people, after an ample interval for deliberation, shall have an opportunity to vote on the question whether they desire the Act to become law, notwithstanding such decision."[19]

Direct democracy did not, of course, mean faith in legislatures, and the twentieth-century enthusiasm for democracy might therefore have meant less rather than more confidence in judicial implementation of legislative purpose. But with the New Deal in the 1930s, the centrality of legislative democracy was established, overcoming the doubts associated with the direct democracy movement.

The changing image of democracy and legislation had significant implications for statutory interpretation. The vitality and scope of modern reform legislation invited the view that statutes embodied a purpose that was the guide to their interpretation. And legislative history, in the form of statements in legislative materials about the statute's purpose, provided evidence of what the legislature was trying to achieve, helping to contradict claims that the statute should be narrowly interpreted to preserve the common law.

Although some observers analogized purposive interpretation to traditional "equitable interpretation," that was an oversimplification. The old "equity" often allowed the judge to help out a careless legislature—one which overlooked problems or failed to update laws—either by extending the statute a bit or limiting coverage, often shunting aside the statutory text. Twentieth-century purposivism was different. It reconceived the text as embodying vital legislative purposes. Judges were willing to tilt the text when necessary to give it a possible meaning though not necessarily the most probable one. The closest analogy in past practice was to the way that Wilson and Marshall approached the Constitution. The spirit of the document did not so much "correct" its language (in Plowden's terms) as imbue it with meaning. Moreover, where late nineteenth-century equitable interpretation narrowed the reach of statutes, often through application of the "derogation" canon, purposivism usually extended statutes. Although no one said it in quite this way—it was statutes that twentieth-century judges were expounding.

Images of the Legislative Process

The foundation for purposivism was laid in the early twentieth century by the development of an affirmative image of the legislative process. This resulted from a developing science of legislation and from the reliability of legislative history as a source of information about legislative purpose.

THE SCIENCE OF LEGISLATION

Before democratic legitimacy provided the dominant justification for judicial deference to legislation, a science of legislation established legislative competence, without which arguments about legitimacy might have been unavailing. Roscoe Pound asserted a "scientific" view of legislation in a 1908 article in the *Harvard Law Review*:

> It is fashionable to preach the superiority of judge-made law. It may be well, however, for judges and lawyers to remember that there is coming to be a science of legislation and that modern statutes are not to be disposed of lightly as off-hand products of a crude desire to do something, but represent long and patient study by experts, careful consideration by conferences or congresses or associations, press discussions in which public opinion is focussed upon all important details, and hearings before legislative committees.[20]

And along with praise for legislative competence went suspicion of judging. "It may be well to remember also that while bench and bar are never weary of pointing out the deficiencies of legislation, to others the deficiencies of judge-made law are no less apparent."

This scientific view of the legislative process was elaborated by Ernst Freund,[21] a political scientist who served on the University of Chicago Law School faculty. He argued that a "science of legislation as a distinctive branch of jurisprudence is concerned mainly with tasks for which the upbuilding of the common law furnishes no precedents or standards; with those aspects of statutes, in other words, that find no analogy in principles developed by judicial reasoning." In Freund's view, judicial reasoning consisted of "principle," which was incapable of dealing with modern legal problems. What was needed was "[m]easured quantity, conventional form, administrative arrangements, and (it should be added) compromise and concession"; these were "the exclusive province of statute law," depending on "empirical, psychological, and sociological factors. Such a law the lawyer regards as being on the whole beyond his science, and as characteristic of the social and political sciences, and he will look with skepticism upon a proposed extension of jurisprudence in that direction."

Workers' compensation statutes, which were passed in nearly all U.S. jurisdictions in the first three decades of the twentieth century, are typical examples of what Freund is talking about. Workers' compensation laws were a response to common law tort rules, which were perceived as unduly restrictive of an employee's right to recover damages for industrial accidents. Industrial accidents took a heavy toll, and the common law was considered inadequate both as a method of encouraging safety and as a compensation scheme for injured workers and their families. At common law, an employee suing an employer had to prove fault, and the employer could interpose the defenses of contributory negligence, assumption of risk, and the fellow servant rule. Courts could have abolished these defenses, and they sometimes did, but elimination of the fault requirement would have seemed too radical for judges. The problem was ripe for legislation that broke with the past, made concessions to employers by way of compromise, fixed recovery amounts applicable to all cases, and established administrative agencies to handle the litigation.

Workers' compensation did all that. Common law defenses were eliminated, and employers were liable without fault for injuries occurring by accident if they arose from and in the course of employment. In exchange, employers were usually liable only to the extent of fixed amounts set forth in schedules, based on previous wages and the severity of the physical impairment. Industrial accident commissions (or similarly named agencies) were established to administer the program. Funding came from insurance premiums or self-insurance financed by employers, which varied with accident experience. It took a statute to achieve these reforms. Courts could not have done the job, at least not courts as we know them.

Even as late as 1961, Judge Henry Friendly expressed similar thoughts about a science of legislation, though (borrowing from Benjamin Cardozo) he referred to a "sociology of method." In "Reactions of a Lawyer—Newly Become Judge,"[22] Friendly discussed whether "in a personal injury action under the Federal Employers' Liability Act, the jury should be instructed to make a deduction, from the portion of the award representing loss of earning power, for the income taxes the plaintiff would have had to pay on the lost earnings." He argued that "the issue . . . was not one adapted to the techniques of judicial law making. . . ." The problem was *not* one of judicial legitimacy in creating law, but the relative competence of judging and legislation. "The more important reasons [why the issue was inappropriate for judicial solution] are that [judges] lacked the factual data needed for a right answer and, still worse, there was no right answer we could give even if the data had been available." Among the needed facts were what went on in the jury room, "how much of the verdicts go for attorneys' fees and other expenses of litigation, what plaintiffs do with the sums awarded, and whether the lump sum recovery, determined in advance of the fact on the basis of averages, is still suitable, especially in an age of new cures that may make it too high, and of increased longevity and inflation which may make it too low."

Moreover, legislatures (unlike courts) were free

[to] establish a small—or no—percentage deduction on awards up to a certain annual figure, and a higher percentage on those above. . . . Alternatively, the legislature might decide to require the portion of the award representing loss of earnings, or so much of it as was left after deducting expenses of litigation, to be paid into court and disbursed over a period of years, then being subject to income tax, and thereby end the whole problem. Almost any of these solutions would be better than the best a court can achieve.

LEGISLATIVE HISTORY

Along with a science of legislation went a shift in judicial attitude toward the use of legislative history,[23] which became a competent and reliable source of information about what the legislature was doing. If it was true, as Theodore Sedgwick had argued in the mid-nineteenth century,[24] that judges were becoming distant from legislatures, legislative history could fill that void, giving courts the information they needed to implement legislative purpose.

In a famous late nineteenth-century case—Holy Trinity v. United States[25]—the Supreme Court interpreted a statute to avoid criminalizing the importation of a pastor into the United States. Holy Trinity is best known for its willingness to trump a clear text to prevent an "absurd" result and to apply the statute in accordance with its purpose. However, the decision's reliance on purpose, which was to prevent importing "cheap unskilled labor" to compete with domestic labor,[26] is not especially important as a harbinger of twentieth-century purposivism. The religious implications of applying the statute to importing a pastor seemed to dominate the decision, and the statutory purpose was invoked for the very premodern objective of limiting the statute's reach rather than to expansively apply its purpose. But the decision is highly important as the most prominent early example of embracing legislative materials to prove legislative purpose. It therefore marks the onset of the use of conventional legislative history to interpret statutes, which was essential to modern purposivism.

Although prior judicial practice had excluded evidence of statutory meaning from written legislative materials, the Court slid into considering committee reports as though it was the most natural thing to do. It quoted the following statement from a report issued by the U.S. Senate Committee on Education and Labor, recommending passage of the bill: "Especially would the committee have otherwise recommended amendments, substituting for the expression, 'labor and service,' whenever it occurs in the body of the bill, the words 'manual labor' or 'manual service,' as sufficiently broad to accomplish the purposes of the bill," but that "believing that the bill in its present form will be construed as including only those whose labor or service is manual in character, and being very desirous that the bill become a law before the adjournment, [the committee] have reported the bill without change."[27]

Although resorting to legislative materials was a sharp break with the past, it was a natural evolution in response to changing realities in the judicial and legislative process. Judges had always relied on their knowledge of the *public* history of a statute to help determine meaning. Indeed, the Court in Holy Trinity first makes reference to such public history *before* it cites committee reports.[28] All the Court did in Holy Trinity was to recognize that it now had a good source of information about the statute's history that could make up for what judges might not know because they were growing more and more distant from the legislative process, at least at the federal level. As the federal legislature came to operate more and more through committees toward the end of the nineteenth century, committee reports told judges what the legislature was doing.

In retrospect, the real objection to judicial use of legislative history had been its unreliability as evidence of what the document meant. Most of the debate about legislative history in the early nineteenth century centered on the federal Constitution and the impropriety of using what the Constitutional Convention thought it was doing to shed light on what the Constitution's authors, the state ratifying conventions, intended. James Madison had stated as a congressman: "[W]hatever veneration might be entertained for the body of men who formed our Constitution, the sense of that body could never be regarded as the oracular guide in expounding the Constitution . . . [since the Constitution] was nothing more than the draft of a plan . . . until life and validity were breathed into it by the voice of the people, speaking through the several State Conventions."[29] Because objections to Framer legislative history were based on its reliability (it was one step removed from the Constitution's authors), the objections were less forcefully advanced when the history was generated by the state ratifying conventions.[30]

Justice Joseph Story had also appealed to reliability concerns to reject legislative history regarding legislation,[31] stating that "little reliance can or ought to be placed upon such sources of interpretation of a statute. The questions can be, and rarely are, . . . debated upon strictly legal grounds, with a full mastery of the subject and of the just rules of interpretation. The arguments are generally of a mixed character, addressed by way of objections, or of support, rather with a view to carry or defeat a bill, than with the strictness of a judicial decision."[32]

As long as nineteenth-century legislative procedure had not developed to the point where committees could plausibly speak for the legislature, objections to the judicial use of legislative history made sense. Congressional procedure was very British in the sense that legislative history consisted mostly of real debates where no individual could speak for the entire body, and U.S. courts generally followed British practice in rejecting legislative history.[33] Moreover, nineteenth-century legislative materials were not always accurate, although matters improved at the federal level with the midcentury adoption of phonography, the approximation of verbatim reporting in the *Congressional Globe*, and, in 1873, congressional authorization for the Government Printing Office to publish the *Congressional Record*.[34]

But once the legislature began to operate primarily through committees in the later part of the nineteenth century,[35] courts appropriately turned to congressional committee reports to learn about the public history of the statute (which had always been relevant to statutory interpretation).[36] Indeed, we have already seen that at least one state judge (Lemuel Shaw in Massachusetts) considered reports written by the revisers of state law as early as the 1840s, presumably because they were reliable evidence of what the legislature was trying to do. And I suspect that a more thorough canvassing of nineteenth-century state court decisions might uncover more examples of reliance on the revisers, though much of it is probably drafting history (changes in the text as a bill goes through the legislative process) rather than statements about what the legislature is doing.[37]

This evolution toward accepting legislative history as reliable evidence of what the legislature was trying to do can also be traced in the observations of post–Civil War commentators. They showed only the slightest tolerance for legislative materials before the Holy Trinity case. Pomeroy's 1874 edition of Sedgwick was marginally less hostile than Sedgwick had been: the "opinion of individual legislators" is entitled to "little weight, if any."[38] G. A. Endlich's Maxwell in 1888 rejects legislative history because the opinions of a few are not relevant, although he notes that no universal consistency exists regarding the use of committees reports.[39] J. G. Sutherland in 1891 states that "[t]here has been occasionally judicial reference to declarations of members of legislative bodies, but such aids are but slightly relied upon, and the general current of authority is opposed to any resort to such aids."[40] Joel Bishop in 1882 was a bit more generous, stating that the materials lack authority but are relevant as "opinion to persuade."[41]

More sensitive to what lay ahead was a comment in a short practitioner-oriented piece in 1881, agreeing with the Supreme Court's view that opinions of individual members were not helpful but urging reliance on "the course of debate [where it] represent[s] the prevailing sentiment" because "no reason exists for excluding [it] from consideration as tending to throw light on the meaning of a statute."[42] The author notes that "[o]f late years . . . it has become not uncommon for courts to refer to the reports of Congressional committees in construing statutes," although the citations do not support his claim.

However, by the time of Sutherland's 1904 second edition—after Holy Trinity—its author, John Lewis, could state: "The proceedings of the legislature in reference to the passage of an act may be taken into consideration in construing the act."[43] It is true that Holy Trinity had used this new evidence in a traditional way—to limit the statute's coverage. But as legislation became more comprehensive and energetic in the twentieth century, purposivist interpreters would need something more than their own guesses about public history, not only to overcome narrowing judicial interpretations, but also to sustain their enthusiastic elaboration of legislative goals. And that something was legislative history. By 1937 it could be said that committee reports were "freely used" and that legislative debates (which had still been considered unreliable evidence of statutory meaning at the end of the nineteenth century, even after Holy Trinity)[44] were now selectively considered when the speaker was a committee chair or member in charge of a bill.[45] This development seemed to do no more than implement the New Deal revolution and the modern theory of government that the legislature expresses popular will.[46]

Transition to Purposivism

A science of legislation and the reliability of legislative history were necessary but not sufficient conditions for a robust purposivism to develop in statutory interpretation. In the pre–New Deal period, when legislation was still struggling to achieve its status as the paramount source of law, two transitional figures, Roscoe Pound and Oliver Wendell Holmes, Jr., helped lay the groundwork for purposivism.

Pound wrote primarily from an academic perspective. By 1907–8, when he published two influential articles about statutes and the common law, he had served briefly on the Nebraska Supreme Court (1902), but then moved on to be dean of the University of Nebraska Law School (1903). He became professor of law at Northwestern University (1907) and the University of Chicago (1909), and he then went to Harvard Law School in 1910, where he became dean in 1916. His affirmative image of legislation replaced the nineteenth century's faith in a science of common law with a science of legislation. This new approach led Pound to conceive of statutes as "principle[s] from which to reason." Although statutory principle could be used to support a purposivist approach to statutory interpretation, that was not Pound's focus. He was more concerned with rejecting the narrowing interpretation of statutes in derogation of common law and with statutes entering into the broad fabric of the law as a source of principle to influence the development of common law.

Oliver Wendell Holmes Jr., although a prolific author on legal issues, wrote about statutes primarily as a judge. His legal career began in 1866, when he entered law practice in Boston. In 1882, he became a Massachusetts state judge, and he went on the U.S. Supreme Court in 1902, from which he retired in 1932. His opinions, not surprisingly, hover between the nineteenth and twentieth centuries in their approach to statutory interpretation, and his writings on this subject are difficult to categorize, providing something for everybody.

ROSCOE POUND

Roscoe Pound's development of sociological jurisprudence was closely linked to his faith in a science of legislation. As he explained in 1912, sociological jurisprudence took account of the social facts upon which law must proceed, the social effects of institutions and doctrines, the means of making legal rules effective, and the social effects of legal doctrine.[47] This view led him naturally to favor legislation as the best vehicle for accomplishing these goals. He looked to legislative hearings and legislative experts to do the necessary research and accommodate the many interests that were legitimately concerned with social reform.

Pound's adoption of sociological jurisprudence led him to react strongly against the common law lawyers' negative view of legislation and to advance the position that statutes were a vital source of legal principle. His 1908 law review article, "Common Law and Legislation," argued that statutory principle should be either superior or parallel to the common law as a source for the development of the common law, although he admitted that most lawyers would consider this argument "absurd."[48] He hoped for this development in the future, a hope echoed by Chief Justice Harlan F. Stone in a 1936 law review article[49] and eventually realized in the Supreme Court in the Moragne case (where the federal common law of admiralty evolved to include wrongful death actions, based in part on the accretion of state and federal statutes).[50]

As for the meaning of statutes, Pound was primarily concerned that statutory principle would overcome the nineteenth-century judicial penchant for narrowly interpreting statutes in derogation of the common law. He described the "orthodox common law attitude" as "strict and narrow interpretation, holding [the statute] down rigidly to those cases which it covers expressly."[51] Some narrowing interpretations were justified—for example, the rule of lenity: "When acts are to be made penal and are to be visited with loss or impairment of life, liberty, or property, it may well be argued that political liberty requires clear and exact definition of the offense."[52] But

> [the] proposition that statutes in derogation of the common law are to be construed strictly has no such justification. It assumes that legislation is something to be deprecated. As no statute of any consequence dealing with any relation of private law can be anything but in derogation of the common law, the social reformer and the legal reformer, under this doctrine, must always face the situation that the legislative act which represents the fruit of their labors will find no sympathy in those who apply it, will be construed strictly, and will be made to interfere with the *status quo* as little as possible.[53]

The term that Pound used for unsympathetic judicial approaches to statutes was "spurious interpretation,"[54] a phrase he borrowed from John Austin for the title of his 1907 law review article and a concept already implicit in Francis

Lieber's writings, which distinguished construction from interpretation. He described genuine interpretation in terms that would have been familiar to Blackstone: "[S]o long as the ordinary means of interpretation, namely the literal meaning of the language used and the context, are resorted to, there can be no question."[55] He was concerned that "recourse . . . to the reason and spirit of the rule, or to the intrinsic merit of . . . several possible interpretations" could blur the line "between a genuine ascertaining of the meaning of the law, and the making over of the law under guise of interpretation. . . ."[56] It was not that "reason and spirit" were off-limits to the judge, but that resorting to them prematurely could be spurious. In this respect, Pound said much the same thing as Blackstone in explaining the order in which interpretive criteria should be considered by the interpreter. Pound's contribution was his tendentious insistence that, unlike genuine interpretation, "the object of spurious interpretation is to make, unmake, or remake, and not merely to discover. . . . It is essentially a legislative, not a judicial process. . . ."[57]

But Pound then drew a conclusion that Blackstone would never have drawn: "As legislation becomes stronger and more frequent, examples of [spurious] interpretation will finally become less common."[58] In sum, "[s]purious interpretation is an anachronism in an age of legislation."[59]

Pound *can* also be quoted for anticipating purposive interpretation, but it would be a mistake to understand him as a full-fledged purposivist. He certainly advocated "a liberal interpretation to cover the whole field [the statute] was intended to cover,"[60] but reason and spirit were to be considered only *after* the "literal meaning of the language used and the context" failed to provide the answer.[61] This position falls far short of the enthusiastic reliance on purpose to infuse the statutory text with meaning, which comes later in the twentieth century. Pound was primarily concerned with how statutes and common law interacted. When he wrote the article excerpted above in 1907, most of the twentieth century's broad programmatic legislation lay in the future.

Pound's sharp distinction between genuine and spurious interpretation is also unfaithful to modern purposivism. He undoubtedly exaggerated that distinction because he associated spurious interpretation with hostility toward legislation, and he wanted to end that hostility. In the modern context, where courts are no longer hostile to legislation, drawing such a sharp distinction between the spurious and the genuine obscures the element of judicial creativity in purposive interpretation and threatens to pin the "spurious" label on its most common feature—the enthusiastic and sympathetic elaboration of legislative purpose.[62]

OLIVER WENDELL HOLMES JR.

Justice Oliver Wendell Holmes Jr.'s legal career spanned the years from 1866 to 1932—in other words, from just after the Civil War to the New Deal. No wonder that his opinions on statutory interpretation ring of both the nineteenth and twentieth centuries.

His most famous statement about statutory interpretation sounds textualist: "We do not inquire what the legislature meant; we ask only what the statute means."[63] This statement surely means that the judge should not narrow the text to preserve the common law (in a spirit of hostility to the statute) on the basis of some guess about legislative intent. And it also rejects evidence of subjective intent derived from unreliable legislative history. But that may be all Holmes meant; it does not necessarily make him a textualist. Holmes did not say: "we ask only what the statute *says.*"[64]

And, indeed, a lot of Holmes's writings sound purposivist. In one well-known example, Boston Sand & Gravel Co. v. United States, he stated: "It is said that when the meaning of language is plain we are not to resort to evidence in order to raise doubts. That is rather an axiom of experience than a rule of law and does not preclude consideration of persuasive evidence if it exists."[65] And in Irwin v. Gavit,[66] Holmes rejected the dissent's explicitly literalistic approach and interpreted the income tax law to achieve its "general purpose."

The most famous of the Holmes quotations on which purposivists often rely is from Johnson v. United States,[67] where he stated:

A statute may indicate or require as its justification a change in the policy of the law, although it expresses that change only in the specific cases most likely to occur to the mind. The Legislature has the power to decide what the policy of the law shall be, and if it has intimated its will, however indirectly, that will should be recognized and obeyed. The major premise of the conclusion expressed in a statute, the change of policy that induces the enactment, may not be set out in terms, but it is not an adequate discharge of duty for the courts to say: *We see what you are driving at,* but you have not said it, and therefore we shall go on as before. (emphasis added)

However, a closer look at the context of Holmes's decisions containing purposivist quotations suggests that he was not a robust twentieth-century purposivist who enthusiastically elaborated the democratic choices of a dynamic legislature.

First, in Boston Sand & Gravel, Holmes was arguing for only a technical rather than an ordinary meaning of language, based on the way that language had been used in a group of statutes other than the one being interpreted.[68] This is a conventional nineteenth-century "look at surrounding statutes" approach to determine how language was used in a specific statute.[69]

Second, the Irwin v. Gavit tax decision did no more than embrace a nineteenth-century "whole text" approach to make sense of the income tax law. The statute taxed income and exempted gifts of "property." Holmes had no trouble finding that the exemption did not apply to "property" in the form of money paid out of the income from a trust. A modern purposivist judge might have gone on at some length about how any other result would permit tax avoidance that could not have been the purpose of Congress; if the receipt of the money was exempt, wealthy families often could arrange for trust earnings to completely avoid income tax. Holmes's approach is different; he works with the statutory text's contrast between taxable income and exempt gifts of property to reach a sensible result.[70]

Holmes's "see what you are driving at" decision is also relatively old-fashioned, firmly in the equitable interpretation tradition of extending a statutory list just a bit. The statute specified that a litigant's "pleading" could not be used in evidence in a later criminal case against the pleader. All Holmes did was to extend the word "pleading" to a schedule of assets filed by a bankrupt individual. Moreover, he also suggested that the word "pleading," without extensive interpretation, could include the bankrupt's schedule of assets.

In sum, Frankfurter's judgment that Holmes "hug[ged] the shores of the statute itself, without much re-enforcement from without"[71] seems close to the mark. Holmes accepted legislation, most famously in his constitutional dissents objecting to judicial overriding of democratic will,[72] although he snuck in a nineteenth-century Golden Rule perspective, stating that the protection of "liberty" by the Fourteenth Amendment preserved what "a rational and fair man necessarily would admit [were] fundamental principles as they have been understood by the traditions of our people and our law."[73] But Holmes was simply not enthusiastic enough about the democratic legislative process to embrace the purposivist's role of expansively and selectively elaborating statutory purpose. Whether Holmes's belief in the "right of a majority to embody their opinions in law"[74] was grounded in a "lack of emotional involvement" or just "blind faith,"[75] his commitment to democracy was insufficiently fervent to classify him as a purposivist judge. His tools—extending the text a bit; looking at the whole text and related statutes—were those of a pre-twentieth-century judge.

But Holmes was not just a product of the nineteenth century. Sometimes he could not help but selectively and enthusiastically expand legislative purpose. Otherwise, for example, it is difficult to explain his decision in International Stevedoring Co. v. Haverty.[76] A federal statute expanded the opportunity for "seamen" to obtain compensation when injured on the job, but the plaintiff was a longshoreman (or a "stevedore"). Holmes's opinion for the Court held that "seamen" also meant stevedores, doing much more than "seeing what Congress was driving at." Although he admitted that "for most purposes, as the word is commonly used, stevedores are not 'seamen,'" still (he said) "words are flexible."[77]

Holmes proceeded to lace his opinion with that harbinger of aggressive purposive judging: the "we cannot believe that Congress intended" language.[78] He states: "We cannot believe that Congress willingly would have allowed the protection to men engaged upon the same maritime duties to vary with the accident of their being employed by a stevedore rather than by the ship." Apparently, Holmes's disbelief follows from his observation that "[t]he policy of the statute is directed to the safety of the men and to treating compensation for injuries to them as properly part of the cost of the business," leading him to the conclusion "that a wider scope should be given to the words of the act, and that in this statute 'seamen' is to be taken to include stevedores employed in maritime work on navigable waters . . . , whatever it might mean in laws of a different kind."

Obviously, Holmes was doing much more than extending a word slightly (as he had done to include a bankruptcy schedule in the term "pleading"). Providing longshoremen with a legal remedy when injured on the job was a much contested political issue at the time. The Haverty case came at the end of a long legislative and judicial struggle to provide adequate remedies to maritime workers injured on the job. Congressional efforts to give states the authority to provide workers' compensation benefits for such workers had been blocked by an unsympathetic court, prompting Holmes's famous dissenting observation that the law is not a "brooding omnipresence."[79] If longshoremen were not covered by the new law covering "seamen," they were without an effective remedy. Holmes's plea for equal treatment of seamen and longshoremen arrayed him on the side of those judges who enthusiastically, if controversially, embraced the cause of providing workers with adequate benefits through statutory interpretation. The flexibility of the words clearly followed *from* the policy of worker safety, which Holmes sympathetically applied to give the text an expansive meaning.

And yet even Holmes's purposivism in the Haverty opinion might not be as robust as it appears. The field of law was admiralty in which federal courts had a substantive common law power to make law. Although the issue was one of statutory meaning, Holmes might have assumed a greater judicial role because of this underlying common law power.

Purposivism

Before purposivist interpretation could come into its own, something more was needed than Pound's commitment to scientific legislation and Holmes's cautious deference to the legislature, and that something was an affirmative sense of energizing purpose. The early years of the twentieth century were not up to that reconceptualization of statutes. The New Deal had not yet arrived, and state legislatures were still suspect. Because the Populist and Progressive movements considered that state legislatures were captive to private interests, they sought to bypass them through referendums and initiatives. And some observers still associated legislation with "mob" rule, explaining the movement to bypass state legislatures as a middle-class attempt to prevent machine politics from aiding the lower classes.[80] Even James Thayer's famous 1893 law review article, which warned about too much judging,[81] was far from enthusiastic about legislative implementation of popular will. Thayer questioned judicial review, not because he had a robust image of democracy, but because such review drove out a sense of legislative responsibility in matters of justice and right. His view that courts cannot "save a people from ruin" was not a ringing endorsement of democracy.

By the time of the New Deal in 1933, however, legislation acquired a more positive image. James Landis in 1934 still dwelled on "science" as the source of legislative vitality, but this position was becoming an obvious rhetorical device.[82] Scientific expertise was now associated as much with administrative decision-making as with legislation, and agencies were delegated the task of fleshing out general legislative principles. Legislatures came to be viewed as the place where popular democratic will was expressed and the common good enacted into law.[83] Statutes replaced common law custom as the source of social consensus—as the glue that held society together. In historical perspective, the nineteenth century split between the people and the law seemed to be healed, and judges could comfortably put on the mantle of legislative purpose to cooperate in the lawmaking enterprise.

Eventually, this emphasis on democracy would evolve into a countermajoritarian anxiety about judging, including a concern about judicial choices associated with purposive interpretation. But in these years of heady optimism about science, democracy, and legislatures, courts could enthusiastically adopt a role as the creative expositors of legislative purpose. Thus, when Landis said that "legislation [as well as judicial precedent] is assuming . . . a creative aspect of purpose" *and* that the judge is a "creative artist," he made the connection between creative legislating and judging that has characterized modern purposive interpretation.[84] And he was explicit about that link: "The consciousness that the judicial and legislative processes are closely allied both in technique and in aims will inevitably make for greater interdependence in both."[85]

The judicial-legislative link at the heart of purposivism was most famously stated by the Supreme Court in United States v. American Trucking Associations, Inc.[86] The Court affirmed the importance of the text as evidence of purpose. ("There is, of course, no more persuasive evidence of the purpose of a statute than the words by which the legislature undertook to give expession to its wishes.") It also underlined the influence of the Golden Rule. ("When that meaning has led to absurd or futile results, however, this Court has looked beyond the words to the purpose of the act.") But there was more. "Frequently, however, even when the plain meaning did not produce absurd results but merely an unreasonable one 'plainly at variance with the policy of the legislation as a whole' this Court has followed that purpose, rather than the literal words." The Court was explicit, too, in addressing the question of judicial role, shunting aside concerns over separation of powers. Indeed, it was the "duty" of courts to interpret the statute in light of legislative policy. Any danger that the judges' own views would intrude into the decision was worth taking. "The interpretation of the meaning of statutes, as applied to justiciable controversies, is exclusively a judicial function." It was a "duty [which] requires one body of public servants, the judges, to construe the meaning of what another body, the legislators, has said." As for the "danger that the courts' conclusion as to legislative purpose will be unconsciously influenced by the judges' own views or by factors not considered by the enacting body," the best way to address that concern was through a "lively appreciation of the danger."

JUDGES

Purposivist judges operated in an environment in which the creative element in purposive judging was hard to deny; but it also was an environment in which no agreement had been reached about how careful the judge must be to avoid the exercise of judicial discretion. Some, like Learned Hand and Felix Frankfurter, were cautious purposivists. Hand, especially, was concerned with anchoring the judge's role in a Plowden-like effort to imaginatively reconstruct how the legislature which passed the statute would have applied the law to the particular case. Others were more full-bodied purposivists, less cautious about how much judicial discretion went into a decision and more willing to elaborate the legislature's purpose without worrying too much about whether the legislature would have reached the same decision.

Learned Hand

The most articulate judicial exponent of modern purposivism, as well as of the need for a "lively appreciation of the danger" of purposivism, was Judge Learned Hand. Like Holmes, his judicial career spanned many decades—from his appointment to the federal district court in 1909 to his retirement from active status as a federal court of appeals judge in 1951, though he continued to decide cases until ten years later. But, unlike Holmes, he was firmly planted in the twentieth century.

Here is one of Hand's more famous statements favoring purposivism and denigrating textualist reliance on the dictionary:

> Of course it is true that the words used, even in their literal sense, are the primary, and ordinarily the most reliable, source of interpreting the meaning of any writing: be it a statute, a contract, or anything else. But it is one of the surest indexes of a mature and developed jurisprudence not to make a fortress out of the dictionary; but to remember that statutes always have some purpose or object to accomplish, whose sympathetic and imaginative discovery is the surest guide to their meaning.[87]

And he practiced what he preached, not only in the field of labor law, which was the subject of much of the dynamic legislation in the early twentieth century, but also in tax law, where the temptation to be more textual is strong.

Lehigh Valley Coal Co. v. Yensavage,[88] is a typical example of a purposive Hand opinion in the field of labor law. The decision interpreted "employee," not by incorporating a borrowed common law meaning into the statute, but, more broadly, to achieve the statute's purpose. The statute was meant to protect miners who were "employees" and worked in potentially unsafe conditions. The defendant had established a relationship with his workers that avoided the traditional "employment" relationship, but Hand said that the technicalities of employment law did not matter because it would "miss the whole purpose of such statutes, which are meant to protect those who are at an economic disadvantage."[89] He continued: "It is true that the statute uses the word 'employed,' but it must be understood with reference to the purpose of the act, and where all the conditions of the relation require protection, protection ought to be given. It is absurd to class such a miner as an independent contractor. . . . He has no capital, no financial responsibility."[90] And, in a not-so-veiled disapproval of the judicial propensity to protect freedom of contract and to claim that this leaning followed from scientifically objective principles, Hand stated: "Such statutes . . . upset the freedom of contract, and for ulterior purposes put the two contesting sides at unequal advantage; they should be construed, not as theorems of Euclid, but with some imagination of the purposes which lie behind them."[91]

Hand's purposivism was pervasive, not limited to social welfare labor legislation, but extending, for example, to interpretation of the income tax law. Indeed, one of Hand's most famous statutory interpretation opinions is Helvering v. Gregory,[92] denying breaks to a taxpayer whose transaction met the letter but not the underlying purpose of the tax law. The taxpayer had tried to turn ordinary income into preferentially taxed capital gain by an elaborate transaction whereby she ended up acquiring investment property previously owned by her corporation. This acquisition should have been a dividend, taxed as ordinary income, but the transaction appeared to meet the technical statutory language, allowing exemption of stock distributions in "reorganizations" and favorable tax treatment of their sale. Hand rejected dictionary definitions for purposive interpretation:

> We agree . . . that a transaction, otherwise within an exception of the tax law, does not lose its immunity, because it is actuated by a desire to avoid, or, if one choose, to evade, taxation. . . . [I]f what was done here, was what was intended by [the statute], it is of no consequence that it was all an elaborate scheme to get rid of income taxes, as it certainly was. Nevertheless, it does not follow that Congress meant to cover such a transaction, not even though the facts answer the dictionary definitions of each term used in the statutory definition.[93]

Moreover, the statutory detail did not faze him in his search for statutory purpose, which he called the statutory "melody." "It is quite true . . . that as the articulation of a statute increases, the room for interpretation must contract; but the meaning of a sentence may be more than that of the separate words, as a melody is more than the notes, and no degree of particularity can ever obviate recourse to the setting in which all appear, and which all collectively create." Hand then describes the "plain" statutory purpose of the reorganization provisions (citing House and Senate reports) as rearranging enterprise assets while they remained in corporate solution, which had not happened in the Gregory case. Since what the taxpayer did was not what the statute intended (the statutory "melody"), the distribution was not exempt as pursuant to a plan of "reorganization."

To fully appreciate Hand's application of purposivism to the income tax, we should remember what he said about the tax law: "In my own case the words of such an act as the Income Tax . . . merely dance before my eyes in a meaningless procession: . . . leave in my mind only a confused sense of some vitally important, but successfully concealed, purport, which it is my duty to extract, but which is within my power, if at all, only after the most inordinate expenditure of time." [94] (Even Frankfurter had suggested that tax statutes were different from other laws, requiring a different interpretive approach. "The relation of [a labor act to an antitrust act] is not that of a tightly drawn amendment to a technically phrased tax provision.") [95] And yet Hand's tax opinions reveal the same kind of imaginative interpretation as do his labor law cases. [96]

A less well-known but even more striking example of purposive interpretation of the tax law is Hand's opinion in Commissioner v. Ickelheimer. [97] The statute disallowed loss deductions on "direct" and "indirect" sales between related parties, including husband and wife. A wife sold bonds on the New York Stock Exchange, and her husband bought the same issue of bonds on the Exchange a day or two later. The parties did not use a friend as a go-between, and they were subject to the risks of the stock market during the gap in time between sale and repurchase. The majority (Hand was in dissent) applied the term "indirect" sale when a friend was used as a go-between, but they did not apply it to sales in which the parties risked market fluctuations. Hand disagreed, rejecting literalism: "[O]ne would have to be a very convinced literalist to say that the section did not cover a device by which the plain purpose of the statute could be frustrated. . . . Unless we must confine 'indirectly' to cases where the seller passes title to an intermediary who has agreed to pass it to the ultimate buyer at the same price, we should call [what the taxpayer did] an 'indirect sale.' I can see no reason so to confine it." [98]

Hand went on to describe an interpretive credo that purports to rely on Holmes's "see what you are driving at" approach, but one that is much more aggressive in its perception and application of legislative purpose. [99] He argues that "the colloquial words of a statute have not the fixed and artificial content of scientific symbols; they have a penumbra, a dim fringe, a connotation, for they express an attitude of will, into which it is our duty to penetrate and which we must enforce ungrudgingly when we can ascertain it, regardless of imprecision in its expression." And, claiming that he "ha[s] no doubt of the [legislative] purpose," he refuses to "truncate" that purpose by "not includ[ing] transactions by which, in accordance with a preexisting design, property passes by whatever combination of moves at a substantially unchanged price from one member to the other of any of the specified pairs."

But, of course, a good reason existed to confine the statute narrowly, to doubt that legislative purpose applied to the sale between husband and wife, if putting oneself at the risk of the market was enough to avoid the statute's intent in disallowing the loss deduction. At this point, Hand does something that goes further than even Pound could have hoped for: he reasons from one part of the statute to another rather than using statutory principle to influence the common law. He interpreted the statutory provision about "indirect" sales in light of an analogous statutory provision, which disallowed tax losses on "wash sales" (meaning a sale at a loss and a repurchase by the seller within a short period of time). "The 'wash sales' section . . . shows that Congress did not regard the chance taken by an investor who sold and rebought within thirty days, as enough of a break in his ownership to 'realize' a loss; the situation here is somewhat like that." [100] But a judge could as easily have concluded that a legislature which made such careful judgments about wash sales would have been equally explicit had it meant to reach an analogous result for sales between related parties. Hand did not so much see what the legislature was driving at as imaginatively reconstruct a legislative purpose which made sense on the assumption that prevention of tax avoidance was a dynamic and expansive congressional goal.[101]

Hand also wrote at length about judging in several essays brought together in *The Spirit of Liberty*,[102] and some of his comments about purposivist statutory interpretation seem firmly cautionary. For example: "When a judge tries to find out what the government would have intended which it did not say, he puts into its mouth things which he thinks it ought to have said, and that is very close to substituting what he himself thinks right. Let him beware, however, or he will usurp the office of government, even though in a small way he must do so in order to execute its real commands at all." [103] He also cautioned against preferring "common sense" over literalism: "It is easy to . . . say that judges are always too literal and that what is needed are men of more common sense. Men of common sense are always needed, and judges are by no means always men of common sense. They are quite like the rest of us. But it is also easy to go wrong, if one gives them too much latitude." [104] And, although committed to enforcing "the common will expressed by the government," [105] he also says things about legislatures and "common will" that are strange coming from a purposivist, suggesting that not much is coming from the legislature on which the judge can elaborate except what the "powerful" can legislate:

> We think of the legislature as the place for resolving [major conflicts], and so indeed it is. But if we go further and insist that there . . . we have an expression of a common will, it seems to me that for the most part what we mean by a common will is no more than that there shall be an available peaceful means by which law may be changed when it becomes irksome enough to powerful people who can make their will effective.[106]

A judge who makes statements that are so suspicious of what a popularly elected legislature does might seem an unlikely candidate for spearheading the purposive approach to statutory interpretation, which rests on a shared sense of legislative vitality and creative judging. Yet that is exactly what Hand does in his judicial opinions. Indeed, as Gerald Gunther notes, Hand usually enforced New Deal laws "more sympathetically than even the post-1937 Supreme Court." [107]

Why would Hand have been so enthusiastic about purposivism as a technique of statutory interpretation despite his awareness of its potential for judicial lawmaking? Hand was certainly distrustful of the "masses"; he favored judicial restraint in part because he feared that the voters would react against "political" judging by interfering with judicial independence, and he vigorously opposed judicial recall.[108] But he was also distrustful of wealth; Jerome Frank called him a "democratic aristocrat." [109] Politically, Hand was active as a young man in the pro-labor and pro-regulatory causes advanced by Theodore Roosevelt's Progressive Party. He was, Gerald Gunther notes, passionately committed to improving worker conditions,[110] and he even ran for the New York Court of Appeals as a Progressive while he was a sitting federal district court judge.[111] And whatever doubts he had about the common will as expressed legislatively, he did not believe that a common will resided in the common law, an idea that he labeled a "fiction," derived from a period when judges were from the class with political power.[112]

In the historical context of progressive legislation, purposivism allowed

Hand (as well as other judges) to advance political principles with which they were in sympathy, while at the same time fairly claiming that they were advancing the legislature's will. Although Hand may have appeared Hamlet-like to Frankfurter[113]—and probably was in comparison to Frankfurter—Hand's statutory interpretation decisions were often in the progressive spirit of his early years.[114] Moreover, statutory interpretation decisions did not have the effect that Hand most feared—the insulation of law from change in response to popular will—because, unlike judicial review striking down a statute, statutory interpretation did not prohibit legislatures from responding with clarifying legislation.

On a more speculative note, I would hazard a guess that an underlying humanism in Hand's judicial work product stood in striking contrast to Holmes's, as evidenced by their artistic preferences. Holmes was deeply moved by the works of Albrecht Dürer, an artist whose "works [were] dearer to me, and more valued instructors than any books and than any other art."[115] He was especially taken with Dürer's print *Melancholia*, "grave with thought and marked with the care of the world; winged, yet resting sadly on the earth."[116] Contrast this with Hand's love of the humanistic Italian Renaissance, "the love of my mature years, but as strong a love as though it had been youthful."[117] Purposivism resonates comfortably with an optimistic humanistic view of legislating and judging, lacking "grav[ity] of thought" and certainly not "resting sadly on the earth."

In the broader context of his other writings, Hand's caution about purposive interpretation may therefore be nothing more than an admonishment to himself to do what the Supreme Court urged in American Trucking: to have a "lively appreciation" of the "danger that the courts' conclusion as to legislative purpose will be unconsciously influenced by the judges' own views or by factors not considered by the enacting body. . . ." Having alerted himself to this concern, he then advocates a robust purposivism:

[The judge] must try as best he can to put into concrete form what that [legislative] will is, not by slavishly following the words, but by trying honestly to say what was the underlying purpose expressed.[118]

Thus, on the one hand, he cannot go beyond what has been said . . . ; on the other, he cannot suppose that what has been said should clearly frustrate or leave unexecuted its own purpose.[119]

. . . Courts must reconstruct the past solution imaginatively in its setting and project the purposes which inspired it upon the concrete occasions which arise for their decision.[120]

And, sounding a lot like Plowden, Hand asserts: "what [the judge] really does is to take the language before him, . . . and try to find out what the government . . . would have done, if the case before him had been before them. . . . To apply [the words] literally may either pervert what was plainly their general meaning, or leave undisposed of what there is every reason to suppose they meant to provide for." [121]

The better reading of Hand's entire body of work is that he was simply incapable of resolving the potential conflict between creative and deferential judging that he was both perceptive and honest enough to see implicit in purposive interpretation. Although not as full-bodied a purposivist as some others, he is readily characterized as falling on the purposivist side of the ledger. Where Holmes crossed that line only with extreme caution and in a manner that pre-twentieth-century judges would usually have recognized, Hand's purposivism was located firmly in the twentieth century. For all of his angst about the judicial role, and perhaps because of it, he felt free when interpreting statutes to sympathetically embrace the legislature's purpose.

Felix Frankfurter

Felix Frankfurter's writings are a bit more cautious than Hand's. He is explicitly wary of Hand's reference to the "art of interpretation as 'the proliferation of purpose,' " preferring to speak of how purpose is anchored in the text: "[P]olicy is not drawn, like nitrogen, out of the air; it is evinced in the language of the statute, as read in the light of other external manifestations of purpose." [122] Frankfurter reemphasized this point in his opinion in Addison v. Holly Hill Fruit Products, Inc.: "If legislative policy is couched in vague language, easily susceptible of one meaning as well as another in the common speech of men, we should not stifle a policy by a pedantic or grudging process of construction." [123] But he contrasted "let[ting] general words draw nourishment from their purpose" with "draw[ing] on some unexpressed spirit outside the bounds of the normal meaning of words." Statutes differed from the Constitution: "[W]e are here not dealing with the broad terms of the Constitution 'as a continuing instrument of government' but with part of a legislative code 'subject to continuous revision with the changing course of events.' " And in his article "Some Reflections on the Reading of Statutes," [124] he enthusiastically embraces Holmes's statement professing not to "care what [the legislature's] intention" is, only "what the words mean."

But Frankfurter was no Hamlet. He came to the Supreme Court bench in 1939 after almost three decades of active political life, most of which was conducted after becoming a Harvard Law School professor in 1914,[125] and during which he drafted statutes and sent many bright young lawyers to work in the New Deal.[126] Frankfurter's political activism did not escape Hand, who sometimes found his "crusading spirit" to be " 'a bit trying,' even 'intolerable.' " [127]

It is therefore not surprising that Frankfurter's conception of statutes and their texts was neither narrow nor textualist. Statutes are "organisms";[128] "living organisms." [129] As for the text, "[w]ords are intellectual and moral currency," and "words sometimes appreciate or depreciate in value";[130] "[t]he notion that because the words of a statute are plain, its meaning is also plain, is merely pernicious oversimplification." [131] He was, moreover, willing to rely on legislative history to determine the meaning of statutory language, beyond that which could be inferred from ordinary usage. "Congress can be the glossator of the words it legislatively uses either by writing its desired meaning, however odd, into the text of its enactment, or by a contemporaneously authoritative explanation accompanying a statute"; the "Court's task is to construe not English but congressional English. Our problem is not what do ordinary English words mean, but what did Congress mean them to mean." [132]

This conception of statutory language and the role of the legislative author went along with a view of legislatures and judges that linked them both in a common venture. Much as James Landis had argued, Frankfurter said that a "statute is an instrument of government partaking of its practical purposes but also of its infirmities and limitations, of its awkward and groping efforts," and judges were "selected by society to give meaning to what the legislature has done." [133] Exorcizing the ghost of Coke, Frankfurter dedicated his coauthored book, *The Labor Injunction,* to Louis Brandeis with the observation that he was one "for whom law is not a system of artificial reason." [134]

The most interesting aspect of Frankfurter's purposivism is the way he worked out meaning from the accretion of multiple statutes, using their accumulating purpose to interpret *other legislation.* This approach went well beyond Roscoe Pound's urging that judges use statutory principle to influence the common law. In Keifer & Keifer v. Reconstruction Finance Corp.,[135] the issue was whether a federal statute implicitly granted sovereign immunity to a government corporation. Statutes governing at least forty government corporations created during the 1920s and 1930s had explicitly waived government immunity in the statutory text. Frankfurter saw this legislation as the cumulative expression of legislative will with a life of its own: "Such a firm practice is partly an indication of the present climate of opinion which has brought governmental immunity from suit into disfavor, partly it reveals a definite attitude on the part of Congress which should be given hospitable scope." [136]

The only problem was that the statutory text at issue in the case was silent about governmental immunity. But that did not matter:

> It is not a textual problem; for Congress has not expressed its will in words. Congress may not even have had any consciousness of intention. The Congressional will must be divined, and by a process of interpretation which, in effect, is the ascertainment of policy immanent not merely in the single statute from which flow the rights and responsibilities of [the government corporation], but in a series of statutes utilizing corporations for governmental purposes and drawing significance from dominant contemporaneous opinion regarding the immunity of governmental agencies from suit.[137]

Frankfurter goes on to infer a waiver of sovereign immunity, despite the statutory text's silence on this issue, refusing to "impute to Congress a desire for incoherence in a body of affiliated enactments and for drastic legal differentiation when policy justifies none." [138] So much for his warning against not drawing on an "unexpressed spirit" outside the text.

Perhaps the most dramatic of Frankfurter's opinions making sense out of the overall purpose of multiple statutes is United States v. Hutcheson.[139] The 1890 Sherman Antitrust Act made certain labor union activities criminal. A 1914 statute prohibited an injunction and criminal prosecution of union activities, but courts interpreted the prohibition to apply only to union activities against employers. Interunion rivalry activities could still be illegal. Then, in 1932, the Norris-LaGuardia Act explicitly prohibited *injunctions* against interunion rivalry activities as well. The issue in Hutcheson was whether interunion activities could be *criminal*, a question not explicitly resolved in the 1932 statute. Frankfurter held that the 1932 act decriminalized the behavior against which injunctions were prohibited by that statute, stating that "it would be strange" if some act could still be criminal even though it could not be enjoined:

> That is not the way to read the will of Congress, particularly when expressed by a statute which, as we have already indicated, is practically and historically one of a series of enactments touching one of the most sensitive national problems. Such legislation must not be read in a spirit of mutilating narrowness. . . . The appropriate way to read legislation in a situation like the one before us, was indicated by Mr. Justice Holmes on circuit [quoting Holmes's "see what driving at" language from Johnson v. United States].[140]

But Frankfurter was not just "seeing what the legislature was driving at." He was not extending a statutory list slightly or even stretching the meaning of a word (like "pleadings" in the Johnson case). He perceived that the "underlying aim of the [1932 act] was to restore the broad purpose which Congress thought it had formulated in the Clayton Act but which was frustrated, so Congress believed, by unduly restrictive judicial construction. . . . The [1932 act] reasserted the original purpose of the Clayton Act by *infusing* into it the immunized trade union activities as redefined by the later Act" (emphasis added).[141] Consequently, the act decriminalized what could not be enjoined.

Justice Owen Roberts was aghast as Frankfurter's bold approach to statutory interpretation, especially in view of the fact that "the scope of proposed amendments and repeals of the anti-trust laws in respect of labor organizations has been the subject of constant controversy and consideration in Congress."[142] It was "a usurpation by the courts of the function of the Congress [that was] not only novel but fraught, as well, with the most serious dangers to our constitutional system of division of powers."[143] But Justice Frankfurter was an expert in labor law, having argued labor law cases before the Supreme Court, and having coauthored a book on the labor injunction.[144] Perhaps because of this background, he was not about to heed his own caution against Hand's view that "the art of interpretation [is] the proliferation of purpose," or his own enthusiastic embrace of Thayer's view (as interpreted by Hand) that judges should avoid setting themselves up as the "final arbiters of social conflicts."[145]

Full-bodied purposivism

Cautious elements are present in both Hand and Frankfurter, at least in their nonjudicial writings, that we do not see in the judicial opinions of some other judges. Just as the nineteenth-century invocation of the derogation canon came in many guises and had its more moderate and extreme versions, so did twentieth-century purposivism. In the more full-bodied versions of purposivism, the statutory text and evidence of legislative compromise receive less emphasis, and legislative purposes—especially those that implement reform objectives—are more enthusiastically and sympathetically embraced. The judge is less concerned with whether he is faithfully reconstructing how the enacting legislature would have applied the statute to the facts of the case and more concerned with projecting that legislative purpose onto those facts.

A more full-bodied purposivism is well illustrated by two of the opinions in the 1940s case of Lenroot v. Western Union Telegraph Co.,[146] which dealt with a statute prohibiting child labor. In this pre–civil rights era, no political issue attracted more passion than child labor. In his Hammer v. Dagenhart dissent in 1918, Holmes had allowed himself to extend his judicial comments beyond constitutional theory requiring deference to the legislature and to speak of the "ruined lives" of working children: "But if there is any matter upon which civilized countries have agreed . . . it is the evil of premature and excessive child labor. I should have thought that if we were to introduce our own moral conceptions where in my opinion they do not belong, this was preeminently a case for upholding the exercise of all its powers by the United States." [147] And Pound had argued as a lawyer in favor of the constitutionality of congressional power to regulate child labor and had favored a constitutional amendment to permit its prohibition. [148]

The statute in Lenroot stated that "no producer . . . shall ship . . . in commerce any goods produced in an establishment situated in the United States [where] any oppressive child labor has been employed." [149] The question was whether this statute applied to what Western Union did with telegrams. Four opinions were offered: Simon Rifkind for the district court, Hand for the court of appeals, and Robert Jackson for the Supreme Court majority, from which Frank Murphy dissented. Rifkind's and Murphy's opinions illustrate full-bodied purposivism. District Judge Rifkind, in holding that the statute applied to Western Union, referred to the "breadth of congressional policy" that kept commerce "undefiled" and "free from pollution by the sweat of child labor." [150] He explicitly applied the liberal interpretation of remedial statutes canon, objecting to "linguistic purism." Justice Murphy's dissent in the Supreme Court appealed repeatedly to the "intent and spirit" of the law and referred to "oppressive child labor." He preferred to rely on "humanitarian purposes" rather than "grammatical perfection," stating:

> In approaching the problem of whether Western Union is a producer of goods shipped in interstate commerce we should not be unmindful of the humanitarian purposes which led Congress to adopt [the statute]. Oppressive child labor in any industry is a reversion to an outmoded and degenerate code of economic and social behavior. . . . If the existence of oppressive child labor in a particular instance falls within the obvious intent and spirit of [the statute], we should not be too meticulous and exacting in dealing with the statutory language. To sacrifice social gains for the sake of grammatical perfection is not in keeping with the high traditions of the interpretative process. [151]

It is a sign of the difficulty in making generalizations about twentieth-century purposivism that Murphy's opinion was a dissent. The Supreme

Court held for Western Union in an opinion that stuck close to the text, finding that the company neither "produced" nor "shipped" what were admittedly "goods." [152] The Court undoubtedly had Rifkind and Murphy's opinions in mind when it took a slap at their version of purposivism, stating: "But we take the Act as Congress gave it to us, without attempting to conform it to any notions of what Congress would have done if the circumstances of this case had been put before it." [153] And Judge Hand, though finding that the statute *did* cover Western Union, wrote a close-to-the-vest textual analysis of the statute which found that the telegrams were "produced" and "shipped." [154] Hand's only hint that he was not ruled by the text occurred when he discussed the word "ship." He stated that, having treated messages as "goods," "we should stultify ourselves, having gone so far, if we were to refuse to understand it as covering what is here involved." [155] Nothing in Hand's opinion speaks eloquently of the problems of child labor.

COMMENTATORS

Before the 1960s, two major twentieth-century schools of legal thought made important observations about purposivism. These were Legal Realism and Legal Process.

The Legal Realists' heyday was the period immediately before and during the New Deal, at the height of purposivism. As Morton Horwitz explains, Legal Realism was less a coherent view of the law than an "intellectual mood," [156] but that mood had important implications for statutory interpretation. The central message of Legal Realism was to call attention to the discretionary political element in judging. Although this observation could have led to questioning the judge's role in statutory interpretation, it did not. Most of the Legal Realist critique was aimed at common law judging. It was optimistic about legislating, and to the extent it had anything to say about statutory interpretation, it appeared to support a full-bodied purposivism that was optimistic about the lawmaking collaboration between judges and legislators.

The Hart & Sacks Legal Process materials, though developed over several decades,[157] appeared in unpublished form in 1958, at the end of the period of confident modern purposivism.[158] Though still confident about legislation, it displayed much greater caution than the Legal Realists about the judicial interpretive role. Legal Process provided a general theory of government, emphasizing the institutional competence of different institutions.[159] At the same time that it carved out a purposive interpretive role for judges, it also expressed a special concern about judicial competence to exercise political lawmaking discretion.

LEGAL REALISTS

Legislation was very important to the Legal Realists. Many of them had confidence in value-free social science, which led to faith in legislative (and agency) solutions and to political activity aimed at achieving legislative reform.[160] Along with faith in legislation went a devastating critique of common law judging, which made it impossible for anyone to appeal to the judge's "artificial reason" or "legal science" in expounding the law. Behind the objective principles of common law lay judicial political choices.[161] Jerome Frank, for example, in his book *Law and the Modern Mind,* noted that Judge Manfield in eighteenth-century England asserted the need for legal certainty at the same time that he exercised massive amounts of judicial discretion on the sly.[162]

Although the primary objective of the Legal Realists was to reveal how common law judging and the incorporation of the common law into constitutional principle was riddled with lawmaking policy choices, their perception that law and politics intersected also had significant implications for statutory interpretation. First, the judicial appeal to the derogation canon that privileged the common law was out-of-date. Second, traditional interpretive approaches embodied in the substantive canons of interpretation did not provide objective judicial guidelines but were easily manipulated by judges to reach desired substantive results. One of the more famous articles in the Legal Realist genre argued that the interpretive canons came in pairs, each with an equal and opposite principle.[163] The classic example of such pairing was the derogation canon and the contrary principle that remedial statutes should be liberally construed.

The point about judicial discretion in statutory interpretation echoed the dominant Legal Realist concern about judicial discretion generally and might have led to a deep suspicion of purposive interpretation. Indeed, when Max Radin (the Legal Realist commentator most concerned with statutory interpretation) looked at the legislative process, he was unable to identify a reliable source of the "legislative intent" on which purposivist interpreters so often relied. He emphasized that the vast bulk of legislators had not given any thought at all to the specifics of most litigated cases; he further stated that, even if the thought had occurred to them, they would not have agreed about how the statute should apply, and, in any event, that such thoughts were not law. He made a similar point about using legislative purpose, adding that legislators as a group usually had a concatenation of purposes, ranging from the more specific to the more general.[164]

Nonetheless, there was a strong tendency among many Legal Realists to embrace a full-bodied purposivism. Their optimistic belief in a value-free humanistic social science and in the ability of legislatures and agencies to make law based on that science encouraged a creative judicial partnership (as Landis had argued) in which the best way to implement what the legislature had done was through sympathetic purposive interpretation. For example, Jerome Frank took Pound to task for "perpetuat[ing] the feeling that there is something in equity and discretion which is out of line with the course which law should take."[165] And, as a judge, Frank was explicit in adopting a purposive approach to statutory interpretation: "We must heed [congressional] policy, even if not explicit. For it is no longer novel doctrine that a policy plainly implied, although not expressed, in a statute should control in its interpretation [quoting Holmes's 'see what you are driving at' language]."[166]

Radin, too, despite his cautionary comments about the judge identifying legislative intent and purpose, spoke very favorably of the purposivist approach, at the same time that he was realistic about the extent to which it required creative judicial judgment. As a Legal Realist, Radin was simply unable to pretend that purposivism eliminated judicial creativity, but that did not bother him much. He authored an updated version of Heydon's Case in which he frankly admitted that the judge exercises judgment about the value attributed to whatever legislative purpose the judge identifies.[167] Radin based his view on a theory of judging and legislating that was much more hospitable to creative judging than many purposivists allowed; a statute, he contended, was a "ground design," and judges were "statesmen" who could "exercise a judgment on the value of the [statutory] purpose."[168] Legitimacy was simply not a problem: "[O]ur legislature is no more and no less sovereign than administrators or judges; [t]he legislature has no constitutional warrant to demand reverence for the words in which it frames its directives."[169]

Radin was therefore led to "rewrite" Heydon's Case as follows: "The first question the interpreter asks is: What is the purpose of the statute as a whole? . . . Second, Is the statutory purpose one that the court feels is good?"[170] As for the problem of judicial legitimacy, Radin argued that "[w]e need not trouble ourselves about the statement that the court must not legislate. Both the judicial and the executive branches participate in the legislative process. . . . They may not rephrase the statute. They may not reject the purpose, even if they do not find it to be good. But they may . . . exercise a judgment on the value of the purpose, and make that judgment the basis of enforcement of the law."

LEGAL PROCESS

If some of the Legal Realists provided support for a more full-bodied purposivism, the Hart & Sacks 1958 Legal Process materials closed out the era of modern purposivism with an influential defense of the more guarded judicial approach associated with Judge Hand. As it turned out, Legal Process attempted to synthesize the creative elements in judging just when the tensions inherent in purposivism were about to become too great to hold their synthesis together.

Sometimes the judge's creative role was frankly recognized. The Legal Process judge has an "ought" role in determining statutory meaning, as many Legal Realists had urged: "The function of a court in interpreting a statute is to decide what meaning *ought* to be given to the directions of the statute in the respects relevant to the case before it" (emphasis added).[171] And:

> In interpreting a statute a court should:
> 1. Decide what purpose ought to be attributed to the statute . . . ;
> 2. Interpret the words . . . to carry out the purpose as best it can.[172]

Moreover (reminiscent of Plowden), "[i]n determining the more immediate purpose which ought to be attributed to a statute . . . a court should try to put itself in imagination in the position of the legislature which enacted the measure[,]" and it "should not do this in the mood of a cynical political observer, taking account of all the short-run currents of political expedience that swirl around any legislative session."[173]

The "oughtness" of the judge's role in the Legal Process formulation suggests a judge with considerable lawmaking discretion. However, strong indications, reminiscent of Hand's more cautionary comments, contradict this degree of latitude.[174]

> In trying to discharge this function the court should:
> 1. Respect the position of the legislature as the chief policy-determining agency of the society . . . ;
> 4. Be mindful of the nature of language and, in particular, of its special nature when used as a medium for giving authoritative general directions; . . .
> And, in deciding what meaning ought to be attributed, the judge must

"mak[e] sure . . . that it does not give the words . . . a meaning they will not bear. . . ."[175]

The fundamental question about this approach was what to make of the most famous Legal Process injunction of all: "[The court] should assume, unless the contrary unmistakably appears, that the legislature was made up of reasonable persons pursuing reasonable purposes reasonably."[176] Was the judge supposed to hold the legislature to an external standard of reasonableness by interpreting the statute in light of that presumption? Or was the judge supposed to be confident that the legislature acted reasonably and not do too much judging?

The broader Legal Process message favors the more restrained version of the judicial role, based on the Hart & Sacks view of the relative competence of legislature and judge. In a section entitled "The Process of Reasoned Elaboration of Purportedly Determinate Directions,"[177] Hart & Sacks urge the judge to "make as sure as he can that the claimed uncertainty is a real one which he actually has power to resolve. Respect for the principle of institutional settlement demands this. What a legislature has duly determined ought not to be set at naught by any other agency or person."[178] Judicial caution is required by what Eskridge and Frickey refer to as the "centrality of process"[179] in the Legal Process approach: "[D]ecisions which are the duly arrived at result of duly established procedures . . . ought to be accepted as binding upon the whole society. . . ."[180] And it is apparent in the contrast between Alexander Hamilton's willingness to use the term "discretion" in the late eighteenth century to describe judging in the Federalist Papers[181] and Hart & Sacks's flight from that description: "[T]here may be thought to be a justification for describing the act of interpretation as one of discretion. . . . But this would be to obscure what seems to be the vital point—namely, the effort, and the importance of the effort, of each individual deciding officer to reach what *he* thinks is *the* right answer" (emphasis in original).[182]

Underlying this tilt toward judicial restraint is an optimistic image of the legislative and administrative process, in which well-represented groups work out their differences in the public interest, and a sense that each institution should do what it does best—that is, take an institutional competence approach.[183] The judge in this legal environment should not do too much, deferring instead to other more competent decision-makers. Interpretation requires "an appreciation . . . of the official's own function. There may be a difference . . . for example, between a court and an administrative agency."[184]

It may be something of an exaggeration to call the Legal Process approach a "procedure-based positivism," as Eskridge and Frickey do.[185] "Reasoned elaboration" of purpose *did* give the judge a lot to do, and there is no denying the tensions in the Legal Process formulation regarding just how much discretion the judge had (whether or not Hart & Sacks like the word). But as long as there was optimism about legislation, the broader goals of a democratic legal system and the reasoned elaboration by judges of legislative purpose converged to a common end. However, the contemporary wilting scrutiny of the legislative process has exposed what Eskridge describes as the "failure of legal process to develop a robust normative theory of democratic legitimacy," which he views as "a striking deficiency . . . in light of the willingness of legal process theory to turn over so many policy decisions to unelected judges." [186]

The Legal Process perspective on judging is in a long tradition of concern about institutional competence, which we have explored in earlier chapters. When the common law was dominant, courts developed various approaches that allowed them to shape statutory meaning based on the assumption that legislatures did not always get things right and needed a lot of help making law, reinforced in the later part of the nineteenth century by a split between the law and the people. Increased legislative competence forced courts to be less arrogant regarding statutes and their own lawmaking potential, and this change in attitude eventually evolved into purposive interpretation in which the judge's creative role could be grounded in affirmative assumptions about creative legislation and about the link between the law and the people that was supposed to exist in a democracy.

But what if we lose faith in *both* judging and legislating, a reality with which contemporary statutory interpretation now struggles? We lack faith in democracy (in the people), but it is also difficult to revive a robust nineteenth-century faith in judicial lawmaking expertise (in the law). What, then, is a court to do when the optimism about legislation that supported purposivism and that persisted during the first six decades of the twentieth century has evaporated?

Part II

Contemporary Statutory Interpretation

Contemporary statutory interpretation attempts to grapple with the collapse of optimism about legislation on which modern purposivism relied, without a corresponding revival of faith in judging. Part II traces the evolution of those efforts, placing them in their historical context, and concluding with my own attempt to ground the judicial role in statutory interpretation on a weak foundation—what I call "ordinary judging." As the following pages explain, we have gone from strong foundational approaches, which overstate judicial competence, to an indeterminate descriptive pragmatism, which threatens to leave judges without any basis at all for collaborating with legislatures to work out statutory meaning. "Ordinary judging" places judging somewhere between these extremes—although it owes a primary debt to pragmatism—resting the judicial role on an effort to place legislation in its temporal dimension, taking account of both its past and future.

The optimism about legislation on which purposivism depended rested on confidence in a policy science applicable to governmental decision-making and confidence in the democratic process from which statutes were supposed to originate. This optimism about legislation permitted an uneasy combination of purposive interpretation, which allowed the judge to imaginatively reconstruct legislative intent, and a skepticism about too much judging. But confidence in "policy science" did not survive World War II. "Science" had failed to head off fascism and a worldwide war, and it now seemed more associated with the destructive power of the physical sciences (symbolized by the atom bomb) than the creative potential of applied political science (what Benjamin Cardozo called "sociology").

That left democracy. The emphasis on democracy highlighted the contrast between legislatures and courts to the apparent disadvantage of judicial law-making discretion. Still, as long as faith in democracy persisted, purposivism could reconcile democratic values (the will of the people) with creative judging (the law) by having judges elaborate democratically declared purposes. But faith in the democratic process declined soon after the 1958 Hart & Sacks Legal Process materials. The comfortable notion that "the legislature was made up of reasonable persons pursuing reasonable purposes reasonably" withered under assault from both the political Left and the political Right. Rather than embodying purpose, statutes were the result of private-interest manipulation of the political process, either in the form of private feeding at the public trough or private economic bargains. In either case, statutes lacked the potential for creative judicial elaboration. Although statutes often had the *appearance* of being in the public interest, the reality was otherwise. Regulatory legislation was often the product of broad "public good" rhetoric accompanied by narrowing administrative implementation; and redistributionist statutes were the aggregation of special interests making claims on the public treasury rather than the expression of community support for those in need.

This view of legislation came largely from the political Right, which developed models about group organization and legislative behavior to support the view of legislation as being essentially purposeless. But an equally devastating critique came from the political Left, which viewed law as dominated not only by well-organized private interests, but also by cultural elites, unwilling to include marginal groups in a meaningful political dialogue. The result was legislation that failed to embody the public purposes deserving of judicial elaboration.

Without the protective purposivist umbrella that had been cast over the judge's discretionary role in statutory interpretation, the link between the law and the people on which purposivism relied was broken, and courts stood exposed to the Legal Realist critique of political judging, leaving statutory interpretation without a foundation on which to justify judicial discretion in working out the meaning of legislation. Pessimism about both legislation and judging left us without a way for judges to confidently share in the task of lawmaking through statutory interpretation. Some tried to overcome anxiety about "how free the judge was in rendering a decision" by finding new justifications for judicial lawmaking discretion—often going under the label of "Republicanism." Republicanism had procedural and substantive versions. Procedurally, judges made up for shortcomings in the legislative process. Substantively, they brought public values to the determination of statutory meaning. Essentially, Republicanism (as it related to statutory interpretation) was an attempt to do what Chief Justice John Marshall had suggested: to define those values that were fundamental enough to influence statutory meaning.

The other major response was textualist: giving the courts as little to do as possible by sticking closely to statutory language. Modern textualism differs radically in its objectives from nineteenth- and early twentieth-century textualism, when the text was contrasted with substantive background considerations — often the common law that many judges thought to be superior to statutes. The older versions of textualism urged the *priority* of legislation over judging, which helps to explain Oliver Wendell Holmes's and Felix Frankfurter's commitment to what the statute said. However, the evolution of a science of legislation, a commitment to democracy, and the rise of purposivism in the twentieth century ended judicial hostility to statutes. In this context, modern textualism is less an effort to defer to legislatures than to prevent what textualism perceives as too much judging inherent in the judicial elaboration of legislative purpose. Rather than preserving what the legislature has done, modern textualism is pessimistic about judging, trying to prevent judges from doing too much — with one major exception. At least some support for textualism (as chapter 6 explains) rests on an effort to preserve judicial capital to allow judges to play a major but limited role in protecting the most fundamental freedoms on which our constitutional system rests. In this respect, textualism is linked to Republican theories of judging (although it may define the values protected by the judge quite differently) and, in this limited setting, to an optimism about judging in regard to a narrowly defined set of fundamental values.

Finally, as the twentieth century comes to a close and the Republicans and textualists have had their say, a sense grows that no single approach — purposivism, Republicanism, or textualism — can explain statutory interpretation. A "pragmatic" mood has set in, giving each approach its due, as well as blending a strong measure of comparative institutional competence into the interpretive mix. This mood is nowhere more apparent than in William N. Eskridge Jr.'s shift away from a foundationalism grounded in both an evolutionary/dynamic and a Republican/fundamental approach to statutory interpretation and toward a commitment to pragmatism, even though the title of Eskridge's 1994 book, *Dynamic Statutory Interpretation*, echoes an earlier period in his thinking. The rigorous antifoundationalism of contemporary pragmatism imparts a sense of realism to the interpretive process, but it remains to be seen whether the pragmatic turn provides a sufficiently robust conception of judging to sustain an affirmative judicial role in statutory interpretation.

Part II explores these contemporary developments in the evolution of statutory interpretation, concluding with my own suggestions for a modest justification of a creative judicial role. Chapter 5 discusses modern textualism and its goal of giving the judge as little to do as possible in determining statutory meaning. In the chapter, I first look critically at the empirical assumptions underlying the law and economics critique of purposivism, which is one source of modern textualism. I then consider the various normative assumptions about legislating and judging that underlie modern textualism, including those that provide the necessary link between the law and economics empirical critique and a textualist approach to statutory interpretation and those that rely on a commitment to the statutory text to implement substantive values inherent in our conception of law and a constitutional system. Finally, I examine the problems which modern textualists encounter in providing a definition of the "text" that is independent of their normative vision of legislating and judging. It turns out that the concept of a "text" (not just the meaning of specific words) is so pliable that the textualist judge cannot avoid *choosing* how to determine its meaning rather than relying on some neutral independent textual standard.

Chapter 6 looks at theories that try to give the judge something—maybe a great deal—to do. We look first at Republicanism. I argue that Republicanism's emphasis on the judicial role in protecting fundamental values is too ambitious; it advances a case for judging that cannot be sustained, and it leaves the discretionary judicial role in statutory interpretation without an adequate foundation. I then consider the effort to find an affirmative interpretive role for judges through reliance on the substantive canons of interpretation. I focus on the textualists' willingness (with occasional misgivings) to permit such substantive value-laden criteria into the judicial interpretive arsenal, despite its inconsistency with a commitment to the text. I suggest that this inconsistency rests on an assumption that the canons will be clear enough in application to accommodate an interpretive role for judges in making substantive judgments while still leaving them with as little as possible to do. I conclude, however, that the canons lack the certainty needed to minimize judging in the way that textualists prefer because of the complexity of interaction between the canons and the statutes whose meaning they purport to influence, and because the weights of the values underlying the canons change over time.

Chapter 7 tries to pick up the pieces of contemporary statutory interpretation that have been left shattered by the broken link between the law and the people (undermining purposivism) and by the failed attempts to limit the judicial role (through textualism) and to justify an aggressive judicial role (through Republicanism). It fleshes out the modern inclination toward pragmatism[1] by locating the judicial role in "ordinary judging," which is a revival of the inherited English tradition of undifferentiated judicial competence, but a competence drained of "artificial reason" and a science of the law on which a belief in judicial superiority thrived for so long.

I will argue in chapter 7 that ordinary judging justifies the judge's interpretive role with the minimum foundational claim that can be made for judicial competence—the placing of statutes in their temporal context (both their past and their future). Moreover, not only is this an affirmative claim of competence, but it is also an acquiescence to the inevitable; there is no way a judge can apply texts to facts (that is, decide cases or controversies) without thinking about and thereby choosing how the text fits into its past and future. That process allows for the glimmer of truth in the otherwise hollow assertion that judges try to implement legislative intent when they interpret a text; "intent" implies the exercise of choice, which must be exercised in determining the meaning of a text.

In sum, ordinary judging avoids making the larger claims for judging that we often encounter. Fundamental values are no more relevant to judging than are matters of inconvenience; judicial concern with defects in the legislative process is not the unifying principle that explains the judicial interpretive role; and the dynamic adaptation of statutes to the future is no more privileged than anchoring a statute in its past. The judge, in making interpretive judgments, will certainly be sensitive to both substantive values and the lawmaking strengths and weaknesses of different institutions, but these are simply the byproducts of fitting statutes into their temporal setting; they do not justify the judge's affirmative interpretive role in the first place. This more modest claim for judging will, I hope, place judicial discretion in statutory interpretation on a more secure footing and establish judges as collaborators in the interpretive process, albeit as junior partners.

5 Giving Judges as Little to Do as Possible:

The Rise of Modern Textualism

William N. Eskridge Jr. reminds us that modern statutory interpretation is stronger if multiple strands converge to support a result.[2] Modern textualism—giving judges as little to do as possible—can benefit from multiple arguments that weave together three strands, each of which supports reliance on the text. One strand is empirical and two are normative conceptions of how legislating and judging fit into the law.

The first strand, built on the law and economics *empirical* critique of modern purposivism, argues that no expansive legislative purpose exists for the judge to elaborate. Consequently, the judge has nothing to do except rely on the text as a default criterion.

The second strand rests on a *normative* conception of the relationship between judging and legislating. It assumes that legislation is a radically separate source of law, not part of a broader legal fabric that the judge has a responsibility to develop. This is the airtight compartment theory of separation of powers (discussed in chapter 2), which was one of several conceptions of separation of powers extant around the time of the Founding. Once the court identifies what the legislature has done, the court has no further role to play.

The airtight compartment conception of legislation and judging marks out two paths to textualism, one based on a negative view of judging, the other on an affirmative view of legislation. The first path, which assumes that the judiciary has no role to play in making up for legislative shortcomings, is the one taken by those who adopt the law and economics empirical critique. Indeed, without this assumption, the law and economics critique would be bereft of a theory to explain why its view of legislation as purposeless leads to textualism. The law and economics approach to statutory interpretation is based on the assumption that the judge has nothing to do except defer to the legislature, either the statutory text it adopts or the legislative intent underlying the text. Finding no intent worth elaborating, the judge is left with nothing to do except fall back on the text.

The second path by which the airtight compartment view of legislating and judging leads to textualism relies on an affirmative view of legislation — i.e., that legislation *is* its text. In this view, the law and economics empirical critique of purposivism is beside the point. The correct constitutional conception of statutes is that they are texts (not intents or purposes), because the text is all that the legislature passes and the executive signs.

The third strand in modern thinking that leads to textualism accepts the view that judges have an affirmative *normative* role to play in fitting statutes into the broader fabric of the law, but it denies that this affirmative role leads to anything other than a commitment to rely on the text. This strand also marks out two paths to textualism. The first is the "rule of law" principle, which is associated with certainty and a minimum of lawmaking discretion: to permit individual planning and prevent arbitrary government. In statutory interpretation, its implications go well beyond textualism to include, for example, a strong defense of stare decisis. But it also implies deference to the statutory text.

The second path by which a textualist judge accepts a role in fitting statutes into the law is based on two assumptions: (1) that judges are the last bastion of protection for fundamental rights, and (2) that public support for this judicial role will erode (judicial political capital will dissipate) if judges are perceived as being too political. In this view, textualism will prevent that erosion from occurring, preserving the political capital of judges so that they can be the guardians of fundamental rights.

This chapter looks critically at all of these strands to see how strongly they support modern textualism. We first question the accuracy of the law and economics empirical models of legislation, which are meant to undermine purposivism, contrasting public choice models of the legislative process with the more realistic empiricism about legislation in the literature of positive political theory. We then critique the normative foundations of textualism: (1) the radical separation of legislating and judging, which deprives judges of a role in fitting legislation into the legal landscape; and (2) the two ways in which textualists assume judges can fit statutes into the broader fabric of the law — to implement rule-of-law values and to preserve judicial political capital to protect fundamental rights.

All of these arguments for textualism imply that the "text" exists independent of the empirical or normative assumptions that favor its use to determine statutory meaning. But the text can be many things, and the modern textualist selects a conception of the text that implements the normative goals of minimizing judicial discretion. This flaw is not fatal. If the normative arguments against too much judging are weighty, then the judge can sensibly adopt a conception of the text that minimizes judging. But it is important to expose the extent to which modern textualism chooses a particular version of the text in order to force the argument back to the essential questions: what is a statute? and what is the judicial role in determining its meaning? This chapter therefore concludes with a discussion of the various conceptions of the text, explaining which conception implements the normative objectives underlying modern textualism.

I do not claim that all those with textualist leanings will agree to everything that I ascribe to them. Indeed, the differences of opinion among textualists about which normative theory of legislating and judging to adopt and about what constitutes the "text" are important points to note in uncovering the extent to which textualism, like other theories of interpretation, depends on pretextualist conceptions of good government, and in deciding whether textualism can deliver on its promise of providing the desired level of certainty in statutory interpretation.

The Law and Economics Critique: Empirical Models

The law and economics critique of purposivism consists of empirical models that question the optimistic view of legislation on which modern purposivism relied. Much of this critique (both its strengths and weaknesses) is well-known,[3] but it is important to review how persuasive its empiricism really is, because no judge interpreting a statute would be completely indifferent to the presence or absence of legislative purpose. Suspicion that there is *no* purpose for the judge to elaborate would weigh in the balance, discouraging (though not completely eliminating) the inclination to engage in purposive interpretation, however strong the normative arguments for doing so might be.

Indeed, the main objective of the law and economics empirical critique is not to demonstrate that all statutes lack an energizing purpose, but to shift the operative judicial presumption, forcing an *affirmative* showing that a particular statute is animated by a purpose worthy of judicial elaboration. Because the real historical facts behind a statute are so hard for busy lawyers and judges to demonstrate in particular cases, the critique changes the empirical background assumptions in light of which judges interpret legislation. Instead of purposivism, fueled by optimistic assumptions about legislation (which also were not proven in individual cases), a more cynical perspective on the legislative process would prevail.

The law and economics empirical critique launched two major attacks on the optimistic assumption that legislation produced a purpose worthy of judicial elaboration. It argued that legislation was usually the result of private-interest bargaining without an expansive purpose, and that legislation was often the result of agenda manipulation, not an expression of genuine majority will.

Private-interest bargaining

One branch of the law and economics model of legislation posits that legislation is usually the product of private-interest bargaining. Two assumptions lead to that conclusion—the advantage that powerful private interests have in forming politically effective groups, and the impact that these groups have on legislative bargaining.

Group formation. The law and economics view of the legislative process asserts that private interests are likely to dominate the political process. Their advantage in group formation results from the familiar problem of free-riders and the difficulty of overcoming the transaction costs of bringing people together—known as the collective action problem. I present a brief description of the problem here and provide a longer explanation, with a numerical example, in appendix A to this chapter.[4]

When something is to be gained (including avoiding a burden), and whenever it is impossible to exclude others from sharing in the fruits of the joint effort (the free-rider problem), a person would rather let those others be the ones to commit their time and effort to organizing to obtain the benefits. Laws often provide such benefits, routinely so with laws that implement public values. All members of society, for example, enjoy the benefit of implementing a fair distribution of income (a "public value"). Economic goods distributed politically also may have this characteristic because, once the law is adopted, all those eligible will share in the benefits. Farmers enjoy price supports; workers get minimum wages; and many manufacturers benefit from trade protection. Confronted with the opportunity and capability to free-ride on the efforts of others, people hold back and refuse to join in organizing political groups.

Countervailing considerations are present. People may realize that, by not joining together, nothing will happen. But at the same time they do not want to be suckers by being among the few to commit to an organization while others hold back, thus throwing time and effort down the drain. In addition, the time and effort of organizing (transaction costs) dampens enthusiasm for creating political groups. In combination, then, the potential to free-ride and the desire to avoid wasting resources on group formation are powerful incentives not to join together in a politically effective organization.

Conversely, the easier it is to get together with others and the greater the payoff to be earned by committing resources to what is admittedly a risky venture, the more likely it is that people will join to form an effective political group. That is why large economic payoffs to small groups are thought to provide the greatest incentives to group formation. These payoffs are substantial enough to justify the risk of participating in organizational efforts. In addition, the smaller the group, the easier it is to overcome the problems of coordinating and maintaining its organization.

Bargaining. The existence of politically strong groups is not itself sufficient to explain legislation in the law and economics model. Group strength must translate into legislation. In its rawest form, group strength produces legislation benefitting only one group or benefitting only groups who logroll to their mutual advantage; there is no bargaining with an adverse party. This type of legislation was much more common in the nineteenth century and has long been prohibited at the state level, at least in theory, by numerous state constitutional provisions against special legislation (or similar prohibitions).[5] In any event, laws focused on providing targeted benefits to a narrow group rarely raise difficult interpretive issues.

More common (and more relevant to our concern with statutory interpretation) is legislation resulting from bargains among adverse political groups, in which each group seeks as much advantage as possible. This arguably leads to results which lack an expansive purpose hospitable to judicial elaboration, because mutual compromise deprives both sides of the bargain of any expansive growing power. Consequently, as Frank Easterbrook argues, the judge

> treats the statute as a contract. . . . A judge . . . implements the bargain as a faithful agent but without enthusiasm; asked to extend the scope of a back-room deal, he refuses unless the proof of the deal's scope is compelling. Omissions are evidence that no bargain was struck: some issues were left for the future, or perhaps one party was unwilling to pay the price of a resolution in its favor. Sometimes the compromise may be to toss an issue to the courts for resolution, but this too is a term of the bargain, to be demonstrated rather than presumed.[6]

This leads to what Easterbrook calls "the beady-eyed contractual approach" to statutory interpretation.[7]

Easterbrook leaves no doubt that the beady-eyed approach rejects purposivism. He contrasts it with "attribut[ing] to [the statute] certain purposes (evils to be redressed), and then bring[ing] within the statute the class of activities that produce the same or similar objectionable results. The statute's reach goes on expanding so long as there are unredressed objectionable results. The judge interprets omissions and vague terms in the statute as evidence of want of time or foresight and fills in these gaps with more in the same vein." The rejected approach is clearly recognizable as the kind of sympathetic and imaginative reconstruction of legislative intent about which purposivists like Judge Hand wrote. In Easterbrook's imagery, a statute has not only direction (purpose), but also length, limited by the countervailing forces that bargain to produce a law.[8]

Agenda control

Another branch of the law and economics empirical model is concerned with the impact of agenda control on legislation. Purposivists like to think that a majority will exists independently of the political process through which it is expressed. Such a process supports the image of a legislature energized by public purposes, on which sympathetic and imaginative judicial interpretation depends. The work of Kenneth Arrow suggests that the legislative process cannot be so optimistically described[9]—that political results are subject to manipulation by nondemocratic forces and are therefore arbitrary. The ultimate majority position depends on how outside intervention structures the legislative vote.

An example illustrates how this might work. Assume that there are three voters with different rank ordering of preferences. Voters A (industry), B (charities), and C (unions) have the following preferences for positions N, M, and $ on adopting workers' compensation. Preference N is for (N)o workers' compensation program at all; preference M is for a (M)oderate program with modest dollar benefits; and preference $ is for a program with generous $ benefits.

Vote	Rank Order of Preferences
A (industry)	N, M, $
B (charities)	M, $, N
C (unions)	$, N, M

This array of preferences might occur for the following reasons. Voter A represents an industry group which believes that tort reform is not coming, so there is no need to compromise, and that workers' compensation will be expensive for the industry. Hence, voter A opposes any program, but his second choice is one with modest benefits—that is, N, M, $ in that order. Voter B represents charities, which would be covered by the bill, and which have a sense of public values that results in their favoring workers' compensation coverage (even for themselves), despite their immunity from tort liability. However, they prefer more modest payment schedules to the more generous program. Hence, M, $, N in that order. Voter C represents the unions, which believe that tort reform is coming. Voter C prefers a generous workers' compensation program because of the certainty of recovery it provides, but he would otherwise like to gamble on tort reform (providing even better employee recoveries), rejecting a modest workers' compensation program that might dampen political enthusiasm for more thorough reform. Hence, $, N, M in that order.

As a result of this set of preferences, the order and pairing of votes is critical. If the vote is taken first on N vs. M, N wins, eliminating M. In the next vote between N and $, $ wins. If the first vote had been between N and $, however, $ would have won, but a runoff between $ and M produces a victory for M. Likewise, an initial pairing of M vs. $ leads to M winning, but N is the winner in a runoff against M.

The results can therefore be manipulated so that one point of view wins. Party leadership might force an all or nothing showdown between N (no program) and $ (generous program), by prohibiting consideration of the alternative favoring modest benefits (M). Or, if an amendment to consider M were allowed, the first vote might be between N and M (none vs. modest), which would reject the modest proposal. The run-off between N and $ would result in a victory for $. Agenda control is therefore critical.[10]

In this picture of the legislative process, there is a majority winner, because the winner gets a majority of the votes. But nothing like a majority purpose has prevailed, in the sense of a public policy that either exists independently in the society or has been forged by the legislative process. All we have is agenda manipulation.

CRITIQUE OF THE EMPIRICAL MODEL

How persuasive is the law and economics empirical critique of purposivism? Do private interest groups dominate political bargaining in the way that the model predicts? Does manipulative agenda control exist and does it have the negative implications for purposivism that the model suggests? Both empirical claims are subject to important qualifications, much of which is developed in modern positive political theory.[11] I do not mean to suggest that positive political theory can provide us with anything like an accurate characterization of legislation—about whether it is really dominated by private interest bargaining or by a public value consensus. What I do suggest is that the empirical reality is far murkier than the public choice model intimates.[12]

Private-interest bargaining

Group formation. The formation of politically powerful economic interest groups is hard to deny, but there are (just as obviously) other politically effective groups. One reason, consistent with the law and economics model, is that public values can provide an incentive for group formation. All that is needed is an ideological commitment to public values which is the equivalent of an economic reward large enough to overcome incentives to free-ride.[13]

There are, moreover, incentives to group formation which might overcome problems identified by the law and economics model. First, there are economic incentives to group formation for nonpolitical reasons, which might lead to the evolution of politically effective groups. Economic goods (such as low-cost insurance for members) provide some incentives for group formation. Second, social cohesiveness can have a similar impact. A sense of professionalism among lawyers, doctors, and business executives, for example, encourages group formation. And social pressure to cooperate might result from stigmatizing noncooperation. People might also be inherently more cooperative than the law and economics model implies, more anxious to get together with others to achieve goals unless there is evidence of betrayal or noncooperation.

There may also be sources of leadership which help to overcome the problems of developing group cohesion. For example, the government might play a role in forming some groups. Some government programs require that a recipient group be formed to receive technical or financial aid, as in the case of farm programs. There are also private policy entrepreneurs, whose careers are committed to working for and financing group formation. Sometimes a few dynamic individuals might be important, such as a Ralph Nader. Sometimes private foundations or wealthy people give money to create and sustain interest groups. In this way, the need for broad-based group membership support is lessened.

The impact of these incentives for group formation is unclear. They may simply reinforce the tendency of already powerful economic interests to form politically powerful groups—as in the case of social cohesion among business executives who form trade associations. They also may have a greater impact in sustaining than in forming groups, which is likely to be true of economic fringe benefits, such as low-cost insurance. And they may work best at encouraging small groups of people to get together (such as local union or religious groups). In any event, they present a richer picture of the opportunities for political group formation than a simplified law and economics model suggests.

Bargaining. What of the assumption that private interest *bargaining* dominates legislation, justifying the beady-eyed contractual approach to statutory interpretation? Easterbrook admits that not all laws are private interest bargains. For example: "Some laws (the prohibition of murder, for example) are general-interest laws, and others (such as tobacco subsidies) are private-interest laws, but most reflect a mixture of objectives."[14] This invites the observation that the usefulness of the private interest bargaining model depends on having reliable criteria for identifying which legislation fits that description. But such criteria are very hard to apply, as we can see by looking critically at those that Easterbrook suggests.

First, Easterbrook would look at whether the text is "specific or general": "[t]he more detailed the law, the more evidence of interest-group compromise and therefore the less liberty judges possess."[15] But legislative detail is often a very weak indicator of a constraining private interest bargain. Learned Hand once decided that one of the most detailed provisions of the income tax law enacted a *melody* that was more than the notes of the statutory text. What looked like a legislative blueprint for how a taxpayer might reduce taxes was instead subject to a business purpose requirement, read into the statute to assure that the taxpayer had more than a tax avoidance objective for rearranging corporate assets.[16]

Second, Easterbrook looks for "the indicia of rent-seeking legislation: limitations on new entry into the business, subsidies of one group by another, prohibitions of private contracting in response to the new statutory entitlements."[17] But identifying the rent-seeking background of a statute can be difficult; the usual indicators might mislead. This lesson is gathered from Langevoort's study of banking legislation.[18] The Glass-Steagall Act, adopted in 1933, imposed barriers to investment banking by commercial banks. In the older view of banking, investment bankers offered securities for sale to the public, and commercial banks loaned to businesses. The law and economics analysis of this legislation concludes that the statute originated in efforts by investment bankers to protect themselves from commercial banks—to retain economic rents. The facts, Langevoort finds, are otherwise. He acknowledges that commercial banks moved into investment banking in the 1920s, but he notes that no major study cites special interest pleading as a significant factor in the passage of legislation separating commercial and investment banking. He concedes the possibility of a cover-up, but he then provides an alternative explanation for the statute, which was to channel bank loans in the traditional direction of commercial and agricultural lending.[19]

Third, Easterbrook counsels examining the legislative process for evidence of bargaining. "Who lobbied for the legislation? What deals were struck in the cloakrooms? Who demanded what and who gave up what?"[20] But as textualists like Easterbrook so often remind us, legislative history may be an unreliable guide to what legislatures are doing. A legislator, anxious to curry favor with a constituent or campaign contributor, might salt the legislative history with statements demonstrating how effective he had been in advancing their interests, but history suggesting a special interest bargain is no more reliable than general statements of purpose.

The broad point is that it is always hard to know what to make of evidence of legislative intent. We live in a cynical age that is as ready to believe in private-interest legislative bargaining as an earlier generation was to believe in public purposes underlying statutes. But both assumptions are likely to remain unsubstantiated, with the result that empirical studies of legislation are unlikely to be all that helpful in interpreting specific legislation.

First, empirical political science is often about legislation in general, indiscriminately lumping together logrolling statutes with civil rights and environmental laws. But evidence about the origins of logrolling legislation, which is rarely subject to interpretive doubt, is unlikely to shed light on the meaning of broad programmatic legislation, which is likely to raise interpretive questions. Second, good empirical work on specific statutes cannot be undertaken by busy counsel and judges when they try to interpret legislation.[21] Impressive scholarship about some specific legislation has focused on interpretive issues,[22] but such scholarship is time-consuming and so subject to qualification regarding the interaction of private interest and public purpose that it is unlikely to compel or even strongly guide the judge toward a particular result.

The difficulty in determining legislative intent makes it important to emphasize Easterbrook's concession that most legislation "reflect[s] a *mixture* of [private-interest and general-interest] objectives" (emphasis added).[23] The very same legislative result often will be supported by both private interests and public values. This occurs, for example, when the Food Stamps program is advocated for distinctly different reasons by farmers, needy people, and those advocating public values in the form of a fair distribution of income. In such a complex legislative environment, where statutory provisions are as likely to be based on public values as private interests, it becomes extremely difficult for a judge to sort out the best way to characterize what the legislature has done.

Indeed, a judge with a law and economics bias is as likely as anyone else to misread legislative intent. Easterbrook may have fallen into just such an error in finding an interest-group compromise when none was reached in Washington Metropolitan Area Transit Authority v. Johnson (WMATA).[24]

In WMATA, the Court exempted a general contractor from tort liability to a *subcontractor's* employee because the employee was covered by workers' compensation purchased by the general contractor. Workers' compensation statutes typically provide that, in exchange for purchasing the statutory remedy for workers, the employer is exempt from common law tort recoveries. Easterbrook asserts that this case demonstrates the interest-group approach to statutory interpretation: "[L]ook for and enforce the bargain, but do not elaborate."[25] But did the statute really apply to insulate the general contractor from liability to a subcontractor's employee? The general contractor purchased workers' compensation benefits, not because the subcontractors refused to buy coverage, but because the general contractor could do so more cheaply.

The dissent in WMATA argued that the statute did not give a general contractor immunity unless it bought workers' compensation *after* the subcontractor refused to do so. The dissenting opinion further claimed that the majority "takes a 1927 statute and reads into it the 'modern view' of workers' compensation, whereby both the contractor and the subcontractor receive immunity from tort suits provided somebody secures compensation for injured employees of the subcontractor. . . . The Court has simply fixed upon what it believes to be good policy and then patched together a rationale as best it could."[26] According to the dissent, the Court had included within the statute's coverage those who were *not* part of the original bargain (the general contractor), sympathetically and imaginatively extending a bargain to those who were not contracting parties. The dissent turned out to be right, at least in predicting what the then-current Congress thought; in 1984, Congress wrote the dissent's interpretation into the law.[27]

Agenda control

The negative image of legislation as subject to manipulation through agenda control also has several weaknesses.[28] First, voting indeterminacy is often overcome by preference intensity. Even though each legislator has one vote, intensity can still be accounted for through bargaining. Referring back to the prior example, assume that the union is so intent on $ (generous program) winning, that it strikes a deal with the charities, that it will oppose a bill opening a charity's finances to attorney general inspection in exchange for the charities placing $ at the top of their preference list. Now, with charities wanting $, M, N, in that order, $ will win regardless of which votes are taken first.

Second, legislators may not enter political deliberation with completely fixed and pre-formed points of view. Discussion (often outside public hearing) may shape and reshape the legislator's position.[29] While this is not a complete bar to indeterminacy and manipulation of political results, it makes it more difficult to identify each legislator's preferences and engage in agenda control.

Third, and most importantly, the assumption that agenda control drains legislation of an animating purpose is questionable. Agenda manipulation has that effect if legislative purpose can only reside in the raw aggregation of a majority vote. But that is not necessarily the source of majority purpose which underlies a statute. Democracy has many forms—town meeting, majority representation, and reliance on leadership within the legislature—and none is more privileged than the other as a working theory of democracy. No one would deny the label democratic to the English Parliament even though its legislation is the product of dominant party control. The role of leadership is intrinsic to our political system and choices made by leaders cannot casually be described pejoratively as the manipulation of political results.

Indeed, the choices made by legislative leaders may be more assertive of public values than of private interests, and therefore those choices may be welcomed by individual legislators as a shield behind which they can hide in order to justify a more public-oriented result than pressures on them by lobbyists might allow. Legislative leaders might be more like independent "political entrepreneurs" with ambitions for office that lead them to pay more attention to the public interest. Some legislators want to achieve committee or party leadership within the body to which they belong; or they want to advance to a position of greater prominence (perhaps the Senate or the presidency); or they simply want to have an impact on public policy in *some* field of law for reasons of personal satisfaction. To achieve these goals, legislators stake out broader public positions rather than yield to the influence of private-interest groups who finance their reelection. Some particular legislators come to mind. Senator Warren Magnuson staked out a position as a specialist in consumer concerns and Senator Edmund Muskie of Maine specialized in environmental legislation.[30] Both used committee chairmanships to their ends.

Some countervailing considerations, however, diminish the independence of the political entrepreneur; instead, they tie the legislator to the private-interest influences associated with campaign financing. First, legislative leadership still depends on being reelected, and reelection depends on campaign financing. Second, leadership positions on important legislative committees provide opportunities to help not only constituents who can reelect the legislator, but also those throughout the country who finance campaigns. Campaign money is therefore attracted to legislators who control important committees with national impact. Moreover, some legislative leaders consolidate their positions by forming political action committees (PACs) to receive campaign contributions, and those PACs then dole out funds to other members of Congress for their campaigns. Obviously, these members develop loyalty to the leader, linking PAC funding to leadership positions.

In sum, the law and economics critique is meant to drain the judge's confidence that legislation has a purpose which judges can elaborate. If statutory interpretation is normatively tied to the democratic ideal of implementing legislative will, once legislative will is dominated by private-interest compromise or agenda manipulation, judges have little to do in determining statutory meaning except to defer to the text. But the reality is likely to be much more murky and difficult to ascertain in particular cases than the law and economics model allows. The model is just that: a presumption that encourages a beady-eyed approach in contrast to the wide-eyed purposivism that prevailed for much of the twentieth century. Positive political theory helps bring a greater sense of reality to understanding the legislative process, but it is unlikely to guide interpretation in particular cases. Its primary impact is to undermine the single-mindedness of public-choice models by calling attention to the complex interaction of private interest and public purposes in shaping legislation and forcing us to rest interpretive theory on normative theories of judging.

Indeed, normative assumptions about judging are far more important in making the case for textualism than is the law and economics empirical critique of the legislative process. First, the empirical critique leads to textualism only on the basis of a normative assumption about the role of judges. Second, the excessive attention paid to law and economics models in recent years has sometimes obscured the more important arguments for textualism, which rest on normative conceptions of legislating and judging that are independent of empirical assumptions about how legislation is made.

Normative Foundations of Textualism

Two normative conceptions of the relationship between legislating and judging have been rivals throughout our history. In one view, legislating and judging exist in airtight compartments. Only legislatures make law, not judges. Once the court identifies what the legislature has done (evidenced by either the statutory text or legislative intent), the court has no further role to play.

In the other view, the law is something that various lawmaking institutions strive to achieve. Both statutes and the common law play a role in that effort, and courts are required to help work out the interaction of statutes to the broader fabric of the law. This inherited English tradition is expressed most clearly in the Hale and Blackstone view that statutes (as well as judicial opinions) are only evidence of the law.

Each normative view of legislating and judging can be developed—though not without controversy, to support a textualist approach to statutory interpretation.

AIRTIGHT COMPARTMENT VERSION OF SEPARATION OF POWERS

The airtight compartment conception of legislating and judging assumes that statutory meaning is determined by either legislative intent or statutory text, both of which purport to trace meaning exclusively to the legislature. This assumption can lead to textualism in either of two ways. First, legislative intent is the preferred criterion of statutory meaning, but no intent exists about the case the court is deciding and no purpose exists for the judge to elaborate; consequently, the interpreter defaults to the text. Second, constitutionally, the statute is its text—nothing more.

Default to the text

The law and economics empirical critique of legislation does not start with a commitment to textualism, although it ends up there. It begins instead with the assumption that statutory law must come from the legislature (which means either legislative intent or statutory text) and that, if possible, legislative intent determines statutory meaning. But intent is unavailing as a standard for applying statutes to particular cases. There is rarely a specific intent about the issues arising in litigated cases, and, when the judge turns to purpose, all he finds is private-interest bargaining and agenda control, which provides little in the way of statutory purpose to elaborate. In this legislative environment, the text becomes the default interpretive criterion to which the judge retreats once it is clear that legislative intent is unavailable.

But this result depends on the premise that the judge has no normative role to play in fitting statutes into the broader fabric of the law, an assumption that breaks faith with our historical traditions. Both the English and American histories of statutory interpretation have been strongly influenced by the relative competence of legislation and judging—whether it be the English common law judge's exercise of artificial reason and sagelike wisdom; the American judge's ability to rely on "common sense" or "practical good sense" in the late eighteenth and early nineteenth centuries; Sedgwick's mid-nineteenth-century emphasis on legislative competence and judicial incompetence to explain the decline of equitable interpretation; the resurgence of judicial claims to superior lawmaking in the second half of the nineteenth century, based on a science of the common law; or twentieth-century purposivism's image of legislative competence and the ability of judges to elaborate legislative purpose. In light of this tradition, the rather dismal law and economics picture of the legislative process would be expected to lead to greater rather than lesser judicial lawmaking discretion in statutory interpretation to make up for legislative incompetence rather than to default to the text. Indeed, as chapter 6 will explain, some commentators make just such an argument for a more aggressive judicial role. In the meantime, we should observe that the airtight compartment view of legislating and judging, which would deny judges a role in compensating for legislative shortcomings, requires a normative justification that is untrue to our legal traditions.

Legislation is the text

Another variation on the airtight compartment view of legislating and judging also leads to textualism, but it does not rely on the law and economics empirical critique of legislation. In this view, the statute *is* the text, not by default, but because that is what a statute is under the Constitution. Constitutionally, the text is what the legislature passes and the chief executive signs. As a consequence, that is all the judge has to work with to determine statutory meaning.

This, too, is a departure from historical tradition. Commitments to the text have always been accompanied by exceptions based on the judge's perception of important values—namely, the Golden Rule's concern with injustice and absurdity; Alexander Hamilton's concern with unjust and partial laws; John Marshall's concern for protecting fundamental values; Francis Lieber's willingness to allow "construction" to preserve justice; the late nineteenth-century commentators' view that common law concerned with "common right" should not be easily overridden by statutes; and the sympathy and imagination with which twentieth-century purposivists elaborated statutory meaning. One need not resort to spurious interpretation—the invocation of an extreme version of the canon that statutes in derogation of the common law should be narrowly construed—to make the point that the text has never been *the* sole criterion. Even modern textualists are insistent that substantive canons continue to play an important role in statutory interpretation, imposing clear statement rules which insist that certain values not be overridden unless the statute explicitly so provides. As Justice Antonin Scalia argues, the judge should rely on ordinary usage *and* the meaning "most compatible with the surrounding body of law into which the provision must be integrated— a compatibility which, by a benign fiction, we assume Congress always has in mind." [31]

If it seems odd that modern textualism is so out of touch with earlier traditions in its insistence on the airtight compartment version of legislating and judging, the strangeness disappears when we observe that modern textualism is a new way to approach statutory interpretation. Much of the battle over statutory interpretation during the last few centuries has been fought to assert legislative dominance—to get judges to be respectful of legislatures—and, to that end, to discourage judicial lawmaking discretion. Modern textualism is different. It is more concerned with minimizing judging than deferring to the legislature.

This shift explains why a modern textualist like Easterbrook is so determined to attack judicial competence at the same time that he argues against a legislative intent worthy of judicial elaboration. He argues that judicial ability to carry on a dialogue with the departed legislature to re-create an intent about contemporary facts—the Plowden-Hand approach to statutory interpretation—is extraordinarily hard to do: "The number of judges living at any time who can, with plausible claim to accuracy, 'think [themselves] . . . into the minds of the enacting legislators and imagine how they would have wanted the statute applied to the case at bar,' may be counted on one hand"; [32] indeed, it is so hard that "even the best intentioned [judge] will find that the imagined dialogues of departed legislators have much in common with their own conceptions of the good."

And, of course, Easterbrook is right. The attempt by moderate purposivists to imaginatively reconstruct how the enacting legislature would decide the case, illustrated by Judge Hand and the Hart & Sacks Legal Process approach, cannot successfully deny Easterbrook's allegation that the judge will slip imperceptibly into what I call full-bodied purposivism in chapter 4. There is too much of the judge's imagination in imaginative reconstruction to avoid that result. Moreover, the idea of imaginative reconstruction is inherently unstable. The question "How would the enacting legislature have decided the case?" elides into the question "How would the legislature have decided the case, knowing what the judge knows today?" In answering this latter question, the judge inevitably brings his own conception of the good to statutory interpretation. But, as the following section emphasizes, textualism itself also rests on the judge's normative conception of the good and cannot insulate itself from debate over what balance of institutional lawmaking responsibility is most conducive to that end.

FITTING STATUTES INTO THE LAW

The rival to the airtight compartment view of legislating and judging allows judges to fit statutes into the broader fabric of the law. This affirmative judicial role can still lead to textualism based on either of two theories: a commitment to the rule of law, or a desire to preserve judicial capital so that judges can protect fundamental rights. The adoption of either theory requires an initial exercise of judicial judgment to adopt textualism as the best way to fit statutes into the law, but thereafter (it is hoped) judging ceases. The judge ties himself to the textualist mast and is deaf to further appeals to exercise lawmaking discretion.

Rule of law

The rule of law is associated with certainty (a law of rules), which in turn requires minimizing judicial lawmaking discretion.[33] This will lead, it is hoped, to greater autonomy of individual planning and freedom from arbitrary government action. Textualism follows from this premise, assuming that textual clarity is sufficiently possible to satisfy rule of law criteria (an inference that I criticize later in this chapter). A commitment to rule of law values also explains why modern textualists are willing to rely on traditional substantive canons of interpretation. These canons, it is hoped, will produce a maximum of judicial agreement, minimizing judicial discretion (a view I also criticize in chapter 6).

Even assuming that certainty were attainable, however, the insistence on rule of law values as *the* way to fit statutes into the law is hard to sustain. Rule of law values, of course, have always been important in statutory interpretation. As we saw in chapter 1, Blackstone's defense of law over equity was probably based on the desire for certainty in the law, not on a theoretical commitment to legislative sovereignty. But it is difficult to argue that rule of law principles have unqualified dominance in our legal system. The prominence of state legislation in the early nineteenth century[34] and the eventual rise of federal legislation in the twentieth century undermine the argument that an affirmative commitment to stability is an unrivaled principle in our law. Legislation, even though technically prospective, is too likely to alter the expectations on which previous activities are based for legal stability to enjoy such pride of place. Moreover, the inherited English tradition of equitable interpretation and the early nineteenth-century judicial practice of instrumental evolution of the common law also support the view that stability is not the sole criterion by which to judge lawmaking.

An inordinate emphasis on rule of law values probably traces to the *post*-Civil War tradition of "liberal" principles,[35] which purported to favor minimal government and a broad scope for private planning and entrepreneurship. But our historical tradition has always been one in which the "rule of law" must vie with other values in the dispute over how judges fit statutes into the fabric of the law.

Preserving judicial capital

Textualism might also follow from a conception of judging in which judges have a critical role to play as guardians of the individual's fundamental rights. This concept is a variation of the Golden Rule and Chief Justice Marshall's commitment to interpreting statutes to preserve fundamental values, which even Justice Holmes might have adopted. In Holmes's famous dissent in the Lochner case, he not only insisted on judicial deference to the legislature, but he also affirmed an *aggressive* judicial role when "it c[ould] be said that a rational and fair man necessarily would admit that the statute proposed would infringe fundamental principles as they have been understood by the traditions of our people and our law."[36]

The modern textualist's concern for individual rights derives from a deep mistrust of the political system—legislatures and judges alike. One task that judges are competent to perform, however, is that of protecting the individual from the government. Thus, the textualist judge Scalia joined the Supreme Court's majority in deciding that a law against burning the American flag was an unconstitutional violation of free speech,[37] despite the substantively non-conservative values associated with flag burning. It turns out that textualists, usually so anxious to minimize judging, place an inordinate faith in judges to perform the vital task of protecting fundamental rights,[38] despite Thayer's warning that courts cannot "save a people from ruin."[39]

The link between this judicial role and textualism is that the popular perception of judges exercising lawmaking discretion threatens to politicize judging and deprive judges of the public support that they need to make a principled stand for individual rights. Writing primarily about constitutional interpretation, but with obvious implications for statutory interpretation as well, Justice Scalia argues: "If the courts are free to write the Constitution anew, they will, by God, write it the way the majority wants; the appointment and confirmation process will see to that. This, of course, is the end of the Bill of Rights, whose meaning will be committed to the very body it was meant to protect against: the majority."[40] Textualism, by reducing judicial discretion, is supposed to preserve the judges' political capital so that they can successfully protect fundamental rights.[41] The textualist might even call on Judge Learned Hand to support this view. Hand certainly feared that the judicial elaboration of vacuous constitutional phrases like due process would arouse the public to destroy the judicial independence necessary to protect the more specific rights provided by the Constitution (such as free speech).[42]

This view of the imperatives of judging probably draws sustenance from the twentieth-century specter of totalitarianism and the need for courts to protect against political disaster. The fear is that when judges try to encourage the good, they may lose their ability to prevent the worst. This loss may seem especially dangerous in our increasingly fractured society, where civic decency is on the wane.

The difficulty with relying on textualism to preserve the judge's political capital is that the empirical evidence about what leads the public to place confidence in judging does not support such a view.[43] Social scientists have had difficulty identifying what makes the public accept judicial decisions. The strongest argument which the data can sustain is that "diffuse support" among the public is capable of surviving adverse reaction to specific judicial decisions. The evidence suggests, however, that this support does not result from the process by which courts determine the meaning of a statute, but from agreement or disagreement with specific judicial decisions and from ideology and party affiliation, suggesting that the public views courts as political institutions. The apolitical image of courts above the fray is probably a legal professional's image of judging—which survives the Legal Realist's critique—rather than an accurate description of the public's view. Certainly, the political process for choosing judges in the United States does not suggest that judges are apolitical, and it is unlikely that this fact escapes public notice.

Not only are many state judges elected or required to stand for public approval, but the federal confirmation process often makes it clear that political values and judging are linked.[44]

The difference between public and professional views of judging is suggested by the reaction to several modern cases, which were viewed by many in the legal profession as overstepping the boundaries of judicial competence. Contrary to Ernst Freund's warning that judges could not adopt numerical formulas and behavioral codes,[45] courts sometimes did just that. They adopted numerically precise rules to require one-person, one-vote in reapportioning legislatures[46] and to make abortion rights depend on the trimester in which the abortion might be performed.[47] And Miranda warnings set forth a detailed code of police behavior.[48] Despite the legal profession's criticism of the "legislative" style of these opinions, I suspect that the public has been more focused on their substantive impact, with varying reactions among different groups. Certainly, no evidence suggest that these decisions undermined public acceptance of unpopular constitutional decisions protecting individual rights. And evidence is even scanter that the judicial practice of textualism, which purports to keep judges out of "politics," would be viewed by the public as more innocent of discretionary "political" choices than any other interpretive approach. This state of things suggests that Holmes was wrong in insisting that courts are concerned only with the molecular and not the molar.[49] Courts might well make "molar" judgments to goad the more political branches of government into action, always expecting that permanent change depends ultimately on popular implementation and approval.

Although I cannot prove it, I suspect that the public's "diffuse" faith in judges—to the extent that it rests on considerations of process—depends on its confidence that judges are not acting in a narrowly partisan way and are simply trying to do their best to make the system work. No more exalted an image of judges is needed to make their judgments stick, if, in the long run, they can be made to stick at all.

Text

An implicit premise underlying textualism is that a coherent conception of the "text" exists independent of the normative theory of judging and good government, both of which justify relying on the text in the first place. All theories leading to textualism—defaulting to the text; the statute is the text, adhering to rule of law principles, preserving the judge's political capital—imply that the text is a stable and reliable source of information about statutory meaning on which the judge can rely. This inference simply is wrong. The "text" can derive meaning from a variety of possible sources, with the interpreter operating well within the boundaries of what it means to understand a "text," and nothing in textualism can predetermine which of these sources should be dispositive. The need for judicial choice among these possibilities deprives the "text" of the stability that supports the normative theories justifying textualism.

Not that modern textualism is mute concerning which sources of textual meaning *should* be relied on by the judge. The normative foundations of textualism all suggest adopting a single conception of the text that minimizes judicial discretion. But for two reasons, the various ways in which a text can be understood undermine the textualist's goal. First, the possible sources of textual meaning are sufficiently varied that it is hard to agree on which source(s) should be used to minimize judicial discretion and thereby either preserve an airtight compartment approach to legislating and judging or protect rule of law values and the judge's political capital. These uncertainties in determining the meaning of a text go far to provide a response to Justice Scalia's argument that the charge of formalism against the modern textualist is "mindless."[50] The charge of formalism is a shorthand for saying that the formalist cannot fulfill the promise of sufficient certainty to implement rule of law values. As long as the conception of a text is as indeterminate as the following pages explain, it is the formalist claim that deference to the text implements rule of law values that is cognitively challenged.

Second, once the text loses its independent status as a reliable source of meaning and is replaced by a *particular* textual conception, it becomes even more obvious that the modern textualist is doing what he would like to conceal, namely, bringing a set of normative values to the task of deciding what a statute means rather than passively deferring to textual meaning. That, in turn, reminds us that the values underlying formalism must compete with other values, including those embodied in the statute's purpose and the substantive background considerations contained in the legal landscape.

The many sources of textual meaning are suggested by these questions, each of which is addressed in the rest of this chapter: (1) who is the author and audience for a statutory text? (2) how do statutory authors and audiences understand statutory language? and (3) what is the statutory text?[51]

Lay vs. technical meanings

How does an interpreter decide whether a statute's text uses a lay meaning or a technical one? The usual "rule" is that lay meaning prevails unless there is evidence of technical meaning;[52] but what counts as evidence of a technical meaning?[53]

Is the statutory author the entire legislature (with a heavy representation of lay people) or a committee (with a more specialized technical background)? Modern textualists do not seem anxious to answer this question. One textualist's view is that the entire Congress is the author,[54] but another well-known textualist defends the use of legislative history in committee reports to determine the text's meaning.[55]

Even assuming that we know the statutory author's identity, who is the audience? Nothing inherent in the conception of a text (certainly not a statutory text) privileges the author's understanding rather than that of the audience. And someone committed to rule of law values certainly would be concerned with the *audience's* understanding. Some support exists among textualists for relying on the audience that is *intended* by the statutory author[56] —a kind of intentionalist textualism—but it is unclear why the author should be allowed to choose the audience. One even might urge that the actual audience (not necessarily the one chosen by the author) has a better claim on the text in certain areas such as tax or criminal law.

No problem exists, of course, in choosing between the author and audience, if the audience shares the same understanding as the author. Indeed, genuine textualism relies on the conjunction of understandings between author and audience.[57] But what if the meaning intended by a technically savvy author conflicts with the meaning understood by an audience lacking that degree of sophistication.[58] Suppose, for example, that the following statutory language created an exemption from the estate tax: "[Certain property] . . . shall be exempt from all taxation now or hereafter imposed." Does this language apply to an estate tax? How could it *not* apply? When confronted with this issue, however, the Supreme Court held that the exemption was inapplicable, stating: "Well before [this act] was passed, an exemption of property from all taxation had an understood meaning: the property was exempt from *direct* taxation, but certain privileges of ownership, such as the right to transfer the property, could be taxed" (emphasis in original).[59] The property was therefore subject to estate tax, which was a tax on a *transfer* of property, not a "direct" tax on property. An audience of general practitioners (not tax specialists) in a small county seat might be surprised by this technical reading of the statute. And it is hard to see how a judge could avoid making choices about whether the author or the audience had the better claim on the statutory text.

Historical vs. contemporary audience

Does the text speak to a future audience or only to the historical audience when the statute is drafted? The modern textualist rejects the claims on a text of a future audience.[60] But why? Statutes that lack a sunset clause do not expire and are presumably written for the future as well as for the present. Nothing in the concept of a text precludes the future audience from having a claim on the text's meaning.[61]

An example is a case applying the word "family" in a law adopted in 1946, right after World War II.[62] The issue was whether a gay couple formed a "family." Pursuant to statute, a regulation prohibited eviction from a rent-controlled apartment of "either the surviving spouse of the deceased tenant or some other member of the deceased tenant's family who has been living with the tenant." Although the earlier lawmakers could not have imagined a gay couple as a "family," neither could the earlier legislature have imagined the current world in which their 1946 law would operate. The legislature had simply failed to address a contemporary situation that it could not have contemplated.

A 1989 court interpreted the law in light of a contemporary audience's perspective on the text. It held that "family" should not be "rigidly restricted to those people who have formalized their relationship by obtaining, for instance, a marriage certificate or an adoption order," thereby adapting the statute to the understanding of a future audience and refusing to limit "[t]he intended protection [of the statute] against sudden eviction [based] on fictitious legal distinctions or genetic history, but instead [relying on a] foundation in the reality of family life." The court stated that "[i]n the context of eviction, a more realistic, and certainly equally valid, view of a family includes two adult lifetime partners whose relationship is long term and characterized by an emotional and financial commitment and interdependence. This view comports both with our society's traditional concept of 'family' and with the expectations of individuals who live in such nuclear units."

As this decision suggests, the textualist's view that the understanding of the *historical* author and audience is determinative—that gaps in the historical understanding should go unfilled—rests securely but controversially on the desire to prevent the kind of judicial discretion that accompanies updating a law to account for modern understandings outside the boundaries of histori-cal experience. Such adaptation of old law to the future necessarily involves speculation about what judicial answer best relates the statute to "the sur-rounding body of law into which the provision must be integrated."[63]

HOW DO AUTHORS AND AUDIENCES UNDERSTAND STATUTORY TEXTS?

Let us now assume that no controversy exists about which author or audience has the dominant claim on the statutory text. That is not the end of con-troversy about how to determine the meaning of the statutory language. The modern textualist has a distinct theory of how statutory language acquires meaning, which is to insist on "ordinary meaning" over other possible mean-ings. "[O]ur job is not to scavenge the world of English usage to discover whether there is any possible meaning of [a statutory term] which suits our preconception . . . ; our job is to determine . . . the ordinary meaning . . .";[64] "[t]he Court does not appear to grasp the distinction between how a word *can be* used and how it *ordinarily is* used" (emphasis in original).[65]

The conception of statutory language that underlies the ordinary meaning approach is that a storehouse of textual meaning is out there in the real world which is borrowed by statutes for use in legislation; further, that this ap-proach rejects purposivism as a tool for determining textual meaning. "[The statute] is not some all-purpose weapon for well-intentioned judges to wield as they please. . . . It is a statute."[66] But just as the textualist is correct in pointing out how substantive values intrude into the elaboration of legislative purpose, so purpose intrudes into the way that authors and audiences deter-mine the meaning of a statutory text.

For example, consider the example of the phrase "grocery store" in three different statutes. Is there an ordinary meaning that the court can borrow, or must the court consider statutory purpose and the values associated with that purpose in defining the term? One statute exempts a grocery store from the minimum wage for employees; another prohibits sale of liquor by a gro-cery store; and a third imposes health inspection requirements on a grocery store.[67] Now assume three stores that sell groceries in the following percent-ages: 100 percent (the typical grocery store), 51 percent (a discount store that also sells appliances, etc.), and 5 percent (a pharmacy that also sells candy, snacks, and the like). Is there an ordinary usage for all three statutes, inde-pendent of the legislative purpose, that can determine which of these three stores that sell groceries is a "grocery store"?

Surely, statutory purpose could appropriately influence how much grocery selling must occur to meet the statutory term "grocery store," leading to a different definition for each statute. The minimum wage exemption might apply only to a store selling close to 100 percent groceries (the traditional small business); sale of liquor might be prohibited only if more than half the sales were groceries; and health inspection might be required when only a small (say, 5 percent) of sales were groceries. Interpreting the liquor-sale prohibition statute might be complicated by an assumption that the statute imposes barriers to entry lobbied for by liquor stores, leading to a narrow construction of the statute's coverage—the beady-eyed contractual approach. But that assumption might be historically inaccurate if the law had been passed in the 1920s, substituting a modern law and economics perspective for a prohibition-inspired anti-liquor consumption animus.

Another more controversial example is the decision in Chisom v. Roemer,[68] where the Court held that statutory protection from race discrimination in the election of "representatives" (the word used by the statute) applied to elected judges. Can you resolve this issue without noting the origins of the law as an effort to deal with the voting rights of minorities? Surely, authors and audiences would consider how best to make sense of *this* text and, to that end, would consider what the text was trying to do and what meaning the text could bear. After all, this was a voting rights law assuring minority participation in the electoral process, a policy that has energized legislatures on numerous occasions.

The important question suggested by this discussion is whether purposivism is really a violation of the way in which people understand language. Asking how "ordinary people" understand language may be the wrong question. Different language genres use words differently, and legislative language is just another genre. The proper question to ask, if we are to insist on a link to ordinary language usage, is *not* what do words ordinarily mean, but how would ordinary people want language to be interpreted in specialized settings?[69] Despite objections to legalese, people might accept the fact that words acquire specialized meanings in statutory contexts, even if those people do not always understand the usage. They therefore would expect the statute itself to shape the meaning of the text it uses rather than simply to borrow ordinary usage.

The modern textualist's real objection to rejecting the storehouse of meaning approach to statutory interpretation is the discretion that it affords to judges. But many things still limit the judge, pointing toward moderate rather than full-bodied purposivism.[70] Even a purposivist like Justice John Paul Stevens will stick closely to the text and adopt a beady-eyed approach when the evidence of legislative compromise is strong.[71] And *some* areas of law (perhaps tax law) may be more text-bound on rule of law grounds, even for a purposivist like Stevens.[72] But that is a context-specific approach to interpreting statutory language that does not rely on a storehouse of meaning to determine how authors and audiences understand statutory texts.

WHAT IS THE TEXT?

The final issue that textualists must address, if the text is to fulfill its promise of providing an independent standard for statutory meaning, is identification of the text. But the "text" is a notoriously slippery concept. In the examples discussed (defining "representatives," "grocery store," "family," and "exemption from taxation"), disputes about meaning all headed up in one or two words whose meaning was in question, but no doubts arose about identifying the text. In the following pages we confront the problem of deciding how narrowly or broadly to define the text.

By asking this question, we do not stop inquiring about who the author and audience are and how authors and audience understand statutory texts. Indeed, trying to define the "text" highlights the difficulty in answering this question. There is a tendency in modern textualism to either narrow or broaden the text in ways that border on literalism (that is, spurious textualism), relying on textual evidence without actually relying on how authors and audiences understand statutory language.

Narrowing the text

An old canon of linguistic interpretation requires the interpreter to understand the meaning of a word along with its neighboring language. The Latin for this approach is *noscitur a sociis* (a word is known by its neighbors), and it is one component of nineteenth-century "whole text" textualism.[73]

It is hard to reject this approach to comprehending how authors and audiences understand language. Surely, people understand texts by considering their entire linguistic context, whatever else they might exclude. But at least one judge with textualist leanings rejected the whole text approach (Justice Clarence Thomas's dissent in the Gustafson case), arguing that the neighboring words should be considered "*only* in cases of ambiguity" (emphasis added).[74] In other words, the whole text should be considered, not as part of the initial effort to understand language, but only *after* textual uncertainty has been identified. This view is especially puzzling, given the frequency with which all judges—textualists and nontextualists alike—usually affirm the need to examine the whole text. The following comment is typical: "[A] text consists of words living 'a communal existence,' . . . the meaning of each word informing the others. . . . Statutory construction 'is a holistic endeavor,' and, at a minimum, must account for a statute's full text, language as well as punctuation, structure, and subject matter."[75]

The answer to the puzzle lies, as usual, in concerns over judicial discretion. The case from which the "communal existence" quotation was taken involved what was clearly a scrivener's error (misplaced quotation marks), which distorted the meaning suggested by other internal textual evidence. Examining the whole text helped to avoid a careless drafting mistake, but it did not draw the judge into the kind of policy judgment that purposivism often requires and that modern textualists try so hard to prevent. By contrast, in the Gustafson case (in which Thomas's dissent warned against relying on the whole text in the absence of ambiguity), the majority's resort to the whole text was driven by a specific policy concern. The statute at issue was a securities law prohibiting material misstatements and the majority's whole text approach prevented applying the statutory prohibition *too* broadly to include a private sale as well as public offerings.[76]

Another possible reason why a modern textualist might want to narrow the range of textual evidence of statutory meaning is that examining the whole text raises at least the possibility that a statute *creates* its own meaning, and that is something the modern textualist is reluctant to admit. An example is Third National Bank v. IMPAC Limited, Inc.,[77] where the statute prohibited an "attachment, injunction, or execution." The Court held that "injunction" only applied to legal action taken against a debtor. Although the word "injunction" in ordinary usage applies to actions against both creditors and debtors, it was sandwiched between "attachment" and "execution" in this particular statute, both of which apply only to actions against debtors. The whole text (the word "injunction" and its neighbors) *created* a different and unusual meaning for the word "injunction."

Broadening the text

At the other extreme, some modern textualists broaden the statutory text to include different statutes without regard to the fact that the statutes have multiple authors and audiences whose understanding of the language might not link the texts together. For example, in Lukhard v. Reed,[78] a welfare statute said nothing about whether personal injury awards counted in a claimant's income, a figure needed to determine eligibility. This text contrasted with the income tax statute, which explicitly excluded such awards from income.

The contrast between the two statutory texts suggested to Justice Scalia that the personal injury award *was* income in the welfare statute.

But the notion that two statutes, written by different authors and read by different audiences, should be read as though they were a single text struck Judge Richard Posner as fanciful: "[T]he United States Code is not the work of a single omniscient intellect."[79] And, as noted in chapter 4, Justice Frankfurter refused to read multiple statutes as a single text, relying instead on a more realistic view of the drafting process[80] to conclude that variations in phrasing in different statutes written at different times dealing with different subjects did not mean that the statutes had different meanings.[81]

Frankfurter's suspicion of lumping together multiple statutes is even clearer in his opinion in Keifer & Keifer v. Reconstruction Finance Corp,[82] an opinion that suggests why the modern textualist might be so anxious to reject Frankfurter's approach and instead lump multiple statutes into a single text. The issue was whether a federal statute implicitly waived sovereign immunity for a government corporation. Statutes governing at least forty government corporations created during the 1920s and 1930s had explicitly waived immunity, but that fact did not prevent Frankfurter from concluding that a statute which did *not* explicitly so provide *also* waived government immunity from suit. He argued that "[i]t is not a textual problem; for Congress has not expressed its will in words." The judge's role is to be concerned with the coherence of legislative policy: "The Congressional will must be *divined,* and by a process of interpretation which, in effect, is the ascertainment of policy immanent not merely in the single statute . . . , but in a series of statutes. . . ." Frankfurter goes on to infer a waiver of sovereign immunity, refusing to "impute to Congress a desire for incoherence in a body of affiliated enactments and for drastic legal differentiation where policy justifies none."

Someone determined to prevent judicial judgment about the policy coherence or incoherence of a body of multiple statutes would obviously be attracted to the simplifying assumption that such statutes are a single text.[83] And that is why the modern textualist, intent on preventing judicial discretion, is drawn toward broadening the text beyond what the actual authors intended or what actual audiences might understand in reading the statutory language.[84]

In sum, modern textualists often make exaggerated claims for the clarity with which the meaning of the "text" can be ascertained. The problem is not that words are often unclear (e.g., vague or ambiguous), but that the meaning of a "text" itself can be determined by many criteria, for example: the meaning intended by the author vs. the meaning understood by the real-world audience; or by the historical vs. future audience; or the meaning borrowed from ordinary usage vs. the meaning shaped by the purpose of the host statute; or one or two words vs. the entire text; or multiple statutes forcibly integrated into a single text vs. reading each statute independently. Many modern textualists tend to adopt the first over the second of each of these choices in the hope that the first approach will provide greater certainty and reduce judicial discretion. But the choice is unlikely to afford the kind of certainty to which the textualist aspires, given the fact that the "text" itself offers up such a broad array of interpretive criteria. In any event, it should be clear that the textualist is making choices about which criteria of textual meaning should prevail because of a normative view that too much judging is bad government.

Appendix A
Free Riders and Collective Goods

Effective political organization requires overcoming the collective action problem. The problem arises when the distribution of a "collective good" is at issue. A "collective good" is one characterized by nonexclusion of people from benefits, once the benefits have been provided. (The term "benefit" includes the avoidance of burdens.)

The collective enjoyment of legislation suggests this question. Why would anyone contribute money or time to a political interest group when they can sit back and let others organize the group and still enjoy its benefits (the "free-rider" problem)? Assume that joint efforts by a significant number of people would produce a collective good, providing enjoyment worth $10 per person, at a cost of $4 per person. This produces a clear $60 gain for a group of ten people. Would you help form a group to obtain these benefits? Consider this explanation for why you might not join. If I do not pay my dues (or provide equivalent value in labor), the benefit will be provided anyway by the efforts of the other nine people cooperating to form a politically effective group, so I will enjoy $10 in any event. Why spend $4 for nothing? If this strategy of free riding occurs to all potential joiners, everyone will hold back and no political group will form. Instead of a $6 gain for everyone ($10 per person minus a $4 cost), everyone will get $0.

One reason why this result might not occur is that it will be obvious to all potential free riders that nothing will happen if they do not join together. In politics, sufficient political clout is often an all-or-nothing proposition. Unless enough people join together, nothing gets done. This fact will appear obvious to all potential free riders, and therefore they might have an incentive to band together.

But the obvious inability to free-ride successfully does not necessarily produce a decision to join. If joining means pouring $4 down the drain because others may not join, it might seem better to leave the status quo where it is (no one joins to form a political group), rather than be a sucker and lose $4.

This decision-making process can be represented schematically (see table). Each cell presents a combination of payoffs to you and to each other person in the potential political group, depending on whether you join or do not join, and whether the rest of the potential group joins or does not join to produce the benefit. Your payoff is always the first of the two figures.

You	Rest of the Group	
Join	Join	Do not join
	6,6	−4,0
	(cooperate)	(sucker)
Do not join	Join	Do not join
	10,6	0,0
	(free rider)	(uncooperative)

This analysis suggests that the decision to join will depend on what each person thinks others are likely to do, and that decision in turn depends on the gains that appear likely from joining together. If there is a 50/50 chance that a $10 gain per person will be produced only by joining together to form the group, the $10 is the equivalent of a $5 benefit (50 percent of $10). This suggests that the size of the gain per person is a critical factor in whether the group will form. If the potential gains, discounted for uncertainty that the gain will not be realized, exceed the $4 cost, the potential joiners will conclude that the $4 cost will not go down the drain and the group will form among those people (unless more profitable uses are found for the $4).

This discussion lends some support to the commonly held view that the formation of a political group is more likely when benefits of political action are concentrated on a small group of people than when benefits are distributed widely over a large group. First, when benefits are concentrated on a small group, it will be obvious to each potential member that nothing will happen unless they all join together and that the political impact will depend on each person contributing. Second, benefits that accrue to a small group are more likely to provide group members with large political payoffs, if only because governmental budget restraints keep individual benefits down when the numbers are large. Examples of concentrated benefits include a tariff or a tax break favoring an industry. Widely distributed benefits are illustrated by a tax decrease for all taxpayers. "Benefits" in the sense of avoiding burdens also can be concentrated or diffuse. Concentrated burdens include a potential tax on one industry (e.g., cigarettes or alcohol) and regulation of a profession. Widely distributed burdens are illustrated by an increase in taxes for the general public and higher prices from inflation.

Appendix B
Routine Sources of Uncertainty

The text discusses fundamental sources of textual uncertainty which arise from the fact that the plain meaning of language requires agreement among various authors and audiences, and identification of the author and audience is both a difficult and politically charged task. However, some routine sources of textual uncertainty are discussed below.

1. *Vagueness.* Vagueness is the phenomenon of one meaning shading off into another, black or white into gray. A legal example would involve determining whether a person is a "guest" in a car, as defined in a statute prohibiting "guests" from suing the negligent driver. Someone sitting in the front seat is a guest; someone waiting to be picked up by a car is not. But what of someone alighting from a vehicle during a temporary stop? Concerns about fraudulent lawsuits, financed by deep-pockets insurance companies, undeniably influence the answer to this question. Whether judicial reliance on such concerns implements legislative purpose or contemporary values is unclear.[1]

2. *Ambiguity.* An ambiguous text is one that can refer to two clearly divergent meanings, as understood in two entirely divergent settings. Examples of semantic ambiguity include the phrase "monarch," referring to a butterfly or ruler; and "heat," referring to temperature or a track and field or swimming event. Legislative purpose, evidenced by the surrounding text (that is, internal context), often resolves this type of uncertainty. It will be immediately obvious, for example, from other statutory language whether the subject matter of a statute using the term "monarch" is fauna or government. Indeed, semantic ambiguity is often resolved so effortlessly that the text hardly seems unclear in the first place.

Syntactic ambiguity is also possible, as when the placement of a comma might affect meaning. A typical problem is whether a modifying phrase applies to every item on a preceding list. A comma before the modifying phrase and after the last-listed item *suggests* application to the entire list, as in "A, B, and C, on condition that . . . ," compared to "A, B, and C on condition that. . . ."

3. *Open-ended.* Some texts are "open-ended," in the sense that uncertainty can be resolved only by weighing multiple factors whose significance evolves over time. Terms like "reasonable," "unconscionable," and "good faith" are examples.

4. *Incomplete text—gaps.* Sometimes a statutory text fails to address a problem, but the court must fill the statutory gap. The extent to which a statute has gaps is itself a controversial interpretive issue. Professor Easterbrook argues that many statutes simply fail to address certain problems; rather than leave gaps to be filled by the court, the best interpretation of the statute is that no legislation covers the issue one way or other.[2] In some cases, however, the statute obviously applies; there is a gap that the judge must fill. For example, the income tax law taxes net income, "including

income derived from salaries, wages, or compensation for personal service." A tax-payer assigns personal service earnings to a relative before they are earned. Who is the taxpayer, the assignor or assignee? The statute must identify the taxpayer in order to impose a tax and *must* therefore fill a gap that the text did not address.[3]

NOTES

1   See, e.g., Tallios v. Tallios, 112 N.E.2d 723 (Ill. App. 1953).
2   Frank Easterbrook, "Statutes' Domains," 50 *U. Chi. Law Rev.* 533, 544–45 (1983).
3   Lucas v. Earl, 281 U.S. 111 (1930).

6 Giving Judges Something to Do:

Republicanism and Substantive Canons

It should be obvious from the discussion in chapter 5 that a normative conception of the relationship between legislating and judging underlies all approaches to statutory interpretation, including textualism. The two approaches discussed in this chapter make no pretense of concealing that link.

We look first at modern Republicanism's emphasis on a judicial role in implementing fundamental values. Although statutory interpretation is not the primary concern of Republican scholarship, Republicanism has implications for how judges determine statutory meaning. I argue that Republicanism's emphasis on fundamental values makes ambitious claims for judging that cannot be sustained and, consequently, provides an inadequate account of the judge's interpretive role.

Next, we look at the reliance on traditional substantive canons of interpretation by modern textualists. Textualists rely on the canons because canons offer the hope of fitting statutes into the broader fabric of the law with a minimum of judicial discretion. But, I will argue, the canons cannot provide the certainty that the textualists seek.

Republicanism

Modern Republicanism adopts an ideal of an inclusive political process in which all groups deliberate respectfully for the common good and in which judges need not apologize for playing an affirmative role in advancing this goal. The historical roots of Republicanism are traceable to the time of the Founding—to the Anti-Federalists' conception of a public-spirited citizenry committed to the pursuit of civic virtue. Thomas Jefferson's view was paradigmatic: "[t]he moral sense is as much a part of our constitution as that of feeling, seeing, or hearing; . . . [and] every human mind feels pleasure in doing good to another."[1] The historical details of this ideal in 1789 are obviously too narrow for us today (since the 1789 ideal excluded women, minorities, and the unpropertied), but the ideal was capable of shaking off its limits and growing into an attractive model of politics. Indeed, contemporary feminist writings are a dominant strain in the modern updating of Republican ideals.[2]

The empirical strand in modern Republicanism views the law and economics critique of the legislative process as incomplete, too preoccupied with economic calculus and too little aware of the social and cultural reality that shapes political choices. The Republican empirical critique calls attention to the exclusionary aspects of the political process, resulting in traditional blindness to the needs and experiences of others. The problem with the legislative process lies at least as much with social and cultural attitudes as with the mechanics of interest-group formation and bargaining emphasized by the law and economics view of legislation. Overcoming the free-rider problem to political organization, for example, still would leave many groups out in the political cold because they would be seen as the "other," not as full participants in the political process. Consequently, even civic-minded politics would be exclusionary from the perspective of groups not accepted into the broader political family. In Legal Process terms, it would be difficult for the dominant political groups to include the "others" among the "reasonable persons" who could "pursu[e] reasonable purposes reasonably."

This Republican view of politics was strongly influenced by the country's experience during the 1960s and 1970s. The civil rights movement made it clear that various groups were shut out of both (1) the electoral process (African Americans often could not vote, and women often could not get elected), and (2) the legislative process (for example, seniority rules in the Senate usually kept civil rights legislation in committee). Opposition to the Vietnam war proved effective precisely because it bypassed the legislature and moved to the streets. By the late 1960s, the assassination of Martin Luther King, Jr., when he was forging multiracial links among the working class and the poor, suggested that political reform coalitions were doomed to failure. And by the 1970s, the Watergate scandal confirmed a lack of confidence in the political system.

The Republican critique of politics has appeared under several banners—critical legal studies, feminist jurisprudence, critical race theory, and gay legal studies. Although far from homogeneous in their perspective on the political system, adherents of these schools of thought agree that the legislative process often produces a systematic (if not always self-conscious) pattern of exclusion. From this perspective, the most striking feature of the Legal Process view of the legal system was not its optimism about the reasonableness of legislating but its inattention to minority rights. One of the more surprising aspects of the legal literature in the late 1950s was the difficulty that legal academics encountered in justifying desegregation decisions protecting African Americans from discrimination. Learned Hand, for example, in his later years, criticized the Supreme Court's 1954 decision in Brown v. Board of Education as an example of judicial second-guessing of legislative choices.[3]

It was ironic that the 1960s and 1970s, when these views took shape, were periods of considerable legal reform, which often included groups that were omitted. The Voting Rights Acts ended many of the old exclusionary practices. The legislature relaxed some of its procedures that entrenched seniority. And post-Watergate legislation tried to do something about the impact of money in politics. Government also did more than simply adjust the political process. The War on Poverty and civil rights legislation tried to end disadvantage and discrimination in the workplace, which would (it was hoped) eventually result in meaningful participation in both the economic and political life of the country. "Maximum feasible participation,"[4] a phrase which has disappeared from our political language, was supposed to bring previously excluded groups into grassroots political participation.

Ultimately, these reforms did little to head off a loss of faith in the government generally and the legislature in particular. Indeed, by creating expectations that were not realized, the reforms contributed to the view that the government was ineffective. Some of those people who were left out saw themselves fall further behind, and those who were included often expressed the frustrations associated with rising expectations. Moreover, legislation aimed at limiting the influence of money in politics proved ineffective (PAC contributions and "soft money" expenditures exploded), suggesting that the legislative process could not fix itself.

None of these things surprised many on the Left. If politics was strongly influenced by social and cultural forces, no wonder that the disadvantaged were not helped by legislative reforms and no wonder that old biases did not yield to legislative correction.

The normative strands in modern Republicanism are responses to these inadequacies in the political process, both those identified by the law and economics critique and those excluded by the broader cultural myopia that shapes political choices. Republicanism has both procedural and substantive versions. Procedural Republicanism is concerned with making up for inadequate representation of political interests. "As if" Republicanism is substantively more ambitious, emphasizing the judge's role in simulating the substantive results of an inclusive and deliberative process that seeks the common good.

Like textualism, Republicanism comprises a variety of approaches, and not everyone claiming an affinity for Republican approaches to judging will agree with my description, even allowing for the distinction between procedural and substantive versions. But there is a common theme among "Republicans," which grounds the judge's lawmaking role in protecting fundamental values. And it is the ambition underlying this claim that, in the end, undermines Republicanism's ability to justify the judge's discretionary role in statutory interpretation.

PROCEDURAL REPUBLICANISM

Procedural Republicanism relies on judges to make up for procedural defects in the process of making legislation.[5] It tries to be substantively unaggressive, relying on the long tradition of judges making up for legislative incompetence, compensating for shortcomings in the legislative process.

Attractions of proceduralism

An emphasis on assuring proper procedures has always seemed an attractive way for judges to avoid the appearance of substantive lawmaking.[6] Most of the familiar procedural protections in our legal system deal with the application, not the formation, of rules. There is a well-developed body of constitutional, statutory, and common law about requirements for notices and hearings when courts and administrative agencies apply law.[7] Procedural requirements for *rule-making* are less well-developed. As a matter of practice, judges usually publish opinions explaining how judicial rules evolve, and administrative agencies are often required by statute to provide notice and an opportunity for written comment before they make rules. But the *legislative* rule-making process is relatively untouched by explicit procedural standards.

Some process requirements for legislative rule-making are established. State constitutions often require three readings of a bill and a wait of several days before a vote. In addition, bills are limited to one subject, changing a bill's subject matter is prohibited as it passes through the legislature, the introduction of substantive law is forbidden in appropriations bills, and titles describing the subject matter of bills are required. The rationale for these rules is to improve the legislator's and public's awareness of what the legislature is doing and to reduce the impact of powerful private-interest groups that might otherwise capture the legislative process.[8]

Few explicit constitutional requirements about how statutes are made exist at the federal level, certainly nothing like the detailed rules found in state constitutions to encourage a meaningful deliberative process.[9] The House and Senate have their own procedural rules, but these rules are not legally enforceable in court.[10] Although public participation in the legislative process is routinely permitted on important legislation (assuming someone knows about the bill and has the means to participate), no explicit constitutional requirement demands that the legislature permit such participation.[11] Procedural Republicanism seeks to fill this gap in procedural protections at the legislative level, providing a substantively neutral way to improve the substantive results of the political process.

Concerns about procedural defects in the legislative process have had great impact on thinking about constitutional law in the work of John Hart Ely.[12] Groups excluded from politics deserve special constitutional protection, according to Ely, implementing what he calls the "representation-reinforcing" principle.[13] This insight built on the famous Carolene Products footnote,[14] which expressed concern for those discrete and insular minorities that had been excluded from the "pluralist's bazaar"[15] (a phrase synonymous with the bargaining of interest groups). Ely's conception of exclusion was expansive, taking account of the fact that some people could not (really) get a hearing because no one would listen. Prejudice, as modern Republicanism emphasizes, could as effectively foreclose access as more obvious barriers such as obstacles to the vote, the inability to form effective political organizations, and legislative inertia.

Statutory interpretation

These Republican insights into the procedural shortcomings of the legislative process were also relevant to statutory interpretation. First, courts could make up for inadequate access to the political process by tilting interpretation in favor of those groups least able to organize effectively. This approach suggested extending protection beyond those discrete and insular minorities who might be better able to organize (such as racial minorities) to include the poor, who lack the time or money to be politically active.[16] An example of this practice in relation to the poor is the Supreme Court's generous approach to interpreting welfare legislation in the late 1960s and early 1970s.[17]

Second, statutory interpretation could help to level the political playing field by interpreting a statute in favor of those least likely to be listened to in the legislature, even if they are politically active. For example, what chance does an unpopular gay couple have to persuade a legislature that it is a "family"?

Third, as Jonathan Macey has argued, courts could help groups that are at a procedural advantage by relying on the public values rhetoric that so often works its way into statutory language.[18] Legislators like to have it "both ways," voting for texts that seem to implement public values while hoping that legislative history or agency rules will confine the statute to protect well-organized political interests. Courts could counter this ploy by implementing the public values language.

SUBSTANTIVE "AS IF" REPUBLICANISM[19]

No procedure without substance

The most trenchant criticism of Procedural Republicanism is that its compensation for procedural defects cannot adequately explain the judicial role. Substantive judgments cannot be excluded.

Proceduralism purports to identify only those excluded from politics, without trying to identify those whose exclusion is "unjustified."[20] But substantive justification is necessarily part of the judge's concern in deciding whom to protect. Once we get past the problem of extreme examples of blocking access to the ballot, it is too hard for courts to distinguish the political loser from the politically excluded. A difficulty in organizing politically may simply reflect a lack of political intensity (which cannot be characterized as a defect in the democratic process) or a lack of money (which is arguably an unfair way to distribute society's wealth but is not itself a failure of the democratic process).

The concept of prejudice (the refusal to listen) is also hard to distinguish from political disagreement. As Gerald Postema's discussion of Edmund Burke suggests, a lot of prejudice can be characterized as "untaught intuition," not "blind, unthinking bias," and the "wise and prudent person" might seek the "latent wisdom" in prejudices which "initially appear ungrounded."[21] For example, regarding gender issues, it is often said that men just do not get it; hence, arguments made by women, though they are an electoral majority and are well-organized politically, are not "heard." Homophobia creates similar problems for gays. Although it is certainly possible to characterize the problem of "unheard" voices as a procedural defect, if we listen carefully to those who (allegedly) do not hear certain arguments, we quickly uncover a substantive worldview that might express itself this way: "Sure, I hear you. You're just wrong. My embrace of traditional 'family' values is self-conscious and purposeful. Traditional family relationships are the backbone of our society." We are, quite simply, a diverse society, where the "problem" is as much diversity (disagreement) as prejudice (refusing to listen). The fact cannot be avoided that the appropriate vision of society, the individual, and the relationship of individuals, and the appropriate distribution of society's wealth are substantive issues that cannot help but affect judicial decisions.

In fact, our legal tradition does not unlink procedure from substance; procedures are fine-tuned to account for substantive impact. The "beyond a reasonable doubt" rule in criminal law is the best-known example, but judicial review of agency rules has always been sensitive to the substantive values at stake. For example, prior hearings are constitutionally required before welfare based on needs can be reduced, but no prior hearings are required if the benefits are not needs-based.[22]

Judicial review of legislative rule-making is also adjusted to take account of substantive values. Although the Constitution does not explicitly impose procedural requirements on the federal legislature, it does so indirectly (through application of the equal protection and due process clauses) by insisting on the elements of a high-quality deliberative process; these process requirements are relaxed as substantive values diminish in importance. For example, when a statute imposes burdens on fundamental interests, the courts require information about the legislature's *actual* purpose (the legislative end) and a close fit between legislative means and ends. This requirement helps to assure that the legislature will explicitly confront any decisions that might impair fundamental values rather than carelessly interfere with such interests. Thus, the Court upheld an exemption from military draft registration for women,[23] even though such discrimination would usually be suspect, in part on the ground that "[t]his case is quite different from several of the gender-based discrimination cases we have considered in that . . . Congress did not act 'unthinkingly' or 'reflexively and not for any considered reason.' The question of registering women for the draft . . . was extensively considered by Congress in hearings, floor debate, and in committee." The Court concluded therefore "that the decision to exempt women from registration was not the 'accidental by-product of a traditional way of thinking about females.'"

However, if the legislature is not (in the court's view) impairing a fundamental interest, the deliberative standard is less stringent, though exactly what is required is controversial. Some judges will accept virtually any government claim about legislative purpose (with little solid evidence that the legislature had any such thing in mind) and a weak fit between statutory means and ends.[24] Others insist on some showing of a means/end fit, but not necessarily a close fit based on actual legislative purpose: "I . . . believe that we must discover a correlation between the [statutory] classification and either the actual purpose of the statute or a legitimate purpose that we may reasonably presume to have motivated an impartial legislature."[25] And some judges will rely on evidence from the legislative history about how carefully the legislature considered the ends and the means-end fit and the extent to which affected parties were able to present their concerns to the legislature.[26] Despite the uncertainty in the standard, however, the degree of required procedural care is clearly a function of the substantive values at stake.

The search for substance

"As if" Republicanism attempts to make up for the substantive myopia of Procedural Republicanism[27] by deciding cases "as if" the Republican ideal worked well, not stopping with procedural concerns. It urges judges to implement public values more directly—to simulate the results of an inclusive and deliberative process that produces legislation for the common good. But where does "as if" Republicanism get its substantive vision? There is a tendency to build substantive values on a procedural foundation, treating procedure as not just an instrumental value (a means of getting a result), but as a way of doing things that rests on substantive values requiring respect and concern for multiple points of view; this further implies a normative conception about which views are *entitled* to attention in the deliberative process.

This reasoning holds procedural and substantive concerns in a delicate balance, as Frank Michelman's explanation of Republicanism makes clear. In Michelman's view, the respect/concern requirement insists that points of view are entitled to political inclusion when they involve "self-identification" whose recognition is a precondition for mutual respect. Michelman develops this theme in discussing homosexuality,[28] which (he argues) is "not just a certain sort of inclination that 'anyone' might feel, but a more personally constitutive and distinctive way, or ways, of being"; it has "come to be experienced, claimed, socially reflected and—if ambiguously—confirmed as an aspect of identity demanding respect."[29]

The requirement of respect/concern also affirms that "[d]ifference is what we most fundamentally have in common," that "openness to 'otherness' [is] a way toward recognition not only of the other, but also of oneself."[30] The emphasis is on a particular way of deliberating—hearing voices that are conventionally unheard, or in Michelman's image, "confront[ing] the parties in the flesh" (a theme he discusses in the context of an army rule forbidding a

Jew from wearing a yarmulke). This requirement is not substantively inno-cent. It insists that the judge replicate a result that listens to multiple points of view which ought to be included in the deliberative process.[31]

Statutory interpretation

"As if" Republicanism would accomplish its substantive goals in the context of statutory interpretation by either or both of the traditional tools of inter-pretation—purposivism and substantive canons. First, the judge would sym-pathetically elaborate statutory purposes that further such values (as Radin had suggested). An example is the decision in Chisom v. Roemer,[32] where the Court concluded that *statutory* protection from race discrimination in the election of "representatives" applied to elected judges. The Constitution clearly did *not* require this result,[33] but the Court just as clearly tilted the statute in the direction of coverage because the Republican values of a race-neutral voting process were at stake.[34] This sympathetic incorporation of substantive values into a purposivist interpretation of the statute was obvious from the way the court bracketed the beginning and end of its opinion with references to the statute's purpose of protecting voting rights.[35]

Second, as Cass Sunstein argues, the Republican judge would selectively apply substantive canons of statutory interpretation that embody Republican values.[36] The rule of lenity, based on a concern for the fundamental rights of the criminal accused, is an example.

Justifying judging

How successful is "as if" Republicanism in its effort to justify judging? By building substantive values on procedural foundations, it tries to carve out a modest yet assertive judicial role. Michelman refers to a "process-based, republican-not-pluralist" approach,[37] which has led to the observation that "as if" Republicanism has a "relative[ly] empt[y]"[38] normative vision and is a "[f]light from [s]ubstance."[39] Indeed, Michelman's substantivism is, by his own admission, relatively weak; it seeks "a process of normative justification without ultimate objectivist foundations. . . ."[40]

However, enough substance can be found in "as if" Republicanism to re-quire a justification for judges to play an active lawmaking role. Michel-man's view is that courts "represent[] to us the possibility of practical reason" capable of implementing Republican ideals of the "common good" and "civic virtue."[41] The most refreshing element of his argument is his abandoning of the fiction of democratic rhetoric, frankly admitting that the "Court is, vis-à-vis the people, irredeemably an undemocratic institution."[42] But in justifying the judicial role on substantive grounds, "as if" Republicanism refocuses our attention from legislative process to judicial process. For example, Michelman emphasizes the procedural advantages that judges have in playing an affirmative role in constructing Republican values. The judicial process is insulated from interest-group politics and is capable of "listening for voices from the margins."[43] Even more important is the courts' deliberative tradition, which consists of reflective thought (fostered by a collegial bench)[44] and, I would add, the need to write publicly available opinions justifying results and taking responsibility for the decision and its rationale.

This procedural defense of what judges do invites a closer look at judging, not always with Michelman's optimism. The Left's critique of an exclusionary political process also applies to judges. Where the Legal Realists saw more or less random political choices by the judiciary, the contemporary Left perceived a more systematic political bias placing those who had traditionally been marginalized by society at a disadvantage. In this view, the optimism underlying "as if" Republican judging provides false comfort. Judges exercise power, with a tendency toward what Robert Cover called the "jurispathic" rather than the "jurisgenerative."[45] "Interpretation always takes place in the shadow of coercion,"[46] excluding meaning in the act of creating it. The façade of Republicanism or any other ism that conceals the exercise of power through the determination of meaning can even deflect rather than bring about real reform and change.

This critique of the judicial process highlights the tendency of courts to be dominated by particular ideologies or class biases, perhaps the very traditions that ought to be questioned. It is therefore not surprising that early Supreme Court decisions favoring the poor eventually gave way to a rejection of any special concern about the impact of school financing on poor families and a refusal to define the poor as a specially protected group.[47]

Decisions about gay rights also illustrate how hard it is to generalize about where protection for particular groups is best obtained. The Court's negative attitude toward gays was obvious not only in the 1967 case of Boutilier v. INS,[48] where the Court interpreted "psychopathic personality" in the immigration law to include homosexuality, but also in the 1986 decision in Bowers v. Hardwick,[49] upholding a sodomy conviction of gay partners. Congress overrode Boutilier in the Immigration Act of 1990.[50] But, more recently, the Court in Romer v. Evans[51] held that a state constitutional amendment prohibiting laws and government policies protecting gays from discrimination violated the Constitution's minimum rationality test for legislation. It was Congress that adopted a federal ban on recognition of gay marriages, although the Senate came within a vote of deciding that gays deserved protection from employment discrimination.[52] Observations like these lend some credence to Robin West's mistrust of the judiciary on the ground that judging leans toward the traditional and incremental, and that legislatures, for all their faults, are where we should look for political change.[53]

In sum, Republicanism's efforts to re-create an ideal of inclusive and deliberative politics has just enough substance to attract the concerns that plague all substantively aggressive approaches to judging—the difficulty of justifying the judicial advancement of selected substantive values. Republicanism, focused as it is on the judge's role in protecting fundamental values, makes claims for judging that are too ambitious to provide us with an adequate explanation of the judge's interpretive role. Viewed from the perspective of the long history of statutory interpretation, it is yet another effort to define those "fundamental" values that influence statutory meaning, something which Chief Justice John Marshall and others advocated many years ago. From a modern perspective, however, those of us living in a post-Legal Realist world are properly suspicious of judicial claims to special expertise in distinguishing fundamental from other interests, just as the uncertainties in the Golden Rule (drawing a line between "absurdity" and "inconvenience") should have been palpable to earlier observers.

I do not mean that it is inappropriate for judges to care deeply about "fundamental" values, even to pay them particular heed. English judges of the sixteenth and seventeenth centuries were certainly concerned with such matters. But they did not justify the judicial role in those terms, and neither should we. The point is that no judicial expertise based on knowledge of community consensus,[54] artificial reason, or scientific principles gives judges any special ability to identify fundamental values any more than they can help to resolve matters of mere inconvenience. It might even make more sense for judges to conclude that fundamental principles are so much more controversial than matters of mere inconvenience that judges should, on that account, be less concerned with the fundamental than the inconvenient; consequently, *more* room exists for the exercise of judicial discretion when the issues involve the merely inconvenient rather than the fundamental.

What we need, therefore, is a theory of statutory interpretation that justifies judicial lawmaking discretion regarding the entire range of substantive issues, whether the issues are fundamental or merely inconvenient. In chapter 7, a theory of "ordinary judging" will be suggested, which, I hope, is equal to that task. But first we should look at the other major contemporary effort to explain how judges fit statutes into the broader fabric of the law—the modern textualist's reliance on the traditional substantive canons of interpretation.

Substantive Canons and Modern Textualism

Another traditional way to give judges something to do—to fit statutes into the broader fabric of the law—is to rely on the traditional substantive canons of interpretation, which insist on clear statutory statements before the statute can override the values embodied in the canon. "Republicans" do this selectively, making judgments about which canons implement fundamental values. But reliance on the canons is not limited to those who espouse a Republican approach to judging. Indeed, it finds a defense—oddly enough—among textualists, who usually are opposed to judges' use of substantive values external to the legislation in determining statutory meaning.

The rationale for the modern textualists' embrace of traditional canons involves two steps.[55] First, modern textualists are unable to deny a judicial role in fitting statutes into the broader fabric of the law; too much contrary historical tradition exists. Second, the canons hold out some promise of fulfilling this role with a minimum of judicial discretion. The idea is that implementing substantive canons that are part of our established tradition will, it is hoped, have a clarity in application that minimizes judging.[56] Selection from among the established canons, however, is not permitted, for that would imply excessive judicial choice. The modern textualist must therefore adopt the substantively questionable practice of accepting tradition as self-justifying in order to avoid too much judicial discretion.[57]

But my concern here is not to critique the substantive implications of incorporating tradition into the legal system. It is easy enough to observe that some aspects of our tradition are odious, but it also is hard to deny that tradition itself has some value in providing continuity.[58] My concern is different. Because the canons are no clearer in application than are statutory texts, I deny that the textualist can deliver on the promise that following established canons will minimize judging. This point is not limited to the obviously open-ended canons—for example, requiring a liberal interpretation of remedial statutes. It also applies to canons with more specific content, such as the federalism canon and rule of lenity canon discussed below. Indeed, at least some textualists hint at this concern. As Scalia notes, "To the honest textualist, [the substantive canons] are a lot of trouble."[59]

The substantive canons are incapable of providing clarity in application for two reasons. First, the interaction of the canons with both the statute's text and purpose varies too widely to provide much certainty. This variation results from the different weights that the substantive values embodied in the canons can have in influencing statutory meaning, operating as presumptions in three possible ways—strong, weak, and in-between presumptions. A strong presumption operates as a clear statement rule, insisting that a particular result can be achieved only if the text (and not legislative history) says so in no uncertain terms. A weak presumption operates *after* the judge has done everything that would normally be done to interpret a statute, but the answer is still uncertain—after the judge seizes "every thing from which aid can be derived."[60] In other words, the presumption acts as a tie-breaker. Finally, the presumption might operate (and usually does) between these two extremes thrown into the interpretive mix to be weighed in uncertain fashion along with other interpretive criteria.[61] Attributing the appropriate weight to a canon as a tool of interpretation lacks the precision required to satisfy the textualist's standard for interpretive certainty.

Second, the canons cannot provide sufficient certainty in application because their weight varies over time. The one constant in our tradition has been change, a point conveyed vividly in Matthew Hale's analogy of the law to the Argonauts' ship, whose physical contents completely altered during the voyage. The second Justice Harlan expressed a similar idea when he affirmed that the tradition on which judges rely is "a living thing."[62]

The impact of change on a canon's weight is complicated by the fact that statutes are part of the tradition on which the court must draw to determine the vitality of values embodied in a canon. The tradition does not stand outside the statute but is shaped in part by it. For example, the increasing importance of revenue in the modern state undermines the canon that favored a narrow interpretation of statutes imposing taxes; the use of criminal statutes to regulate rather than punish behavior weakens the rule of lenity; and the dominance of statute law in modern government requires reconsideration of the presumption that statutes are prospective,[63] and that statutes in derogation of the common law should be narrowly construed. No judge can discover the tradition without judging it, based in part on the statute whose meaning the tradition influences.

The uncertainty created by the complexity of the interaction between the canons and a statute and by the change in a canon's weight over time are best illustrated by considering some examples. Two canons are discussed here: (1) the federalism canon, which presumes that federal statutes do not interfere with the states; and (2) the rule of lenity, which presumes that a statute does not impose criminal penalties.

FEDERALISM

The federalism canon has been invoked in numerous settings, including the following: (a) to prevent inferring that a federal statute overrides state sovereign immunity in federal courts;[64] (b) to prevent inferring a cause of action against states based on a federal statute;[65] and (c) to prevent inferring that a federal statute interferes with areas traditionally regulated by the states.[66] The different settings in which the federalism canon applies illustrate both the variety of ways in which canons can interact with a statute and the change in a canon's weight over time, producing uncertainty in the canon's application.

The strength of the values underlying the canon—even when applied to its core case of state sovereign immunity in federal court—is relatively new.[67] The Constitution's Supremacy Clause (Article VI), stating that federal law "shall be the supreme law of the Land," is a rival to federalism principles favoring the states. The Supreme Court today unquestionably believes strongly in federalism principles. A majority affirms that "Congress may abrogate the States' constitutionally secured immunity from suit in federal court only by making its intention unmistakably clear in the language of the statute"[68]— that is, a strong presumption.

Recently, the Supreme Court has even gone so far as to reject Congress's power to legislate away a state's sovereign immunity in federal court when acting under Article I of the U.S. Constitution (the Commerce Clause).[69] *Some* exercises of federal power are therefore constitutionally impermissible; they simply are not issues of statutory interpretation. But the 1996 vintage of this denial of legislative power, reversing a 1989 decision, is clearly demonstrated by Justice David Souter's long and thoroughly researched dissent.[70] Sovereign immunity was an element of the common law when the Constitution was adopted, and it could therefore be superseded by legislation like any other common law principle. Souter refers correctly to the "pervasive understanding" at the time of the Founding that the common law "was always subject to legislative amendment."[71] The contemporary Supreme Court's response to this dissent is in the tradition that now should be recognized as a commitment to protecting fundamental values, claiming that sovereign immunity is even more basic than the common law, that it "found its roots not solely in the common law . . . , but in the much more fundamental 'jurisprudence in all civilized nations.'"[72]

In any event, despite the newly established constitutional disability to legislate away state immunity in federal court when acting under the Commerce Clause, congressional power to abrogate state sovereign immunity in federal court unquestionably persists when Congress legislates under the Fourteenth Amendment (to preserve equal protection and due process rights) or adopts legislation making grants-in-aid to the states. In such cases, the contemporary shift toward a strong interpretive presumption that favors the states is still relevant.

This shift toward a strong version of the federalism canon is less certain when the issue is not immunity in federal court. When the question is whether a federal statute creates a cause of action against a state in a *state* (not federal) court, the Supreme Court sometimes infers a cause of action and overrides the state's interest in protecting itself from lawsuits. In a 1991 case raising this question, the Court stressed that the issue is "merely" one of statutory interpretation, lacking the same constitutional significance as cases involving suits in federal court,[73] but the dissent considered constitutional federalism principles to be equally applicable whether the lawsuit was in federal or state court.[74]

Uncertainty over the weight of the federalism canon is even clearer in the variety of cases concerned with whether a federal statute should be interpreted to avoid interfering in areas traditionally regulated by the states. The Court has held that the federal Hobbs Act definition of "extortion" included bribery, even though a major impact of the decision was to apply federal criminal law to state officials.[75] And the Court has interpreted a federal antidiscrimination law to prevent a group home for ten to twelve adults recovering from alcoholism and drug addiction from being kept out of a neighborhood zoned for single-family residences.[76] The dissents in both cases appealed to federalism principles. As for the federal crime of extortion, the dissent objected that "[t]he Court's construction of the Hobbs Act is repugnant . . . to basic tenets of federalism. Over the past 20 years, the Hobbs Act has served as the engine for a stunning expansion of federal criminal jurisdiction into a field traditionally policed by state and local laws—acts of public corruption by state and local officials."[77] And in the zoning case the dissent argued that "land use . . . is an area traditionally regulated by the States rather than by Congress, and that land use regulation is one of the historic powers of the States."[78]

But federal law will not always be interpreted to interfere with the state's regulatory power. The regulation of corruption by state officials turned out to be a lesser interference with federalism principles than the federal regulation of retirement ages for state judges. Consequently, a federal statute prohibiting a mandatory retirement age did not apply to appointed state judges because the power to determine judicial qualifications was a fundamental and traditional state function.[79]

In sum, the weight of the federalism canon has varied over time and changes widely depending on the statutory setting. It is, of course, always open for a judge to argue that the federalism canon *should* be more consistently applied. But however one comes out on this argument's merits, it is difficult to defend the canon on the ground that in practice it can provide the certainty to which modern textualism aspires.

The rule of lenity, by tilting statutory interpretation in favor of the criminal accused, serves a number of functions. It makes sure that the legislature has confronted the implications of criminalizing behavior. It gives notice to the accused. And it limits prosecutorial discretion. Even Roscoe Pound, without explanation, spoke favorably of the rule of lenity in contrast to the "derogation of common law" canon.[80] But the weight of the rule of lenity, like other canons, varies over time and statutory setting.

The importance of the rule of lenity canon has clearly declined during the twentieth century.[81] Some states actually reject the rule of lenity by statute.[82] And the 1993 Uniform Statute and Rule Construction Act declined to include it in its Rules of Construction, citing its rejection by statute in several states and its inconsistent application.[83]

Two reasons can be found for the decline in importance of the lenity canon. First, the criminal law has been used more and more, not just to condemn evil behavior, but to regulate economic activity. Jail sentences and stigmas are less likely to attach, either by law or in practice. In that setting, a generalized tilt toward the accused loses some of its attraction. Second, as public concern about crime increases, the inclination to adopt an across-the-board presumption in favor of the accused weakens. Legislatures have provided a nudge in this direction by stating that some specific criminal statutes should be liberally construed, not in accordance with the rule of lenity.[84]

This change in the canon's weight has contributed to uncertainty in application, as illustrated by two gun control cases. In Scarborough v. United States,[85] the petitioner was convicted of possessing a firearm in violation of Title VII of the Omnibus Crime Control and Safe Streets Act of 1968, which prohibited felons from possessing guns under certain circumstances. The Court admitted that the statute was not "a model of clarity," that the "language was ambiguous at best," but it nonetheless held that the statute applied to the defendant, noting that it "was a last-minute amendment to the Omnibus Crime Control Act enacted hastily." This led the Court to rely on legislative history to apply the statute to the accused: "The legislative history in its entirety, while brief, further supports the view that Congress sought to rule broadly to keep guns out of the hands of those who have demonstrated that 'they may not be trusted to possess a firearm without becoming a threat to society.'" The Court added that upholding the defendant's position would "create serious loopholes in the congressional plan to 'make it unlawful for a firearm . . . to be in the possession of a convicted felon. . . .'"

As for the rule of lenity, the Court, clearly downgrading the canon to tie-breaker status, made the following statement about how much doubt the judge must have before indulging a substantive presumption about the statute's meaning.[86]

> Petitioner . . . overlooks the fact that we [do] not turn to [the rule of lenity unless] we ha[ve] concluded that "[a]fter 'seizing every thing from which aid can be derived,' . . . we are left with an ambiguous statute." The [rule is] applicable only when we are uncertain about the statute's meaning. . . . In this case, the [legislative] history is unambiguous and the text consistent with it.

The dissent expressed the more traditional view that the Court's approach was "inconsistent with the time-honored rule of lenity in construing federal criminal statutes"; "it is appropriate, before we choose the harsher alternative, to require that Congress should have spoken in language that is clear and definite. We should not derive criminal outlawry from some ambiguous implication."[87] The point, seemingly well-taken, was that a statute which was not a "model of clarity" (the majority's phrase) would normally be "leniently" interpreted to avoid a broad definition of a crime. And, as Justice Antonin Scalia noted elsewhere, the use of legislative history to resolve ambiguity violates the stricter clear statement version of the rule of lenity.[88]

Although the rule of lenity was unavailing in Scarborough, it was successfully invoked in United States v. Thompson/Center Arms Co.[89] The statute imposed both a tax and a criminal sanction (without proof of willfulness) on anyone "making" a "firearm." The question was whether a gun manufacturer "makes" a firearm when it packages a mail-order kit, which can be used to make both a firearm and another weapon, which did not fit the technical statutory definition of "firearm." A majority of the Court applied the rule of lenity, based on the text's "ambiguity." The fact that the defendant was the gun manufacturer—not the gun user—explains why in this case the values embodied in the rule of lenity carried more weight in the interaction with statutory policy.[90] There was no unpalatable combination of guns and felons that existed in Scarborough.

In sum, the variety of statutory settings in which substantive canons interact with the statute's text and purpose and the evolution in the importance and influence of these canons over time make their application extremely variable. Their persistence in statutory interpretation is testimony to the inevitability of judicial efforts to fit statutes into the broader fabric of the law, but the canons cannot provide the kind of certainty that the modern textualist seeks in statutory interpretation. Indeed, the use of the canons is as likely to reflect the judge's "own conception of the good" as the effort by purposivist judges to carry on an imagined dialogue with a departed legislature to apply a statute to contemporary facts.

7 Ordinary Judging

Now my charms are all o'erthrown,
And what strength I have's mine own. . . .
— *Shakespeare,* The Tempest

Most efforts to explain the judicial role in statutory interpretation have failed because they are too ambitious. Those who favor or oppose too much judging in statutory interpretation exaggerate the virtues of what they advocate and the defects of what they oppose, often insisting that the issues involve legitimacy rather than institutional competence or making excessive claims about the competence of different institutions.

Ample evidence of this practice has been given. Judges for a long time claimed a special competence, first, by appealing to artificial reason to dominate the relationship between judges and legislatures, and, then, in the nineteenth century, by turning to a science of the common law that would defend the common law from statutory encroachment. The twentieth-century critique of judging also was exaggerated, placing too much faith in the "people" and their legislative representatives and implying that judges made unconstrained and random political choices.

None of these claims proved fatal to twentieth-century purposivism (the sympathetic and imaginative elaboration of legislative purpose). But purposivism also rested on exaggerated claims, specifically, that the legislature consisted of "reasonable persons pursuing reasonable purposes reasonably," and that judges were especially good at conducting imagined dialogues with departed legislatures to apply statutes to specific cases. Subsequent critiques undermined this optimistic view of legislation and judging, leaving judges without a foundation for a creative role in interpreting statutes.

Modern efforts to rebuild that foundation also have failed, producing at best an incomplete picture of the judicial role in statutory interpretation. On the one hand, modern textualism rests on a denial of judicial competence and legitimacy that is unfaithful to our traditions of statutory interpretation, which are less pessimistic about judging and do not so narrowly circumscribe the judge's lawmaking role; and, further, it is grounded on an exaggerated confidence in the judge's ability to apply the statutory text to specific cases with certainty. On the other hand, modern efforts to ground the judge's interpretive role on inflated claims about judicial ability also are inadequate to the task. Republicanism is too committed (however cautiously) to an optimistic view of judging and too wedded to limiting the judicial role to implementing fundamental values. And dynamic statutory interpretation[1] places too much emphasis on the judge's role in fitting statutes into an evolving legal landscape as *the* justifying principle for the judge's collaborative interpretive role.

Given that political power is at stake, exaggerated claims about the strengths and weaknesses of both judging and legislating are certainly understandable. The language of political debate tends to galvanize adherents and demonize opponents, in part to overcome the inherent conservatism of existing political practices. The academic author who best reflects this style is Ronald Dworkin, who paints the judge as Hercules, capable of obtaining the right result.[2] But exaggeration has its price. Superheroes are too easy a foil for those who object to judicial discretion; when claims turn out to be indefensible, the defended institution is set adrift. At the very least, exaggeration produces an unnecessary anxiety about the judge's (inevitable) lawmaking role that should be familiar to those raised in the Learned Hand tradition.[3] It is far better to paint the judge as engaged more modestly in a struggle to determine statutory meaning (Sisyphus, if we must have a Greek model), without claiming extraordinary abilities.[4]

The better route to justifying judicial discretion in statutory interpretation is to accept the notion that judging is an ordinary activity, neither grounded in any exceptional skill or expertise, nor threatening to usurp legislative power. In H. L. A. Hart's terminology, judging is neither a noble dream (discovering law, not creating it) nor a nightmare (the equivalent of legislation),[5] but a conscientious effort by judges to help out in the lawmaking process.

Ordinary judging builds on that part of our historical tradition that is concerned with institutional competence rather than legitimacy. Competence has always played an important role in the debate about statutory interpretation. Legislative incompetence was for years a major justification for equitable interpretation, and judges were emboldened to play a major interpretive role because of their competence in bringing artificial reason and a knowledge of legal science to their job. During the nineteenth century, views about the relative competence of legislatures and judges began to change. Some commentators noted a growing distance between judges and legislatures, supporting a retreat to the Golden Rule (avoiding absurd results) and placing greater weight on the statutory text. By the early twentieth century, legislative competence in the guise of a science of legislation began to replace a science of the common law; it became obvious that judges could not do what modern legislatures did well—gather data, make compromises, and adjust to change. And the Legal Realists demolished the view that judges could competently identify apolitical, objectively valid principles of law. The emphasis in the Legal Process approach in the late 1950s on the relative competence of different lawmaking institutions[6] is only the latest variation in a long history of concern about who best can make law, going back to Aristotle's observation about the legislator's inability to foresee many details.

The case for judging based on competence, however, must be carefully constructed to prevent it from making claims that are too strong. Defenders and opponents of judicial discretion are as likely to exaggerate the competence and incompetence of institutions as they are to overstate claims about legitimacy. In recent years, most prominently in the Law and Economics and Procedural Republicanism literature, the tendency has been to emphasize legislative incompetence—calling attention to the nonlevel playing field that results from the difficulties of political organization and cultural bias—and the judge's ability to decide when to make up for these procedural defects. But the positive political science needed to make secure judgments about legislative behavior is not well enough developed to confidently guide judges. Although judges cannot avoid making guesses about how the legislative process works when deciding specific cases, their guesses about whether political success results from unfair procedural imbalance are too speculative to provide a foundational justification for the judicial role in statutory interpretation. Moreover, the implication that judges are especially good at making procedural but not substantive judgments is unfounded. It is no more difficult for judges to make guesses about which *substantive* decision best fits statutes into the law than to decide about the strengths and weaknesses of the legislative process.

Similarly, foundational claims about judicial competence to make substantive judgments are as hard to sustain as those based on legislative incompetence. The judge's procedural advantages (based on collegial and dispassionate debate and the publication of reasoned judgments) are too often not realized in the rush to judgment and the sophistic and manipulative argumentation of many judicial opinions. Moreover, judicial claims of expertise in identifying fundamental values are equally vulnerable; the judge's selection of fundamental values is too often the result of obvious conservative or liberal biases, and, in any event, judges have as much trouble identifying fundamental values as in resolving problems of statutory interpretation involving the "merely inconvenient." Even the textualist's effort to promote an image of apolitical judging in order to preserve the judge's ability to protect fundamental rights is likely to founder, not only on an inability to persuade people that textualism is apolitical, but also on the difficulty of defining what rights are fundamental.

It is not that fair lawmaking procedures and fundamental values are irrelevant or unimportant to the judge, only that judges are as unsure of identifying what is fair and fundamental as they are of any other values they enforce. They cannot therefore ground their interpretive lawmaking role on these criteria.

The better case for judging lies in making a weaker competence argument, one based on the fact that judges are good at contextualizing their decisions. Of course, as with all modern efforts to explain the role of context in judging, what we mean by context is crucial. If the appeal to context is simply to "take account of all the relevant factors"—the facts of the case and the statute's broad substantive and institutional setting—contextualization becomes both trivial and vacuous, as an explanation of judging. We want to make the most general claim possible, without emptying the idea of content, about how contextualizing decisions justifies the exercise of judicial discretion in determining statutory meaning.

In statutory interpretation, judges contextualize by taking account of the statute's temporal dimension—fitting the law into its past and future. The conception of legislation that underlies this view of judging is that a statute is but one frame in a motion picture—with a past and a future. Interpretation is therefore neither inherently forward-looking and dynamic, as William N. Eskridge Jr. has suggested,[7] nor inherently conservative, as many judges and others emphasized before the twentieth century.[8] It is both conservative and dynamic.

The judge's ability to fit statutes into their temporal dimension, which is the essence of ordinary judging, is what justifies their collaborative lawmaking role in determining statutory meaning. I do not mean that judges are alone in having the competence to understand what went before a statute and what comes after it. Other institutions can play this role, such as agencies and the legislature itself, if and when the legislators revisit the law. That is why the *comparative* institutional competence of different lawmaking institutions is relevant to modern debates about statutory interpretation. But judges are uniquely situated to consider how best to fit statutes into the broader temporal evolution of the law and to umpire claims of institutional competence.

Judges are uniquely situated for two reasons. First, they have the time to do it. We need not posit anything invidious or unbalanced about the politics of group formation, legislative bargaining, and agenda control in the legislative process to make this claim for judging. Legislatures are simply preoccupied with issues pushed onto their agenda—issues that often lead them to pay too little attention to how the law interacts with its past and its future. All we need to justify a collaborative judicial role in statutory interpretation is to conclude that *some* decision-maker should be concerned with how a statute fits into its past and its future and should make judgments about the competence of various institutions to perform this task. No other institution but the judiciary can perform this function with the sustained attention to the complexities of applying law to particular cases, which is desirable in a well-ordered government.

Second, the imperative toward ordinary judging and the collaborative judicial role it requires is all but inevitable once the judge's mind is set to the task of deciding cases and controversies. Included within a case or controversy are not only the specific facts, but the facts that make up the statute's temporal context. The simple act of thinking about the meaning of statutory language in this broader context—which the judge must do—requires judgment about how the text should interact with its past and future. That is why, despite its being an obvious fiction, the judge when engaged in statutory interpretation is unable to do without the concept of legislative intent. Intent is matched with text as an essential aspect of statutory meaning, not because the judge has any confidence that legislative intent is knowable, but because "intent" (or "will") captures the idea that choices *must* be made in order to apply a text to facts. Legislative intent is a useful judicial construct because the judge is required to make the choices that best express the statutory text's meaning.

It bears repeating that, once courts accept the collaborative task of considering the statute's dynamic *and* traditional context, no way can be found to turn a blind eye to substantive concerns and procedural considerations about institutional competence; however, the practice of making these judgments does not provide the foundation for the judge's interpretive role. Ordinary judging is no more dynamic than it is traditional; no more committed to fundamental values than it is to the merely inconvenient; and no more concerned with process than it is with substance. Ordinary judging simply responds to the judicial imperative to decide how a statute fits into the broader fabric of the law. In doing so, it makes guesses about *both* the procedural strengths and weaknesses of different institutions *and* substantive values without claiming foundational insight into any of these concerns. These judicial guesses *follow from* the imperatives of ordinary judging; they do not provide its foundation. In this way, ordinary judging avoids the pitfalls of a foundationalism focused on fundamental values and dynamic, future-oriented interpretation without lapsing into a descriptive pragmatism that gives up all attempts to justify judicial discretion in statutory interpretation.

This argument for judicial discretion in statutory interpretation puts aside several issues. First, I do not question whether there is any such thing as a broader fabric of the law into which judges fit statutes. Despite Justice Oliver Wendell Holmes's objection to viewing law as a "brooding omnipresence," everyone—textualist and nontextualist alike—agrees that this concept (however it is described) has enough substance to form the basis of *some* judging. Thus, a textualist like Justice Scalia describes the judge's job as "mak[ing] sense" of the corpus juris "[w]here a statutory term . . . is ambiguous";[9] and Frank Easterbrook welcomes the judge's developing of a common law when properly authorized by legislation.[10] Although these commentators would allow judicial lawmaking only when the plain meaning of the text fails to resolve an issue, they do not dispute the existence of a broader fabric of law as an operative judicial concept, only the circumstances in which it can be invoked.

Second, we do not look in one obvious place to locate the justification for judicial discretion—namely, the political selection process for judges, which is based on appointment and approval by political officials at the federal level and election (or at least standing for electoral approval) in many states. The fact that no one (to my knowledge) makes this argument for judicial discretion may be a tribute to the legal profession's apolitical self-image, so carefully nurtured during the nineteenth century and so persistent despite the Legal Realists' efforts. But I think the reason lies deeper. The argument based on the selection process is concerned with legitimacy, and, as I have repeatedly suggested, the issue of competence is far more important in deciding what judges can and should do. The nature of competent judging, not the judge's political pedigree, explains the judge's lawmaking role.

However, linking the judge's political connections to a sense of institutional competence—of being politically savvy—is another matter.[11] We noted the legislative experience of English and nineteenth-century state judges in the United States, an experience bound to give them a sense of shared institutional competence with legislators in figuring out statutory meaning. Analogous observations can be made about the political experience of contemporary judges. For example, Herbert Jacob reports the percentage of state judges holding previous political office[12]—either elected law enforcement or legislative—broken down by selection criteria and by types of judicial office

Table 7.1   State Judges with Previous Political Office

			Selection Criteria (in percentages)		
	Governor	Legislature	Missouri plan	Partisan election	Nonpartisan election
Total	56.8	95.1	16.7	53.6	30.4
Law enforcement	39.1	19.2	100	78.6	71.7
Legislature	66.6	80.7	—	24.5	22.1

	Types of Judicial Office (in percentages)	
	Supreme court	Trial judges
Total	64.4	47.1
Law enforcement	53.6	65.9
Legislature	51.2	34.0

(see table 7.1). More generally, the selection process (whether by election or appointment) is so tied to state politics that it is likely to produce judges who think of themselves as politically knowledgeable.[13]

I am not aware of similar data on federal judges, but the selection process also is likely to elevate individuals with a sense of their own political savvy. One study finds that over 50 percent of federal judicial appointees were "active" politically.[14] Kenneth Abraham's study of 102 U.S. Supreme Court justices finds that all of them had "considerable experience in public life," even though only fifteen held elected political office at the time of appointment (the exclusion of judgeships from the "elected political office" category may understate this figure).[15] Certainly, no one would consider Felix Frankfurter (a professor when appointed), Thurgood Marshall (a court of appeals judge), or Louis Brandeis (a practicing lawyer) as politically naïve. Finally, the process of senatorial courtesy for district judges and senatorial clearance for court of appeals judges suggests that many if not most appointees will have political experience.[16]

But political savvy is not the principle justifying the judge's collaborative interpretive role. To be sure, political savvy is one determinant of how aggressively the judge makes judgments. For example, I noted Justice Frankfurter's propensity to use his labor law expertise to boldly interpret labor legislation. And one explanation for modern textualism at the federal level, urging a minimal exercise of lawmaking discretion, is a decline in confidence that judges understand what is going on in any particular area of statute law, and a desire to leave the complex issues raised by statutory interpretation for legislative resolution. But the judge's level of confidence about lawmaking does not establish the existence of judicial interpretive discretion in statutory interpretation, even though it might embolden or discourage its exercise. That discretion follows from the process of ordinary judging, whereby the judge fits statutes into their past and future.

Before explaining ordinary judging as it applies to statutory interpretation, I should briefly discuss why my own background makes me less anxious about judging and more confident about the judge's discretionary interpretive role. First, much of the twentieth-century angst about judging arose because judges were reading the Constitution to freeze the law, rejecting legislative attempts at legal change. By contrast, my professional interest in law emphasizes statutory rather than constitutional interpretation, which poses less of a threat to the evolution of the law because the judge's interpretive decision can be overridden by the legislature. Second, the preoccupation of most American academic commentators is with *federal* law, raising questions of federal power that are not common to *all* judging. A good part of my own experience with statutory interpretation has been with state judges, whose interpretation of state legislation is not troubled by concerns about aggrandizing the power of the central government, including the federal judiciary. Third, my own substantive legal specialty is mundane—the income tax code—where the role of courts in helping to reach sensible conclusions has long been a routine activity (often with Learned Hand in the lead).

In examining contextualization, statutory interpretation, and ordinary judging in this chapter, I look first at contemporary arguments for judicial contextualization that build on the confluence of two philosophical traditions: (1) the mental process of judging (Kant's *Critique of Judgment*) and (2) political action (Aristotelian practical reason and its distant descendant, American pragmatism). Both approaches insist on *some* form of contextualization, but they also require us to fill in the details. The remainder of the chapter is then devoted to arguing that the details of judicial contextualization in statutory interpretation are concerned with how judges fit statutes into their temporal dimension.

Contextualization: Two Philosophical Traditions

Two philosophical traditions contribute to contemporary efforts to explain how judges contextualize decisions. One builds on Kant's *Critique of Judgment*, concerned with how the judicial mind both engages (sympathizes) with and separates (distances) from the object of judgment. The Kantian tradition's primary contemporary contribution is to explain how the mental process of ordinary judging can reasonably lay claim to public acceptance. The other tradition relies on Aristotle's conception of practical judgment and American Pragmatism, which calls attention to the broader political setting into which a judgment must fit.

I do not pretend to be confident about exactly what the originators of these traditions might say about modern political judgment, modern judging, or statutory interpretation, or whether they would agree with any of the modern uses made of their philosophies. At the very least, it must look strange to wed an account of practical reason (historically tied to a communitarian city-state society in which citizens found meaning through political action)[17] with modern pragmatism (so often associated with the efficiency of individual choices). But that should not stop us. The point of modern applications of these theories is that it is up to us to apply their general perspectives on judgment to contemporary judicial practices.

My account of how this might be done draws in the case of Kant on the work of Hannah Arendt, Ronald Beiner, and Anthony Kronman, and for Aristotle and American Pragmatism on the writings of Eskridge and Philip Frickey, as well as Beiner. As my references indicate, Beiner's work looks at how *both* traditions contribute to a more complete understanding of judgment, and my primary objective is the same.

THE JUDICIAL MIND: KANTIAN JUDGMENT;
SYMPATHY AND DETACHMENT

Kant's *Critique of Judgment* was explicitly concerned with aesthetic judgment, but Hannah Arendt argued cogently that it contained the seeds of a political philosophy.[18] In her view, Kant's political sense was offended by the subjective arbitrariness of aesthetic taste.[19] Rather than being subjective and individualistic, judgment was inherently social and public, seeking to persuade others about what we share in common, and to develop a shared perspective out of an awareness of the plurality of experience.[20] In Beiner's view, Kant believed that judgments of beauty do not just affirm preferences but "solicit the rational assent of everyone else,"[21] a mental frame of mind with obvious political implications.

We might resist these efforts to apply Kant's *Critique* to political and legal judgment because we are so accustomed to viewing matters of aesthetic taste as outside the boundaries of rational argument—"there is no accounting for taste." But late eighteenth-century thought considered taste and judgment as similar faculties (the original title of the *Critique of Judgment* was "A Critique of Taste").[22] Although it may be hard for us to recapture the late eighteenth-century perspective that argued rationally and publicly about how to make judgments, it is worth our while to make the attempt for both historical and contemporary reasons.

Historically, the "centrality of the concepts of taste and judgment in eighteenth-century British empiricist thought"[23] paralleled Kant's views on taste and judgment and undoubtedly influenced the views of many Founders about the meaning of judgment exercised by courts under the Article III Judicial Power. For example, Henry Home, Lord Kames (an author well-known to late eighteenth-century American lawyers),[24] devoted a chapter in his 1762 book, *Elements of Criticism*, to "disproving the 'dangerous' maxim 'There is no disputing about taste,'" arguing instead that people had standards of taste, based on a "sense or conviction of a common nature."[25] And the American James Wilson (both a Supreme Court justice and "one of the principal founders of our distinctly American constitutional jurisprudence")[26] agreed. Wilson rejected the view that it is "fruitless to dispute concerning matters of taste." "Nothing," he said, "can be farther from the truth."[27]

Contemporary commentatory (by Judge Robert Bork) has also analogized *judicial* discretion to aesthetic judgment.[28] Although Bork means this analogy as a criticism of what he considers arbitrary judging, it might be turned to good use to defend rather than disapprove of judicial discretion. At least one observer has argued that "[i]f Kant had been an Englishman he might have noticed that the same sort of reflective judgment [as in aesthetics] seems to work in the common-law tradition. . . ."[29]

The central point in Kant's *Critique of Judgment* that is relevant for contemporary judging is that decision-making can be defended in specific situations when there is no objective truth—that is, when practical reason is no longer "pure" and cannot rely on the generalities of the categorical imperative. As one observer notes, the issue is whether "one [can] judge the particular without reference to a general concept or universal rule, and [whether] judgment [can] have any validity beyond the judging subject, that is for others." [30]

The Kantian tradition gives us a defense of judgment by relying on the twin concepts of distance (or detachment) and sympathy. Distance refers to the judge's position as a "spectator," providing an objective stance. This concept of objectivity is a weak one, meaning only that the judge works hard to avoid bringing a partial perspective to the task of judgment. The theme is familiar in the image of the blindfolded judge, which originally conveyed the notion of judicial distance from the (willful) sovereign. [31]

Nowadays, we are appropriately suspicious of claims that judicial distance will succeed in overcoming partiality. Indeed, the aura of objectivity is seductive, potentially obscuring the biases that the judge brings to judging. That is where sympathy plays an important role, enabling the judge, in Kronman's account, [32] "to see and feel, from within, what each [alternative] would be like," to "understand the experience of other people." Or, as Arendt put it, the judge achieves an "enlarged mentality," putting himself in imagination into another's shoes. [33] But sympathy is not the same as empathy, [34] which yields to the preferences of one party to a dispute. Sympathy draws the judge away from an overconfident objectivity, but it does not equate judgment with any one perspective. Indeed, sympathy contributes to establishing distance because the judge is forced by the multiplicity of perspectives to be detached from any single point of view.

This commitment to *both* sympathy and distance allows the judge "genuinely to make a decision among the alternatives rather than merely be swept along by the tide of feeling that any sympathetic association . . . can easily arouse." [35] It leads to a kind of "objectivity," though nothing like the objective truth that rests on principles established outside the judging process. Indeed, "those thinkers who developed the theory of taste or judgment were in opposition to the subjective/objective dichotomy which has ruled modern thought. . . ." [36]

The "objective" force of sympathetic-but-distanced judging arises from the judge's need to seek acceptance for a judgment committed to multiple perspectives *without* an external standard of truth—to "woo the consent" of the audience [37] and to "solicit the rational assent of everyone else." [38] In Arendt's view, judgment does not compel, but persuades. [39] And, as Beiner puts it: "Judgment allows us to comport ourselves to the world without dependence upon rules or methods, and allows us to defeat subjectivity by asserting claims that seek general assent." [40]

The relationship between "wooing consent" and a search for general assent (that is, a grounding in *some* conception of democracy) is as problematic for the Kantian judge as it is for us today. The sought-for acceptance cannot be equated with popular consensus;[41] and yet it derives some normative force through its appeal to experience shared with others, communicable to others, and rooted in common sense.[42] We may simply have to admit that the defense of "objective" taste and judgment in Kant and other late-eighteenth-century thinkers was linked to an optimism about the *common* sense of the people and the implications that this view had for democracy but that we may not share.

This portrait of the Kantian judge has several lessons for modern judging. First, the judge's appeal for acceptance must include persuasive argument. Without a "common" sense to fall back on, the combination of detachment and sympathy can hope to produce "objective" agreement only from the way the judge reasons to a conclusion. Indeed, as democratic forces questioned the judge's ability to implement either common sense or artificial reason, the widespread introduction of writing and reporting of judicial opinions in the early-nineteenth-century United States was undoubtedly associated with the need for judges to "woo consent." In this political climate, many states required judges to write opinions to limit their discretion;[43] and judges such as James Kent and Joseph Story viewed the reporting of written opinions as a technique for enhancing judicial authority.[44]

Second, the Kantian judge should be modest and restrained, willing to reveal doubts. The lack of objective truth and the need to woo consent should make the judge painfully aware of how difficult judging is and the responsibility it entails. Although judges are not generally inclined to admit to doubt in their published opinions,[45] a tradition of judicial doubt has historical roots in Matthew Hale's and Sir William Blackstone's view that all decisions are only evidence of law and in Lord Mansfield's notion of the law working itself pure.

The Kantian perspective on judging can take us only so far. First, the Kantian judge reflects more on the past than he actively participates in shaping the future. This limitation is a major shortcoming for understanding political judgment, including the element of political choice in judicial judgment. A judge of the law cannot be innocent of the political impact of judgment on future behavior, even if an aesthetic judge can separate himself from the effects of judgment on what future artists do or art critics perceive. Second, despite Arendt's observation about the political and moral relevance of Kant's *Critique of Judgment,* its political/moral implications are far from clear. Beiner argues that its relevance for political judgment is "highly problematical"; and he contends that Kant's aesthetic judgment is nonmoral, because it is disinterested and contemplative, not practical.[46]

Nonetheless, the concepts of judicial distance and sympathy help us to understand that judging is a process with its own internal dynamic—wooing consent with arguments sensitive to multiple perspectives but without yielding unreflectively to popular consensus. And this process can provide an internal justification of its own results, as long as it is not relied on to make exaggerated claims of judicial competence but is viewed as an ideal that judges strive for when engaged in the mundane process of ordinary judging.

POLITICAL ACTION: ARISTOTLE'S PRACTICAL REASON AND AMERICAN PRAGMATISM

Whatever relevance Kant's *Critique of Judgment* may have for an understanding of political and legal judgment, there is no denying that its central concern is not political action, and that no account of judging would be complete today without considering the judge as a political actor. For a more complete understanding of modern judging, we must look to commentary that builds on Aristotle's notion of practical reason and American Pragmatism,[47] which William James explicitly linked to Aristotle.[48]

We should be clear in what respects practical reason and pragmatism add something to our understanding of contemporary judging beyond what we can derive from Kant. The difference does *not* lie in a concern for the particulars of experience. A judge exercising Aristotelian practical reason "moves back and forth, from universal to particular, and from particular to universal,"[49] but so does the Kantian judge.[50] And a modern pragmatist would share Kant's view that judgment can be practiced but not taught.[51] The difference lies instead in the emphasis on political action in Aristotle and problem-solving in American pragmatism, both of which require the political actor to consider a wide range of factors to make a decision.

Aristotelian practical reason is judgment embodied in action,[52] whereas the Kantian judge has a more limited focus, concerned primarily with the way that the judicial mind engages with the specific object(s) of judgment. Consequently, the Aristotelian judge adopts a broader perspective than the Kantian judge, taking account of how judgments fit, both substantively and institutionally, into the larger political system. In the modern setting, this perspective requires the judge to consider the impact of a judgment on those other than parties to a dispute (both the incentive and distributional effects, as well as public acceptability) and the institutional alternatives to a judicial decision.

The problem-solving orientation of American pragmatism is obvious from William James's conception of truth. Truth is what "works"; "truth *happens* to an idea"; truth is determined by its "cash-value"; truth is an "event"; "truth is *made* . . . in the course of experience." [53] James also left no doubt that common law judging was an example of pragmatic problem-solving, whatever a nineteenth-century judge might claim: "Common-law judges sometimes talk about the law . . . in a way to make their hearers think they mean entities pre-existent to the decisions. . . . But the slightest exercise of reflexion makes us see that . . . law [is a] result. Distinctions between the lawful and the unlawful in conduct . . . have grown up incidentally among the interactions of men's experiences in detail. . . . Given previous law and a novel case, . . . the judge will twist them into fresh law." [54]

Indeed, some nineteenth-century commentators had a strong pragmatic streak, rejecting the view that the law consisted primarily of formal categories. For example, Theodore Sedgwick (in midcentury) sounded like a Jamesian pragmatist, emphasizing that "[w]hat is required . . . is not formal rules . . ."; "[o]urs is eminently a practical science. It is only by an intimate acquaintance with its application to the affairs of life, as they actually occur, that we can acquire that sagacity requisite to decide new and doubtful cases." [55] Francis Lieber also had a strong pragmatic streak, appealing to "[c]ommon sense and good faith [as] the leading stars of all genuine interpretation." [56] And Roscoe Pound in the early twentieth century linked sociological jurisprudence to modern pragmatism, expressing unhappiness that "discussion of general principles goes on and a pragmatist philosophy of law is yet to come." [57]

The most obvious implication for judging of Aristotle's practical reason and American pragmatism is to reject reliance on formal rules and theories that pay insufficient attention to the experience or context of decision-making. [58] This notion is vague, to be sure, reflecting the fact that these ideas are more concerned with what they reject than (ironically) with what they might concretely require of the judge. Exactly what experience or context the judge should consider is less important than making sure that no general rule should dictate meaning. We need, therefore, to flesh out a concept of pragmatic judging if it is to have relevance for modern statutory interpretation. Before I offer my own suggestions, however, three modern theories of judging with pragmatic roots, all of them relevant to statutory interpretation, require some comment.

First, Cass Sunstein explains the judicial role as concerned with incompletely theorized conclusions. [59] Judging, in this view, is statecraft, intent on finding the point of agreement among multiple points of view, without always insisting on *the* right rationale (hence the incompleteness of the conclusions). This theory "works" by serving the broader political goals of providing mutual respect for a variety of perspectives and avoiding divisive political controversy where possible—emphasizing the theme of public acceptance for the judgment.[60] In the context of statutory interpretation, this approach has much in common with Charles Peirce's image of a "cable, weav[ing] together several mutually supporting threads" to provide the strongest interpretation, an image that Eskridge also finds attractive.[61]

Much is to be said for Sunstein's approach and for Peirce/Eskridge cable-weaving, but judicial opinions about statutory interpretation suggest caution in our embrace of this pragmatic justification for judging. Judicial opinions about statutory interpretation are, to be sure, often written as though multiple criteria lead to the same result—for example, arguing that text, purpose, legislative history, and policy considerations favor the same conclusion. But the opinions, rather than weaving together mutually reinforcing strands, will often strike the reader as somewhat far-fetched in their reliance on multiple arguments, appearing too manipulative in their indiscriminate appeal to multiple criteria. Cable-weaving seems more pragmatically descriptive than normatively persuasive as a justification for the judge's interpretive approach. In other words, a theory of judicial statecraft can be too little concerned with justifying the criteria that the judge *should* consider. The threads that make up judging are not unlimited, and *some* criteria are more appropriate than others; the judge, like any politician, can do too much "wooing."

One possible version of the multistrand approach *is* judgmental about which criteria the judge ought to consider. This version sensibly argues that the weights accorded to the various interpretive criteria (e.g., text, purpose, and background considerations) *ought* to vary, depending on which substantive area of law is addressed by the statute. For example, a tax statute *might* be approached with greater deference to the text; a civil rights law with more attention to purpose; environment statutes with greater concern for the institutional shortcomings of judge-made law; etc. We certainly need interpretive theories in which scholars in particular areas of statute law wed their specialized expertise to a sophisticated understanding of statutory interpretation. But I cannot pursue this line of thought here, except to support the undertaking. My concern is with finding a more general pragmatic theory of statutory interpretation, not one limited to a particular area of statute law.

Second, Learned Hand's pragmatic philosophy, directly traceable to the influence of his philosophy professors in the late nineteenth century (including the pragmatist William James),[62] led him to embrace judicial "craft" as the source of judicial legitimacy. For several reasons, however, this justification is inadequate. There is, first, the fact that few judges can aspire to Hand's level of judicial craft. Easterbrook makes this point indirectly in questioning the purposivist's effort to implement legislative intent by carrying on imagined dialogue with the spirits of the departed legislature.[63] Easterbrook's suggestion that conversing with such spirits is more likely to produce results desired by the judge suggests that as much craftiness as craft may infuse the judge's imaginative interpretation of legislation. Second, Hand is forthright (in his nonjudicial writings) that the exercise of craft resembles the existential effort to impose order on a chaotic legal universe rather than to extract meaning put there by someone else. "By some happy fortuity, man is a projector, a designer, a builder, a craftsman; it is among his most dependable joys to impose upon the flux that passes before him some mark of himself, aware though he always must be of the odds against him. His reward is not so much in the work as in its making; not so much in the prize as in the race. . . ."[64] This confession is unlikely to put at ease those who view pragmatism as an open invitation to willful judging.

Third, and somewhat surprisingly, textualism can lay some claim to being a pragmatic theory of statutory interpretation. Textualism might make a strong claim to pragmatic acceptance in light of the broader political system—to work better than other theories—by weaving together several strands that contribute to interpretive theory. First, textualists argue that judicial discretion, by associating judging with politics, denies judges the popular respect that they need to make difficult decisions,[65] a problem with serious consequences in a fractured society where the threat of converting disagreement into disrespect is close to the surface. Second, it is better to leave contentious issues to the legislature where a chance exists of forging a more lasting consensus.[66] Third, too much judging deprives legislatures of the incentives to face up to their political and drafting responsibilities. Fourth, judges lack the competence to go behind the text to make sound pragmatic judgments about statutory meaning. In light of these observations, a single textual strand might "work" best,[67] at least in this modern period of diminished confidence in government and threat of political discord.

Although this pragmatist case for textualism cannot be ruled out a priori, it will prove difficult to sustain as long as we insist on the pragmatic test of examining how well an interpretive approach works. The following discussion of how contextualization occurs in statutory interpretation suggests that textualism cannot survive the judge's confrontation with the tug of past and future on statutory meaning.

Contextualization: The Statute's Temporal Dimension

Modern adaptations of Kantian judgment, Aristotelian practical reason, and American pragmatism all argue for contextualized judging, but what context should the judge consider? The insight that Kant provides is that the job of ordinary judging consists not only of detachment associated with the traditionally blindfolded judge, but also of engagement with the multiple points of view that contribute to the decision of the case. This concept is neither a nightmare nor a noble dream as long as it is an ideal for the judge to approach with humility, not the foundation for making exaggerated claims of judicial expertise. The contribution of Aristotelian practical reason and American pragmatism is that the judge must consider the broader political context into which the decision must fit. Unfortunately, these traditions embolden the judge to make discretionary lawmaking choices without providing much guidance.

The remainder of this chapter argues that these traditions should lead the modern judge engaged in statutory interpretation to take account of the statute's temporal dimension—fitting statutes substantively into their past and future. This role is one aspect of ordinary judging. Judges do it because they are good at it—because they are well-situated to decide how to fit statutes into their broader temporal evolution, free of the distractions that lead legislatures to overlook the past and the future. Moreover, judges do it because it is an inevitable result of trying to determine the meaning of a text as applied to facts, which necessarily include the statute's past and future.

However, nothing about this judicial process is particularly exalted. Judging is an "ordinary" activity, which cannot be sustained by putting on the mantle of special expertise (such as artificial reason or legal science), or appealing to an optimistic view of judging—such as Republicanism (oriented either toward compensating for defects in the legislative process or enforcing fundamental rights), or dynamic statutory interpretation (focusing primarily on the future evolution of statutory meaning). Ordinary judging requires the judge to consider substantive values with due regard to comparative institutional lawmaking competence, but these are byproducts of interpretation, not justifications for the judge's interpretive role.

Implicit in this claim for ordinary judging is the idea that competence analysis is preferable to a concern with judicial legitimacy. It rejects reliance on the airtight compartment theory of separation of powers that underlies much of the legitimacy-based objections to a discretionary role for judges in statutory interpretation. To be sure, a risk of error is present when a judge interprets a statute, but Justice Anthony Kennedy's warning that there is "too great a risk that the Court [will] exercis[e] its own 'Will instead of Judgment' "[68] is more alarmist than realistic.

In the following discussion I make frequent use of examples, not to provide a thorough picture of the law of statutory interpretation, but to illustrate the nature of ordinary judging. Selective examples, of course, do not provide a complete description of judging or a normative justification for what the judge does. But no pragmatic account of judging can do without them. They provide the reader with a sense of what judging is like, and they invite ("woo") the reader to accept the examples as illustrative of the way that judging must proceed.

My overall objective is to explain how ordinary judging requires a discretionary judicial role in fitting statutes into their temporal dimension without leaning too far toward either strong foundationalism or descriptive pragmatism. To that end, many examples deal with mundane legal issues (is a haybine a "mower"? is a prisoners' association a "person" entitled to a waiver of court fees to advance a claim for free smoking tobacco?). These matters lack the firepower we associate with more "fundamental" legal issues, such as civil rights, but the way in which judges deal with the mundane provides us with a more accurate picture of judging than a focus on questions that some might consider more "fundamental." Indeed, an important feature of ordinary judging is that it is concerned as much about the merely inconvenient as it is about matters of fundamental principle.

We look first at how judges determine the meaning of a statute by taking account of the future after passage of legislation, and then we examine how they integrate legislation with its past history.

THE FUTURE

Arguments about the judge's interpretive role in taking account of the future can be framed in terms of either competence or legitimacy. I look first at how considerations of competence lead a judge to consider change, with special attention to the unsuccessful efforts by a well-known textualist professor-judge to avoid the choices that change requires. I then critique legitimacy arguments against judicial adaptation of statutes to the future, suggesting that these arguments fail to do a good job of explaining the judicial role in statutory interpretation.[69] Finally, I present some examples of interpretive criteria that might help a judge decide whether to leave a decision to other lawmakers.

The operative word here is "decision." All statutory interpretation leaves an "issue" for legislative resolution; legislatures can always change the statute to override what the judge has done. The correct question is whether a decision to favor a particular result is best left to nonjudicial resolution.

The best way to understand why judges necessarily make judgments about substantive values and institutional competence when they adapt statutes to the future is to ask which institution is most competent to make law. Imagine a judge being asked to apply a statute only to facts existing when the text was adopted. On lawmaking competence grounds, that seems silly. It makes little sense to insist that a legislature revisit a statute whenever some change occurs. Legislatures are simply unable to function efficiently in this way, and it would be a waste of time for the legal system to require them to do so.

For example, suppose an old statute requires banks to keep "banker's books."[70] Many years later, microfilm is invented. No judge would have trouble interpreting the statute to include the microfilm, which is the modern equivalent of a book, even though the legislature did not have microfilm in mind when it used the word "book." It would be a waste of the legislature's time for the court to insist that a statute redefine books to include microfilm. Consequently, the judge would act appropriately to help out the legislature by extending the statute beyond the shared historical understanding of the word "book" when the statute was passed.

The functional adaptation of an old text to future facts—so that microfilm is a banker's book—is usually considered a trivial point, with no broader implications for statutory interpretation. That is wrong. Functional adaptation can be made less obvious by injecting a few as yet unconsidered possibilities into the example. Suppose the switch to microfilm is very expensive (much more than keeping books); and suppose that the statute does not require nonbanks to maintain these records, giving them a competitive advantage over banks; further suppose that the reasons for keeping the books (checking up on bank solvency and preventing bank fraud) were no longer important because of regulatory measures passed after the banker's book statute. These questions illustrate that the interpretation cannot be narrowly focused on what a "book" means. The facts to which a statute applies do not exist in airtight compartments separate from the background from which the statute arises—from either the values that shaped the legislative purpose, or the traditions against which the legislature acted. When that background changes or new facts do not fit neatly into the historical background, the understanding on which the statute was based is unsettled. Microfilm might not be a book.

But the judge has no way to resolve this issue without making substantive judgments about what to do if the fit is not perfect. The purposivist's effort to avoid these choices hides behind an "imagined dialogue" with the departed legislator. But as soon as the judge begins to imagine what that dialogue might consist of—what would the legislator want to do about expensive microfilm, about competitive advantages for nonbanks, about the impact of new banking regulations—the judge is drawn into substantive speculations that cannot honestly be described as re-creating the historical legislature's intent in the modern world.[71] Moreover, such substantive speculations do not end the matter. The technical and political complexities of reaching a particular decision might urge that it be left to the legislature (or agency) to reach. Consequently, issues of comparative institutional competence cannot be avoided.

These substantive and institutional speculations are not just the product of the judge's sense of institutional competence in adjusting an old text to new facts. They are, in fact, inevitable. Modern textualists assert otherwise by insisting that texts *necessarily* have a functional meaning: that is, microfilm is a book because it functions as a book.[72] But nothing inherent in the idea of a text insists on its being expanded functionally rather than tied to the facts existing when it was written. The necessary process of thinking about how a text applies to facts leads to making this choice, which, in turn, requires speculation about substantive values and the allocation of institutional lawmaking authority. Judges often describe this process as one of determining legislative intent, but it would be less misleading to speak of the "statute's intent," a phrase that exposes judicial choice (which meaning was intended?), without pretending that the judge is confidently re-creating actual legislative intent.

Consider, for example, this more modern example. Is the recording of a 911 emergency telephone call a "statement" in a statute defining that term to include an "electrical, or other recording . . . which is a substantially verbatim recital of an oral statement made by a person and recorded contemporaneously. . . ?" Under the statute, "statements" must be provided by prosecutors to defendants. Surely, the text clearly applies to 911 calls. But what of the huge financial costs to municipal police departments of keeping such records and the fact that the 911 system postdated adoption of the statute requiring "statements" to be provided? Is it either desirable or possible for a judge to think about this statute without taking into account the costs and the temporal relationship between the adoption of the statute and the events to which the statute might apply?[73]

A textualist's judicial opinion. The inevitability of judicial speculation about substantive values and comparative institutional competence is strongly suggested by the contrast between Judge Easterbrook and Professor Easterbrook. As a professor, Easterbrook counseled putting the statute down once events outstripped the historical understanding that underlaid it:

> [T]he domain of the statute should be restricted to cases anticipated by its framers and expressly resolved in the legislative process. Unless the party relying on the statute could establish either express resolution or creation of the common law power of revision, the court would hold the matter in question outside the statute's domain. The statute would become irrelevant, the parties (and court) remitted to whatever other sources of law might be applicable.[74]

As a court of appeals judge, Easterbrook abandoned this textualist approach, apparently unable to avoid thinking about how new facts unsettled the meaning of an old statute and how the judge should update the law.

We should not be surprised that a gap exists between the scholar and the judge, given the scholar's greater time and expertise and a penchant to exaggerate in order to influence an otherwise recalcitrant and traditional judiciary.[75] But there is more to the difference between the academic and judicial sides of the profession. Judging forces the judge to think about applying the text to the facts, which leads (as Max Radin noted) to a judgment about the statute's substantive purpose(s), its historical and evolving context, and the institutional background considerations that suggest who should make law.[76]

The decision by Judge Easterbrook that we examine involved a 1935 Wisconsin statute that exempted mowers owned by farmer-debtors from a creditor's claim.[77] Since 1935, mowers had changed considerably, developing from the kind driven by friction with the ground to those powered by the tractor's drive shaft. Eventually, the haybine effectively replaced mowers. A haybine was a mower-plus because it not only mowed in ways not common in 1935, but it also conditioned hay. When Professor Easterbrook urged that a statute should cover only that which was "anticipated by its framers," he advocated what I would label "narrow denotation," tying a text to those particulars existing or anticipated when the text was written. As I noted, this is a difficult position to sustain because it means that technological change could never be included in a text written before the change occurs. Judge Easterbrook is aware of this point and responds with a theory of language. A word, he says, conveys a function not limited to the particulars extant when the word was first used. Call this "broad denotation."

But nothing in textualism mandates that result. Authors and audiences understand texts in terms of particulars, and they do not reach agreement on particulars of which they are unaware. There are, as mentioned, many good reasons why it would be silly to limit a word to its narrow denotation. But it would not be silly to exclude the fruits of technological change either—is an eight-month-old fetus who can survive outside the mother's womb a "person"? Once Easterbrook admits, as he does in his opinion, that "the age of th[e] statute prevents 'literal' application to today's farm equipment," [78] the interpreter's approach to change becomes a problem of judicial allocation of lawmaking authority, not resolvable within the boundaries of textualism.

Judge Easterbrook does in fact go further and becomes a purposivist,[79] trying to fit the old statute to contemporary facts. First, he admits the relevance of the fact that the law's intended purpose was to protect assets owned by a small farm from creditors. Second, he further admits that this "remedial" purpose is relevant to interpreting the statute. Third, he worries about whether implementing this remedial purpose by including the haybine within the statute would really help farmers, given the fact that exempting debtor property from seizure by creditors might dry up credit. But why are these purposes relevant to statutory interpretation when the statute's authors never considered including a haybine within the statutory term "mower"? Purpose does not *have* to be invoked to arbitrate between a narrow and broad denotational meaning of a word such as "mower." The statute can just as easily be put down when new facts fall outside the narrow denotational meaning of a statutory text. Certainly, the fact that the statute is "remedial" can be disregarded, as Easterbrook urged in another setting.[80] But, *as a judge,* Easterbrook says that remedial purpose is relevant to include in the statute very fast mowers that were unknown in 1935, but that this remedial purpose does not help in deciding whether a "mower-plus" (a haybine) is a mower. No explanation is given for such fine-tuning of the judge's reliance on the statute's remedial purpose.

Easterbrook's last argument—that exempting debtors might not help farmers—is especially interesting because it is advanced without any attention to whether that approach was likely to be a legislative concern in 1935. My best guess about what the legislature intended in this depression-era law in a farmer-dominated state (Wisconsin) would be that farmers' immediate needs were of central concern rather than the long-term impact of the law on extending credit. I also would hazard the guess that worrying about drying up credit if the law favors debtors is a distinctly modern perspective on law and economics and on what policy makes the most sense. This modern perspective is appropriate for a judge concerned with adapting a statute to changing values, but it is hard to reconcile with the views of a judge who claims to be committed to sticking to historical understandings of a text.

Why is Judge Easterbrook unable to avoid considering statutory purpose and contemporary values to determine how an old statute applies in the modern world? He tells us that change has made literal application of the text impossible, but that is not true. It is perfectly possible to limit the text to 1935 mowers, or at least to mowers and not haybines (a mower-plus). The reason that Judge Easterbrook cannot act in this way is that the experience of applying texts to changed circumstances shatters the agreement on which textualism depends: the agreement between author and audience. Put more technically, the mistake that the textualist makes is to assert that language usage is necessarily dichotomized between a text that either plainly hands courts a common law power or is restricted to cases anticipated by its framers. That is not how language works. Language operates along a spectrum that includes the extremes of broad delegation of interpretive authority and narrow denotation, but stopping places are many in between. In most instances, the judge chooses how broadly or narrowly to read an older statutory text rather than passively acquiescing in the text's meaning. And to make this choice, the judge cannot help but exercise substantive discretion about how to adapt the statute to new events.

Nor can the judge avoid issues of comparative institutional competence. That is also apparent in Judge Easterbrook's decision, which begins and ends with a textualist's plea for institutional help to avoid judicial choice—starting with the observation that "technology has done more to change farm implements than the Wisconsin legislature had done to change" the law, and ending with deference to the lower court's interpretation: "The law has need of tie-breakers, and if this case be a tie (it comes close), the nod goes to the district court's construction."[81] But there is no escaping judicial responsibility for making this decision to allocate lawmaking responsibility. Change forces the judge to look beyond the statutory author to the future audience and that, in turn, forces the judge to ask questions that cannot insulate him from becoming engaged in policy concerns and judicial choices that have not been resolved by the historical legislature. An imagined dialogue with a departed legislature takes on a life of its own, and the decision to defer to the lower court (or legislature or agency) is the judge's to make.

229

The alternative to comparative institutional competence as the way to think about judging is legitimacy. There are three ways to question the legitimacy of how judges interpret statutes to adapt to change. That none of them is persuasive (or so I will argue) does not *prove* that judges should exercise political judgment to adapt to change, but it strongly suggests such a conclusion by removing a major objection to judges playing that role.

The first legitimacy concern is the countermajoritarian problem of judges threatening to undermine legislative decisions. In my view, the charge of countermajoritarianism leveled against the judge's exercise of interpretive discretion to adapt to change comes much closer to being "mindless" than the charge of formalism against the modern textualist.[82] The concern expressed by the countermajoritarian anxiety is that judges who try to update the law will undermine what the historical legislature has done. The countermajoritarian objection to adapting statutes to change is spurious, as Eskridge and Daniel Farber have explained.[83] Change means that something new has occurred which the legislature did not anticipate, in which case judging does not "counter" legislative decisions. Moreover, statutory interpretation differs from constitutional adjudication, which can strike down a law and thereby pose a greater risk of defeating the historical legislature's decision. I do not mean that questions concerning the judicial role dissipate just because decisions are not countermajoritarian. The judge must still decide whether or not a particular decision favoring one side of a dispute should be left to the legislature (or agency). The problems are those of comparative institutional competence, not legitimacy.

The second legitimacy argument regarding judicial adaptation of statutes to change is the airtight compartment theory of judging. (Indeed, I suspect that the charge of countermajoritarianism is really leveled misleadingly against the judicial exercise of interpretive discretion, even though that discretion does not counter anything the legislature has done.) In this view, judges are not allowed to make the political choices necessary to adapt the statute to change; that is a legislative function. But this argument assumes that all law is legislative, which is a difficult position to sustain in our legal tradition. Not only are judges accustomed to making common law, but they routinely work out the interaction of statutes with substantive values embodied in canons that are not derived from the statute itself—an obvious lawmaking function. Of course, a reasonable argument can be offered that certain political choices should not be made by judges under certain circumstances—that judges are not competent to make such choices. However, such an analysis is situation-specific, based on the comparative competence of judges and legislatures, not a legitimacy argument.

The third legitimacy argument denying judicial discretion to update statutes is concerned with legislative inertia. When a judge takes account of change, he often decides that legislative inertia prevents the legislature from addressing the problem and that the judge can properly step in to make up for this imperfection in the lawmaking process. Easterbrook argues that such an action takes the judge beyond the legitimate sphere of judicial concern[84] because inertia is an important check on legislation, analogous to more familiar checks and balances on government power built into our constitutional structure.

Easterbrook refers to "a number of checks [on the legislature's power] from the demands of its internal procedures to bicameralism to the need to obtain the executive's assent," and he then makes the leap that is meant to undermine judicial concern about legislative inertia: "The foremost of these checks [on legislation] is time. Each session of Congress, for example, lasts but two years, after which the whole House and one-third of the Senate stand for re-election. What . . . a Congress might have done, had it the time, is simply left unresolved. The unaddressed problem is handled by a new legislature with new instructions from the voters." Because

> time is classified with the veto as a limit on the power of legislatures, . . . one customary argument for judicial gap filling—that legislatures lack the time and foresight to resolve every problem—is a reason why judges should *not* attempt to fill statutory gaps. . . . In a sense, gap-filling construction has the same effects as extending the term of the legislature *and* allowing that legislature to avoid submitting its plan to the executive for veto.

There is no gainsaying the inventiveness of this argument against courts taking account of legislative inertia, although one wonders what "new instructions from the voters" we can really expect regarding most of the detailed changes occurring after passage of a statute that will produce problems of statutory interpretation. In any event, it is difficult to make the case that this limit on judging is hard-wired into the Constitution's conception of judicial power. The problem of the legislature's inability to anticipate change and the need for judges to help out in such cases goes back to Aristotle and has been part of the judicial tradition for too long to be ruled out by inference,[85] based on a creative analogy between the expiration of legislatures and those checks and balances explicitly set forth in the Constitution.

What, then, does the judge do when thinking about how to adapt a statute to change? The "trivial" case of defining a book to include microfilm led to a concern with substantive policies and the comparative institutional competence of legislatures and judges, and we must follow that lead to expand our understanding of the judicial role. The following examples illustrate how certain concerns intrude into the interpretive decision—specifically, a judicial concern with political controversy and technical complexity; with overcoming legislative inertia; with the impact of decisions on the incentive to legislate; with lawmaking responsibility; and with the judge as "expert" in particular areas of law.

These are more or less familiar themes in current discussions of statutory interpretation, but they include two major shifts of emphasis. First, the modern judge resents being forced to decide difficult cases by a legislature that does not face up to its lawmaking responsibility. This theme will not prevail at all times among all judges in all jurisdictions. But as the sense of political savvy among judges declines (at least at the federal level), the court is less and less likely to accept the task of making tough interpretive decisions willingly and gracefully. This unwillingness has nothing to do with the legitimacy of the judge's interpretive discretion, but it does concern the declining sense of confidence in one's own lawmaking competence that influences the way in which the judge interprets legislation. Second, an inexorable interaction exists between procedural concerns and substantive decisions. Thus, political controversy—a reason to withhold decisions—is often associated with substantive values about which judges, with good reason, feel strongly; and evidence about lack of legislative inertia (counseling against a decision) often correlates with evidence that the legal landscape is evolving in a particular substantive direction (counseling for a decision).

Political controversy and technical complexity

The judge will be concerned with whether the application of the old text in a new setting raises issues that are technically complex and/or politically controversial, suggesting that a decision might be left to the legislature (or an agency). The issue of political controversy is troublesome, however, because contentious issues are often those to which the judge has the strongest substantive commitment.

Example 1. Suppose in a statute making it a crime to commit vehicular homicide that a judge must decide whether a fetus capable of living outside the womb (a "viable" fetus) is a "person."[86] These statutes date to a time when an unborn fetus was not legally a "person," but technology has made survival of a prematurely born fetus much more likely today. If the fetus is viable, it is technologically no less a person than a microfilm is a banker's book. But the issue feels sharply different, and for good reason. Expansive definition of "person" seems to embroil the court in a potentially volatile political controversy over when life begins. It also makes something a crime, which might undermine the protection for the accused embodied in the traditional rule of lenity. A court might therefore decide that criminalizing such behavior requires an explicit legislative judgment.

But the tug of contemporary values is extremely strong. A judge who enthusiastically embraces the antidrunk driving policy of vehicular homicide statutes is unlikely to be going against the grain of modern policy.

Still, the criminal setting might give the judge pause. That explains why only four state courts to date have interpreted criminal statutes to apply to a fetus,[87] but statutes dealing with *civil* damage claims for wrongful death have more often than not been interpreted to define "person" to include a viable fetus.[88]

Example 2. Inflation can raise issues which are both technically complex and politically controversial.[89] Suppose an income tax statute uses a dollar amount to determine the deduction for depreciation. This rule was adopted when inflation was moderate, but assume that today inflation is out of control. Should the judge treat the statutory text as providing inflation-adjusted figures? The implications of making inflation adjustments to investment cost will vary among industries, depending (among other things) on the balance of labor and capital. Moreover, making adjustments for owners distorts investment decisions unless corresponding adjustments are made to the tax rules that apply to debtors in order to reflect repayment in deflated currency, a matter of considerable technical complexity. Finally, historical cost is only one of many examples of dollar figures in the income tax, each raising different policy concerns. Some fixed-dollar rules might deserve the obsolescence that inflation provides (for example, maximums on certain deductions provided as a tax incentive), if only to force Congress to revisit the rule. Courts are unlikely to be confident enough to address either the political or technical aspects of inflation adjustments without legislative guidance.

Overcoming legislative inertia

The judge will consider whether relevant interest groups can effectively get the legislature to listen and respond to change. Absent the likelihood of a legislative response, judges who would otherwise be reluctant to make aggressive substantive choices might nonetheless be willing to make them, even to become embroiled in technically complex and politically controversial issues. This is a central concern of Procedural Republicanism, discussed in chapter 6.

Legislative attention to a problem is a broadly applicable criterion for judging, relevant to the evolution of the common law as well as statutory interpretation. For example, the Supreme Court cut short its previously aggressive development of common law wrongful death damage recoveries (which compensate for losses from the death of a relative) and instead left development of the law to Congress: "We no longer live in an era when seamen and their loved ones must look primarily to the courts as a source of substantive legal protection from injury and death; Congress and the States have legislated extensively in these areas."[90] Similar considerations are relevant when judges interpret statutes.

Example 3. Suppose a statute provided the elderly with tax rebates if they owned property interests appearing on a list that did not include "life care" arrangements.[91] These arrangements call for the taxpayer to pay money to a retirement community for lifetime care, but the taxpayer does not, technically, own a "property" interest listed in the statute.[92] When this case arose in New Jersey, the court refused to extend the statutory list to help the elderly. Clearly, the judicial habit of judicial extension had eroded by the twentieth century. The judge's first instinct is that these decisions are now the legislature's job, not the judge's; the judge is no longer confident about what the legislature is "driving at." But the decision also can be defended by a more situation-specific analysis of comparative lawmaking competence. In fact, evidence existed that the statutory list had been frequently supplemented by legislative amendment, suggesting that the legislature was paying attention to the problems of the elderly, who could take care of themselves politically.

But the example of a legislature responding to the elderly suggests the substantive ambiguity of evidence about legislative inertia, suggesting how hard it is to fall back on procedural criteria. The same evidence indicating lack of inertia (the legislative extension of statutory lists of exempt property) might also reassure the court that *substantive* public policy favors those capable of getting the legislature's ear (the elderly). Consequently, judicial extension of the statutory list might be the better substantive decision.

Incentive to legislate

The judge worries about whether updating a statute will actively discourage legislative attention to an issue. The overall competence of the lawmaking system might best be served by the judge withholding a decision because carving out a judicial solution to only part of a problem might defuse the legislature's incentive to address broader issues.

Example 4. Taxpayers frequently develop new tax avoidance schemes, and courts are asked to decide whether they are legal. A popular scheme involved borrowing and deducting prepaid interest. In many of these cases, the opportunity for economic gain through use of the borrowed funds was virtually nil, except for the tax break in the form of interest deductions. This was a bizarre situation; taxpayers had incentives to make economically profitless investments because of the income tax law, even though no legislature had ever focused on whether these investments ought to be encouraged.

Courts might conclude that this absurd result should not be tolerated and deny the deduction, and they often did so.[93] But this problem can be looked at in another way. The tax avoidance technique of deducting interest is useful in situations much broader than those which the courts addressed. The court cases involved situations where economic profit apart from taxes was all but impossible, but many tax avoidance schemes involve some (albeit speculative) possibility of economic profit. Courts are able to fashion antitax avoidance doctrine only for cases in which profits are virtually nil, where the tax break seems absurd. But by making such decisions—carving out an area where tax avoidance is prevented—they leave untouched the more common tax avoidance schemes that only Congress can prevent through statutory amendment. And, by addressing only the most extreme cases, courts remove an incentive for the legislature to address the problem.

The incentive effects of judging on legislative behavior, however, are difficult to predict. In fact, judicial decisions disallowing extreme tax avoidance schemes that relied on the interest deduction did not discourage Congress from addressing the broader problem of combining tax avoidance and interest deductions.[94] The courts turned out to have a good anticipatory sense of what substantive values the legislature would later adopt, suggesting that judges can be as confident of guesses about substance as they are about the legislative process.

Lawmaking responsibility

A twentieth-century judge concerned with overall lawmaking competence would worry not only about whether the legislature is in fact paying attention to an issue and about the incentive effects of judicial decisions on the legislature's agenda, but also about whether a substantive decision *should* be the legislature's responsibility rather than the judge's. Much of the strength underlying the argument for a special judicial role in protecting fundamental values relies on the assumption that nurturing such values is a special *judicial* responsibility.

A concern with lawmaking responsibility forces the judge to think about whether change has occurred after passage of the statute. When change has *not* occurred, the case for legislative rather than judicial responsibility to make a decision is strongest, based on the theory that the legislature should not pass the buck to the courts to do what the legislature *could* have done with its potential awareness of a problem. Change, by precluding the possibility of legislative awareness, weakens the argument favoring legislative as opposed to judicial responsibility.

Example 5. Suppose a statute deals with the theft of a "vehicle." Is a plane a vehicle? A modern textualist might say, simply, that people do not use the term this way. But Justice Holmes was not ready to take that approach.[95] Holmes, after all, was willing to "see what the legislature was driving at." Nonetheless, he concluded that planes were not vehicles, in part because planes existed when the statute was adopted and the contrast between planes and more conventional vehicles would (or, at least, should) have been obvious to the drafting legislature. In such cases, the legislature has the responsibility of defining the boundaries of legislation if it wants to adopt the more extensive meaning.

In deciding whether the legislature could have been aware of an issue, however, we must not confuse the potential to be aware of "raw" facts with awareness of their political significance. The change relevant to lawmaking responsibility is a function of the fact's significance, not some easy-to-identify objective "reality"; and a fact's significance is a function of the substantive background values into which it fits, as the following example illustrates.

Example 6. Suppose a statute requires the government to compensate an American Indian whose property was stolen by a "white person," if the thief did not pay compensation.[96] This 1834 statute was carefully written to exclude compensation when the thief was black (an 1834 amendment had changed the text identifying the nonpaying thief from "citizen or other person" to "white person"), because Congress wanted to encourage hostility between Indians and fugitive black slaves. What should a court do when the case arises *after* the Civil War and the value system that encouraged hostility to fugitive slaves had crumbled? Should it decide that "white person" means "not an Indian"? Has the "fact" of being "white," to which the legislature paid explicit attention in 1834, changed its significance and therefore its meaning since the Civil War?

When the Supreme Court decided this case, it did not stop with the obvious textualist position that "white" meant white. But it nevertheless denied compensation because the historical legislature had clearly focused on whether recovery was limited to situations in which the thief was "white."

Consider, however, just what the historical legislature knew. It certainly did not know that all blacks were free citizens. The significance of being white and black *after* the Civil War was foreign to the historical legislature. Indeed, the Court recognized that fact but insisted that, because it was interpreting a statute, judicial adaptation to change was improper, in contrast to the common law. But that adaptation to change is *precisely* the question of interpretive theory that must be addressed: what *should* a court do with a statute when change alters the significance of old facts in a contemporary setting?

A judge who is cautious about helping out the historical legislature that fails to discharge its political responsibility to deal with facts of which it could have been aware might take a less diffident approach when a different kind of legislative failure occurs, such as careless drafting errors. Such errors are the legislature's fault, but they do not arise from a failure of *political* responsibility such as ducking a politically contentious issue. In fact, there is a willingness to correct such errors when the text carelessly refers to dates on which nothing has occurred relevant to the statute's objective (otherwise the statute is "absurd"),[97] and when there is internal textual evidence of the mistake.[98] Whether judges should help out a careless legislature is more controversial when the text could apply to real-world events and there is no internal textual evidence of a drafting error.[99]

The judge as "expert"

It is obvious from previous discussion that the pull of substance operates on the judge in tension with concerns about which institution should make certain decisions. Therefore, it is not surprising that the enthusiasm with which courts defer to other decision-makers is a function of how expert—how competent—the judge considers himself. For example, if judges are especially knowledgeable because they serve on specialized courts, they might be expected to take a bolder interpretive role. One commentator on bankruptcy decisions has made just this observation regarding the more policy-oriented approach of lower courts, including bankruptcy judges, compared to the Supreme Court,[100] which is less knowledgeable about bankruptcy matters. And Frederick Schauer hints at the relevance of expertise when he justifies textualism in part as a response to judicial inability to handle complex issues.[101]

It is also apparent that judges who believe they are experts in a field are more willing to be bold in adapting statutes to change. Frankfurter's aggressive interpretation of the antitrust law's application to labor unions is explicable on these grounds. As a labor law expert,[102] he was willing to read a later statute denying injunctions against labor unions for possible antitrust violations as *implicitly* repealing a criminal penalty imposed by an earlier law, a result characterized by the dissent as "a process of construction never . . . heretofore indulged by this court." [103]

This discussion of "competent" statutory interpretation clearly demonstrates how indeterminate ordinary judging can be. It is hard to know when an issue is too politically controversial or technically complex, when legislative inertia plays a role, what impact judging has on legislative incentives, how judicial vs. legislative responsibility can be determined, and how expert a judge may be. The discussion also demonstrates how procedural criteria for allocating lawmaking authority interact with substantive considerations—political controversy often correlates with strong substantive commitments; evidence that legislative inertia has been overcome also suggests a momentum for certain substantive policies; substantive judicial choices often anticipate rather than discourage legislative action; and allocation of lawmaking responsibility is a function of changing substantive values and, by some accounts, of the judge's role in protecting certain values.

Two divergent inferences can be drawn from this indeterminacy and interaction. One can conclude that judging is too political (H. L. A. Hart's "nightmare") and work hard to minimize judicial discretion (as textualists do). Or one can conclude that political judgment is intrinsic to judging—the result of both the need to rely on the judge's competence in adapting statutes to the future and the inevitability of that process once the judge thinks about how to apply a text to the facts. As long as good government requires someone to work out how statutes fit into the future development of the law, judges are often the best people to do it, or at least they are the best to help out in the collaborative lawmaking venture. Specific decisions interpreting a statute can be criticized, but not the general enterprise of judges helping to make law.

THE PAST: MULTIPLE STATUTES

Statutes interact with their past as well as their future. Indeed, some argue that judging is inherently conservative, although they may disagree about whether that is a good idea.[104] The truth is that judges are as properly concerned with a statute's past—its interaction with policies predating its passage—as they are with a statute's dynamic evolution. In both instances, the question of judicial role is the same: how does the judge place the statute in its broader temporal context?

Nineteenth-century statutes often interacted with prior common law, but in the modern setting the statute's past is as likely to be a prior statute (*more* likely at the federal level). Chapter 3 has provided numerous illustrations of how legislation interacted with prior common law, suggesting that as much of a claim on the judge is exercised by the past as by the future. For that reason, the following discussion of how judges take account of a statute's past focuses on prior legislation, not prior common law.

In working out the interaction of a statute with its past, textualists try to dampen judicial discretion by one of two routes. They either rely on a clear later statutory text, even if relying on that language to override prior law would make little policy sense. Or they rely on a clear earlier statutory text that controls how a later law is made, even though such control would prevent the most sensible interpretation of the later legislation. These efforts to deny judicial discretion have proved unavailing, even in some instances for textualist-oriented judges, suggesting once again that judicial discretion in working out the interaction of later law and earlier law is an essential aspect of ordinary judging.

And the reason, once again, is that a text cannot be relied on to make sense of its interaction with its own historical setting—the past as well as the future. We would not want a judge to avoid asking whether prior law is superseded despite what the later statute said any more than we would want the judge to avoid thinking about how the law adapts to its future. Moreover, it is hard for the judge to adopt the tunnel vision needed to avoid this perspective, once application of the text to the facts highlights the problem of overriding prior law.

Later text vs. prior statute

When later law made dramatic changes in the common law, courts often balked. We have been so accustomed to criticizing the judicial preference for prior common law that we tend to reject the judge's inclination to preserve the past in light of later legislation. But preserving the past is as legitimate an enterprise as adapting to the future. Both aspects of judging fall—over a wide range—within the judge's legitimate role in fitting statutes into their temporal setting, and a political judgment to favor the past cannot be ruled out a priori. The discussion in chapter 3 concerning the interaction between statutes and prior common law during the late nineteenth century made that point in discussing statutes dealing with attachment, mechanic's liens, wrongful death, and married women's property. Indeed, late-nineteenth-century commentators never denied that taking account of past law was a legitimate judicial practice, only that prior common law was no *more* privileged than prior statute law. They urged that the old interpretive canon, which presumptively rejected the implied repeal of prior law, should apply equally to both prior common law and legislation. And, on a more modern note, those who rely on American pragmatism to help explain modern judging should recall William James's affirmation of the importance of the past in determining the truth: "[O]ur theory must mediate between all previous truths and certain new experiences. It must derange common sense and previous belief as little as possible. . . ."[105]

Modern textualists would apply the canon against implied repeal of prior legislation in a restrictive fashion, making it hostage to language. A clear later statutory text would preclude the judge from making policy sense of the interaction of a later statute with earlier law. In the most extreme view, clear later texts prevent judicial discretion to decide whether or not later law prevails over a prior statute. Justice Scalia puts it this way: "[W]here . . . the meaning of [a later] term prevents [an] accommodation [between prior and later law], it is not our function to eliminate clearly expressed inconsistency of policy. . . ."[106] He denies that the judicial interpreter can take account of the realities of legislative authorship. "The facile attribution of congressional 'forgetfulness' cannot justify such a [judicial] usurpation [of power]. . . . [T]he attribution of forgetfulness rests in reality upon the judge's assessment that the later statute contains the better disposition. But that is not for judges to prescribe."[107] A more moderate textual approach allows judicial accommodation of two statutes to prefer the *earlier* law when the later law uses a clear but general text that appears to override earlier, more specific statutory language.[108] But that is as far as a textualist judge can go.

In the textualist's view, reasonable guesses about legislative intent or judicial efforts to make policy sense of the interaction of two statutes are off-limits, absent some previously identified linguistic weakness in the later legislation. But courts are not prevented from "mak[ing] sense of the corpus juris"[109] when the later statutory text is "clear"—whether the prior law is statute or common law.

Example 7. An earlier law allocated revenues from oil and gas leases on national wildlife refuges *reserved* from public lands: 90 percent of the revenue to the state and 10 percent to the United States.[110] A *later* law, which was aimed at softening the revenue loss when lands were *acquired* from localities for refuge purposes, allocated revenues from mineral leases on such lands—including revenues from oil and gas leases—in a different way: 25 percent to the country and 75 percent to the United States. But the text of the later law inadvertently applied to wildlife refuges reserved from public lands as well as refuges on land acquired from localities, with the arguably unintentional result of changing the prior statute's allocation formula. The text of the later law was not enforced by the Court to apply to reserved lands in deference to likely legislative intent (evidenced by some legislative history) and a sense of policy coherence (the later law's introduction of a 25 percent share for the county made good sense only for acquired lands, because it compensated counties for acquired land removed from the county's property tax base).

We have in this example what Chief Justice Marshall would have called a matter of "inconvenience" or "political regulation," a mundane issue of ordinary judging, where the court nonetheless helped out the legislature to achieve a sensible result. The Supreme Court might easily have said that the legislature could have been aware of this problem, that a judicial bailout would reduce legislative incentives to be careful in writing laws, and that it was therefore the legislature's responsibility to get it right. But the issue was not technically complex or politically controversial, and the Court took it upon itself to work out a sensible solution.

When the issues are more politically controversial and no one solution takes obvious precedence, a court is more likely to let the clear text of a later law override a prior statute, even when strong evidence suggests that the result indicated by the later statutory text was inadvertent.

Example 8. An earlier statute gave poor working families a subsidy (called an earned income credit). This credit, as a matter of statutory mechanics, was treated as a tax "refund" of an "overpayment" of a percentage of wages.[111] However, the credit was granted even when there was no withheld overpaid tax to refund; that is, even when no "overpayment" occurred, in the colloquial sense. Thus, a taxpayer with $3,000 wages and no tax obligation would get a percentage of the $3,000 as a subsidy for working. The text of a *later* law required prospective refunds of "overpayments" to be turned over by the federal government to a state government, which previously had provided welfare to support the child of a person eligible for the refund. The question was whether this later law applied only to "real" overpayments, where the taxpayer had too much tax withheld, or whether it also applied to the earned income credit that exceeded prior withheld taxes.

The Court insisted that the later statutory text was clear, applying to "refunds" of "overpayments," even when no prior tax was withheld, based on the fact that the earlier earned income credit and the child support repayment rules appeared in two adjacent statutory sections of the Internal Revenue Code. But the two statutes were drafted at different times, and the later law was part of an immensely long statute, written in a very short time. The dissent was probably correct in surmising that the implications of the child support repayment rule for the earned income credit had not been worked out carefully, any more than (in the previous example) the new rules about compensating state and local governments when oil revenue was derived from reserved lands had not been thoughtfully considered.

Nonetheless, the Court's decision was reasonable. The political interests—the needs of poor families and state claims to repayment of prior welfare payments—were in equipoise. Indeed, behind the textualist façade of the majority opinion, the Court implies that the priority of these policies was too close to call, stating that "[t]he ordering of *competing* social policies is a quintessentially legislative function" (emphasis added). In this political environment, the Court's adherence to the text of the later law made sense.

Earlier text vs. later statute

Another way that a statutory text might try to limit judicial discretion in working out the relation of past and future legislation is for an earlier text to control how later law is made. Doctrinally, it is clear that an earlier law cannot control future lawmaking in any formal sense. To do so would entrench prior law, something that violates both the American and English constitutions.[112] For example, a statute specifying that later law can be made only after consideration by a specific legislative committee would not bind later legislatures. But prior law, in effect, binds later law if the prior law adopts a definition of language used in a later law, and the definition controls the meaning of the later legislation.[113] Statutory codes often contain such "Dictionary Acts" in their introductory titles. These definitional statutes usually contain their own escape hatch—binding only if the "context" of the later law does not otherwise "require" or "indicate." But that does not dispose of questions about the binding impact of the prior law's text, if the "context" that the prior law would countenance is narrower than the interpretive criteria the court would consider in interpreting the later law without encumbrance by the earlier definitional statute.

The following extended discussion of a recent case dealing with the U.S. Dictionary Act illustrates how rhetorical deference to textualism mingles with a practice of making policy sense of the interaction of two statutes, further suggesting the inevitability of a discretionary, policy-oriented role for judges when a prior statutory text tries to control later law. The case of Rowland v. California Men's Colony[114] involved the question of whether a prisoners' association could take advantage of a statute allowing poor persons not to pay certain fees in connection with litigation (that is, to proceed *in forma pauperis*). The case is a classic example of mundane ordinary judging, involving a legal issue of relatively minor importance. Moreover, the prisoners' substantive claim—indigent prisoners wanted free smoking tobacco—seemed trivial. But we can learn more about judicial method from cases involving such matters of "inconvenience" than from a single-minded focus on how the courts address more "fundamental" matters.

Two statutes dealt with this issue. The older statute was the Dictionary Act, which defined a "person" for purposes of the U.S. Code, "unless the context [of the statute using the word person] otherwise indicates." This act was originally adopted by Congress in 1871,[115] but its definition of "person" was expanded to include an "association" in 1948. A later statute stated that a poor "person" could litigate *in forma pauperis*. Before 1959, this statute stated that only "citizens" had this privilege; but, in 1959, the "citizen" language was replaced by "person." [116] The issue was how the earlier Dictionary Act's definition of "person" (to include "associations") interacted with the use of the word "person" in the later *in forma pauperis* statute.

All nine judges took a textualist approach to interpreting the interaction of these two laws, or at least they claimed to do so. First, they held that the prior Dictionary Act determined the meaning of later law. The only open question was whether the context of the later statute "indicated" a different meaning, as the prior law permitted.[117] The later law apparently had no independent significance in determining the meaning of "person," outside the boundaries of what prior law allowed. This result is one that a textualist would obviously relish. It relies on a dictionary of the legislature's own making to define language used at a later time; and it avoids looking too closely at what the later statute using the defined term might mean, avoiding questions about the interaction with the earlier statutory definition of the text, purpose, and background of the later law.

But this result is doctrinally odd. No prior statute can mandate later law, and definitional statutes are no exception. Indeed, the Court's holding to this effect in Rowland was contrary to many prior decisions.[118] The occasional prior case to the contrary could be explained on the ground that the definitional statute and the statute in which the defined term appeared were passed at about the same time. The definitional statute was therefore good evidence of linguistic usage extant when the drafting legislature wrote the law.[119]

As a practical matter, discussion of whether the definitional statute is mandatory often can be avoided, because the definitional statute itself contains its own escape hatch — that is, it allows a departure from the Dictionary Act definition if the "context" of the later host statute otherwise indicates. But a potential for conflict between the earlier and later laws remains if the word "context" in the Dictionary Act receives a textualist reading, which is what happened in the Rowland decision. All nine judges agreed that the term "context" in the earlier Dictionary Act meant *textual* context, not the broader context, such as the legislative history or the purposes and policy background of the later law. The justices *explicitly* rejected the inclusion of legislative history as "context." [120] And, in what obviously was question-begging, the Court acknowledged that a broader meaning of "context" than textual context existed, but they stated that, *because this was an act of Congress,* the narrower meaning was more appropriate.[121]

Textualism provided the analytical framework for the analysis by every member of the Court but *not* for the Court's actual decision. Five judges proceeded to interpret the later statute to conclude that the prisoners' association was *not* a "person." The Court relied on practical policy concerns posed by including artificial entities (such as associations) in the meaning of "persons," despite the Dictionary Act's definition of "person" to include an "association." It noted that an affiant must certify the person's poverty to be entitled to *in forma pauperis* status under the statute, that serious problems are involved both in identifying whether the affiant has authority to speak for an entity and in imposing effective penalties on perjury.[122] In addition, applying the "inability to pay" standard to artificial entities was extremely difficult, both regarding the choice of insolvency definitions and deciding when to pierce the entity's veil to consider the owners' or members' economic condition.

The Court claimed that its analysis relied on the internal textual context of the later law, as the prior Dictionary Act allowed, but it had in fact lost all touch with the text of the later statute, appealing to what the dissent called "classic policy considerations" [123] and "look[ing] beyond the words of [the] statute . . . to consider the policy judgments on which those words may or may not be based." [124] This approach makes sense, of course, if the broader *nontextual* context of the later statute had been thrown into the balance to work out the interaction of earlier and later legislation. But it does not adhere to the textualist framework that the majority claimed for its analysis, which insisted that the text of the prior Dictionary Act controlled the meaning of the later statute.[125]

Why was the reality of statutory interpretation, as opposed to its rhetoric, cut loose from the textualist moorings provided by the earlier statutory definition? Why did the Court fail to stick to its textualist guns in this case involving matters of mere inconvenience, a prisoner's right to proceed *in forma pauperis?* The Court, clearly, was not tilting an interpretation to favor a group disadvantaged in the legislative process; if the legislature was likely to disadvantage anyone, it would probably have been the prisoners who wanted free smoking tobacco, and they lost the lawsuit. Moreover, the legislature could have known about the earlier law (the Dictionary Act) if it had paid attention when it changed the statutory text from "citizen" to "person," and judicial failure to adhere to the earlier definition deprives the legislature of an incentive to be more careful in writing legislation. The judges surely could have left this mundane issue to the legislature to be worked out in accordance with its preferences. What judicial imperative took the Court beyond the text to reach a sensible result?

The answer is apparent once we recall the three ways that earlier law can influence the meaning of later law. First, prior law might prevail as a matter of legislative intent because the later legislature might actually take account of prior law when it writes a later statute. But that inference often rests on a fanciful portrayal of how legislative drafters work. Second, the earlier law might be binding because earlier law is binding. But that is bad constitutional law.

Third, rather than struggle to find reasons to rely on the earlier law, a court might go in the other direction—that is, disregard it when interpreting a later statute. But if courts cannot treat prior law as binding, neither are they willing to disregard it. The earlier statute is, after all, a law passed by the legislature, and it should be entitled to some weight in making sense of the interaction between earlier and later legislation,[126] just as prior common law is entitled to some weight in determining the meaning of a later statute. And it is this process of integrating past and present in accordance with the weight of the earlier and later laws that opens the door to discretionary judging by taking some account of prior law. The earlier law is neither dispositive nor irrelevant. And the only way to work out the interaction is for the judge to consider the values embodied in the two laws, without insisting on the letter of either the later or earlier statute. The past, like the future, stakes a claim on judicial choice.

For example, in the Rowland case, the thought processes working out the interaction of the earlier Dictionary Act and the later *in forma pauperis* law probably developed in the following way. Earlier Dictionary Acts serve important functions as stabilizing default rules for legislatures and lawyers who pay attention to the statute book, and they should not be lightly regarded, absent strong policy reasons favoring a different meaning when a defined term crops up in a later law. In Rowland, however, the practical problems of determining when an association is "poor" were sufficiently weighty to overcome the prior definition, especially in light of legislative history indicating that the text had been changed from "citizen" to "person" to make aliens eligible to litigate *in forma pauperis*. These problems and the relevant legislative history were not part of the later law's "textual context," but they still weakened the gravitational pull of the prior statute in the interpretive mix of prior and later law. Consequently, although the court would not disregard the indications of the prior text, ordinary judging in this case chose later law over earlier law.

Conclusion

The search for a theory that would sustain a judicial lawmaking role in statutory interpretation started with history rather than contemporary theory because no theory can sustain itself unless it is linked to the historical legal culture in which it arose. That legal history highlighted the importance of institutional competence rather than legitimacy in deciding how judges should interpret statutes,[127] and it led to the conclusion that "ordinary judging" was the best way to justify the judge's collaborative role in determining statutory meaning. More specifically, the judge is uniquely competent to place statutes in their temporal setting, taking account of what happens both before and after a statute is passed. Moreover, the exercise of this competence inevitably results from applying texts to facts, an exercise that forces the judge to think about how a text's meaning interacts with the past and the future (about the statute's intent). Once this thought process begins, judgment requires thinking about substantive values and comparative institutional competence; however, these are the results of ordinary judging, not a foundation for its exercise. Ordinary judging, so understood, has survived the pre-twentieth-century judicial arrogance that historically elevated the common law over legislation, and the twentieth-century reaction, which threatened to undermine a judicial lawmaking role by exposing its political content. It is often accompanied by a sense of political savvy among judges (probably more so at the state level than at the federal). It has proved to be a robust if mundane activity.

In historical perspective, this is what happened. In the old view, statutes were identified as static, isolated, and sterile pronouncements, and the common law was viewed as the creative and evolving source of law. In such a setting, judges (as the expositors of the common law) dominated lawmaking. Hence, the common view that statutes in derogation of common law should be narrowly construed and that detailed statutes were static, incapable of adaptation to the future. By the twentieth century the source of creative and evolving law had been transferred from judging to legislation, supporting an active judicial role only in the guise of elaborating legislative purpose. When modern critiques of legislation revived the view of statutes as sterile pronouncements without restoring a robust judicial lawmaking role, that apparently left judges without much to do; or that, at least, was the modern textualist's position.

But another perspective on law, legislating, and judging suits the modern legal world of increased skepticism about government. The creative and evolving image of the law remains as an ideal, no longer confidently located in either legislating or judging, but persisting in the collaborative efforts of both legislatures and judges. In that environment, judicial lawmaking dominance is out of the question, but so is a sterile image of judging. A modest confidence in ordinary judging survives as the best way to explain the collaborative judicial role in statutory interpretation. In this conception of the law, statutes are neither static nor innocent of their past, and judges can help legislatures make law.

Those who urge that ordinary judging implies a judicial lawmaking responsibility in statutory interpretation are often put on the defensive by the example of Humpty-Dumpty, who tells Alice that a word "means just what I choose it to mean. . . . The question is . . . which is to be master—that's all." [128] This view reduces disputes over meaning to raw political power, questioning the legitimacy of pervasive judicial discretion. But the greater danger is the judge as Pontius Pilate, washing his hands of responsibility for making decisions.

Judges, of course, may get the answer wrong. At times, judges do too much; at times, too little. "Law, even statutory construction, is not a science. It is merely an effort by human beings, albeit judges, to do their best with imperfect tools to arrive at a correct result." [129] But the judges' job is to work out the relationship of specific statements of law (whether from common law decisions or statutes) to the broader fabric of the law, sensitive to the institutional competence of various lawmaking institutions. Statutory interpretation has always been less about what the statutory words mean, or even what the statute means, than about who should decide what issues and when.

Appendix A
Legislative History: Competence or Legitimacy?

The contemporary dispute over the judicial use of legislative history focuses on legitimacy, that is, the questioning of the link between legislative history and either the statutory text or legislative intent. Because the only text with legal status is the statute itself, passed by the legislature and signed by the executive,[1] legislative history should not be used to determine what the statute means. And because the drafters of the legislative history are not the legislature, their intent cannot equate with legislative intent.

There are some qualifications to this broad rejection of legislative history on legitimacy grounds. First, if the history helps the interpreter understand the way in which language is used, then it is legitimately useful, just like any other contextual evidence of linguistic usage.[2] Second, legislative history is not an illegitimate source of nondispositive evidence about legislative purpose, although its competence as evidence of purpose may be questioned; and the judge's use of legislative purpose to interpret statutes may raise legitimacy issues, whether the evidence of purpose comes from legislative history or any other historical materials.

The critical legitimacy concern regarding the use of legislative history arises when the judge relies on statements about *specific* legislative intent. For example, suppose the text of a statute with the purpose of preventing manual laborers from entering the United States also appears to prevent pastors from coming into the country, but the legislative history specifically states that pastors can immigrate.[3] When a court relies on such statements about specific legislative intent to interpret the statute, the legislative history sets up a rival text to the statutory text, and that conflict raises legitimacy concerns.

The scope of this objection should not be understated. It applies whether the statutory text is unclear or clear. Sometimes the argument goes that legislative history is more properly used when the statutory text is unclear, but the legitimacy objection cannot be so limited. If the concern is that legislative history is an illegitimate text establishing specific legislative intent, then the objection applies whether or not the statutory language is uncertain.

One way to defend the use of legislative history is a tribute to the tenacity of legitimacy analysis, but it will not work. Legislative history sometimes is said to shed light on legislative intent, which gives it a legitimate pedigree traceable to the legislature itself. This claim, however, is spurious. First, legislative history is rarely a genuine part of the context on which legislators base their votes, especially with regard to details for which courts often cite the legislative history. Second, the hope that authors of legislative history reflect the views of the parent chamber is often ephemeral. Many (though not all) committees consist of legislators with positions more extreme than the parent body (so-called "outliers").[4] Third, although legislative committees (which write most legislative history) are in fact agents of the legislative body,[5] the fact that a committee may be the agent of the legislature does not overcome the legitimacy objection to judicial reliance on that agency relationship.

The proper response to legitimacy-based objections to using legislative history is to note that courts do *not* treat legislative history as binding. If they did, then the objection that courts are setting up legislative history as a rival to the statutory text would be persuasive. But courts only treat statements in legislative history as one factor in the interpretive mix. The Constitution only forbids mandating law through legislative history, not using it as one among many factors to determine statutory meaning. Consequently, the INS v. Chadha decision,[6] which prohibited making law through a process short of passing a statute (specifically, through a legislative veto of executive action), is irrelevant to the debate over legislative history.

This does not mean that judicial reliance on legislative history is uncontroversial, but the problems concern comparative institutional competence. A lot of legislative history might not fare well as a competent source of statutory meaning. A major problem is that the process of creating legislative history might be politically manipulative, even more so than the process of writing and passing a legislative text. As Bruce Ackerman and William Hassler explain,[7] advocates of a political position may salt legislative history with statements that might be too weak to pass as legislation or, at least, are too politically controversial to run the risk of being put to an explicit vote.

But when measured by competence criteria, legislative history is not all that bad. The process by which legislative history is created often contains checks that reduce the problem of political manipulation. It is hard to sneak through one-sided legislative history on a contentious political issue. An Ackerman and Hassler story about legislative history suggests as much. Their example involves House conferees in a conference committee trying to achieve a political result opposed by the Senate. But Senate conferees introduced their own legislative history that contradicted the House view, producing a stalemate. Rival neutralizing legislative history is probably common on politically controversial issues, minimizing the chance that history will distort the legal result.[8] Moreover, statutory texts as well as legislative history can be manipulated to confuse legislators when they vote on statutory language.[9]

Focusing on the potential for political abuse of legislative history also fails to give a complete picture of the advantages of its judicial use. Some political uses of legislative history are not manipulative at all. First, it is sometimes too hard to agree on a firm all-or-nothing position, but legislative history can express a preference for one view unless circumstances identified on a case-by-case basis strongly favor a different result. Justice Stephen Breyer recounts an example.[10] The issue was whether a provision of federal law preempted state law. The bill dealt with federal aid to states for urban mass transit and provided that the state had to protect the interests of employees affected by transit funding. Unambiguous and uncontested legislative history said that the "employee protection" provision did not preempt state law. Although the "employee protection" rule was controversial in Congress, the "no preemption" legislative history was not. So why not put the "no preemption" language explicitly into the statutory text? Because stating the guiding principle in legislative history left room for the occasional judicial exception as the court encountered specific cases.

Second, when uncertainty arises about how best to apply a general rule to specific cases, it sometimes makes better sense for the legislature to suggest the answer in legislative history. Overburdening the statute with specific detail might produce a virtually incomprehensible text rather than a clear expression of legislative intent.

Third, in some political settings, an attempt to force legislative agreement on specific statutory language, rather than resolving the issue in legislative history, might doom an entire bill. It might reopen the full text to amendment, either within a committee or on the floor of Congress (perhaps inviting a filibuster in the Senate), resulting in political stalemate.

Fourth, *later* legislative history—that is, comments made in committee reports postdating adoption of a statute—also may be a good guide to statutory meaning, even if it does not accompany passage of the law. As long as the entire meaning of a statute is not fixed at birth, its meaning can evolve, and it is appropriate (though not mandatory) for a court to seek clues to that evolution from later legislative history.[11]

Under these circumstances, using legislative history to resolve certain issues is not political manipulation but political accommodation. Although the possibility remains that unchallenged legislative history on a politically controversial issue will sneak through, that is no reason for rejecting legislative history out of hand.

Moreover, lawmaking competence must be gauged from the perspective of the entire lawmaking system. Competence is comparative. If the judge rejects legislative history, on what does he rely? First, judges lack the expertise to resolve many questions confidently, and their reliance on legislative history often can provide suitable answers. Second, when legislative history is compared to other interpretive criteria, such as substantive canons, it is far from clear which criteria as a general matter should be preferred. Third, if the public audience for a law relies on legislative history, it is hard to argue that judicial reliance on such history works badly. Rule-of-law considerations, which often favor deferring to the statutory text on grounds that it provides notice to the affected public, would favor reliance on legislative history in areas of law in which such history is routinely consulted.

A comparative institutional perspective also goes a long way toward defusing the objections to the role of staff in writing legislative history. The legitimacy argument emphasizes that staff are unelected and that "routine deference to the detail of committee reports, and the predictable expansion in that detail which routine deference has produced, are converting a system of judicial construction into a system of committee-staff prescription."[12] But objections to staff-written legislative history do not add much to the objections to legislative history from committee sources. The fact is that *statutes* are also a committee-staff product. Committees operate as minibureaucracies that require staff to play a significant role. And although staff are not elected, they respond to the elected officials for whom they work, submitting their work for review, and relying on their own ability to second-guess their superiors' wishes most of the time. As unelected officials unprotected by civil service tenure, they must realize that they cannot get away with more than one mistake.[13]

More fundamentally, from the perspective of the competence of the overall law-making process, advantages are evident in judicial reliance on staff-written legislative history. Staff are experts. Some legislative detail may not be spelled out adequately in the text, and explanations by the staff may fill that gap. They are similar to agency regulations, although they lack the procedural advantages provided by public notice and comment.

Competence analysis of judicial use of legislative history also provides a good way for courts to decide whether to defer to agency rules or to legislative history. From a perspective of competence, agency rules are often preferable,[14] having gone through a process in which the public receives notice and an opportunity to be heard.[15] Legitimacy analysis, if it successfully equates legislative history with legislative intent, threatens to shunt an agency rule aside as weaker evidence of what the legislature wanted.

In sum, legislative history has political uses as well as abuses, and efforts to delegitimize judicial reliance on legislative history result from the same kind of exaggeration that affects most debates over the judicial role in statutory interpretation. Some legislative history is competent and some is not. Judges will not always get it right, but that is no more true of legislative history than other criteria of statutory meaning, such as text, purpose, and background considerations.

NOTES

1   Matter of Sinclair, 870 F.2d 1340, 1343 (7th Cir. 1989) (Easterbrook, J.) ("Statutes are law, not evidence of law"); Wisconsin Public Intervenor v. Mortier, 501 U.S. 597, 621 (1991) (Scalia, J., concurring in the judgment) ("[W]e are a Government of laws, not of committee reports").

2   Matter of Sinclair, 870 F.2d 1340, 1341–43 (7th Cir. 1989).

3   This example is based on Holy Trinity v. United States, 143 U.S. 457, 459, 464–65 (1892), where the statutory text seemed to prevent pastors from coming to the United States, but there was no specific legislative history of the kind mentioned in my hypothetical example.

4   See Keith Krehbiel, "Are Congressional Committees Composed of Preference Outliers?" 84 *Amer. Pol. Sci. Rev.* 149 (1990).

5   See SEC v. Robert Collier & Co., 76 F.2d 939, 941 (2d Cir. 1935).

6   462 U.S. 919 (1983).

7   See Bruce Ackerman and William Hassler, "Beyond the New Deal: Coal and the Clean Air Act," 89 *Yale L. J.* 1466, 1505–11 (1980).

8 See e.g., Landgraf v. USI Film Products, 511 U.S. 244, 262–63 n.15 (1994) (retroactivity of the Civil Rights Act of 1991); International Brotherhood of Electrical Workers v. NLRB, 814 F.2d 697, 701–2 (D.C. Cir. 1987) (debate over extending the National Labor Relations Act to employees of nonprofit health care employers).

9 Arthur Maass reports an example regarding the 1977 Clean Air Act amendments in *Congress and the Common Good*, pp. 115–16 (1983). The House in 1977 undertook to repeal the Environmental Protection Agency's authority to require reduction of air pollution in major cities by restricting parking facilities through what is known as "indirect source review." The Senate committee, however, had a different view. Senate staffers did two things. They inserted language into the conference report that apparently supported opposition to EPA authority, stating that "the administrator would be prohibited outright from requiring indirect source review, either directly or indirectly." But they wrote language into the statute that left the door open on parking regulation and, therefore, did not match the legislative intent stated in the conference report. When this issue arose in a case, Manchester Environmental Coalition v. EPA, 612 F.2d 56, 59–61 (2d Cir. 1979), the court followed the statutory language despite the legislative history's contrary implication. Devotion to the statutory text over the legislative history in this case could *not* be characterized as judicial protection of the legislative process from manipulation.

10 Stephen Breyer, "On the Uses of Legislative History in Interpreting Statutes," 65 *S. Cal. L. Rev.* 845, 857–61 (1992).

11 See, generally, James Brudney, "Congressional Commentary on Judicial Interpretations of Statutes: Idle Chatter or Telling Response?" 93 *Mich. L. Rev.* 1 (1994).

12 Hirschey v. FERC, 777 F.2d 1, 8 (D.C. Cir. 1985) (Scalia, J., concurring). See also Matter of Sinclair, 870 F.2d 1340, 1343 (7th Cir. 1989) (Judge Easterbrook) ("legislative history is a poor guide to legislators' intent because it is written by the staff rather than by members of Congress"); Blanchard v. Bergerson, 489 U.S. 87, 98 (1989) (Scalia, J., concurring in part and concurring in the judgment) (reports are written by, at best, staff and, at worst, lobbyists). See also Report to the Attorney General, *Using and Misusing Legislative History: A Re-evaluation of the Status of Legislative History in Statutory Interpretation*, pp. 15, 55 n. 223, and 56 (U.S. Dept. of Justice, 1989).

13 See David Farber and Philip Frickey, "Legislative Intent and Public Choice," 74 *Va. L. Rev.* 423, 437–42 (1988) (discussing a charge that the staff ran amok and arguing that Justice Scalia's example of staff independence in creating legislative history is misperceived).

14 See United States v. Shreveport Grain & Elevator Co., 287 U.S. 77, 84 (1932) (preferring agency regulation to legislative history, but emphasizing that regulation was contemporaneous with passage of the statute).

15 Judicial deference to agency rules is also best resolved by competence rather than by legitimacy analysis, although courts have varied in their approaches. In the late

nineteenth century the increasing use of agencies to make law produced a challenge to their legitimacy, which was eventually rejected by the Supreme Court. See Verkuil, "The Emerging Concept of Administrative Procedure," 78 *Colum. L. Rev.* 258, 262–64 (1978) (early twentieth-century Supreme Court decisions legitimized administrative lawmaking).

A tenuous link to legitimacy was still maintained by requiring that legislative delegation to the agency contain some standards, however uncertain. But the judicial approach to sustaining agency rules was based on the decision-maker's competence. See, e.g., Skidmore v. Swift & Co., 323 U.S. 134, 140 (1944) ("the thoroughness evident in its consideration, the validity of its reasoning, its consistency with earlier and later pronouncements, and all those factors which give it power to persuade, if lacking power to control"). Among the competence criteria that courts have considered over the years were political responsiveness of the agency; public participation in agency proceedings; the rationality of the agency's reasoning process; agency expertise in dealing with technical problems; agency "bias"; the importance of obtaining a legislative (rather than an agency) decision on certain issues; and the importance of protecting persons from serious harm.

More recently, the Supreme Court appears to have reverted to a legitimacy approach, but one that now favors rather than disfavors agency rule-making. As long as Congress has given an agency the task of addressing a problem but has not expressed its intent clearly (as determined by traditional tools of statutory construction), *any* reasonable agency resolution will be sustained on the theory that the agency is acting under legislative authority. Chevron, U.S.A., Inc. v. Natural Resources Defense Council, Inc., 467 U.S. 837 (1984). In fact, the application of the Chevron doctrine has probably reverted to an institutional competence approach, implicitly or explicitly considering the competence criteria that had previously been favored. First, this application of the institutional competence approach can occur explicitly under the second branch of the Chevron test, which is that the agency rule must be "reasonable." Courts have little trouble reaching the "reasonableness" test, given the difficulty in agreeing whether Congress has clearly expressed its intent. See, e.g., Regions Hospital v. Shalala, 118 S.Ct. 909 (1998) (majority and dissent disagree whether the text is clear). Second, competence considerations also influence the court's decision to give less (though some) deference to agency decisions that are not issued after public notice and comment because inadequate public participation reduces the quality of agency rule-making. See Reno v. Koray, 515 U.S. 50, 61 (1995) ("But [the Bureau's] internal agency guideline, which is akin to an 'interpretive rule' that 'do[es] not require notice-and-comment,' is still entitled to some deference since it is a 'permissible construction of the statute'"). See, generally, Cass Sunstein, "Law and Administration After Chevron," 90 *Colum. L. Rev.* 2071 (1990); Richard Pierce, "The Supreme Court's New Hypertextualism," 95 *Colum. L. Rev.* 749 (1995).

Appendix B
Inferring a Private Cause of Action—Competence or Legitimacy?

The rivalry between legitimacy and competence analysis is a pervasive theme in the recent dispute over how courts should decide whether to infer private causes of action from statutes which do not explicitly provide them. There is an old principle of law that every right has a remedy, which comes from an age when statutes often did little more than identify a legal wrong, leaving it to the common law to supply a remedy.[1] But the courts extended this approach to infer a private cause of action even when the statute already provided specific (often administrative) remedies.[2]

The Court has recently retreated from an expansive inference of private remedies, first adopting a four-part test which imposed some limits on inferring a private cause of action,[3] and then shifting to a legislative intent test.[4] The "intent" test made it very difficult to infer a remedy, given silence in the legislative history about available remedies.

The analytical framework for this evolution in the law of remedies has been hotly disputed, some relying on legitimacy arguments and others on competence concerns. Some judges argued that it is illegitimate for judges to infer causes of action not provided in the statute. Justice Lewis Powell put it most forthrightly in his dissent in Cannon v. University of Chicago,[5] where he stated that the Article III judicial power did not include the power to imply private causes of action from silent statutes (a legitimacy claim). Justice Stevens took a very different view of the legitimacy issue, stressing that conservative judges of an earlier stripe were quite comfortable with inferring causes of action when the statute was silent.[6]

However, many judges have been willing to go along with the change in judicial approach based, not on legitimacy concerns, but on concerns about comparative institutional competence. Inferring private remedies now seems likely to require difficult judgments about the complexities of enforcement,[7] often beyond what judges can reliably determine. Even Justice Stevens has been wary of inferring remedies because of the impact on an expanding federal judicial workload: "The increased complexity of federal legislation and the increased volume of federal litigation strongly supported the desirability of a more careful scrutiny of legislative intent than [an earlier case] had required";[8] and "a Court that is properly concerned about the burdens imposed upon the federal judiciary . . . has been more and more reluctant to open the courthouse door to the injured citizen."[9]

NOTES

1 Sedgwick, pp. 74–76.

2 See Rosado v. Wyman, 397 U.S. 397, 420–21 (1970) (welfare recipients can obtain an injunction against the state that violated conditions of a federal grant-in-aid; federal cutoff of funds is not the exclusive remedy); Cannon v. University of Chicago, 441 U.S. 677 (1979) (injunction against the university for gender dis-

crimination in violation of federal grant-in-aid conditions); Merrill Lynch, Pierce, Fenner & Smith, Inc. v. Curran, 456 U.S. 353, 365 (1982) (the securities' laws supported a damage claim by the injured private parties, not just lawsuits by the agencies that were explicitly charged with enforcing the statute).

3 Cort v. Ash, 422 U.S. 66, 78 (1975).

4 Middlesex County Sewerage Authority v. National Sea Clammers Assn., 453 U.S. 1, 25 (1981) (Stevens, J., concurring in the judgment in part and dissenting in part) ("The touchstone now is legislative intent"); Merrill Lynch, Pierce, Fenner & Smith, Inc. v. Curran, 456 U.S. 353, 388 (1982) (Stevens, J.) ("In view of our construction of the intent of the Legislature there is no need for us to 'trudge through all four of the [Cort v. Ash] factors when the dispositive question of legislative intent has been resolved' ").

5 441 U.S., at 730–31 (Powell, J., dissenting).

6 Middlesex County, 453 U.S. at 23–24 (Stevens, J., concurring in the judgment in part and dissenting in part) ("our truly conservative federal judges . . . readily concluded that it was appropriate to allow private parties who had been injured by a violation of a statute enacted for their special benefit to obtain judicial relief"); Merrill Lynch, 456 U.S. at 375–76. ("Because the Rigsby approach prevailed throughout most of our history, there is no merit to the argument . . . that the judicial recognition of an implied private remedy violates the separation-of-powers doctrine.")

7 Cannon, 441 U.S. at 748–49 (Powell, J., dissenting); Middlesex County, 453 U.S. at 13–14.

8 Merrill Lynch, 456 U.S. at 377.

9 Middlesex, 453 U.S. at 24–25 (Stevens, J., concurring in the judgment in part and dissenting in part).

Notes

Introduction

1 See Erwin Griswold, "The Explosive Growth of Law Through Legislation and the Need for Legislative Scholarship," 20 *Harv. J. on Leg.* 267 (1983); Robert Williams, "Statutory Law in Legal Education: Still Second Class After All These Years," 35 *Mercer L. Rev.* 803 (1984); Antonin Scalia, *A Matter of Interpretation*, 115 (1997).

2 Quoted in Eugene Gerhart, *America's Advocate: Robert H. Jackson*, 86 (1958).

3 The easiest way to gain access to the literature is to read everything written by William N. Eskridge Jr. For starters, see Eskridge, *Dynamic Statutory Interpretation* (1994). See also Guido Calabresi, *A Common Law for the Age of Statutes* (1982); Cass Sunstein, "Interpreting Statutes in the Regulatory State," 103 *Harv. L. Rev.* 405 (1989).

4 See Eskridge, "Dynamic Statutory Interpretation," 135 *U. Pa. L. Rev.* 1479, 1479–80, 1484–85 (1987) (hereafter Eskridge, "Dynamic"); Eskridge, "Public Values in Statutory Interpretation," 137 *U. Pa. L. Rev.* 1007, 1036 (1989) (hereafter Eskridge, "Public Values"). There are occasional sympathetic references in the works cited in this note to interpreting statutes in light of what happened *before* a statute's passage, especially the common law (see, e.g., Eskridge, "Public Values," 1051), but their tenor is largely critical of a judicial commitment to obsolete and establishment values (Eskridge, "Public Values," 1055–61, 1086–91). Arguably, Eskridge's emphasis on dynamic evolution should be taken less as an example of strong foundationalism and more as an attempt to correct for the court's earlier traditionalism and to reject the legitimacy problems in an evolutionary interpretive approach that many see.

5 An emphasis on fundamental values appears in Eskridge, "Public Values," 1008, 1015–16, 1019–36 (constitutional source for values); 1041–42, 1047–48 (Native Americans). Admittedly, the issue is one of emphasis. Eskridge also refers to values of less than fundamental concern (see Eskridge, "Public Values," 1045–46, 1048–49). See also Eskridge and Philip Frickey, "Statutory Interpretation as

Practical Reasoning," 42 *Stan. L. Rev.* 321, 367–71 (1990) (hereafter Eskridge and Frickey, "Practical Reasoning").

6 See Eskridge and Frickey, "Practical Reasoning," 345, 348–53, 364–71, where the authors develop a positive political model which explains the complex set of factors that influence judicial decisions and critique Supreme Court decisions for failing to live up to that model. The authors go on to make a normative argument about the Court's behavior, largely from a dynamic evolutionary perspective; at 371–78.

7 Quoted in David Lieberman, *The Province of Legislation Determined*, 91 (1989).

1 English History

1 The following description of early English legal history relies heavily on Theodore Plucknett, *Statutes and Their Interpretation in the First Half of the Fourteenth Century* (1922) (hereafter Plucknett, *Statutes*); *A Discourse Upon the Exposicion and Understandings of Statutes* (Samuel Thorne, ed., 1942); Charles McIlwain, *The High Court of Parliament and Its Supremacy* (Archon Books, 1962) (1910) (hereafter McIlwain).

2 Aumeye v. Anon., Y.B. 33 & 35, Edward I, 78–82 (approx. 1305 to 1307), reported in Plucknett, *Statutes*, 184. See also Henry Richardson and George Sayles, "The Early Statutes," 50 *Law Quart. Rev.* 540, 545 (1934) (early judges drafted statutes).

3 See Barbara Shapiro, "Codification of the Laws in Seventeenth Century England," 1974 *Wis. L. Rev.* 428.

4 See Ash v. Abdy, 36 Eng. Rep. 1014, 1014 (1678) (one member of the House of Lords—Nottingham, sitting as a judge in chancery appeals—claimed to know the meaning of a statute (the Statute of Frauds) because he had proposed the bill).

5 John Dawson, *The Oracles of the Law* 89–90 (1968) (hereafter Dawson).

6 The following Plowden quotations and examples come from Plowden's commentaries on Eyston v. Studd, 75 Eng. Rep. 688, 695–96, 698–99 (K.B. 1574).

7 Partridge v. Strange & Croker, 75 Eng. Rep. 123, 130 (K.B. 1553).

8 Christopher Hatton, *A Treatise Concerning Statutes or Acts of Parliament and the Exposition Thereof*, 30 (1677) (hereafter Hatton). Hatton's work was written between the late 1560s and the late 1570s but published in the seventeenth century. Ian Maclean, *Interpretation and Meaning in the Renaissance: The Case of Law*, 182 (1992) (hereafter Maclean). There is some possibility that Hatton did not, in fact, write the cited treatise. *Dictionary of National Biography*, vol. 9, 162 (Leslie Stephen and Sideny Lee, eds., 1949–50).

9 Samuel Thorne, "The Equity of a Statute and Heydon's Case," 31 *Ill. L. Rev.* 202, 213 (1936) (hereafter Thorne, "Equity").

10 Hatton, 66, 73, and introductory table to his ch. 7.

11 Plowden also is critical of a decision interpreting a statute denying the benefit of clergy (which prevented execution) whenever "horses" were stolen so that it did not apply to stealing *one* horse. He notes that this interpretation, neglecting "equity," forced a legislative change to explicitly deny benefit of clergy for stealing one horse. 75 Eng. Rep. at 699.

12 Hatton, 32–34, 42, and 51–53. Another example seems more ambitious, extending a statute specifying the Bishop of Norwich to apply to *all* bishops because such an extension was conducive to the "publick good." Hatton, 40–41.

13 Thorne, "Equity," 202, 210. The Landis reference is to his article, "Statutes and the Sources of Law," *Harvard Legal Essays*, 213 (1934).

14 Thorne, "Equity," 210.

15 76 Eng. Rep. 809, 815–16 (1601).

16 Quoted in McIlwain, 260.

17 Quoted in Hans Baade, "The *Casus Omissus:* A Pre-History of Statutory Analogy," 20 *Syr. J. Intl. Law & Comm.* 45, 84–85 (1994) (hereafter Baade).

18 Quoted in Baade, 76, from the decision in Sheffield v. Ratcliffe.

19 Sir William Holdsworth, *A History of English Law*, vol. 4, 467, 472–73 (1924) (hereafter Holdsworth). See also David Lieberman, *The Province of Legislation Determined*, 53 (1989) (hereafter Lieberman, *Province*) (lawyers get around Statutes of Uses).

20 Arthur Corbin, *On Contracts*, vol. 2, ch. 12, sec. 277, 17–18 (1950).

21 Holdsworth, vol. 6, 387–94. See also Simon v. Metivier, 96 Eng. Rep. 347, 347 (K.B. 1766) ("The key to the construction of the Act is the intent of the Legislature; and therefore many cases, though seemingly within the letter, have been let out of it," both in law and equity courts, where the rule is the same).

22 Quoted in Samuel Thorne, "Dr. Bonham's Case," 54 *Law Quart. Rev.* 543, 544 (1938) (hereafter Thorne, "Bonham").

23 Coke, generally concerned with the widespread potential for judicial corruption at this time, advocated replacing the system of judicial fees with salaries. Donald Veall, *The Popular Movement for Law Reform, 1640-1660*, 68 (1970).

24 Thorne, "Bonham," 544–45, 548. For the contrary view of the sixteenth-century significance of Bonham's Case, see Barbara Black, "The Constitution of Empire: The Case for the Colonists," 124 *U. Pa. L. Rev.* 1157, 1207–8 (1976). See also Theodore Plucknett, "Bonham's Case and Judicial Review," 40 *Harv. L. Rev.* 30, 34 (1926) (hereafter Plucknett, "Bonham").

25 See Catherine Drinker Bowen, *The Lion and the Throne*, 20–21, 483–504 (1956) (hereafter Bowen).

26 Cited in Gerald Postema, *Bentham and the Common Law Tradition*, 30–31 n. 65 (1986) (hereafter Postema) ("Then the king said, that he thought the law was founded upon reason, and that he and others had reason as well as the judges: to which it was answered by me, that true it was, that God had endowed his Majesty with excellent science, and great endowments of nature; but his Majesty

was not learned in the laws of his realm of England, and causes which concern the life, or inheritance, or goods, or fortunes of his subjects are not to be decided by natural reason, but by the artificial reason and judgment of law, which law is an act which requires long study and experience before that a man can attain to the knowledge of it"). See also Bowen, 304–5, 316.

27 See Henry Hallam, *The Constitutional History of England*, vol. 1, 335 n. (Garland Pub. Co., 1978) (1846) (hereafter Hallam).

28 Hallam, 441.

29 Coke never spoke of Parliament as a legislature, only as a court declaring law. W. Ivor Jennings, *The Law and the Constitution*, 321 (5th ed., 1959).

30 Even when statutes were deemed to provide an exclusive remedy, they were viewed against a common law background. For example, many statutes enacted remedies not available at common law. Courts could (if they wanted) preserve the common law by finding that remedies supplemented rather than displaced it. A famous example concerns the eighteenth-century dispute over whether a statutory remedy for copyright violation eliminated common law remedies. In Millar v. Taylor, 98 Eng. Rep. 201 (K.B.) (1769), the court held that the statutory remedy did *not* preclude common law remedies. In the parlance of the day, this statute in derogation of the common law was not extended to preclude application of common law remedies. When the House of Lords reversed this decision, Donaldson v. Beckett, 98 Eng. Rep. 257 (1774), it did so on the ground that no natural law copyright protection existed and that therefore the statute displaced the common law. See Lieberman, *Province*, 97.

31 Quoted in Baade, 84.

32 Colehan v. Cooke, 125 Eng. Rep. 1231, 1233 (1742).

33 Baade, 89.

34 The quotations from Blackstone in these four paragraphs are from William Blackstone, vol. 1, *Commentaries on the Laws of England*, 59–62 (1765) (hereafter Blackstone). See, generally, Albert Alschuler, "Rediscovering Blackstone," 145 *U. Penn. L. Rev.* 1 (1996).

35 Blackstone, vol. 1, 91.

36 Lieberman, *Province*, 18.

37 David Lieberman, "Blackstone's Science of Legislation," 27 *J. Brit. Stud.* 117, 140–41 (1988) (hereafter Lieberman, "Science").

38 James Oldham, *The Mansfield Manuscripts*, vol. 1, 195 (1992) (hereafter Oldham, *Mansfield*).

39 Blackstone, vol. 1, 10.

40 Blackstone, vol. 1, 365.

41 Quoted in Lieberman, *Province*, 61.

42 Blackstone, vol. 1, 10–11. See also Blackstone, vol. 1, 71 ("artificial reason" of old judicial precedent may not be obvious to everybody).

43 Blackstone, vol. 1, 70.

44 Craig Klafter, "The Americanization of Blackstone's *Commentaries*," 44–45, in *Essays on English Law and the American Experience* (1994).

45 Quoted in Lieberman, *Province*, 91.

46 McIlwain, 141. McIlwain reconciles Coke's apparently conflicting views of judicial and legislative power on the ground that it was Parliament's *judicial* powers that were "transcendent" (142–43).

47 See, generally, Lieberman, *Province*, 222–36. Thomas Hobbes is probably the first modern political theorist to adopt this view; see McIlwain, 95 (Hobbes's view that only legislative power can make law of the common law). For a similar argument in the United States, see Robert Rantoul, "All Law Must Be Legislation," reprinted in Jamil Zainaldin, *Law in Antebellum Society: Legal Change and Economic Expansion*, 84 (1983).

48 See Baade, 77; McIlwain, 293 (discussing Lord Ellesmere's criticism of common law judges). Some criticism of Mansfield's more creative judicial efforts accused him of behaving like an equity judge rather than the more constrained judge of the King's Bench, which he was. See Oldham, *Mansfield*, vol. 2, 1240.

49 Lieberman, *Province*, 55. See also Plucknett, "Bonham," 57–58 (eighteenth-century judges "treat[ed] statutes with scant respect, but without giving any constitutional justification . . ."; Statutes of Frauds is an example).

50 Charles Haines, *The American Doctrine of Judicial Supremacy*, 36 (1959).

51 Postema, 25–26.

52 Blackstone, vol. 1, 70–71.

53 See John Miller, "Crown, Parliament, and the People," in *Liberty Secured? Britain Before and After 1688*, 80–84 (J. R. Jones, ed., 1992). See also Lieberman, "Science," p. 132; Michael Lobban, "Blackstone and the Science of Law," 30 *The Historical J.* 311, 326 (1987).

54 Richard Posner, "Blackstone and Bentham," 19 *J. Law and Econ.* 569, 585 (1976).

55 Baade, 90.

56 John Reid, "Another Origin of Judicial Review: The Constitutional Crisis of 1776 and the Need for a Dernier Judge," 64 *N.Y.U. L. Rev.* 963, 971–72 (1989).

57 Blackstone, vol. 1, 63.

58 Blackstone, vol. I, 87–88.

59 See also Lieberman, "Science," 121 (Blackstone wrote for future lawyers and educated laymen). See also David Lockmiller, *Sir William Blackstone*, 47–48 (1938) (hereafter Lockmiller) ("[T]he laws of England should be taught to all Englishmen and not merely to the few who wished to become professional lawyers").

60 Oldham, *Mansfield*, vol. 2, 1353–55 (Mansfield's judicial modification of this ancient rule).

61 James Oldham, "From Blackstone to Bentham: Common Law Versus Legislation in Eighteenth-Century Britain," 89 *Mich. L. Rev.* 1637, 1649–50 (1991). See also Lockmiller, 112–114.

62 Oldham, *Mansfield*, vol. 1, 199.

63 Blackstone, vol. 1, 70.

64 Blackstone, vol. 1, 91.

65 Blackstone, vol. 1, 61.

66 Blackstone, vol. 1, 89.

67 W. J. Jones, *Politics and the Bench*, 47 (1971) (hereafter Jones).

68 W. R. Cornish and G. de N. Clark, *Law and Society in England: 1750–1950*, 48 (1989) (hereafter Cornish and Clark).

69 Cornish and Clark, 10.

70 Daniel Duman, *The Judicial Bench in England: 1727–1875*, 1 (1982) (hereafter Duman).

71 Duman, 21. See Supreme Court of Judicature Act, 1873, ch. 66, sec. 9 (Eng.).

72 Duman, 17.

73 Duman, 43.

74 Duman, 45.

75 Duman, 78–80, 84–88. To this day, the Lord Chancellor is head of the judiciary, a member of the cabinet, and a member of Parliament, who sometimes sits with the law lords. See, e.g., Pepper v. Hart [1993] 1 All E.R. 42 (H.L.) (Lord Chancellor Mackay).

76 Lockmiller, 88–89, 108.

77 Mansfield, vol. 1, 16, 22, 33–35. This eighteenth-century pattern continued that of the sixteenth and seventeenth centuries. Lord Coke certainly moved easily between what we would call the executive, legislative, and judicial branches (1592 —solicitor general; 1594—attorney general; 1606-16—chief justice of common pleas and then chief justice of the King's Bench; 1621-28—member of Parliament); see Samuel Thorne, *Sir Edward Coke*, p. 4 (1957). This confluence of lawmaking activity might help to explain how Coke's theoretical view that Parliament had "transcendent and absolute" power (McIlwain, 141) could coexist with his bold assertions of judicial power to decide whether a statute that violated common right or reason could survive (in Bonham's Case). See also Jones, 47 (committees of the House of Commons often met at the Inns of Court in the seventeenth century); 39, 42 ("The [seventeenth-century] bench was associated both with the bar from which it was sprung and with the men who made government policy" in "an age when it was . . . impossible to separate judges from politics").

78 Giles Jacob, *A New Law Dictionary* (8th ed., 1762) (quotation appears under "Statute" heading; no page) (hereafter Jacob's Dictionary). The Jacob's Dictionary was the most-owned law dictionary in eighteenth-century American law libraries (Herbert Johnson, *Imported Eighteenth-Century Law Treatises in American Libraries, 1700-1799*, 61 [1978]), although quantity does not necessarily equate with influence; Donald Lutz, The Relative Influence of European

Writers on Late Eighteenth-Century American Political Thought," 78 *Amer. Pol. Sci. Rev.* 189, 190 (1984).

2   United States: From the Revolution to the Founding

1   The English picture is complicated by the fact that judges could be removed by address of Parliament with consent of the king, although the king's assent was expected from about the mid-eighteenth century. Barbara Black, "Massachusetts and the Judges: Judicial Independence in Perspective," 3 *Law & Hist. Rev.* 101, 105–8 (1985). This removal power was not limited to impeachment grounds. See also Joseph Smith, "An Independent Judiciary: The Colonial Background," 124 *U. Pa. L. Rev.* 1104, 1109–10 (1976).

2   Jamil Zainaldin, *Law in Antebellum Society: Legal Change and Economic Expansion,* 83 (1983). See also Maxwell Bloomfield, *American Lawyers in a Changing Society, 1776–1876,* 57 (1976).

3   Gordon Wood, *The Creation of the American Republic, 1776–1787,* 160–61 (1969) (hereafter Wood).

4   Shannon Stimson, *The American Revolution in the Law,* 49 (1990) (hereafter Stimson); Note, "The Changing Role of the Jury in the Nineteenth Century," 74 *Yale L. J.* 170, 173 (1964).

5   Seminole Tribe of Florida v. Florida, 517 U.S. 44, 161 n. 55 (1996) (Souter, J. dissenting).

6   Wood, 300–301.

7   See Plaut v. Spendthrift Farm, Inc., 514 U.S. 211, 218–23 (1995) (discussing the history of legislative reversal of court judgments).

8   Cynthia Jordan, " 'Old Words' in 'New Circumstances': Language and Leadership in Post-Revolutionary America," 40 *American Quart.* 491, 495 (1988). Some might trace this view of interpretive power to the well-known statement about interpretive discretion by Bishop Hoadly. Benjamin Hoadly, "The Nature of the Kingdom, or Church, of Christ: A Sermon Preached Before the King at the Royal Chapel of St. James, March 31, 1717, Published at His Majesty's Special Command," p. 17 (Portsmouth, N. H.: Peirce, 1802) ("Whoever has an absolute authority to interpret any written or spoken laws; it is he, who is truly the Law giver to all intents and purposes, and not the person who first wrote or spoke them.") But this statement was directed at the interpretation of religious principles, not legal texts. Herbert Vaughan, *From Anne to Victoria,* 62–63 (1931).

9   Wood, 301.

10   Morton Horwitz, *The Transformation of American Law, 1780–1860,* 5 (1977). See also Wood, 304 n. 75 (Jefferson's concern with equitable construction).

11   Wood, 161.

12   Julius Waterman, "Thomas Jefferson and Blackstone's *Commentaries,*" in *Essays*

in the History of Early American Law, 465–67 (David Flaherty, ed., 1969) (hereafter Waterman).

13   Waterman, 459, 462. Jefferson's 1790 and 1814 list of law books for students did, indeed, include Blackstone, but the 1814 list referred to the more "Republican" Tucker edition (460–61).

14   Waterman, 468–69.

15   Wood, 302–3; Edward Corwin, "The Progress of Constitutional Theory Between the Declaration of Independence and the Meeting of the Philadelphia Convention," 30 *Amer. Hist. Rev.* 511, 534 (1924–25) (hereafter Corwin).

16   Thomas Jefferson, *Notes on the State of Virginia*, 123 (1829).

17   Corwin, 514; Charles Haines, *The American Doctrine of Judicial Supremacy*, 70–71 (1959) (hereafter Haines).

18   Aviam Soifer, "The Supreme Judicial Court of Massachusetts and the 1780 Constitution," 214–15, in *The History of the Law in Massachusetts: The Supreme Judicial Court, 1692-1992* (Russell Osgood, ed., 1992); Frank Grinnell, "The Judicial System and the Bar," in *Commonwealth History of Massachusetts*, 38 (Albert Hart, ed., 1930).

19   Haines, 88–121; Wood, 453–63; Leslie Goldstein, "Popular Sovereignty, the Origins of Judicial Review, and the Revival of Unwritten Law," 48 *J. Pol.* 51, 62 (1986).

20   See Stimson, 133–36 (discussing James Wilson).

21   First Continental Congress Declaration and Resolves (1774), in Documents Illustrative of the Formation of the Union of the American States, H.R. Doc. No. 398, 69th Cong., 1st sess., 1, 3 (Charles Tansill, ed., 1927).

22   John Dawson, *The Oracles of the Law*, 376 (1968) (hereafter Dawson).

23   Dawson, 379.

24   Dawson, 376.

25   Dawson, 376–80.

26   G. Edward White, *The American Judicial Tradition*, 43–45 (1988) (judges such as Kent and Story favored the reporting of written opinions as a technique for enhancing judicial authority).

27   The French attitude toward precedent also reflects the differences in legal culture. To the French, insistence on judicial precedent aggrandizes judicial power against legislation. Dawson, 413–14. The usual role of precedent in the common law tradition is to limit judicial authority to remake law. The English House of Lords even froze judicial precedent from 1898 to 1966. Dawson, 92–94.

28   Philip Kurland, "The Rise and Fall of the 'Doctrine' of Separation of Powers," 85 *Mich. L. Rev.* 592, 601 (1986) (goal was "minimalist government").

29   The reference to a council needs some explanation. The states were familiar with "councils" from their colonial experience. The colonial councils were usually appointed by the king on the advice of the colonial governor and often sat as the upper house of the legislature, as the highest court of appeal, and as advisers to

the governor, mixing legislative, executive, and judicial functions. Many early state constitutions provided for councils, which performed a more modest role than their colonial predecessors. They were usually elected by the legislature or people, participated with the governor in making certain decisions, and acted as checks on gubernatorial power.

30 Haines, 255–59 (impeachment proceedings in Ohio and Kentucky for declaring laws unconstitutional).

31 See *Federalist Papers* 79, 403 (Max Beloff, ed., 1987) (hereafter *Federalist*) ("Some [states] have declared that *permanent* salaries should be established for the judges; but the experience has, in some instances, shown that such expressions are not sufficiently definite to preclude legislative evasions.")

32 There is an impression, perhaps traceable to Corwin, 514, that most states had such separation of powers provisions. However, Corwin's cite for this position is to *Federalist*, 47, 248–51, in which Madison explains that state constitutions provide for checks and balances, not separation of powers.

33 Massachusetts Declaration of Rights (1780), art. 30, reprinted in *The Federal and State Constitutions, Colonial Charters, and Other Organic Laws of the United States*, Part 1, 960 (Benjamin Poore, 2d ed., 1878) (hereafter, Poore).

The original proposal at the 1780 Massachusetts convention focused only on judicial independence: "The judicial department of the state ought to be separate from, and independent of, the legislative and executive powers." Another proposed section stated: "In the government of the Commonwealth of Massachusetts, the legislative, executive, and judicial power shall be placed in separate departments, to the end that it might be a government of laws, and not of men." However, without any explanation of which we are aware, the texts of the two proposals were combined and modified to read as above. See *Works of John Adams*, vol. 4, 230 (Charles Adams, 1851). John Adams had drafted the proposals, but he was in France when the final draft was completed. Ellen Brennan, *Plural Office-Holding in Massachusetts, 1760–1780*, 138–42 (1945).

34 New Hampshire Constitution, Bill of Rights, art. 1, sec. 37, Poore, Part 2, 1283 ("In the government of this state, the three essential powers thereof, to wit, the legislative, executive and judicial, ought to be kept as separate from and independent of each other, as the nature of a free government will admit, or as is consistent with that chain of connection that binds the whole fabric of the constitution in one indissoluble bond of union and amity").

35 North Carolina, Declaration of Rights, art. 4 (1776): "That the legislative, executive, and supreme judicial powers of government, ought to be forever separate and distinct from each other." Poore, Part 2, 1409.

Maryland, Declaration of Rights, art. 6 (1776): "That the legislative, executive, and judicial powers of government ought to be forever separate and distinct from each other." Poore, Part 1, 818.

Virginia, Const., 2d para. (1776): "The legislative, executive, and judiciary department, shall be separate and distinct, so that neither exercise the powers properly belonging to the other. . . ." Poore, Part 2, 1910.

Georgia, Const., art. 1 (1777): "The legislative, executive, and judiciary departments shall be separate and distinct, so that neither exercise the powers properly belonging to the other." Poore, Part 1, 378.

36 The proposed text: "The powers delegated by this constitution, are appropriated to the departments to which they are respectively distributed: so that the legislative department shall never exercise the powers vested in the executive or judicial; nor the executive exercise the powers vested in the legislative or judicial; nor the judicial exercise the powers vested in the legislative or executive departments." Gerhard Casper, "An Essay in Separation of Powers: Some Early Versions and Practices," 30 *Wm. & Mary L. Rev.* 211, 221 (1989) (hereafter Casper).

37 Casper, pp. 221–22.

38 See, generally, W. B. Gwyn, *The Meaning of the Separation of Powers* (1965).

39 *Federalist* 78, 396.

40 *Federalist* 78, 399. Hamilton was not alone in his willingness to use the word "discretion" to describe judging. See United States v. The William, 28 Fed. Cases 614, 620 (1808) ("Legal discretion is limited. . . . Political discretion has a far wider range"); James Kent, *Commentaries on American Law*, vol. 1, lecture 20, "Of Statute Law," 421 (DaCapo, 1971) (1826) ("legal discretion").

41 The explanation in this paragraph and the following one relies on Gerald Postema, *Bentham and the Common Law Tradition*, 3–38 (1986) (hereafter Postema).

42 Philip Hamburger, "The Constitution's Accommodation of Social Change," 88 *Mich. L. Rev.* 239, 255 (1989).

43 Quoted in Postema, 6.

44 Gregory Alexander, "Time and Property in the American Republican Legal Culture," 66 *N.Y.U. L. Rev.* 273, 320–21 (1991) (influence on late eighteenth-century American lawyers); Henry May, *The Enlightenment in America,* 346 (1976) (hereafter May); Jay Fliegelman, *Declaring Independence,* 74 (1993) (hereafter Fliegelman) (influence on Jefferson).

45 David Lieberman, *The Province of Legislation Determined,* 165 (1989).

46 One can hear echoes of this view of judging in some of Hamilton's statements in the *Federalist Papers*. See *Federalist* 22, 108, where Hamilton acknowledges the "diversities in the opinions" of judges.

47 William Blackstone, *Commentaries on the Law of England,* vol. 1, 70 (1765) (hereafter Blackstone).

48 May, 346 (Jefferson considered Dugold Stewart, one of the prominent spokesmen for common sense philosophy in America, as "one of the greatest thinkers.").

49 Stimson, 92, 128 (Reid's influence on Jefferson and Wilson).

50 One commentator on Reid asserts that common sense does not leave decision

to the "verdict of the vulgar," but that "[c]ommon sense is like common law" whose "general rule of decision . . . must be left to the jurist." *The Works of Thomas Reid*, vol. 2, 751–52 (William Hamilton, 6th ed., 1863) (hereafter Reid). See also *The Works of James Wilson*, vol. 1, 209 (Robert McCloskey, ed., 1967) (hereafter Wilson) ("common sense is that degree of judgment, which is to be expected in men of common education and common understanding"); Daniel Howe, "The Political Psychology of *The Federalist*," 44 *Wm. & Mary Quart.* 485, 496–97 (1987) (*Federalist Papers* addressed to "judicious part of community," contrasted with the "turbulent" and "short-sighted masses").

51 Fliegelman, 74.

52 Wilson, vol. 1, 377.

53 May, 296.

54 Reid, vol. 1, 421, 423. See also Reid, vol. 2, 674–75; Wilson, vol. 1, 213 (no "real opposition" between common sense and reason); Wilson, vol. 1, 223 ("reason has no other root than the principles of common sense"); Wilson, vol. 1, 394 ("[j]udgment . . . is frequently denominated common sense").

55 Reid, vol. 2, 674.

56 Reid, vol. 2, 676–77.

57 Robert Ferguson, *Law and Letters in American Culture*, 16 (1984).

58 Thomas Gustafson, *Representative Words*, 200 (1992). See also Cynthia Jordan, " 'Old Words' in 'New Circumstances': Language and Leadership in Post-Revolutionary America," 40 *American Quarterly* 491 (1988); Michael Kramer, *Imagining Language in America* (1992); Shannon Stimson, *The American Revolution in the Law* (1990); May.

59 *Federalist* 83, 424.

60 Stimson, 131–36.

61 Stimson, 135.

62 *Federalist* 37, 178. Compare *Federalist* 51, 264 ("each department [executive, legislative, and judiciary] should have a will of its own").

63 Reid, vol. 1, 426.

64 *Federalist* 78, 398.

65 See, generally, James Barry, "The Council of Revision and the Limits of Judicial Power," 56 *U. Chi. L. Rev.* 235 (1989); Alfred Street, *The Council of Revision of the State of New York* (1859).

66 The council originated as a compromise between too much legislative power and too much executive power; a veto on legislation was considered necessary, but a governor veto seemed too monarchical. The solution was to involve judges in the veto process. Council membership included the governor, the chancellor (chief judge for the equity branch of the judiciary), and state supreme court justices. Although some people favored a council of revision to protect judges from legislative encroachment, the council's power clearly extended further to include political policy judgments.

67 *Federalist 78*, 400–401.

68 Some delegates to the Constitutional Convention, including Madison, favored a New York-style council of revision with power to veto legislation, consisting of the "Executive and a convenient number of the National Judiciary" (Resolution 8 of the Virginia Plan proposed to the Constitutional Convention). Max Farrand, *The Records of the Federal Convention of 1787*, vol. 1, 211 (hereafter Farrand). Madison supported the council for four reasons at the convention: first, it gave the judiciary a defense against legislative encroachment; second, it gave "additional confidence" to the executive veto; third, echoing the tradition of artificial reason, legal wisdom would help provide "consistency, conciseness, perspicuity, and technical propriety in the laws"; and, fourth, it was a way of preventing "unwise and unjust measures." Farrand, vol. 2, 74; also at 77 (judicial association with the executive does not violate the maxim that departments "be kept separate and distinct.")

69 Farrand, vol. 1, 97–98. See also vol. 2, 74–75, 78.

70 *The Writings of James Madison*, vol. 8, 406–7 (Gaillard Hunt, ed., 1908).

71 Corwin, 516 (commenting on Jefferson's *Notes on Virginia*). See, generally, Brennan, *Plural Office-Holding*.

72 State of Massachusetts, *Colony to Commonwealth: Documents on the Formation of Its Constitution, 1775–1780*, 79–80 (Robert Taylor, ed., 1961).

73 Blackstone, vol. 1, 58 (warning against letting legislatures interpret the law because that "affords great room for partiality and oppression").

74 Nine states restricted judges from holding at least some legislative office: North Carolina, Const., art. 29 (1776), Poore, Part 2, 1413; Virginia, Const. (1776), Poore, Part 2, 1911; New Jersey, Const., art. 20 (1776), Poore, Part 2, 1313; Delaware, Const., art. 18 (1776), Poore, Part 1, 276; Maryland, Declaration of Rights, art. 30 (1776), Poore, Part 1, 819; Massachusetts, Const., ch. 6, art. 2 (1780), Poore, Part 2, 971–72; New Hampshire, Const. (1784), Poore, Part 2, 1292; New York, Const., art. 25 (1777), Poore, Part 2, 1336; Pennsylvania, Const., sec. 23 (1776), Poore, Part 2, 1545–46. The federal constitution prohibits any officeholder (including judges) from being a member of Congress. U.S. Const., art 1, sec. 6.

75 Akhil Amar, "The Bill of Rights and Our Posterity," 42 *Cleve. St. L. Rev.* 573, 575 (1994).

76 Helen Michael, "The Role of Natural Law in Early American Constitutionalism: Did the Founders Contemplate Judicial Enforcement of 'Unwritten' Individual Rights?" 69 *N.C.L. Rev.* 421, 445 n. 137 (1991).

77 Jared Sparks, *The Life of Gouverneur Morris*, vol. 3, 323 (1832).

78 See, generally, William Nelson, "Changing Conceptions of Judicial Review: The Evolution of Constitutional Theory in the States, 1790–1860," 120 *U. Pa. L. Rev.* 1166 (1972).

79 See the argument for the plaintiff in Robin v. Hardaway (1772), citing Bonham's

Case, reported by Thomas Jefferson, *Reports of Cases Determined in the General Court of Virginia*, 114 (William S. Hein & Co., 1981). Haines cites other examples of judicial reliance on Coke for a power of judicial review; Haines, 63, 148–49, 158, 169. But compare *The Law Practice of Alexander Hamilton*, vol. 1, 284 (Julius Goebel, ed., 1964) (hereafter Hamilton, *Law Practice*) (arguing that Blackstone's *Commentaries* led to abandonment of reliance on Dr. Bonham's Case in the debates over Parliament's right to legislate for the colonies before the Revolution).

80 3 U.S. 386, 388 (1798). Justice Iredell dissented from Chase's view and denied that courts had a power to void statutes on natural justice grounds; 3 U.S. at 398–99. See also Charles Haines, "The Law of Nature in State and Federal Decisions," 25 *Yale L. J.* 617, 625–31 (1916).

81 Haines, 36.

82 1 Bay 93, 98 (S. Car. 1789). This merging of judicial review and statutory interpretation also appeared in an 1816 New York opinion, Gardner v. Village of Newburgh, 2 Johns. ch. 161, 168 (New York, 1816), written by Chancellor Kent. The case held that a statute was unconstitutional and then interpreted it to avoid that result, stating that "it would be unjust, and contrary to the first principles of government, and equally contrary to the intention of this statute, to take [property without compensation]." For a discussion of nineteenth-century courts' inclination to find a statute unconstitutional and then interpret it to avoid that result, see Nagle, "Delaware & Hudson Revisited," 72 *Notre Dame L. Rev.* 1495 (1997).

83 Hamilton, *Law Practice*, vol. 1, 396.

84 Hamilton, *Law Practice*, vol. 1, 415.

85 Stimson, 115–16. See also Haines, 101 (case subject of mass meetings).

86 Hamilton, *Law Practice*, vol. 1, 311.

87 Eskridge, "Textualism, The Unknown Ideal?," book review of Antonin Scalia, *A Matter of Interpretation*, 96 *Mich. L. Rev.* 1509, 1524–26 (1998).

88 1 Virg. (1 Wash.) 341, 352 (Va. 1794).

89 1 Virg. (2 Wash.) 116, 121 (Va. 1795).

90 1 Virg. (2 Wash.) 282, 299 (Va. 1796).

91 1 N.J.L. 224, 225, 227 (1793).

92 1 N.J.L. 246, 247 (1794).

93 See Matter of Erickson, 815 F.2d 1090, 1093 (7th Cir. 1987).

94 Case of Mayo, 2 Yeates 30, 31 (Pa. 1795).

95 *The Debate on the Constitution*, Part 2, Brutus XI, 1/31/1788, 131 (Bernard Bailyn selection 1993) (hereafter Brutus).

96 Brutus, XV, 3/20/1788, 375.

97 Brutus, XII, 2/7/1788 and 2/14/1788, 173.

98 Brutus, XV, 3/20/1788, 372.

99 Calder v. Bull, 3 U.S. 386, 387 (1798).

100   St. George Tucker, Blackstone's *Commentaries,* vol. 1, appendix, 150–54, 423 (1803).

101   *Federalist* 81, 412.

102   *Federalist* 83, 424.

103   *Federalist* 78, 399.

104   *Federalist* 83, 425. See also Madison's contrast between "plain reason, as well as . . . legal axioms" in *Federalist* 40, 197.

105   U.S. Constitution, Amendment 9. See also Joseph Story, *Commentaries on the Constitution of the United States,* 154–55 (Carolina Academic Press, 1987) (specifically cautioning about the use of the *expressio* maxim, Story states: "the natural and obvious sense of its provisions, apart from any technical or artificial rules, is the true criterion of construction").

106   Fliegelman, 48.

107   John Taylor, *Constitution Construed and Constitutions Vindicated,* 21 (1820). Concerning Taylor's criticism of Marshall, see Robert Clinton, "Original Understanding, Legal Realism and the Interpretation of 'This Constitution,' " 72 *Iowa L. Rev.* 1177, 1213 (1987).

108   *The Papers of Alexander Hamilton,* vol. 8, 105 (Harold Syrett, ed., 1965) (hereafter Hamilton, *Papers*).

109   Hamilton, *Papers,* vol. 8, 48.

110   We sometimes encounter the contrary argument—that there was no distinction between constitutional and statutory interpretation. But this argument results from emphasizing that late eighteenth-century observers rejected reliance on evidence of subjective intent, especially through legislative history, whether the document was the U.S. Constitution or a statute. See H. Jefferson Powell, "The Original Understanding of Original Intent," 98 *Harv. L. Rev.* 885, 894–96, 899–900, 931 (1985). It is true that subjective intent was rejected as a criterion of meaning for *both* documents, but the similarity in interpretive approaches disappears if we focus on how liberally ("equitably") the court approached the text of each type of document.

111   Hamilton, *Papers,* vol. 8, 105.

112   Priestman v. United States, 4 U.S. 28, 30–31 (1800) (observations made by Justice Chase sitting as presiding judge on circuit).

113   2 U.S. 419 (1793).

114   Stephen Conrad, "James Wilson's 'Assimilation of the Common-Law Mind,' " 84 *Nw. U. L. Rev.* 186, 189 (1989) (hereafter Conrad) ("[W]hen [Wilson] contemplated 'the Common Law' as 'a system of law,' [he] was inclined to speak nothing short of 'poetically.' With language that anticipated Keats himself, he praised the Common Law as not only 'just' but 'beautiful'; indeed, 'to every age,' he said, 'it has disclosed new beauties and new truths.' ").

115   Conrad, 207.

116   Stimson, 134–35 (discussing James Wilson).

117   2 U.S. 419, 453 (1793).

118   *Federalist* 81, 417.

119   2 U.S. at 453-54.

120   2 U.S. at 465.

121   2 U.S. at 465.

122   2 U.S. at 465.

123   Chief Justice John Jay's opinion in the same case invoked the traditional interpretive canon—that remedial statutes should be liberally interpreted—to permit
suits against states. 2 U.S. at 476. A recognizable lineage can be traced between
that canon and later purposive interpretation.

3   The United States: Nineteenth Century

1   Morton Horwitz, *The Transformation of American Law, 1780-1860* (1977) (hereafter Horwitz, *1780-1860*).

2   William Novak, "Salus Populi: The Roots of Regulation in America, 1787-
1873" (Ph.D. diss., 1991) (hereafter Novak, "Salus Populi"); William Novak,
"Common Regulation: Legal Origins of State Power in America," 45 *Hastings
L. J.* 1061 (1994). See also William Novak, *The People's Welfare* (1996).

3   I admit to the difficulty of researching judicial opinions during this period,
which makes my study incomplete; the body of judicial opinions is vast and
Lexis/Westlaw search tools cover only a limited sample. I selected for study
Chief Justice John Marshall's opinions at the federal level and (primarily) Chief
Judge Lemuel Shaw's (Massachusetts) at the state level.

4   Novak, "Salus Populi," 6-7, 107-25.

5   Drew McCoy, *The Last of the Fathers*, 92-99 (1989).

6   James Richardson, *A Compilation of the Messages and Papers of the Presidents*,
vol. 5, 247-56 (1897).

7   Act of June 20, 1874, 43d Cong., 1st Sess., ch. 333, 18 Stat. 113 (1874).

8   Elizabeth McPherson, "The History of Reporting the Debates and Proceedings
of Congress," 210 (Ph.D. diss., 1940).

9   The "enacting" clause language was adopted by early American legislatures
from England. J. G. Sutherland, *Statutes and Statutory Construction*, sec. 20.06,
vol. 1A, 88-89 (Singer, 5th ed., 1992). Congress explicitly required statutes to
begin with an enacting clause by Act of Feb. 25, 1871, ch. 71, 16 Stat. 431 (1871),
but this approach had been the congressional practice from the outset, illustrated by the first statute passed in each of the first five Congresses, which begins
with the phrase "be it enacted": Act of June 1, 1789, ch. 1, 1 Stat. 23 (1789); Act
of Nov. 8, 1791, ch. 1, 1 Stat. 226 (1791); Act of Jan. 13, 1794, ch. 1, 1 Stat. 341
(1794); Act of Feb. 5, 1796, ch. 1, 1 Stat. 445 (1796); Act of June 14, 1797, ch. 1,
1 Stat. 520 (1797).

10   Francis Hilliard, *The Elements of Law*, 5 (Arno Press, 1972) (1835).

11 Joseph Story, "Law, Legislation and Codes," in *Encyclopedia Americana*, appendix 7, 576, 586 (Francis Lieber, ed., 1831) (hereafter Story, *Encyclopedia*) (citations are to the 1836 New Edition of *Encyclopedia Americana*).

12 Joseph Story et al., "Codification of the Common Law of Massachusetts." Report of the commissioners appointed to consider and report upon the practicability and expediency of reducing to a written and systematic code the Common Law of Massachusetts, or any part thereof, 17 *American Jurist* 17, 27 (1837) (hereafter Story, "Codification").

13 David Hoffman, *A Course of Legal Study,* 573 (Arno Press, 1972) (1836).

14 Note, "Fitness of Lawyers for Legislation," 23 *American Jurist* 491–92 (1840) (referring to the lawyer's "indifference [to] the convenience or inconvenience of [legislation]").

15 "Opening Address by Professor Francis Wayland before the American Social Science Association," 14 *J. Soc. Sci.* 1, 20 (1881) (hereafter Wayland).

16 Wayland, 23.

17 See Allison Dunham, "A History of the National Conference of Commissioners on Uniform State Laws," 30 *Law & Cont. Prob.* 233 (1965).

18 St. George Tucker, Blackstone's *Commentaries,* vol. 1, appendix, 151–54, 369–70, 423–24 (Augustus Kelley, 1969) (1803).

19 James Kent, *Commentaries on American Law,* vol. 1, lecture 20—"Of Statute Law," 419–38 (1826) (hereafter Kent).

20 Story, *Encyclopedia,* 576–92.

21 Francis Lieber, *Legal and Political Hermeneutics* (Charles Little & James Brown, 1839) (hereafter Lieber). The 1839 book was an expanded version of an essay entitled "Political Hermeneutics," which originally appeared in 1837. Herz, "A Symposium on Legal and Political Hermeneutics," 16 *Cardozo L. Rev.* 1879 (1995).

22 E. Fitch Smith, *Commentaries on Statute and Constitutional Law and Statutory and Constitutional Construction,* x–xi (1848) (hereafter Smith).

23 See *Dictionary of American Biography,* vol. 16, 551–52 (Dumas Malone, ed., 1943) (hereafter *Dictionary/Biography*).

24 Theodore Sedgwick, *A Treatise on the Rules Which Govern the Interpretation and Construction of Statutory and Constitutional Law* (1857) (all cites are to the Pomeroy ed., 1874) (hereafter Sedgwick).

25 Platt Potter, *A General Treatise on Statutes by Dwarris* (1871) (all cites are to the 1885 ed.) (hereafter Potter).

26 G. A. Endlich, *A Commentary on the Interpretation of Statutes Founded on Maxwell's Treatise* (1888) (hereafter Endlich).

27 Joel Bishop, *Commentaries on the Written Laws and Their Interpretation* (1882) (hereafter Bishop).

28 J. G. Sutherland, *Statutes and Statutory Construction* (1891) (hereafter Sutherland, 1st).

29 Henry Black, *Construction and Interpretation of the Laws* (1896) (hereafter Black).

30 Thomas Cooley, *Commentaries on the Laws of England by William Blackstone*, vol. 1, 58–61 nn. 13–22 and 86–90 nn. 14–26 (2d ed., 1872) (hereafter Cooley).

31 Bishop, 3, sec. 2.

32 Sutherland, 1st, iii–iv.

33 Black, iii.

34 Bishop, 3, sec. 3.

35 Sutherland, 1st, 373, sec. 289.

36 Quoted in David Raack, "'To Preserve the Best Fruits': The Legal Thought of Chancellor James Kent," 33 *Amer. J. Leg. Hist.* 320, 354 (1989) (hereafter Raack). Kent made this point in connection with objections to statutory rigidity: "The great objection to legislative rules and to all kinds of codification, when it runs into detail, is, that the rules are not malleable; they cannot accommodate circumstances. . . ."

37 Slee v. Bloom, 5 Johns. ch. 366, 377–79 (New York, 1821) (remedy provided by statute that makes shareholders liable on corporate dissolution is not available at common law and is narrowly construed; dissolution must be "judicially ascertained and declared" and only "by regular [judicial] process"); Tenbrook v. Lansing, 4 Johns. ch. 601, 602–3 (New York, 1820) (case not within the "equity or policy of the act"); Livingston v. Gibbons, 4 Johns. ch. 571, 572 (1820) ("unusual" and "severe" remedy was not extended by equitable construction).

38 Jerome v. Ross, 7 Johns. ch. 315, 341–42 (New York, 1823). This was the last judicial opinion that Kent wrote; at 346. On the interaction of law, compensation, canal building, and nineteenth-century law, see Horwitz, *1780–1860*, 63–69.

39 Kent, vol. 1, 431. He did occasionally speak favorably, if cautiously, of some statutory modifications of the common law in his 1826 *Commentaries on American Law*; see Raack, 339, 357.

40 Kent, vol. 1, 434.

41 Kent, vol. 1, 433.

42 "Letter from Chancellor Kent to Edward Livingston—Penal Code," 16 *American Jurist* 361, 370 (1837).

43 The "body" referred to the "whole text": "'[T]he intention of the lawgiver is to be deduced from a view of the whole, and of every part of a statute, taken and compared together'—not a cramped and narrow literalism." Kent, vol. 1, 431–32.

44 R. Kent Newmyer, *Supreme Court Justice Joseph Story: Statesman of the Old Republic*, 45, 48, 53, 59, 63–64, 71–72 (1985) (hereafter Newmyer).

45 United States v. Dickson, 40 U.S. 141, 163–64 (1841).

46 McCreery v. Somerville, 22 U.S. 354, 361 (1824).

47 Charles River Bridge v. Warren Bridge, 36 U.S. 420, 588 (1837) (Story, J., dissenting). The majority affirmed that the United States, in adopting English jurisprudence, had also adopted its rules for statutory construction. 36 U.S. at 545.

48 See also United States v. State Bank of North Carolina, 31 U.S. 29, 35 (1832) (strict construction should be avoided when interpreting an uncertain text to achieve the "public good"); Gardner v. Collins, 27 U.S. 58, 87 (1829) (a change in language between two statutes was accidental).

49 Story, *Encyclopedia,* 587.

50 Story, *Encyclopedia,* 585–86.

51 United States v. Coolidge, 25 F. Cas. 619, 621 (C.C. Mass. 1813), reversed, 14 U.S. 415 (1816); Kent, 314–22.

52 41 U.S. 1 (1842). In order to defend his interpretation of the 1789 Rules of Decision Act that deference to state laws did not include the entire body of state common law, Story's opinion adopts Blackstone's view of judge-made law (without attribution) as only evidence of the law, not law itself. 41 U.S. at 18.

53 Story, *Encyclopedia,* 588.

54 Story, *Encyclopedia,* 591.

55 Quotes from Story in the remainder of this section are from Story, *Encyclopedia,* 583–84.

56 Kent, vol. 1, 433.

57 Wolfgang Holdheim, "A Hermeneutic Thinker," 16 *Cardozo L. Rev.* 2153–54 (1995). Soifer calls him a protopragmatist. Aviam Soifer, "Facts, Things, and the Orphans and Girard College: Francis Lieber: ProtoPragmatist," 16 *Cardozo L. Rev.* 2305 (1995). But Carrington suggests that Lieber may have contributed to formalism. Paul Carrington, "William Gardiner Hammond and the Lieber Revival," 16 *Cardozo L. Rev.* 2135, 2139–40 (1995).

58 Michael Herz, "Rediscovering Francis Lieber: An Afterword and Introduction," 16 *Cardozo L. Rev.* 2107, 2110–13 (1995).

59 Lieber, 113.

60 Lieber, 64.

61 Lieber, 71, 81.

62 Roscoe Pound, "Spurious Interpretation," 7 *Colum. L. Rev.* 379 (1907).

63 Lieber, 89. He especially appealed to common sense to reject "literalism," although this appeal might imply little more than Blackstone's requirement that words be understood in their linguistic context. Thus, "shedding blood" does not apply to a surgeon because the phrase implies violence (69), and "Christian" in Spain means only a Catholic (108–9). Lieber associated literal interpretation with "artful interpretation" (68–69): "If we understand by literal interpretation, a species, which by way of adhering to the letter, substitutes a false sense for the true one, it has no more meaning than the term 'false facts.' It is false, deceptive, or artful interpretation, if we do not give that sense to words which they ought to have, according to good faith, common sense, the use which the utterer made of them, &c."

64 Lieber, 56.

65 Lieber, 121.

66 Lieber, 136.

67 Lieber, 116-17.

68 Lieber, 115.

69 Lieber, 121. See also Lieber, 163 ("generality . . . requires construction").

70 Lieber, 134.

71 Lieber, 139-40. The linking of judging to the difficulty of foreseeing change is as old as Aristotle, but one can also see in Lieber's concern for the interaction of change and subjects of "elementary, vital and absorbing importance" an anticipation of modern dynamic statutory interpretation concerned with fundamental values. See William N. Eskridge Jr., *Dynamic Statutory Interpretation* (1994).

72 Smith, 830-31.

73 Smith, 831.

74 Priestman v. United States, 4 U.S. 28 (1800).

75 Smith, 831-32.

76 Smith, 580.

77 Smith, 588-89.

78 Sedgwick, 193.

79 Sedgwick, 253.

80 *Dictionary/Biography*, 551-52.

81 Sedgwick, 265, 314.

82 Sedgwick, 184.

83 Sedgwick, 265-66.

84 Sedgwick, 205.

85 Sedgwick, 205.

86 James Willard Hurst, *The Growth of American Law: The Law Makers*, 141 (1950).

87 Kent (G. Edward White, *The American Judicial Tradition*, 37 (1988) (hereafter White); Shaw (White, 37); Gibson (Frank M. Eastman, *Courts and Lawyers of Pennsylvania—1623-1923*, vol. 2, 441 (1922)); Blackford (Charles W. Taylor, *Biographical Sketches and Review of the Bench and Bar of Indiana*, 33 (1895) (hereafter Taylor)); Ruffin (*Dictionary/Biography*, vol. 16, 216).

88 John Reid, "Chief Justice—The Judicial World of Charles Doe," 60-74 (1967) (explaining Doe's active political life); *Dictionary/Biography*, vol. 5, 354.

89 Cooley (*Dictionary/Biography*, vol. 4, 392-93).

90 *A History of the Court and Lawyers of Ohio*, vol. 1, 231-65 (Carrington Marshall, ed., 1934).

91 Taylor, 32-36, 39, 41.

92 Sedgwick, 267-75.

93 Sedgwick, 273.

94 Sedgwick, 191-92.

95 White, 18, 21-22, 24.

96 See, generally, John Yoo, "Marshall's Plan: The Early Supreme Court and Statutory Interpretation," 101 *Yale L. J.* 1607 (1992).

97 Kirkpatrick v. Gibson, 14 F. Cas. 683, 684 (1828).

98 Marshall, however, was willing to correct a text which contained an obvious drafting error—for example, where the text refers to two periods, only one of which is possible. Huidekoper's Lessee v. Douglass, 7 U.S. 1, 65–70 (1805). Moreover, a more modest judicial discretion to tilt the text *might* survive: "Courts still construe words liberally, to reach that intention which the words themselves import, but [they] seldom insert a description of persons omitted by the statute, because, in the opinion of the court, there is the same reason for comprehending those persons within its provisions, as for comprehending those who are actually enumerated." 14 F. Cas. at 684.

99 Pennington v. Coxe, 6 U.S. 33, 52 (1804) (relying on the whole text).

100 Oneale v. Thornton, 10 U.S. 53, 68 (1810).

101 Schooner Paulina's Cargo, 11 U.S. 52, 60 (1812).

102 Thomson v. United States, 23 F. Cas. 1107, 1109 (1820).

103 6 U.S. 358 (1805).

104 6 U.S. at 386.

105 6 U.S. at 386.

106 This quotation and others from Chief Justice Marshall in this paragraph are from U.S. v. Fisher, 6 U.S. at 390.

107 *Federalist* 78, 400–401 (Max Beloff, ed.).

108 Gordon Wood, *The Creation of the American Republic,* 291–92 (1969) (hereafter Wood).

109 William Nelson, "The Eighteenth-Century Background of John Marshall's Constitutional Jurisprudence," 76 *Mich. L. Rev.* 893, 901-2, 936, 953 (1978) (hereafter Nelson).

110 Nelson, 932.

111 See, generally, Veronica Dougherty, "Absurdity and the Limits of Literalism: Defining the Absurd Result Principle in Statutory Interpretation," 44 *Amer. Univ. L. Rev.* 127 (1994).

112 Becke v. Smith, 150 Eng. Rep. 724, 726 (Exch. 1836). See also Perry v. Skinner, 150 Eng. Rep. 843, 845 (Exch. 1837) ("construe [words] in their ordinary sense, unless it would lead to any absurdity or manifest injustice . . .").

113 River Wear Comm'rs. v. Adamson, (1877) 2 App. Cas. 743, 764-65 (H.L.). See also King v. Pease, 110 Eng. Rep. 366, 371 (1832) (K.B.) ("construe . . . according to the ordinary sense of the words, unless such construction would lead to some unreasonable result, or be inconsistent with, or contrary to, the declared or implied intention of the framer of the law, in which case the grammatical sense of the words may be extended or modified . . .").

114 U.S. v. Fisher, 6 U.S. at 386.

115 Bond v. Ross, 3 F. Cas. 842, 845 (D. Virg. 1815). This case dealt with what Marshall called the "strange negligence of the legislature" in providing for the

recording of mortgages of land but not personal property. Convinced that the legislature intended to provide for recording of personal property mortgages, he "aid[ed] the words" of the statute, by borrowing recording rules explicitly provided in the law so that they applied to personalty. Marshall also treated habeas corpus as a fundamental right. Ex Parte Bollman, 8 U.S. 75, 95 (1807). A statute dealing with the writ of habeas corpus took the following grammatical form—"situations A,B,C, which . . .," where the "which" clause listed situations in which habeas corpus would *not* be available. Usual grammatical construction principles (because of the comma after C) would make the "which" clause modify all three items on the list. But the habeas corpus writ was guaranteed by the Constitution, and the statute was passed in the first Congress, which "felt [the] force" of the constitutional mandate. Marshall therefore expansively interpreted the statute to authorize the writ, limiting the "which" clause to the last item on the list, although there was a dissent (a rarity at the time).

116 2 U.S. 419 (1793).

117 5 U.S. 137 (1803).

118 5 U.S. at 174.

119 22 U.S. 1 (1824).

120 Quotations in this paragraph are at 22 U.S. at 187–88.

121 17 U.S. 316 (1819).

122 17 U.S. at 407.

123 17 U.S. at 402–6.

124 17 U.S. at 407.

125 17 U.S. at 415.

126 There is no reason to think that Marshall believed in an evolving constitution, as opposed to evolving legislative power. Joseph Story made this point explicitly in *Commentaries on the Constitution of the United States*, 145, 158 (Carolina Academic Press, 1987): "The constitution is not to be subject to . . . fluctuations [of policy]. It is to have a fixed, uniform, permanent construction;" and "the daily language of life in one generation sometimes requires the aid of a glossary in another."

127 17 U.S. 122 (1819). Quotations from this decision are at 17 U.S. at 202–3, 205.

128 25 U.S. 213 (1827).

129 Quotations from the Marshall dissent are at 25 U.S. at 334–36, 354–55.

130 25 U.S. at 266–67. The full text of the constitutional provision is: "Art. I, Sec. 10. No state shall enter into any treaty, alliance, or confederation; grant letters of marque and reprisal; coin money; emit bills of credit; make anything but gold and silver coin a tender in payment of debts; pass any bill of attainder, ex post facto law, or law impairing the obligation of contracts; or grant any title of nobility."

131 Sedgwick, 179.

132 Sedgwick, 266.

133 "On Construing Statutes by Equity," 3 *Quart. L. J.* 150, 156–65 (1858).

134 Sedgwick, 263.

135 3 *Quart. L. J.* at 161. The reviewer also disagreed (3 *Quart. L. J.* at 152–54) with Sedgwick's hostility toward equitable interpretation. He argued that a narrowing equity made better sense than expansive equity to fulfill legislative intent: "All men, knowing what it is they do contemplate, are apt to use words which are large enough to embrace it; but all men, being unconscious necessarily of what they do not contemplate, are liable to employ general words that (literally taken) have a sense more comprehensible than is suited to their present design. . . . Restraining equity, therefore, is only a candid interpretation of the lawgiver's language. . . ."

136 Smith, 591.

137 Martha Lamb and Burton Harrison, *History of the City of New York,* vol. 3, 725–26 (1877).

138 The material in this discussion of cases arising from the New York fire comes from Mayor of New York v. Lord, 17 Wend. 285, 286–87, 291–94, 303–4 (New York, 1837), affirmed, 18 Wend. 126, 131–32, 139 New York, 1837); Stone v. The Mayor of New York, 25 Wend. 157, 179–80 (New York, 1840).

139 See Note, "The Origins and Original Significance of the Just Compensation Clause of the Fifth Amendment," 94 *Yale L. J.* 694 (1985).

140 See Note, "Advisory Opinions," 13 *Iowa L. J.* 188, 189–91 (1928).

141 Brown v. Brown, 1 Del. Cases, 188, 191 (Ct. Common Pleas 1798).

142 Judicial refusal to correct "inconvenience" implies that "absurd" results might still be prevented by the court through statutory interpretation, an approach affirmed in Laws v. Davis, 1 Del. Cases. 256, 259 (Ct. Common Pleas 1800). One midcentury decision also expresses a strong preference for the text over equitable interpretation, although the argument is based on policy concerns—protecting reliance interests—rather than separation of powers (that is, legitimacy). An 1855 Georgia case, Strawbridge v. Mann, 17 Ga. 454, 456, 458–59 (1855), dealt with whether a judgment creditor had to take certain steps to preserve his rights as a creditor. The court first observed that the statute was "one . . . to which this Court has applied the principle of *equitable* interpretation." But the opinion went on to reject that approach for contemporary statutes, arguing that "[t]he words . . . are . . . what the great majority of the people of the State shape their actions by. It is the words only, that are published to them—and when, after they have followed the words of the law, they are told by the Courts that they have not followed the law, they feel, that for them, the law has been turned into a snare. And it is difficult to say that they have not the right so to feel."

143 See, generally, Leonard Levy, *The Law of the Commonwealth and Chief Justice Shaw* (1957) (hereafter Levy).

144 See Oliver W. Holmes Jr. *The Common Law*, 85 (Mark deWolfe Howe, ed.,1963).

145 White, 42–43. See also Kearney v. Boston and Worcester Railroad Corp., 63 Mass. 108, 112 (1851) (Shaw refers to the "plain common sense, and the true meaning of the act").

146 "Chief Justice Shaw," 2 *Amer. L. Rev.* 47, 68 (1867).

147 White, 37.

148 Lemuel Shaw, "Profession of the Law in the United States," 7 *American Jurist* 56, 67 (1832) (hereafter Shaw, "Profession").

149 Gray v. Coffin, 63 Mass. 192, 199 (1852).

150 Jacquins v. Commonwealth, 63 Mass. 279, 282 (1852).

151 Commonwealth v. Anthes, 71 Mass. 185, 187 (1855). This opinion was one of the few by Shaw that was not unanimous. Levy, 294.

152 71 Mass. at 186–87.

153 71 Mass. at 239.

154 Benjamin Kaplan, "Introduction: An Address," in *The History of the Law in Massachusetts: The Supreme Judicial Court: 1692-1992*, 4–5 (Russell Osgood, ed., 1992) (hereafter Osgood).

155 Shaw, "Profession," 68.

156 Jacquins v. Commonwealth, 63 Mass. 279, 282 (1852).

157 Winchester v. Forster, 57 Mass. 366, 369 (1849).

158 Commonwealth v. Dimond, 57 Mass. 235, 237–38 (1849).

159 Drake v. Curtis, 55 Mass. 395, 410 (1848).

160 Brigham v. Bigelow, 53 Mass. 268, 271 (1847).

161 Hartwell v. Inhabitants of Littleton, 30 Mass. 229, 232 (1832).

162 Brown v. Thorndike, 32 Mass. 388, 402 (1834).

163 Parks v. City of Boston, 32 Mass. 198, 203 (1834).

164 Sawyer v. Inhabitants of Northfield, 61 Mass. 490, 494 (1851). See also Commonwealth v. Gardner, 77 Mass. 438, 443 (1858) ("taking the whole statute together").

165 Harwood v. City of Lowell, 58 Mass. 310, 312 (1849).

166 Inhabitants of Newburyport v. County Commissioners of Essex, 53 Mass. 211, 216–17 (1846).

167 See discussion in chapter 4.

168 Kidder v. Browne, 63 Mass. 400, 401 (1852); Howard v. Merriam, 59 Mass. 563, 565 (1850); Britton v. Commonwealth, 55 Mass. 302, 305 (1848); Commonwealth v. Mash, 48 Mass. 472, 474 (1844); Williams v. Hadley, 36 Mass. 379, 380 (1837); Tower v. Tower, 35 Mass. 262, 263 (1836).

169 Wright v. Oakley, 46 Mass. 400, 402 (1843) ("reasons . . . stated by the commissioners for revising the statutes, in their note to . . . their report"); Morrison v. Underwood, 59 Mass. 52, 54 (1849) ("report of the revising commissioners, in their comments"); Marshall v. Crehore, 54 Mass. 462, 466 (1847) ("[t]he com-

missioners, by their note, [*in loco*] indicate what was their purpose"); Newcomb
v. Williams, 50 Mass. 525, 536 (1845) ("fully explained by the report of the commissioners for making that revision").

170 Putnam v. Longley, 28 Mass. 487, 489–90 (1831).

171 Barnicoat v. Folling, 69 Mass. 134, 136 (1854).

172 Sedgwick, 192.

173 See, generally, Paul Kahn, *Legitimacy and History* (1992) (hereafter Kahn).

174 William Nelson, "Changing Conceptions of Judicial Review: The Evolution of
Constitutional Theory in the States, 1790–1860," 120 *U. Pa. L. Rev.* 1166, 1177
(1972). See also G. Edward White, "The Marshall Court and Cultural Change,
1815–35," in *History of the Supreme Court of the United States*, vols. 3–5, 195–
200 (1988) (drawing a distinction between partisan politics and the consensual
political theory).

175 *Federalist* 51, 265.

176 Shannon Stimson, "Judgment and the Concept of Judicial Space," 119 (Ph.D.
diss., 1984) (hereafter Stimson, "Ph.D."). But see Stimson's more cautious comments about Jefferson in *The American Revolution in the Law*, 87–88 (1990)
(Jefferson did not favor a jury deciding the law; jury service was an education
in civic virtue).

177 Stephen Conrad, "James Wilson's 'Assimilation of the Common-Law Mind,' "
84 *Nw. U. L. Rev.* 186, 188–91 (1989). See also Arthur Schlesinger Jr., *The Age
of Jackson*, 330 (1945) (for the Whigs, common law was "the law of the people,"
but statutes were "further off from the people: they are formal things").

178 Akhil Amar, "The Bill of Rights as a Constitution," 100 *Yale L. J.* 1131, 1133,
1182–99 (1991).

179 It is not that the franchise had been drastically limited. Bailyn reports that 50–
75 percent of the adult white male population could vote in Colonial America.
But the franchise was underexercised. Bernard Bailyn, *The Origins of American Politics*, 86–88 (1968); Bernard Bailyn, "Political Experience and Enlightenment Ideas in Eighteenth-Century America," 67 *Amer. Hist. Rev.* 339, 342,
346–47 (1962).

180 Richard Ellis, *The Union at Risk*, 15 (1987).

181 Note, "The Changing Role of the Jury in the Nineteenth Century," 74 *Yale L.
J.* 170, 170, 192 (1964) (hereafter "Changing Role").

182 Daniel Boorstin, *The Mysterious Science of the Law*, 11–30 (1941) (hereafter
Boorstin, *Science*).

183 Boorstin, *Science*, p. 30.

184 See Robert Gordon, Book review of "Cook, *The American Codification Movement*," 36 *Vand. L. Rev.* 431, 445-46, 455-58 (1983) (hereafter Gordon). Horwitz, *1860-1960*, 5-6, 12-13, 22; Kahn, 79-80, 97.

185 Kahn, 79-80 (discussing the work of Tiedeman, whom Kahn describes as the

most influential constitutional theorist of the later nineteenth century after Cooley (77).

186   Robert Stevens, *Law School: Legal Education in America from the 1850s to the 1980s*, 52–53 (1983).

187   Roscoe Pound, *The Lawyer from Antiquity to Modern Times*, 254, 259 (1953).

188   Evan Haynes, *The Selection and Tenure of Judges*, 89 (1944) (hereafter Haynes).

189   Democratic sentiments did, however, have an indirect effect on judging in New York in 1821. Popular dissatisfaction with the judge's political role on the council of revision, on which appointed judges had a veto over proposed legislation, resulted in an 1821 constitutional amendment terminating the council. The council had frequently objected to legislation on grounds that the law would violate the constitution or the "public good." One study states that 55.6 percent of the vetoes were mainly on policy grounds, 21.8 percent on constitutional grounds, and 12.4 percent for other reasons. James Barry, "The Council of Revision and the Limits of Judicial Power," 56 *U. Chi. L. Rev.* 235, 245–46 (1989). See, generally, J. Hampden Dougherty, *Constitutional History of the State of New York* (2d ed., 1915) (hereafter Dougherty); Merrill Peterson, *Democracy, Liberty, and Property: The State Constitutional Conventions of the 1820s*, 125–270 (1966). It may not be an accident that New York courts first held that a statute violated the state constitution in the same year (1821) that the council was abolished. Charles Haines, *The American Doctrine of Judicial Supremacy*, 86 (1959).

190   Haynes, 99–100.

191   Haynes, 100. The move to democratize judicial selection was not universal. The Massachusetts 1820 constitutional convention headed off such attempts. Justice Story chaired the committee on the judiciary at the convention, which proposed *less* popular accountability by increasing the legislative vote needed to remove judges to two-thirds. Russell Osgood, "Isaac Parker: Republican Judge, Federalist Values," in Osgood, 168; *Journal of Debates and Proceedings in the Massachusetts Constitutional Convention, 1820–21*, 136 (1853). The move failed but, perhaps, took some of the steam out of any moves toward electing judges. The 1853 Massachusetts convention also was concerned with limiting judicial discretion. See Aviam Soifer, "The Supreme Judicial Court of Massachusetts and the 1780 Constitution," in Osgood, 208. However, it turned down election of judges, proposing instead ten-year terms, which was defeated at the polls. Frank Grinnell, "The Judicial System and the Bar (1820–1861)," in *Commonwealth History of Massachusetts*, vol. 4, 59–60 (Albert Hart, ed., 1930).

192   See, generally, William Popkin, *Materials on Legislation*, 813–25 (2d ed., 1997) (hereafter Popkin).

193   Peter Galie, *The New York State Constitution*, 12 (1991) (hereafter Galie).

194   Switch from legislative selection: Alabama (1850), Haynes, 101–2; Arkansas (1848), Haynes, 102–3; Florida (1865), Haynes, 107; Georgia (1865), Haynes,

108-9; Illinois (1848), Haynes, 110; Indiana (1851), Haynes, 110; Iowa (1857), Haynes, 111; Michigan (1850), Haynes, 116; North Carolina (1868), Haynes, 124; Ohio (1851), Haynes, 125; Tennessee (1866), Haynes, 130; Vermont (1850), Haynes, 132; Virginia (1850), Haynes, 133. States that switched to popular election of judges from a method other than legislative selection were Kentucky, Louisiana, Maryland, Missouri, New York, Pennsylvania, and Texas; Haynes, 112-13, 115-18, 123, 127, 130-31.

195 "Changing Role," 178 n. 55.

196 The material in these paragraphs on New York developments is based on Francis Bergan, *The History of the New York Court of Appeals, 1847-1932*, 19, 35-36, 95-96, 100, 102, 107, 124, 129-30, 245-47 (1985) (hereafter Bergan). See also William Bishop and William Attree, *Report of the Debates and Proceedings of the Convention for the Revision of the Constitution of the State of New York* (1846).

197 Bergan, 107 (quoting Conger).

198 Dougherty, 365-65.

199 Bergan, 246, 284.

200 Anthony Kaufman, *Cardozo*, 178-79 (1998).

201 David Lieberman, *The Province of Legislation Determined*, 182-84 (1989).

202 Barbara Shapiro, "Codification of the Laws in Seventeenth Century England," 1974 *Wis. L. Rev.* 428, 440 (hereafter Shapiro).

203 Shapiro, 439, 442.

204 Shapiro, 430, 448-56.

205 Charles Cook, *The American Codification Movement*, 74-78 (1981) (hereafter Cook).

206 Gordon, 431.

207 Gordon, 433-36.

208 Bentham wrote to President Madison (among others in the United States), who responded five years later. Livingstone, codifier of Louisiana law, seemed to be his only active U.S. admirer. H. L. A. Hart, *Essays on Bentham*, 76-78 (1982).

209 Cook, 75.

210 See "A Notice of the Most Recent Revisions, Digests, and Collections, of the Statute Laws of the United States, and of the Several States," 18 *American Jurist* 227, 230-53 (1837).

211 Newmyer, 278-79. The report appears at Story, "Codification," 17 *American Jurist* 17 (1837). See also Story, "Codification," 30-32 (cannot codify whole common law but can codify some of it).

212 Kent's *Commentaries on American Law* was published in 1826. Story's eight private law treatises appeared from 1832 through 1845; Newmyer, 281. See also Horwitz, *1780-1860*, 257-58.

213 Note, "Some Forgotten Massachusetts History About Codification and Its Relation to Current Legislative and Judicial Problems," 1 *Mass. Law Q.* 319, 329 (1916).

214 Galie, 12.

215 Cook, 189–90.

216 He was not originally appointed to the "procedural" commission but joined when one member unsympathetic to the endeavor resigned; Cook, 190–91. He was appointed to the second, not the first, "substantive" law commission; Cook, 194–96; Henry Field, *The Life of David Dudley Field*, 74–75, 77 (1898) (Fred B. Rothman, 1995) (hereafter Field, *Life*). See also Lawrence Friedman, *A History of American Law*, 391–98, 403–6 (2d ed., 1985) (hereafter Friedman).

217 Cook, 191.

218 Field, art. no. 5, in "The Completion of the Code: 5 Articles by David Dudley Field," *New York Evening Post* (1851) ("It is indeed no secret, that many of the judges, and some think a majority of them, have felt from the beginning a repugnance to the code . . .").

219 Cook, 194–96.

220 Field, *Life*, 88.

221 Maurice Harrison, "The First Half-Century of the California Civil Code," 10 *Calif. L. Rev.* 185, 187 (1922); Field, *Life*, 89–90.

222 Even Jefferson had questioned codification on the ground that experience was more varied than language. Daniel Boorstin, *The Lost World of Thomas Jefferson*, 136 (1948).

223 1 *Mass. Law Q.* at 332.

224 See James Carter, *Law: Its Origin, Growth, and Function* (1907) (a posthumously published book based on essays and lectures given from 1883 to 1890); James Carter, "The Provinces of the Written and Unwritten Law," 24 *Amer. L. Rev.* 1 (1890).

225 Address of John W. Stevenson, 8 *Report of Amer. Bar Assn.* 149, 150 (1885); Address of Alexander R. Lawton, 6 *Report of Amer. Bar Assn.* 137, 174–75 (1883); Address of Edward J. Phelps, 4 *Report of Amer. Bar Assn.* 141, 170 (1881).

226 Carter's emphasis on *adaptable* common law was outdated. The image of the common law that gained ascendancy after the Civil War was static. The dynamic common law had done its job of revising the law in the earlier decades of the nineteenth century, and it retreated to a position of strength, becoming hostile rather than complementary to legislation. The pre-Civil War idea of a dynamic common law was reincarnated in constitutional law (Kahn, 73–84); now, it was the Constitution that would evolve. The Supreme Court, without any sense of irony, would cite Marshall's assertion that "it is a constitution we are expounding" to *limit* federal legislative power to impose an income tax, rather than to expand federal power. Pollock v. Farmers' Loan & Trust Co., 158 U.S. 601, 617 (1895). And the federal Constitution was interpreted to impose substantive due process limits on federal and state reform legislation, often preventing changes that threatened common law contract and property rights. Kahn, 74 (Cooley identified common law with constitutional law).

227 Quoted in Edwin Patterson, "Historical and Evolutionary Theories of Law," 51 *Colum. L. Rev.* 681, 697 (1951).

228 Friedman, 404 (quoting Carter).

229 Lewis Grossman, "Codification and the California Mentality," 45 *Hastings L. J.* 617, 621–34 (1994). See also Gordon, 457.

230 See, generally, Allison Dunham, "A History of the National Conference of Commissioners on Uniform State Laws," 30 *Law & Cont. Problems* 233 (1965).

231 See Herbert F. Goodrich, "The Story of the American Law Institute," 1951 *Wash. U. L. Q.* 283, 285–86 (quoting By-Laws, 2 A.L.I. Proc. 429 [1923]).

232 Bishop, 3, sec. 2.

233 Sutherland, 1st, iii–iv.

234 Black, iii.

235 7 *Colum. L. Rev.* 379, 380 (1907).

236 Francis v. Western Union Tel. Co., 59 N.W. 1078, 1081 (Minn. 1894).

237 Penoyar v. Kelsey, 44 N.E. 788, 789, 790 (New York, 1896).

238 Walker v. Reamy, 36 Pa. 410, 415–16 (1860).

239 Bishop argued that extension of statutes was more appropriate for briefer older statutes than modern "plethoric" legislation. Bishop, 180–81, sec. 190. Sutherland locates equitable interpretation in a time when acts of Parliament were "brief and general" and the line between legislating and judging was unclear; it is now obsolete, a relic of ancient hermeneutics. Sutherland, 1st, 524–30, secs. 413–14. Potter's Dwarris makes a more political statement: "The judiciary, are removed too far from the people to share much in their prepossessions." Potter, 89. Black links the obsolescence of equitable interpretation to a decline in the "sanctity of the common law." Black, iii. Endlich's Maxwell argues that the "courts can exercise the power of controlling the language in order to give effect to what they suppose to have been the real intention of the law makers," only when the text is ambiguous or doubtful; the judge cannot mold meaning to "meet an alleged convenience or an alleged equity"; "[i]t is inaccurate to speak of the meaning or intent of a statute as something separate or distinct from the meaning of its language"; and that to do so would be an "assumption of legislative powers by the court." Endlich, 6–7, 11–12.

240 Thomas Cooley, *Commentaries on Blackstone's "Laws of England,"* vol. 1, 89 n. 21. (1873).

241 Sedgwick, 267–69 n.(a).

242 Endlich, 172–75.

243 Bishop, 140–41, 178, secs. 155, 189a.

244 Black, 243–44.

245 Sedgwick, 267–69 n.(a).

246 Endlich, 172–75.

247 Sutherland, 1st, 374–75, sec. 291.

248 Potter, 185. We know, however, from Judge Potter's opinion in Billings v. Baker,

28 Barb. 343, 356, 361 (New York, 1859), that he objected to the Kentian approach. His opinion identifies the Married Women's Property Acts as remedial and states: "Is the glory of the ancient common law so dazzling, that the learning of the present day, and all the attempted reforms upon the system to meet the wants of the age, are to be regarded as dangerous experiments?"

249 Sutherland, 1st, 374, sec. 290. Sutherland refers in this paragraph to "fundamental rights."

250 Endlich, 473–74, sec. 341.

251 Francis v. Western Union Tel. Co., 59 N.W. at 1079.

252 C.O. So Relle v. W.U. Telegraph Co., 55 Tex. 308 (1881).

253 59 N.W. at 1080.

254 59 N.W. at 1081. ("The great lights of the law may take some liberties with the law in the way of new applications of old principles that modesty would forbid to ordinary men; and while we are not disposed to look upon everything ancient with slavish reverence merely because it is ancient, it would certainly be presumptuous in us to lightly discard a doctrine which has been so long approved, and which is so firmly established by authority.")

255 John Dawson, *Oracles of the Law*, 91–94 (1968).

256 For example, at common law, real property was exempt from sale on execution of a judgment, but personal property was not. A statute exempted both types of property but was silent regarding insurance proceeds from loss of such property. The court, in Heath v. Griffin, 39 P. 962, 962–63 (Wash. 1895), explicitly noted that a liberal interpretation would exempt the proceeds, but a narrow construction would not. It then concluded that the statute was remedial, calling for a liberal interpretation (so "that the family might have something which would enable them to maintain a home, and live together therein"), even though this was in derogation of the common law.

257 McDonnell v. Alabama Gold Life Ins. Co., 5 So. 120, 122 (Ala. 1888).

258 Roswell Shinn, *A Treatise on the American Law of Attachment and Garnishment*, vol. 1, sec. 8, 10–11 (1900) (strict construction is the dominant though not universal pattern). These statutes predated the nineteenth century. Rhonda Wasserman, "Equity Renewed: Preliminary Injunctions to Secure Potential Money Judgments," 67 *Wash. L. Rev.* 257, 275 n.77 (1992) (90 percent of all eighteenth-century civil suits were debt cases and attachments used primarily in aid of debt collection). See, generally, Robert Millar, *Civil Procedure of the Trial Court in Historical Perspective*, 481–97 (1952).

It is possible that narrow construction of attachment statutes was a phenomenon of the second half of the nineteenth century. An 1855 Mississippi case did *not* interpret an attachment statute strictly, forgiving a harmless procedural lapse, Bank of Augusta v. Conrey, 28 Miss. 667 (1855). But later case law adopted strict construction, Rankin v. Dulaney, 43 Miss. 197 (1870). The contrast between these two cases raises the interesting possibility that narrow interpretation of attachment statutes developed in the second half of the nineteenth century, perhaps because attachment was no longer uniformly sought by a moneyed class against an impecunious debtor class. As debt and bankruptcy became recognized as normal incidents of doing business, attachment might have seemed a more extreme measure.

259 Duxbury v. Dahle, 81 N.W. 198 (Minn. 1899).

260 *Eminent domain.* The case of In re Rochester Electric Ry. Co., 25 N.E. 381 (New York, 1890) involved a railway's exercise of eminent domain to deprive someone of private property. The failure to file a map, required by statute, was fatal, even though in this particular case *no* prejudice would be caused by the procedural failure.

Mortgage enforcement. In Pickle v. Smalley, 58 P. 581, 582 (Wash. 1899), the statute allowed a "sheriff" or "other proper officer" to enforce mortgages. The court held that a "constable" was not authorized by this law to enforce the mortgage. The derogation canon was invoked to prevent extension of the law "beyond the plain import of its terms." The court concluded that "[t]his rule of construction forbids giving to the term 'sheriff' a generic meaning. . . ." It also held that "other proper person" was restrictive, not expansive, applying only to those empowered to act when the sheriff could not, such as a deputy. It further observed that "[i]n carrying out the provisions of the statute accuracy and technical precision are required, in order to pass title to the property sold."

Tax enforcement. The courts insisted on the government following the letter of the law to enforce taxes in Dowell v. City of Portland, 10 P. 308 (Ore. 1886) ("it is to the credit of the common law that no sanction for . . . proceedings [depriving an American of his land] is found in its bosom, and that its wise rule of statutory construction, that statutes in derogation of its principles are to be strictly construed, has not tended to facilitate the divestiture of property by such proceedings . . ."); Judson v. Smith, 15 S.W. 956 (Mo. 1891) (discouraging summary tax remedies).

261 Hayes v. Williams, 30 P. 352, 353 (Colo. 1892).

262 Jaffray v. Jennings, 60 N.W. 52, 53, 54 (Mich. 1894) (statute quoted in dissenting opinion).

263 The existence of a dissent in this case also indicates that not all judges interpreted statutes to preserve the common law. The dissent expressed concern that the court's decision would allow a "partner having a nominal interest [to] incur indebtedness on behalf of the firm fraudulently, and no process c[ould] issue against either the copartnership property or the property of his copartners." 60 N.W. at 55.

264 Penoyar v. Kelsey, 44 N.E. 788, 789–90 (New York, 1896).

265 Mitchell v. W. T. Grant Co., 416 U.S. 600 (1974); Fuentes v. Shevin, 407 U.S. 67 (1972). See also Sniadach v. Family Finance Corp., 395 U.S. 337 (1969) (garnishment).

266 Daniel Hinkel and Richard Dick, *Indiana Mechanic's Lien Law*, sec. 1.2, 2 (1981).

267 This may explain why a statute giving a laborer a preference in insolvency, which created no *new* liability, was liberally interpreted. See In re Black, 47 N.W. 342 (Mich. 1890) (construction of term "labor").

268 53 Am. Jur. 2d, Mechanic's Liens, para. 7, p. 93.

269 Maher v. Shull, 52 P. 1115, 1116 (Colo. 1898) ("[T]he remedial portions of mechanic's lien statutes should be liberally construed, but . . . the other parts, —those upon which the right to the existence of a lien depended,—being in derogation of the common law, should be strictly construed"). See also Cary Hardware Co. v. McCarty, 50 P. 744, 746 (Colo. App. 1897): "Much of the seeming conflict in authority as to the rule for the construction of mechanic's lien statutes is more apparent than real. . . . It is too frequently asserted broadly and hastily that mechanic's lien statutes are in derogation of the common law, and therefore subject to the well-known canon of construction that they must be construed strictly. This is true as to parts of such statutes, but it also may be, and invariably is, the case as to the greater portion of the same statute that its provisions are remedial in their nature, and hence, according to a rule of construction equally well settled, should be liberally construed. . . . No inflexible rule of either strict or liberal construction can be laid down which will be applicable to every part of such a statute. . . ."

270 53 Am. Jur. 2d, paras. 11, 24, pp. 97, 104.

271 Johnston et al. v. Barrills, 41 P. 656, 658 (Ore. 1895).

272 In re Clark, 52 N.W. 637, 637 (Mich. 1892).

273 Some decisions were generous in defining eligible "laborers." See Hand v. Cale, 12 S.W. 922 (Tenn. 1890) (the court defines a traveling salesman to be a "laborer").

274 Butler v. Gain, 21 N.E. 350, 351 (Ill. 1889).

275 See also Pilz v. Killingsworth, 26 P. 305, 306 (Ore. 1891) (mechanic's lien denied when claimant failed to "allege that the property therein described is a lot within [the city] . . ."; In re Hall's Estate, 23 A. 992 (Penn. 1892). See also Minor v. Marshall, 27 P. 481 (N.M. 1891) (the court was willing to relax the letter of the law as to *some* procedures for obtaining a lien but was unwilling to go as far as the dissent, which explicitly opposed strict construction). Statutes protecting the claims of laborers to remuneration, other than mechanic's lien laws, also insisted on formal compliance with the letter of the law. See Quackenbush v. Chicago & W. M. Ry. Co., 51 N.W. 883, 884–85 (Mich. 1892): "[T]he statute is somewhat analogous to those providing for a lien in favor of mechanics and others. Where such a statute requires a claimant to file a claim containing a statement of the terms, time, and conditions of his contract, the requirement is held to be imperative. Again, where the claim must set out the quantity or sum claimed to be due, and the nature or kind of work done, or the kind and amounts of materials furnished and work and labor done, he must

state the amount claimed for each as a distinct item, or the omission will render it totally invalid. . . . In the present case the notices did not show upon their face whether the work charged for was for the plaintiff's personal labor or for team work, nor do the notices state the kind of labor performed, the dates when performed, nor the rate per day, nor how much had been paid upon it. . . ."

276 Hannah & Lay Mercantile Co. v. Mosser, 62 N.W. 1120, 1122 (Mich. 1895).

277 May, Purington & Bonner Brick Co. v. General Engineering Co., 54 N.E. 638, 640–41 (Ill. 1899).

278 Similarly, in Sterner v. Haas, 66 N.W. 348 (Mich. 1896), contractors (not just laborers) could obtain a mechanic's lien but only by filing information about payments to laborers and men who furnished materials, and the amounts due them. The court would not excuse the contractor's failure to provide that information, even though it was agreed that the contractor had paid the workers, and the property owner had not requested the statement. "The lien law is in derogation of the common law, and all rights under it are statutory, and cannot be extended beyond the provisions of the statute."

279 Williams v. Vanderbilt, 34 N.E. 476, 476 (Ill. 1893).

280 Another case, Maher v. Shull, 52 P. 1115, 1116 (Colo. 1898), gives a less clear message regarding the reasonableness of a narrow interpretation of who is subject to the mechanic's lien law. An owner of mining property agreed to sell property to a buyer, if the buyer completed work to develop a mining claim. The buyer hired a contractor to do the work, and the contractor's employees sought a mechanic's lien under a statute that applied to work done pursuant to contracts between an owner and a contractor. But the buyer, who had contracted for the work, was not yet an owner; and the owner had not contracted for the work. The court invoked the derogation canon to deny the claim because the parties were not those described in the mechanic's lien law—the statutory terms "cannot be extended by implication . . . to make one person liable for the debt of another." However, if this arrangement was a device used to avoid the mechanic's lien law (of which the opinion gives no hint), the decision might have allowed property owners to exploit a statutory loophole.

281 May, Purington & Bonner Brick Co. v. General Engineering Co, 54 N.E. 638, 640 (Ill. 1899).

282 In re Hall's Estate, 23 A. 992, 994 (Penn. 1892).

283 See, e.g., Loan Association v. Topeka, 87 U.S. 655, 664 (1874) (this exercise of governmental "power can as readily be employed against one class of individuals and in favor of another, so as to ruin the one class and give unlimited wealth and prosperity to the other," and that "[t]o lay with one hand the power of the government on the property of the citizen, and with the other to bestow it upon favored individuals to aid private enterprise and build up private fortunes, is none the less robbery because it is done under the forms of law and is called taxation").

284   See the British case of Baker v. Bolton, 170 Eng. Rep. 1033 (K.B. 1808).

285   See, generally, Stuart Speiser, Recovery for Wrongful Death, sec. 1.12, 32–33 (2d ed., 1975). Courts were much less hostile to legislation in another group of tort cases that abolished common law defenses in tort actions by employees against an employer. For example, Mobile & B. Ry. Co. v. Holborn, 4 So. 146, 146 (Alabama 1888), dealt with the abolition of the "fellow servant" rule, which had denied employees recovery when the injury occurred as a result of the negligence of a fellow employee: "Being in derogation of the common law, the inference is that the terms of the act clearly import the changes intended, and their operation will not be enlarged by construction further than may be necessary to effectuate the manifest ends. Notwithstanding, a narrow and restrictive view of the act should not be taken. In its construction the court should consider its objects, have regard to the intentions of the legislature, and take a broad view of its provisions, commensurate with the proposed purposes."

286   Sweetland v. Chicago & G. T. R. Co., 75 N.W. 1066, 1071 (Mich. 1898) (Long, C.J., concurring).

287   75 N.W. at 1072, 1076.

288   See, e.g., Turner v. Cross, 18 S.W. 578, 579 (Tex. 1892), in which a statute authorized a cause of action against a "proprietor, owner, charterer, or hirer of any railroad," but the court would not extend the law to apply to a "receiver operating a railway under the appointment and control of a court." A similar cramped though permissible interpretation of the Wrongful Death Act refused to treat a stepfather as a "father." Thornburg v. American Strawboard Co., 40 N.E. 1062 (Ind. 1895).

See also Merkle v. Bennington Tp., 24 N.W. 776, 777 (Mich. 1885), a decision that, unlike the case in the text, was full of praise for wrongful death acts. The court stated that "the [wrongful death] statute . . . is in the strictest sense a remedial statute, and as such it should receive not a strict, but a favorable, construction. It was passed to remedy a great defect in the law, whereby, through the very severity of the injury which a party's negligence or misbehavior had caused, he in many cases escaped responsibility altogether, though these were exactly the cases in which he ought with most certainty to be held chargeable."

Modern decisions are, however, more generous in implementing the purposes of wrongful death acts than were nineteenth-century courts. For example, contemporary state courts usually allow both survival and wrongful death actions, with protection against double recovery of the same damages; William Prosser, Torts, sec. 127, 950 (5th ed., 1984). And a majority of jurisdictions now include an unborn viable fetus within the category of persons whose death supports a wrongful death claim; see, e.g., O'Grady v. Brown, 654 S.W.2d 904, 908 (Mo. 1983) ("wrongful death acts . . . designed to mend the fabric of the common law"), overruling Hardin v. Sanders, 538 S.W.2d 336 (Mo. 1976). More generally, the Restatement of Torts affirms that wrongful death actions are part of the common law, despite their statutory origins (Restatement of Torts, 2d, sec. 925, comment k, 532), a result confirmed in the federal common law of admiralty; Moragne v. States Marine Lines, 398 U.S. 375 (1970).

289 See, generally, Richard Chused, "Married Women's Property Law: 1800–1850," 71 *Geo. L. J.* 1359 (1983); Richard Chused, "Late Nineteenth Century Married Women's Property Law: Reception of the Early Married Women's Property Acts by Courts and Legislatures," 29 *Amer. J. Leg. Hist.* 3 (1985).

290 See Billings v. Baker, 28 Barb. 343, 347–48 (New York, 1859).

291 Board of Trade of City of Seattle v. Hayden, 30 P. 87, 88, 92 (Wash. 1892) (statute quoted in dissenting opinion).

292 Though perhaps not as great as that expressed by an Oregon court in Frarey v. Wheeler, 4 Ore. 190, 195 (1871): "[I]t is the generally received opinion that the sphere of married women's duties . . . precludes the means of acquiring by them that knowledge of law and commercial transactions necessary to enable them . . . to safely and understandingly enter into covenants concerning their real estate."

293 See, e.g., Kohn v. Collison, 27 Atl. 834 (Del. 1893) (a wife cannot sign a promissory note of her husband, lending him her credit—MWPA protects the wife and her signing of his note does the opposite). These decisions were symptomatic of a more general refusal to recognize the wife's separate status when dealing with her husband, as evidenced by cases preventing her from suing her husband. See Siegel, " 'The Rule of Love': Wife Beating as Prerogative and Privacy," 105 *Yale L. J.* 2117, 2163–67 (1996). See also Longendyke v. Longendyke, 44 Barb. 366 (N.Y. Sup. Ct. 1863).

294 Rostker v. Goldberg, 453 U.S. 57 (1981).

295 It is also important to take note of dissenting judicial voices, which (in the partnership case) excoriated the majority for usurping legislative power. Board of Trade of City of Seattle v. Hayden, 30 P. at 91–93. The dissent quoted the statutory text—"every married person can enjoy and dispose of every species of property as if he or she were unmarried"—and referred to "[a]dvancing thought . . . [as recognizing a] woman's independence and capability. . . ." It then objected "that the decision . . . is another instance (too common in the history of the courts of the United States) of the judicial repeal of a statute. It is not only a fundamental principle of our government . . . that the legislative and judicial departments of the government must be kept distinct and separate, but the first warning note sounded by all writers on statutory interpretation is that, when the language of a statute is plain and unambiguous, the duty of interpretation by the court does not arise." Because "there [is no]thing doubtful or ambiguous about that language," the court has no "right . . . to step in, and, under the guise of construction, inject a limitation which the legislature did not provide for, and which, in effect, renders nugatory the law passed by that body[.] It is an easy but a dangerous thing for courts to wander off in hazy theories and speculations concerning what the legislature meant, and to base their conclusions on

the policy or impolicy of the law." And, in an obvious though veiled reference to the Golden Rule, the dissent concluded that "[h]owever unjust, arbitrary, or inconvenient the intention conveyed may be, it must receive its full effect."

296 Corn Exchange Ins. Co. v. Babcock, 42 N.Y. 613 (1870), reversing, 57 Barb. 222 (New York, 1867). But see White v. Wager, 25 N.Y. 328 (1862) (protecting the wife by not allowing her to transfer real estate to her husband). White v. Wager was overridden by statute; see Dean v. Metropolitan Elev. Ry. Co., 23 N.E. 1054, 1055 (New York, 1890) (ch. 537 of New York Laws of 1887).

297 See, e.g., Stramann v. Scheeren, 42 P. 191, 194 (Colo. App. 1895).

298 A similar observation is apt regarding the eloquent statements in the case of Quilty v. Battie, 32 N.E. 47, 48 (New York, 1892), where the court stated that "[this legislation] effectually removes the common-law disability of the wife, which deprived her of the possession and control of her property during coverture, and, to that extent, it extinguished the common-law rights and powers of the husband. Because it is in derogation of his common-law privileges, it is to be rigidly applied, and not extended by implication beyond its strict letter; but it is also a remedial act, and as to its clearly expressed subject-matter it should have a liberal construction. Full and absolute ownership of all property which the wife might have or acquire . . . was evidently conferred upon her by this statute. . . . Her husband is thus placed upon the same footing as a stranger, and has no greater authority than a stranger to impose a burden upon her separate estate, or to restrict or embarrass her in the exercise of exclusive dominion over it." But this case simply allowed the wife to be sued because she failed to control a dog on her property.

299 See, generally, Haskins, Curtesy in the United States, 100 *U. Pa. L. Rev.* 196 (1951).

300 Vallance v. Bausch, 28 Barb. 633 (New York, 1859).

301 This description of the statute is from Billings v. Baker, 28 Barb. 343, 347-48 (New York, 1859), although it is unclear if it is an exact quote from the statutory text. This imprecision in the court's reference to the statute is itself a symptom of the common law courts' casual attitude toward legislation.

302 28 Barb. at 642.

303 Walker v. Reamy, 36 Pa. 410, 414-16 (1860).

304 A New Jersey decision, Johnson v. Cummins, 16 N.J. Eq. 97, 107 (1863), had agreed with the New York decision in Vallance—that the husband's curtesy interest survived. Then, in 1864, the New Jersey legislature agreed with the New Jersey court. See the discussion of the statute in Stoutenburgh v. Hopkins, 12 A. 689, 690 (N.J. Eq. 1888) (Statute of April 12, 1864, P. L. 698 provides that wife has a power to dispose of property by will, *to the extent it does not* defeat husband's curtesy right).

305 28 Barb. 343, 361 (New York, 1859).

306 Schindel v. Schindel, 12 Md. 294, 302, 313-14 (1858).

307 In re Bradwell, 55 Ill. 535, 540 (1869); Ex Parte Goodell, 39 Wis. 232 (1875); In re Leonard, 6 P. 426 (Ore. 1885); Ex Parte Robinson, 131 Mass. 376 (1881). The common law's opposition to women's bar membership was also important when the Supreme Court upheld the Illinois position against a constitutional challenge. Bradwell v. Illinois, 83 U.S. 130, 140 (1872) (Bradley, J., concurring) (opinion relied heavily on the common law to uphold Illinois' denial of bar membership).

308 39 Wis. at 244–45.

309 In Re Leach, 34 N.E. 641 (Ind. 1893) (common law *does not* prevent women from being practicing lawyers); In re Hall, 50 Conn. 131 (1882) (common law evolves); In re Thomas, 27 P. 707 (Colo. 1891) (common law evolves). See also Kirk, "Exclusion to Emancipation: A Comparative Analysis of Women's Citizenship in Australia and the United States, 1869–1921," 97 *W. Virg. L. Rev.* 725, 736–37 (1995) (Iowa allows women to practice law).

310 In Re Leach, 34 N.E. 641, 642 (Ind. 1893).

311 Limiting the reach of legislation was the dominant judicial perspective, even when it was not necessary to preserve the common law, as illustrated by the famous Supreme Court case of Holy Trinity Church v. United States, 143 U.S. 457, 458, 460 (1892). A federal statute made it a crime to bring an alien into the country for "labor or service of any kind." The defendant brought in a pastor from England. The text seemed clear—this was prohibited activity. But the Supreme Court refused to apply the statute to clergy, relying on both the spirit of the law (the statute was aimed at importing *manual* laborers), and on the avoidance of an "absurd" result (a religious nation like ours could not possibly criminalize the importation of a religious cleric).

312 One example of a narrowing construction of a statutory text to preserve the common law, which was not hostile to legislation, was Campbell v. Colorado Coal & Iron Co., 10 P. 248, 250–51 (Colo. 1886). The issue was whether a debtor could make a partial assignment of his property to prefer certain creditors, which was permitted at common law, despite passage of a statute forbidding "an assignment" to defeat the claims of laborers. The court observed that statutes in derogation of the common law, such as this one, were strictly construed. It therefore read the text so that the words which I have placed in parentheses were replaced by the words which I place in square brackets to limit the application of the statute only to "general assignments": "Whenever any person or corporation shall hereafter make (an assignment) [a general assignment] of his or its estate for the benefit of creditors, the assignee . . . shall be required to pay in full, from the proceeds of the estate, all moneys *bona fide* due to the servants, laborers, and employes of such assignor for their wages accruing" during a certain period up to a certain amount. But this rewriting made good sense. A general assignment by debtors to creditors was an early procedure used to deal with insolvency, in which case protecting laborers was sensible policy. Partial

assignments were simply payments to specific creditors, where special protection for laborers was unnecessary. The distinction between general and partial assignments was an old one, as evidenced by an early opinion of Chief Justice Marshall: U.S. v. Hooe, 7 U.S. 73, 91 (1805) ("Had the legislature contemplated a partial assignment, the words '*or part thereof*,' or others of similar import, would have been added"; courts can still protect laborers by treating transfer of all but a small amount of property as a general assignment).

4 From 1900 to the 1960s

1   Federal Food and Drugs Act of 1906, ch. 3915, 34 Stat. 768 (1906).
2   Federal Reserve Act, ch. 6, 38 Stat. 251 (1913).
3   Federal Trade Commission Act, ch. 311, 38 Stat. 717 (1914).
4   Roy Lubove, *The Struggle for Social Security*, 52–54 (1968) (hereafter Lubove).
5   Federal Employees' Compensation Act, ch. 458, 39 Stat. 742 (1916).
6   Longshoreman's and Harbor Workers' Compensation Act, ch. 509, 44 Stat. 1424 (1927).
7   Lubove, 99.
8   Revenue Act of 1913, 38 Stat. 114 (1913).
9   Ives v. South Buffalo Ry. Co., 94 N.E. 431, 442–44 (New York, 1911).
10   Joel Bishop, *Commentaries on the Written Laws and Their Interpretation*, 4, sec. 4 (1882) (hereafter Bishop). Bishop also describes a statute as "a thread of woof woven into a warp which before existed. It is never to be contemplated as a thing alone, but always as a part of a harmonious whole" (4, sec. 5).
11   Muller v. Oregon, 208 U.S. 412 (1908).
12   Roscoe Pound, "The Causes of Popular Dissatisfaction with the Administration of Justice," 40 *Amer. Law Rev.* 729, 736, 740, 748 (1906).
13   Morton Horwitz, "The Constitution of Change: Legal Fundamentality Without Fundamentalism," 107 *Harv. L. Rev.* 30, 57–63 (1993).
14   U.S. Const., Amend. 17 (1913) (Senate election); U.S. Const. Amend., 19 (1920) (women's suffrage).
15   The material in these paragraphs about the Populist and Progressive movements is based in part on Thomas Cronin, *Direct Democracy: The Politics of Initiative, Referendum, and Recall*, 43–54, 125–27 (1989) (hereafter Cronin).
16   Cronin, 51 (table 3.1).
17   Cronin, 125–26 (table 6.1). The election of judges in these seven states is described in Evan Haynes, *The Selection and Tenure of Judges* (1944): 102 (Arizona), 103–4 (California), 104–5 (Colorado), 121 (Nevada), 124 (North Dakota), 126–27 (Oregon), 135 (Wisconsin).
18   J. Leonard Bates, *The United States, 1898-1928: Progressivism and a Society in Transition*, 117–18 (1976).

19   The Progressive Party platform of 1912, reprinted in *The Progressive Movement, 1900–1915,* 130 (Richard Hofstadter, ed., 1963).

20   Roscoe Pound, "Common Law and Legislation," 21 *Harv. L. Rev.* 383, 383–84 (1908) (hereafter Pound, "Common Law").

21   Ernst Freund, "Prolegomena to a Science of Legislation," 13 *Ill. L. Rev.* 264, 269–70 (1918).

22   71 *Yale L. J.* 218, 225–28 (1961).

23   Chapter 7, appendix A, discusses judicial use of legislative history from the point of view of institutional competence.

24   Theodore Sedgwick, *A Treatise on the Rules Which Govern the Interpretation and Application of Statutory and Constitutional Law,* 205 (1857) (John Pomeroy, ed., 1874) (hereafter Sedgwick) ("But in modern societies, where the division of political attributes is so much more nice and rigorous, where the business of legislation has become multifarious and enormous, and especially in this country where the judiciary is so completely separated from the Legislature, it must be untrue in fact that they can have any personal knowledge sufficient really to instruct them as to the legislative intention; and if untrue in fact, any general theory or loose idea of this kind must be dangerous in practice").

25   143 U.S. 457 (1892).

26   The statute had been drafted and lobbied for by labor associations. *Congressional Record,* 48th Cong., 2d Sess., 1778, 1781, 1785 (1885) (noting organized labor's role in drafting the bill and expressing concern for laborers). Another purpose was to prevent immigration of an "ignorant and servile class" of foreign laborers into the country (at 1634); also at 1631 (comments about foreign laborers' ignorance and ethnicity).

27   143 U.S. at 464–65.

28   143 U.S. at 463.

29   5 Annals of Cong., col. 776 (1796). Alexander Hamilton had also criticized Thomas Jefferson, in the debate over the constitutionality of the U.S. Bank, for alluding to what the constitutional Framers had intended when they rejected a specific provision empowering Congress to authorize corporations: "[W]hatever may have been the intention of the framers of the constitution, or of a law, that intention is to be sought for in the instrument itself, according to the usual and established rules of construction." *The Papers of Alexander Hamilton,* vol. 8, 111 (Harold Syrett, ed., 1965).

   Judicial use of the *Federalist Papers* to interpret the Constitution can be traced to Cohens v. Virginia, 19 U.S. 264, 295, 352, 418–19 (1821) (citing *Federalist Papers*). The rationale for this use, however, may have been to demonstrate contemporaneous understanding, not authorial intent. Reliance on contemporary understanding helps to assure stability in the law, independent of what the authors intended.

30 Hans Baade, "'Original Intent' in Historical Perspective: Some Critical Glosses," 69 *Tex. L. Rev.* 1001, 1016–196 (1991) (hereafter Baade). State courts were also sometimes willing to rely on materials from state constitutional conventions to shed light on the meaning of state constitutions. Baade, 1055–57. Thomas Cooley's view, however, was that state constitutional convention material was still one step removed from the authors because ratification was by vote of the people. In his view, state convention material was therefore less useful for interpreting state constitutions than legislative proceedings were for statutory interpretation. Baade, 1059.

31 Mitchell v. Great Works Milling & Manufacturing Co., 17 F. Cas. 496, 498–99 (1843).

32 Story also broached a constitutional argument, not only in his veiled hint that judges, not legislators, were masters of rules of interpretation, but also in his observation that the "opinions of a few [House] members" expressed neither the views of the House nor of the Senate and president whose views are equally weighty. 17 F. Cas. at 498–99.

33 Baade, 1006–11.

34 Elizabeth McPherson, "The History of Reporting the Debates and Proceedings of Congress," 201–2, 205, 210 (Ph.D. diss., 1940).

35 Woodrow Wilson, *Congressional Government,* p. 82 (World Pub. Co., 1956) ("a government by the chairmen of the Standing Committees of Congress").

36 United States v. Union Pacific Railroad Co., 91 U.S. 72 (1875) (public history considered, but not the views of individual members of Congress).

37 See, e.g., Wood v. Caldwell, 54 Ind. 270, 280–81 (drafting history and reviser's note explaining legislative design). Even before Holy Trinity, the Supreme Court had occasionally used drafting history to shed light on what the final text meant. Blake v. National Banks, 90 U.S. 307, 317–19 (1874) (drafting history).

38 Sedgwick, 203–4 n.(a).

39 G. A. Endlich, *A Commentary on the Interpretation of Statutes Founded on Maxwell's Treatise,* 42–43, 88 (1888) (citing a Pennsylvania court's use of a revising commissioner's report).

40 J. G. Sutherland, *Statutes and Statutory Construction,* 384, sec. 300 (John Lewis, 2d ed., 1904).

41 Bishop, 60, sec. 76.

42 "Statutory Construction, Vol. IX," *Washington Law Reporter,* 321 (May 1881).

43 Sutherland, *Statutes and Statutory Construction,* 879, sec. 470. (1st ed., 1891). Black's 1896 treatise, however, approves the use of drafting history, but he still was grudging about relying on opinions of legislators, even after Holy Trinity. Henry Black, *Construction and Interpretation of the Laws,* 224–29, secs. 91–92 (1896). These opinions were "entitled to but little weight," though the author quotes Bishop to the effect that they can "persuade," citing a case (Ex Parte

Farley, 40 Fed. 66, 69 [D. Ark., 1889],) which considered a statement by the chairman of the House Judiciary Committee.

44 United States v. Trans-Missouri Freight Assn., 166 U.S. 290, 317-18 (1897).

45 Note, "Legislative Materials to Aid Statutory Interpretation," 50 *Harv. L. Rev.* 822, 824-25 (1937) (hereafter Note, "Legislative Materials").

46 Baade, 1088.

47 Roscoe Pound, "The Scope and Purpose of Sociological Jurisprudence, III," 25 *Harv. L. Rev.* 489, 512-16 (1912) (hereafter Pound, "Scope").

48 Pound, "Common Law," 385.

49 Harlan Stone, "The Common Law in the United States," 50 *Harv. L. Rev.* 4, 12-13 (1936).

50 Moragne v. State Marine Lines, Inc., 398 U.S. 375 (1970).

51 Pound, "Common Law," 385.

52 Pound, "Common Law," 387.

53 Pound, "Common Law," 387.

54 Roscoe Pound, "Spurious Interpretation," 7 *Colum. L. Rev.* 379, 380 (1907) (hereafter Pound, "Spurious").

55 Pound, "Spurious," 381.

56 Pound, "Spurious," 381.

57 Pound, "Spurious," 382.

58 Pound, "Spurious," 382.

59 Pound, "Spurious," 383.

60 Pound, "Common Law," 385.

61 Pound, "Spurious," 381.

62 Pound's criticism of the Riggs v. Palmer case (see "Spurious," 382), which did not allow a murderer to inherit under a will from his victim, also seems too harsh, as Hart & Sacks suggested. See, e.g., Henry Hart and Albert Sacks, *The Legal Process*, 89-94 (William N. Eskridge Jr. and Philip Frickey, eds., 1994) (implying approval of the Riggs decision). It is highly unlikely that a legislature would intend the murderer to inherit, and a reasonable judge could so infer.

63 Oliver Wendell Holmes Jr., "The Theory of Legal Interpretation," 12 *Harv. L. Rev.* 417, 419 (1899). Holmes also sounded textualist in the following judicial opinions: U.S. v. Officers & Crew of U.S. Steamer Mangrove, 188 U.S. 720, 725 (1903) ("[I]t is impossible not to feel that the prize law had in mind a different kind of case from this. . . . But some rather weak cases must fall within any law which is couched in general words."); U.S. v. Brown, 206 U.S. 240, 244 (1907) ("We do not apprehend any serious consequences. . . . But, whatever the consequences, we must accept the plain meaning of plain words.")

64 Felix Frankfurter quotes a more textualist-sounding observation in a letter written by Holmes describing a statement that Holmes had made at oral argument to counsel: "I don't care what their [the legislature's] intention was. I only want to know what the words mean." Felix Frankfurter, "Some Reflections on the

Reading of Statutes," 47 *Colum. L. Rev.* 527, 538 (1947) (hereafter Frankfurter, "Reflections").

65   278 U.S. 41, 48 (1928).

66   268 U.S. 161, 166 (1925).

67   163 F. 30, 32 (1st Cir. 1908).

68   278 U.S. at 47 ("We are satisfied . . . that the many private acts like the present generally have been understood, before and since the act now in question not to carry interest by the often repeated words now before us.")

69   See also United States v. Whitridge, 197 U.S. 135, 143 (1905) ("the general purpose is a more important aid to the meaning than any rule which grammar or formal logic may lay down"). In this case, Holmes is relying on a series of statutes that continuously refined the method of valuing property subject to tax in order to provide the basis for rejecting grammar for purpose. 197 U.S. at 142–43. ("The history of the statutes shows a series of continually closer approximations to [the true value of property]. . . . The general purpose of this proviso undeniably is to secure a closer approximation still. In construing it we must bear this obvious purpose in mind.")

70   Even when Holmes said that the "meaning of a sentence is to be felt rather than to be proved," he relied heavily on the "whole text," and it was the dissent (!) that relied on purpose, demonstrated by legislative history. United States v. Johnson, 221 U.S. 488, 496–97 (1911); at 502–3. 505 (Hughes, C.J., dissenting). Another Holmes statement, which seems "purposive," also can be given a textualist reading. For example, when he argued that a "word is not a crystal, transparent and unchanged, it is the skin of a living thought and may vary greatly in color and content according to the circumstances and the time in which it is used" (Towne v. Eisner, 245 U.S. 418, 425 (1918)), he might have required attention to only those elements of context that give meaning to language.

71   Frankfurter, "Reflections," 532.

72   Lochner v. New York, 198 U.S. 45, 75 (1905) (Holmes, J., dissenting) ("The Fourteenth Amendment does not enact Mr. Herbert Spencer's Social Statics").

73   198 U.S. at 76.

74   198 U.S. at 75.

75   Thomas Grey, "Holmes, Pragmatism, and Democracy," 71 *Or. L. Rev.* 521, 534, 538 (1992).

76   272 U.S. 50 (1926).

77   272 U.S. at 52.

78   272 U.S. at 52.

79   Southern Pacific Co. v. Jensen, 244 U.S. 205, 222 (1917) (Holmes, J., dissenting).

80   Julian Eule, "Judicial Review of Direct Democracy," 99 *Yale L. J.* 1503, 1512–13 n. 38 (1990).

81   James Thayer, "The Origin and Scope of the American Doctrine of Constitutional Law," 7 *Harv. L. Rev.* 129, 155–56 (1893).

82 James Landis, "Statutes and the Sources of Law," in *Harvard Legal Essays,* 213 (1934) (referring to the influence of "the rise of social sciences" on legislation and a "science of statutory interpretation") (hereafter Landis).

83 See Note, "Legislative Materials," 822; Morton Horwitz, "The Constitution of Change: Legal Fundamentality Without Fundamentalism," 107 *Harv. L. Rev.* 30, 57–63 (1993).

84 Landis, 213, 219.

85 Landis, 233. Landis claimed an ancient lineage for purposivism in the sixteenth- and seventeenth-century practice of equitable interpretation, arguing that, even in that early period, "behind the formal fiat of the statute lay an aim that challenged [the judge's] sympathetic attention, [and] the appropriate exercise of judicial power permitted courts to advance ends so emphatically asserted." Landis, 216. Samuel Thorne may be correct when he argued in the *Illinois Law Review* article, excerpted in chapter 2, above, that sixteenth-century equitable interpretation was less bold than modern purposive interpretation, but Landis is correct that purposive interpretation can trace its roots to the earlier English practice.

86 310 U.S. 534, 543–44 (1940).

87 Cabell v. Markham, 148 F.2d 737, 739 (2d Cir. 1945).

88 218 F. 547 (2d Cir., 1914). A later Supreme Court case also read "employee" in the National Labor Relations Act in light of the history, context, and purpose of the statute rather than adopt its common law or local law meaning. NLRB v. Hearst Publications, Inc., 322 U.S. 111 (1944).

89 218 F. at 552.

90 218 F. at 552–53.

91 218 F. at 553.

92 69 F.2d 809 (2d Cir. 1934), affirmed, 293 U.S. 465 (1935).

93 69 F.2d at 810.

94 Learned Hand, "Thomas Walter Swan," 57 *Yale L. J.* 167, 169 (1947).

95 United States v. Hutcheson, 312 U.S. 219, 235 (1941).

96 Hand's income tax decisions are not aberrational. In the 1920s and 1930s the Supreme Court set a course toward interpreting the language of the income tax law in light of its underlying statutory purpose without (in many instances) sticking too closely to the text. The Supreme Court affirmed Hand's decision in the "reorganization" case, Gregory v. Helvering, 293 U.S. 465 (1935).

Holmes paid little attention to the text in deciding that "attenuated subtleties" would not allow an income earner to avoid tax by assigning the income to a relative. Lucas v. Earl 281 U.S. 111, 114 (1930). This approach was later applied to taxpayers who retained control over trust property (see Helvering v. Clifford, 309 U.S. 331 [1940]), even though Congress had begun to legislate in the area and the Court could have plausibly concluded that resolution of the complexities could be left to the legislature (as the dissent urged); at 340 (Roberts, J., dissenting).

And the word "property" in the capital asset definition did not have its property law meaning, but depended on the income tax law's underlying purpose. Burnet v. Harmel, 287 U.S. 103, 106 (1932) (sale of carved out income interest). See also Commissioner v. Gillette Motor Transport, Inc., 364 U.S. 130, 134–35 (1960) (summarizing history of purposive interpretation of "property").

97   132 F.2d 660 (2d Cir. 1943) (Hand, J., dissenting). The Supreme Court reached the same result in McWilliams v. Commissioner, 331 U.S. 694 (1947).

98   132 F.2d at 662. See also Borella v. Borden Co., 145 F.2d 63, 64–65 (2d Cir. 1944) ("To say that [purposivism] is a hazardous process is indeed a truism, but we cannot escape it, once we abandon literal interpretation — a method far more unreliable."), affirmed, 325 U.S. 679 (1945).

99   132 F.2d at 662.

100 132 F.2d at 662.

101 However, we should be as careful in characterizing Hand's purposivism as we were with Holmes. In context, not all of his affirmations are as bold as they may sound. Cabell v. Markham, 148 F.2d 737, 739 (2d Cir. 1945), in which Hand criticized making a fortress of the dictionary and favored relying on the sympathetic and imaginative discovery of legislative purpose, involved a statute whose text seemed inconsistent with the obvious purpose that the statute be effective during subsequent wars. The "purpose" that Hand implemented was therefore the modest one of assuring that the statute did not expire. See also Borella v. Borden Co., 145 F.2d at 64, where Hand spoke of the need to "reach the meaning . . . , as always, by recourse to the underlying purpose, and, . . . by trying to project upon the specific occasion how we think persons, actuated by such a purpose, would have dealt with it, if it had been presented to them at the time." But he then acknowledged that a purpose "inhere[s] as much in its limitations as in its affirmations." 145 F.2d at 65.

102 Learned Hand, *The Spirit of Liberty* (Irving Dilliard, ed., 1960) (3d ed., enlarged) (hereafter Dilliard).

103 Learned Hand, "How Far Is a Judge Free in Rendering a Decision?" (1935), in Dilliard, 108 (hereafter Hand, "Rendering").

104 Hand, "Rendering," 107–8.

105 Hand, "Rendering," 109.

106 Hand, "Is There a Common Will?" (1929), Dilliard, 53–54 (hereafter Hand, "Common Will"). See also Gerald Gunther, *Learned Hand*, 433 (1994) (hereafter Gunther) (modern democracy is "not as bad as it seems"; though it is not "ideal," it is "tolerable," insuring "continuity" and "slow change").

107 Gunther, 451.

108 Gunther, 212–18, 249.

109 Gunther, 526.

110 Gunther, 190; also at 348 (Hand's praise for pro-worker legislation).

111 Gunther, 231.

112 Hand, "Common Will," 52–53.

113 Gunther, 136.

114 Gunther, ch. 5, 190–269 (The Peak of Political Enthusiasm).

115 Wolfgang Stechow, "Justice Holmes' Notes on Albrecht Dürer," 58 *J. Aesthetics & Art Criticism* 119, 124 (1949) (containing the text of Holmes's notes) (hereafter Stechow). See also David Burton, *Oliver Wendell Holmes, Jr.*, 27–28 (1980).

116 Stechow, 123.

117 Gunther, 371; Gunther describes Hand as "enthusiastically touring [Italian] museums, absorbed in the art of the Renaissance. . . ."

118 Hand, "Rendering," 109. See also Guiseppi v. Walling, 144 F.2d 608, 624 (2d Cir. 1944) (Hand, J., concurring) ("There is no surer way to misread any document than to read it literally"); Peter Pan Fabrics, Inc. v. Martin Weiner Corp., 274 F.2d 487, 489 (2d Cir. 1960) (rejecting "relentless literalism").

119 Hand, "Rendering," 106–7.

120 Hand, "The Contribution of an Independent Judiciary to Civilization" (1942), in Dilliard, 157.

121 Hand, "Rendering," 106. Hand made a similar statement in his judicial opinions: "As nearly as we can, we must put ourselves in the place of those who uttered the words, and try to divine how they would have dealt with the unforeseen situation; and, although their words are by far the most decisive evidence of what they would have done, they are by no means final." Guiseppi v. Walling, 144 F.2d 608, 624 (2d Cir. 1944) (Hand, J., concurring).

122 Frankfurter, "Reflections," 529, 539. Frankfurter repeated this image in Textile Workers' Union v. Lincoln Mills, 353 U.S. 448, 462, 465 (1957) (Frankfurter, J., dissenting) ("This is more than can be fairly asked even from the alchemy of construction"; "cannot be drawn from [a brooding omnipresence] like nitrogen from the air.").

123 322 U.S. 607, 617 (1944).

124 47 *Colum. L. Rev.* 527, 538 (1947).

125 Helen Thomas, *Felix Frankfurter*, 18–41 (1960) (hereafter Thomas).

126 Thomas, 26–31.

127 Gunther, 359–60; also at 389–91, 395–96 (Hand's reaction to Frankfurter).

128 Frankfurter, "Reflections," 541.

129 United States v. Monia, 317 U.S. 424, 432 (1943) (Frankfurter, J., dissenting).

130 Frankfurter, "Reflections," 537–38.

131 317 U.S. at 431.

132 Commissioner v. Acker, 361 U.S. 87, 94–95 (1959) (Frankfurter, J., dissenting).

133 Frankfurter, "Reflections," 528–29.

134 Felix Frankfurter and Nathan Greene, *The Labor Injunction* (dedication page) (1930).

135 306 U.S. 381 (1939).

136 306 U.S. at 390–91.

137   306 U.S. at 389.

138   306 U.S. at 394. In another case, United States v. Monia, 317 U.S. 424, 444–45 (1943) (Frankfurter, J., dissenting), the interpreted legislation was silent regarding whether a subpoenaed witness had to make an explicit claim of the privilege against self-incrimination to obtain immunity from prosecution. Other statutes explicitly conditioned immunity on making the claim. Frankfurter explained the inconsistency as a drafting quirk which resulted from the fact that these statutes lacked a common drafter. He then read the requirement of an explicit claim into the silent statute.

139   312 U.S. 219 (1941).

140   312 U.S. at 235.

141   312 U.S. at 235–36.

142   312 U.S. at 245–46 (Roberts, J., dissenting).

143   312 U.S. at 246.

144   Frankfurter and Greene, *The Labor Injunction*. See also Thomas, 18, 80; Leonard Baker, *Brandeis and Frankfurter*, 138, 147, 205–6 (1984).

145   Gunther, 51 (noting that Frankfurter thought Thayer's article expressing these views to be "the most important article on constitutional law ever published").

146   141 F.2d 400 (2d Cir. 1944), reversed, 323 U.S. 490 (1945).

147   Hammer v. Dagenhart, 247 U.S. 251, 280 (1918) (Holmes, J., dissenting).

148   Paul Sayre, *The Life of Roscoe Pound*, 216–18 (1948).

149   Statutory text quoted in 323 U.S. at 492 n. 2.

150   52 F. Supp. 142, 147–48 (S.D.N.Y. 1943).

151   323 U.S. at 510 (Murphy, J., dissenting).

152   The Court agreed that telegrams were "goods" "because the Act defines 'goods' ... to include among other things 'articles or subjects of commerce of any character.' ... It was long ago settled that telegraph lines when extending through different states are instruments of commerce and ... [t]hat 'ideas, wishes, orders, and intelligence' are 'subjects' of the interstate commerce in which telegraph companies engage. ..." But the Court refused to conclude that Western Union produced the goods. The statute defined "produced" to mean "produced, manufactured, mined, handled, or in any other manner worked on," and the Court did not construe "worked on" or "handled" to include what Western Union did to accomplish the interstate transit or movement of messages in commerce; the Court relied in part on a linguistic canon of interpretation—that words should have a consistent meaning within a statute. Finally, the word "ship" did not, in colloquial usage, include what Western Union did with telegrams. 323 U.S. at 502–6.

153   323 U.S. at 501.

154   Hand simply differed with the Court's conclusion that Western Union did not "handle" or "work on" the goods. At the end of his opinion he states that arguments based on "well-known canons of statutory interpretation" do "not in our

judgment overbear the construction we have adopted." 141 F.2d at 404. I take this statement to be a rejection of the "consistent usage" canon, later relied on by the Supreme Court majority to interpret the meaning of "production."

155 141 F.2d at 403.

156 Morton Horwitz, *The Transformation of American Law, 1870–1960: The Crisis of Legal Orthodoxy*, 169 (1992) (hereafter Horwitz, *1870–1960*).

157 William N. Eskridge Jr. and Philip Frickey, "Commentary: The Making of *The Legal Process*," 107 *Harv. L. Rev.* 2031, 2033–45 (1994) (hereafter Eskridge and Frickey, "Commentary").

158 Henry M. Hart Jr. and Albert M. Sacks, *The Legal Process* (William N. Eskridge Jr. and Philip Frickey, eds., 1994) (hereafter Hart & Sacks). All citations are to the published version.

159 Willian N. Eskridge Jr., *Dynamic Statutory Interpretation*, 141–42 (1994); Eskridge and Frickey, *Commentary*, 2032, 2036, 2040; Horwitz, *1870–1960*, 254.

160 Horwitz, *1870–1960*, 170.

161 See Horwitz, *1870–1960*, chs. 6–8, 169–246.

162 Jerome Frank, *Law and the Modern Mind*, 152 (1970) (hereafter Frank, *Modern Mind*).

163 Karl Llewellyn, "Remarks on the Theory of Appellate Decision and the Rules or Canons About How Statutes Are to Be Construed," 3 *Vand. L. Rev.* 395 (1950). See also Stephen Ross, "Where Have You Gone, Karl Llewellyn? Should Congress Turn Its Lonely Eyes to You?" 45 *Vand. L. Rev.* 561 (1992).

164 Max Radin, "Statutory Interpretation," 43 *Harv. L. Rev.* 863, 870–71, 876–78 (1930).

165 See also Frank, *Modern Mind*, 151. ("The truth is, of course, that what Pound calls law and what he calls non-legal cannot be separated.")

166 Old Colony Bondholders v. New York, N.H. & H.R. Co., 161 F.2d 413, 436 (2d Cir. 1947) (Frank, J., dissenting). Frank also cited (161 F.2d at 436) Hand's view that "[t]here is no surer guide in the interpretation of a statute than its purpose when that is sufficiently disclosed; nor any surer mark of over-solicitude for the letter than to wince at carrying out that purpose because the words used do not formally quite match with it," from Federal Deposit Ins. Corp. v. Tremaine, 133 F.2d 827, 830 (2d Cir. 1943). See also Frank, "Words and Music: Some Remarks on Statutory Interpretation," 47 *Colum. L. Rev.* 1259, 1262 (1947).

167 Max Radin, "A Short Way With Statutes," 56 *Harv. L. Rev.* 388, 421–22 (1942) (hereafter Radin, "Short Way").

168 Radin, "Short Way," 407, 410–11, 422.

169 Radin, "Short Way," 406.

170 Radin, "Short Way," 422.

171 Hart & Sacks, 1374.

172 Hart & Sacks, 1374.

173 Hart & Sacks, 1378.

174 Hart & Sacks, 1374.

175 Hart & Sacks, 1374.

176 Hart & Sacks, 1378.

177 Hart & Sacks, 145–50.

178 Hart & Sacks, 146–47.

179 Introduction to Hart & Sacks, xciv.

180 Hart & Sacks, 4.

181 *Federalist Papers* 78, 399 (Max Beloff, ed., 1987). See also United States v. The William, 28 Fed. Cases 614, 620 (D. Mass. 1808) ("Legal discretion is limited. . . . Political discretion has a far wider range").

182 Hart & Sacks, 149–50.

183 Eskridge and Frickey, "Commentary," 2032–33. See also William N. Eskridge Jr. and Philip Frickey, "Law as Equilibrium," 108 *Harv. L. Rev.* 26, 34 (1994); Edward Rubin, "The New Legal Process, the Synthesis of Discourse, and the Microanalysis of Institutions," 109 *Harv. L. Rev.* 1393, 1425–26 (1996).

184 Hart & Sacks, 147.

185 Introduction to Hart & Sacks, xcvi.

186 Eskridge, *Dynamic Statutory Interpretation.* 161.

5 Giving Judges as Little to Do as Possible

1 We have, it seems, all become pragmatists. Judge Richard Posner, whose single-minded commitment to law and economics as the foundation of law seemed unshakable, has become a pragmatist, perhaps *because* he has shifted roles from professor to judge: "I shall argue in short for a functional, policy-saturated, nonlegalistic, naturalistic, and skeptical, but decidedly not cynical, conception of the legal process; in a word (although, I fear, an inadequate word), for a *pragmatic* jurisprudence" (emphasis in original). Richard Posner, *The Problems of Jurisprudence*, 26 (1990).

2 William N. Eskridge Jr., *Dynamic Statutory Interpretation*, 56 (1994).

3 For a review of the literature, see Daniel Farber and Philip Frickey, *Law and Public Choice* (1991) (hereafter "Farber and Frickey"); Daniel Farber and Philip Frickey, "Foreword: Positive Political Theory in the Nineties," 80 *Geo. L. J.* 457 (1992); Jerry Mashaw, "The Economics of Politics and the Understanding of Public Law," 65 *Chi-Kent L. Rev.* 123 (1989). There is an older critique of purposivism, developed by Dickerson, which also undermines the claim that judges can rely on statutory purpose. In Reed Dickerson, *The Interpretation and Application of Statutes*, 90–91 (1975), the author argues that purpose is often harder rather than easier to identify than specific legislative intent because "[t]he disciplines of the legislative process are directed more to attaining agreement on the specific action to be taken in a bill than to attaining agreement on its legislative purposes. . . ." Dickerson explains: "Even those who are closest to the bill are

likely to focus more sharply on the specific action taken in the bill than on any general statements of purpose. Other legislators, whose knowledge of the bill tends to be general only, are likely to have their own notions of the broader or more remote purposes that it will serve and not so likely, therefore, to adopt the states of mind of others. Indeed, even those who are closely familiar with the specific terms of the bill may agree on the same specific action for a variety of reasons. As a result, there is likely to be less actual agreement on specific ultimate objectives than there is on the action taken in the bill itself."

4 This description relies heavily on Russell Hardin, *Collective Action* (1982). See, generally, Mancur Olsen, *The Logic of Collective Action* (1965).

5 See William D. Popkin, *Materials on Legislation*, 813–25 (2d ed., 1997).

6 Frank Easterbrook, "The Court and the Economic System," 98 *Harv. L. Rev.* 4, 15 (1984) (hereafter Easterbrook, "Economic"). An example of tossing an issue to the courts is the retroactivity of the Civil Rights Act of 1991. An earlier version of this law contained a retroactivity provision, which was one reason for a presidential veto. In debating a later version, senators inserted diverse views about retroactivity into the *Congressional Record*. Senator Bob Dole, in a section-by-section analysis of the bill, asserted that the act was prospective. 137 *Cong. Rec.* S15478 (daily ed., Oct. 30, 1991); also at S15483 (daily ed., Oct. 30, 1991) (Senator Danforth). Senator Ted Kennedy stated his view that the act was retroactive, or at least that the issue was left open for the courts to decide. 137 *Cong. Rec.* S15963 (daily ed., Nov. 5, 1991); at S15485 (daily ed., Oct. 30, 1991). Disagreement was spread all over the *Congressional Record*. The statute was silent on retroactivity, and the Court held that Congress left the issue for judicial resolution. Landgraf v. USI Film Products, 511 U.S. 244, 286–87 (1994) ("highly probable . . . that, because it was unable to resolve the retroactivity issue . . . , Congress viewed the matter as an open issue to be resolved by the courts").

7 The beady-eyed approach is associated with private-interest compromise, *not* the compromise of public values. See Easterbrook, "Economic," 15 ("statutes . . . designed to replace the outcomes of private transactions with monopolistic ones"). See also Frank Easterbrook, "Statutes' Domains," 50 *U. Chi. L. Rev.* 533, 547 (1983) (hereafter Easterbrook, "Domains") (the judge should be "faithful to the nature of compromise in private interest legislation"). It is unclear, however, why the beady-eyed approach should not also apply when the statute compromises public values. Is Easterbrook implicitly suggesting that the judge has a greater role to play when public values are at stake?

8 See In re Erickson, 815 F.2d 1090, 1094 (7th Cir. 1987).

9 See, generally, Kenneth Arrow, *Social Choice and Individual Values* (2d ed., 1963).

10 Legislators might try to counteract agenda control by engaging in strategic voting—that is, voting against their preference-ordering so that the final vote will be more palatable. An example: Assume that the first vote in the earlier workers' compensation case is (N)o benefits vs. (M)oderate benefits; the most generous

program, $, would eventually win in that case. As an industry representative with an N, M, $ preference structure, you might be well-advised to vote for (M)oderate, instead of (N)o benefits on the first vote, so that the next choice will be between (M)oderate and $, in which case (M)oderate wins.

11 See Farber and Frickey, 24–33.

12 In Raines v. Byrd, 117 S.Ct. 2312 (1997), the Court implicitly rejects one of the essential features of the public-choice model of the legislative process—that a law is the result of logrolling to pass a statute that is not likely to pass without the bargain. The Court denies standing for a member of Congress to challenge the constitutionality of the president's line-item veto on the ground that his vote is ineffective in the following hypothetical situation. Assume that one-third of the legislature opposes positions A and B, one-third favors A but not B, and one-third favors B but not A. The A and B advocates join forces to pass the law. The president vetoes A. Even though the law would not have passed without A, and the advocates of position A are thereby denied their say in the passage of the law, the A advocates are denied standing to challenge the veto.

13 I do not mean that a commitment to public values always produces a good political process. Such commitment might result in single-issue politics, which many would consider undesirable.

14 Easterbrook, "Economic," 16.

15 Easterbrook, "Economic," 16.

16 Gregory v. Helvering, 69 F.2d 809, 810–11 (2d Cir. 1934), affirmed, 293 U.S. 465 (1935).

17 Easterbrook, "Economic," 17.

18 Donald Langevoort, "Statutory Obsolescence and the Judicial Process: The Revisionist Role of the Courts in Federal Banking Regulation," 85 *Mich. L. Rev.* 672 (1987) (hereafter Langevoort).

19 Langevoort, 691–98.

20 Easterbrook, "Economic," 17.

21 See Cass Sunstein, *Legal Reasoning and Political Conflict*, 4 (1996) (time constraints on judges contribute to incompletely theorized agreements).

22 See, e.g., Donald Langevoort, "Statutory Obsolescence and the Judicial Process: The Revisionist Role of the Courts in Federal Banking Regulation," 85 *Mich. L. Rev.* 672 (1987); Bruce Ackerman and William Hassler, "Beyond the New Deal: Coal and the Clean Air Act," 89 *Yale L. J.* 1466 (1980); Daniel Shaviro, "Beyond Public Choice and Public Interest: A Study of the Legislative Process as Illustrated by Tax Legislation in the 1980s," 139 *U. Pa. L. Rev.* 1 (1990).

23 Easterbrook, "Economic," 16.

24 467 U.S. 925 (1984).

25 Easterbrook, "Economic," 54.

26 467 U.S. at 941–42 (Rehnquist, J., dissenting).

27 Pub. L. 98-426, para. 4, 98 Stat. 1639, 1641 (1984). The conference committee

stated that the majority in WMATA "changed key components of what had widely been regarded as the proper rules governing contractor and subcontractor liability and immunity under the [Act.]" H.R. Rep. 98-1027, 98th Cong., 2d Sess. 24 (1984).

28 One reason why agenda control might not dominate the legislative process is unpersuasive in the United States. When ideology arrays preferences along a liberal–conservative spectrum (rather than in the form of unstructured rank orderings, as in the previous workers' compensation example), the result will be determined by the median voter, rather than by agenda control. However, the tendency to structure issues along a liberal–conservative spectrum may be minimal in the United States, where political parties are less ideologically oriented and much weaker than in Europe. Politicians have decentralized state and local power bases that discourage central party control, which might otherwise impose a more ideological perspective. Various "reforms" also have weakened the party structure; campaign spending rules have encouraged formation of Political Action Committees (PACS), which give a legislator some independence of traditional party control.

29 See, generally, Cass Sunstein, "Naked Preferences and the Constitution," 84 *Colum. L. Rev.* 1689 (1984).

30 Bernard Asbell, *The Senate Nobody Knows,* 5 (1978) (Muskie is the Senate's "Mr. Environment"). The president also plays a legislative role—exercised through the threat of a veto, party leadership, control of patronage, force of personality, and media access—and in this role he often takes a broad view of public policy. For example, the deregulation of the airline industry, which undermined the oligopolistic control enjoyed by private economic interests, benefitted from presidential leadership that favored deregulation. And protectionist tariff legislation—arguably bad for the nation overall—has been opposed by the president, who has exerted his leadership, even though particular legislators would be inclined to vote otherwise.

31 Green v. Bock Laundry Machine Co., 490 U.S. 504, 528 (1989) (Scalia, J., concurring in the judgment). See also Chisom v. Roemer, 501 U.S. 380, 404 (1991) (Scalia, J., dissenting): "[F]irst, find the ordinary meaning of the language in its textual context," and then "us[e] established canons of construction [to determine] whether there is any clear indication that some permissible meaning other than the ordinary one applies."

32 Easterbrook, "Domains," 550–51.

33 See Antonin Scalia, "The Rule of Law as a Law of Rules," 56 *U. Chi. L. Rev.* 1175 (1989).

34 See, generally, William Novak, "Salus Populi: The Roots of Regulation in America, 1787-1873" (Ph.D. diss., 1991); William Novak, "Common Regulation: Legal Origins of State Power in America," 45 *Hastings L. J.* 1061 (1994).

35 Easterbrook, "Domains," 549–50.

36 Lochner v. New York, 198 U.S. 45, 76 (1905) (Holmes, J., dissenting).

37 Texas v. Johnson, 491 U.S. 397 (1989).

38 See Louis Jaffe, *English and American Judges as Lawmakers*, 20 (1969) (hereafter Jaffe).

39 James Thayer, "The Origin and Scope of the American Doctrine of Constitutional Law," 7 *Harv. L. Rev.* 129, 156 (1893).

40 Antonin Scalia, *A Matter of Interpretation*, 47 (1997). See also remarks of Alexander Bickel, "Arthur Garfield Hays Conference: The Proper Role of the United States Supreme Court in Civil Liberties Cases," 10 *Wayne L. Rev.* 457, 477 (Dorsen, ed., 1964). See, generally, Alexander Bickel, *The Least Dangerous Branch*" (1962).

41 English commentators make a similar point when they argue that judges cannot preserve "justice" if they are perceived as too political. Jaffe, 7–8. Perhaps preserving judicial political capital is more important when the legislature is truly sovereign, as in England.

42 See Gerald Gunther, *Learned Hand* (1994) (hereafter Gunther) (discussing Hand's concern about judicial activism opposing legislative experimentation and his fear of the public's reaction, as evidenced by the recall of judges and judicial decisions (212–19, 249); and discussing Hand's advanced views on free speech, in comparison to Justice Holmes, and his opposition to political witch-hunts during World War I and the McCarthy period (157–61, 586–91)).

43 See William D. Popkin, "An 'Internal' Critique of Justice Scalia's Theory of Statutory Interpretation," 76 *Minn. L. Rev.* 1133, 1173–86 (1992). See also Jaffe, 14 (doubting the English view that the public objects to "political" judging).

44 See Paul Simon, *Advice and Consent: Clarence Thomas, Robert Bork, and the Intriguing History of the Supreme Court's Nomination Battles* (1992).

45 Ernst Freund, "Prolegomena to a Science of Legislation," 13 *U. Ill. L. Rev.* 264, 269–70 (1919).

46 Gray v. Sanders, 372 U.S. 368 (1963); Wesberry v. Sanders, 376 U.S. 1 (1964); Reynolds v. Sims, 377 U.S. 533 (1964).

47 Roe v. Wade, 410 U.S. 113 (1973).

48 Miranda v. Arizona, 384 U.S. 436 (1966).

49 Southern Pacific Co. v. Jensen, 244 U.S. 205, 221 (1917) (Holmes, J., dissenting).

50 Antonin Scalia, *A Matter of Interpretation* 25 (1997).

51 I do not discuss routine sources of uncertainty, such as ambiguity (except for lay vs. technical meaning), vagueness, open-ended texts, and situations in which an obviously incomplete text with gaps must be filled by a judge. Textualists and nontextualists alike agree that something more than textual understanding is needed to resolve these doubts, even if they disagree on what that something might be. I am concerned here with other sources of uncertainty that undermine the textualist's claim to an objective standard of textual meaning independent of the normative interpretive theory that urges reliance on the text in the first

place. Some examples of routine sources of uncertainty are given in appendix B to this chapter.

52 See Nix v. Hedden, 149 U.S. 304 (1893) (because tomatoes are vegetables in colloquial usage, and there is no evidence that the statute meant the more technical botanical definition—in which tomatoes are fruits—the tariff act's use of the term vegetables includes tomatoes.

53 One of the few cases to identify the statute's author and audience in order to decide whether its text has a lay or technical meaning is St. Luke's Hospital Assn. v. United States, 333 F.2d 157 (6th Cir. 1964). The issue was whether "interns" did or did not include residents. Lay understanding when the statute was passed used the broader meaning, but technical usage in the medical field was narrower.

54 Green v. Bock Laundry Machine Co, 490 U.S. 504, 528 (1989) (Scalia, J., concurring in the judgment) (relying on ordinary usage because it is the meaning "most likely to have been understood by the whole Congress which voted on the words of the statute").

55 In re Sinclair, 870 F.2d 1340, 1342–43 (7th Cir. 1989).

56 870 F.2d at 1342 ("assumptions [legislative] authors entertained about how their words would be understood").

57 870 F.2d at 1342 ("Language is a process of communication that works only when authors and readers share a set of rules and meanings").

58 Judges often try to avoid a conflict between author and audience, or among multiple authors or audiences, by finding that lay and technical meanings converge. For example, in Mohasco Corp. v. Silver, 447 U.S. 807, 825 (1980), the Court considered two possible audiences, the lay public and "one who carefully read the entire section"—which I take to mean legal counsel. A statute required filing a discrimination complaint with a federal agency within 180 days, except when states provided their own administrative remedy. In "state remedy" jurisdictions, the complainant had three hundred days to file with the federal agency, except that the complaint could be filed no earlier than sixty days after filing with the state agency (or earlier, if the state agency completed its work more quickly). In Mohasco, the state provided a remedy. The complainant filed with the federal agency within the period (on day 291), but processing was delayed until after the state agency considered the issue. The sixty-day delay period, permitting state agency consideration, extended beyond the 300-day filing period requirement. The issue was whether the filing was timely. The Court held that the simpler lay person's reading of this statute was to require filing within 180 days. The more complex reading (apparent to the trained legal reader) was to require filing within 240 days (in most cases) in "state remedy" jurisdictions, so that the sixty-day delay period would expire within the lengthened 300-day requirement. Under either reading, the complainant was tardy.

59 United States v. Wells Fargo Bank, 485 U.S. 351, 355 (1988).

60 See West Virginia University Hospitals, Inc. v. Casey, 499 U.S. 83, 101 n. 7 (1991)

("The 'will of Congress' we look to is not a will evolving from Session to Session, but a will expressed and fixed in a particular enactment.").

61 See, generally, Lawrence Lessig, "Fidelity in Translation," 71 *Tex. L. Rev.* 1165 (1993).

62 Braschi v. Stahl Associates Co., 543 N.E.2d 49, 52–54 (N.Y. 1989). Some change shatters meaning, often through technology, in which case judicial choice is both necessary and apparent. In Johnson v. Calvert, 851 P.2d 776 (Cal. 1993), affirming, Anna J. v. Mark C., 286 Cal. Rptr. 369 (Ct. App. 1991), a dispute arose about who was the "mother" of an unborn child. Mark and Crispina wanted a child, but Crispina was medically unable to bear children. She did, however, provide an egg that was fertilized by sperm from her husband outside her womb. The embryo was then implanted in Anna's womb for a fee. The contract with Anna provided that Anna waived parental rights. Later, Anna wanted to keep the child. The California Supreme Court held that Crispina was the "natural mother" under the statute. The court admitted that the word could apply to either Anna or Crispina; change had fractured the text. It held that the statute showed no preference for either mother, both of whom "presented acceptable proof of maternity." The court decided to rely on the intentions of the parties in entering the surrogacy relationship, rejecting the argument that the contract was against public policy, and rejecting a "best interests of the child" test, although it suggested that the "intent" test will usually produce a result in the child's best interests.

63 Green v. Bock Laundry Machine Co., 490 U.S. 504, 528 (1989) (Scalia, J., concurring).

64 Chisom v. Roemer, 501 U.S. 380, 410 (1991) (Scalia, J., dissenting).

65 Smith v. U.S., 508 U.S. 223, 242 (1993) (Scalia, J., dissenting). See also Oliver Wendell Holmes Jr., "The Theory of Legal Interpretation," 12 *Harv. L. Rev.* 417, 418 (1899) (relying on meaning determined by a "normal speaker of English" is a "special variety . . . of our old friend the prudent man" and an example of the law's "externality"). But see chapter 4, for a discussion of Holmes's purposivist leanings.

66 501 U.S. at 404 (Scalia, J., dissenting).

67 This example is inspired by Delaware Alcoholic Beverage Control Comm'n. v. Newsome, 690 A.2d 906 (Del. 1996).

68 501 U.S. 380 (1991).

69 Scholars are beginning to study how the public understands particular terms, but not how the public would ordinarily expect statutory meaning to be determined. Clark Cunningham, Judith Levi, Georgia Green, and Jeffrey Kaplan, "Plain Meaning and Hard Cases" (review of Lawrence Solan, *The Language of Judges*), 103 *Yale L. J.* 1561, 1588–1613 (1994). See also Law and Linguistics Conference, 73 *Wash. U. L. Q.* 769–1313 (1995).

70 See the distinction in chapter 4 between cautious and full-bodied purposivism.

71 See Mohasco Corp. v. Silver, 447 U.S. 807, 818–19 (1980) (a heavily filibus-

tered civil rights law passed as a result of compromise). See also U.S. v. Board of Comm'rs. of Sheffield, 435 U.S. 110, 149 n. 12 (1978) (Stevens, J., dissenting) (courts must respect the product of compromise when interpreting the voting rights statute).

72 See, e.g., St. Martin Evangelical Lutheran Church v. South Dakota, 451 U.S. 772, 791 (1981) (Stevens, J., concurring in the judgment) ("Congress has a special duty to choose its words carefully when it is drafting technical and complex laws; we facilitate our work as well as that of Congress when we adhere closely to the statutory text in cases like this [involving coverage of unemployment insurance tax law]"); United California Bank v. United States, 439 U.S. 180, 211 (1978) (Stevens, J., dissenting) ("I firmly believe that the best way to achieve evenhanded administration of our tax laws is to adhere closely to the language used by Congress to define taxpayers' responsibilities. Occasionally there will be clear manifestations of a contrary intent that justify a nonliteral reading, but surely this is not such a case").

73 Pennington v. Coxe, 6 U.S. 33, 52–53 (1804) (Chief Justice Marshall); James Kent, *Commentaries on American Law*, vol. 1, 431–32 (1826); Joseph Story, "Law, Legislation and Codes," in *Encyclopedia Americana*, appendix 7, 584 (Francis Lieber, ed., 1831); Sawyer v. Inhabitants of Northfield, 61 Mass. 490, 494 (1851) (Justice Shaw); Commonwealth v. Gardner, 77 Mass. 438, 443 (1858) (Justice Shaw).

74 Gustafson v. Alloyd Co., Inc., 513 U.S. 561, 586 (1995) (Thomas, J., dissenting) (quoting from Russell Motor Car Co. v. United States, 261 U.S. 514, 519 (1923)): "Noscitur a sociis is a well-established and useful rule of construction where words are of obscure or doubtful meaning; and then, but only then, its aid may be sought to remove the obscurity or doubt by reference to the associated words."

75 United States National Bank of Oregon v. Independent Insurance Agents of America, Inc., 508 U.S. 439, 454–55 (1993).

76 513 U.S. at 571, 578 (majority opinion), at 594 (Thomas, J., dissenting).

77 432 U.S. 312 (1977).

78 481 U.S. 368 (1987).

79 In re Wagner, 808 F.2d 542, 546 (7th Cir. 1986) (the meaning of "gross income" in a bankruptcy statute is determined on the basis of that law's purposes, not the meaning of the same phrase in other statutes).

80 Drafting reality is also an issue when statutes written at different times are codified together. The different authorship suggests that the language of the two laws need not be read as a single text, but the temptation to integrate the texts is considerable in order to avoid the kinds of policy judgments invited by a separate reading. For example, in Sullivan v. Stroop, 496 U.S. 478, 484 (1990), the Court insisted that "identical words used in different parts of the same act are intended to have the same meaning." The phrase at issue was "child support." An earlier public law, codified in Part IV-D of the Social Security Act, defined

"child support" to refer to a parental obligation because it dealt with enforcing a father's obligation to support a child on welfare. A second and later statute, codified in Part IV-A of the Social Security Act, disregarded $50 of "child support" in computing a child's income for computing welfare benefits. The Court held that "child support" in the second law (Part IV-A) did not include government support for the child provided through the Social Security program, in part because Part IV-D referred only to parental support, disregarding the disparate drafting history of the two laws. That history revealed not only that the laws were written at different times, but also that the disregarded $50 made a "sudden appearance" in a House-Senate conference and had not been in either the House or Senate bill. 496 U.S. at 492 (Blackmun, J., dissenting).

In Sorenson v. Secretary of the Treasury, 475 U.S. 851, 863 (1986), the word "overpayment" in 1975 and 1981 statutes was given the same meaning, in part because the laws were codified in two adjacent sections of the Internal Revenue Code. The first law defined an "overpayment" of taxes to include something that was not an overpayment but was treated as such—a percentage of earnings that the government would pay the worker as an Earned Income Credit. The second law required that "overpayments" would be paid to the state to reimburse it for welfare benefits previously paid to the family of the person otherwise entitled to a refund of an overpayment and obligated to support the children. The Court treated these texts as though they were part of an integrated document, claiming to rely on the author's perspective: "[I]t defies belief that Congress was unaware" in 1981 of the 1975 provision placed in the adjacent section of the code. The dissenting justices could not accept the Court's characterization of authorial understanding. They noted that the 1981 amendment was part of a huge omnibus statute and that many legislators were unlikely to be aware of the provision: "With all due respect to the Court and to our hardworking neighbors in the Congress, I think 'it defies belief' to assume that a substantial number of legislators were sufficiently familiar with [the 1981 statute] to realize that somewhere in that vast piece of hurriedly enacted legislation there was a provision that changed the 6-year-old Earned Income Credit Program." 475 U.S. at 867 (Stevens, J., dissenting).

81 United States v. Monia, 317 U.S. 424, 444–45 (1943) (Frankfurter, J., dissenting).

82 306 U.S. 381, 389, 394 (1939).

83 Even texts written at the same time may not use words consistently. For example, in Lawson v. Suwanee Fruit & Steamship Co., 336 U.S. 198 (1949), a workers' compensation statute provided benefits for work-related disability. To achieve that purpose, the statute defined "disability" to mean an incapacity resulting from a work-related injury. Another portion of the statute provided a "second injury" fund, which provided that if an employee who was partially disabled before acquiring a job then suffers a job-related injury that results in permanent and total disability, the employer will be liable only for the disability resulting

from the second injury. This rule is intended to encourage employers to hire the partially disabled, whether or not the partial disability was work-related, by removing the employer's concern about workers' compensation liability for any total disability that later may occur on the job. The court read the word "disability" in the second injury part of the statute to have its colloquial meaning, not the meaning determined by the statutory definition.

84 The best-known modern case to raise this issue is West Virginia University Hospitals, Inc. v. Casey, 499 U.S. 83 (1991). A statute provided for recovery of "attorneys' fees" by a winning party, but it was silent on experts' fees. Other statutes explicitly provided for recovery of both the attorneys' and experts' fees. Justice Scalia read silence regarding experts' fees as evidence that the statute did not provide for recovery of experts' fees, given the explicit affirmation of such recovery in other statutes. Justice John Paul Stevens, the purposivist, argued that the historical context of the specific statute was more important than evidence derived from reading multiple statutes together and that this context indicated congressional intent to allow both attorneys' and experts' fees to be recovered.

6 Giving Judges Something to Do

1 Quoted in Henry May, *The Enlightenment in America*, 296 (1976).
2 See, e.g., Martha Minow, *Making All the Difference: Inclusion, Exclusion, and American Law* (1990); Martha Minow, "Justice Engendered," 101 *Harv. L. Rev.* 10 (1987); Max Radin, "The Pragmatist and the Feminist," 63 *S. Cal. L. Rev.* 1699 (1990). Cass Sunstein argues that a strong case also could be made that James Madison's advocacy of checks and balances in the federal government—to offset the ability of one faction to dominate another—had the additional objective of transforming legislative politics into a deliberative process about public values. A significant strain in Madison's thinking, in other words, was to advance Anti-Federalist goals but by different means. He sought ways to adapt the republican traditions of civic virtue, which were historically associated with small city-states, to the needs and circumstances of a large nation-state. Cass Sunstein, "Interest Groups in American Public Law," 38 *Stan. L. Rev.* 29, 38–45 (1985).
3 Gerald Gunther, *Learned Hand*, 656–71 (1994).
4 Daniel Moynihan, *Maximum Feasible Misunderstanding* (1970).
5 Frank Michelman, "Law's Republic," 97 *Yale L. J.* 1493, 1526–28, 1532–37 (1988) (hereafter Michelman, "Republic").
6 See Lawrence Tribe, "The Puzzling Persistence of Process-Based Constitutional Theories," 89 *Yale L. J.* 1063 (1980).
7 See, generally, Henry Friendly, "Some Kind of Hearing," 123 *U. Pa. L. Rev.* 1267 (1975).
8 The efficacy of these constitutional rules is uncertain. A minority of states (by

judicial fiat) adopt an "enrolled bill" approach, which precludes judicial review for violations of state constitutional rules about legislative procedures. And some states which review for procedural error excuse lapses that seem "harmless" (such as failure to read the bill three times; or violation of the one-subject rule if the title is accurate). See William D. Popkin, *Materials on Legislation*, 782–98 (2d ed., 1997).

9   For example, revenue bills must originate in the House of Representatives (U.S. Const., art. 1, para. 7); and 20 percent of those present can force recording of the yeas and nays in the journal (U.S. Const., art. 1, para. 5).

10 Metzenbaum v. Federal Energy Regulatory Commission, 675 F.2d 1282, 1287–88 (D.C. Cir. 1982).

11 Minnesota State Board for Community Colleges v. Knight, 465 U.S. 271, 283 (1984). But compare Vander Jagt v. O'Neill, 699 F.2d 1166, 1170 (D.C. Cir. 1982) (court reserves power to determine whether party representation on congressional committees so departs from party membership in the parent chamber that it is "manipulated beyond reason").

12 John Hart Ely, *Democracy and Distrust: A Theory of Judicial Review*, 79–83, 102–3, 151–53 (1980) (hereafter Ely).

13 Ely, 87.

14 United States v. Carolene Products Co., 304 U.S. 144, 152 n. 4 (1938) (stricter scrutiny to protect "discrete and insular minorities").

15 Ely, 152.

16 Bruce Ackerman, "Beyond Carolene Products," 98 *Harv. L. Rev.* 713, 729 (1985).

17 See, e.g., King v. Smith, 392 U.S. 309 (1968) (state's definition of "father," which includes a man living with the mother but who has no duty to support children, violates the federal AFDC grant-in-aid statute).

18 Jonathan Macey, "Promoting Public-Regarding Legislation Through Statutory Interpretation: An Interest Group Model," 86 *Colum. L. Rev.* 223, 250–56 (1986).

19 The phrase is borrowed from Jerry Mashaw, "As if Republican Interpretation," 97 *Yale L. J.* 1685 (1988) (hereafter Mashaw).

20 Ely, 153.

21 Gerald Postema, *Bentham and the Common Law Tradition*, 67 (1986).

22 Compare Goldberg v. Kelly, 397 U.S. 254 (1970) (needs-based welfare) with Mathews v. Eldridge, 424 U.S. 319 (1976) (Social Security disability benefits).

23 Rostker v. Goldberg, 453 U.S. 57, 72, 74 (1981).

24 United States Railroad Retirement Board v. Fritz, 449 U.S. 166 (1980) (upholding a statute that denied claims to both railroad and Social Security retirement benefits by long-term railroad workers who had no recent tie to the industry).

25 449 U.S. at 170, 180–89 (Stevens, J., concurring in the judgment).

26 Schweiker v. Wilson, 450 U.S. 221, 243–44 (1981) (Powell, J., dissenting) (classification prevents the mentally ill in state hospitals from obtaining certain cash

welfare benefits). See also United States v. Lopez, 514 U.S. 549, 562–63 (1995) (no showing that Congress made any findings about the connection of regulated activity to interstate commerce).

27 See, generally, Frank Michelman, "Law's Republic," 97 *Yale L. J.* 1493 (1988); Frank Michelman, "Traces of Self-Government," 100 *Harv. L. Rev.* 4 (1986) (hereafter Michelman, "Traces"); Cass Sunstein, "Beyond the Republican Revival," 97 *Yale L. J.* 1539 (1988).

28 Michelman, "Republic," 1532–37.

29 Michelman, "Republic," 1533.

30 Michelman, "Traces," 32–33.

31 See, generally, Lynn Henderson, "Legality and Empathy," 85 *Mich. L. Rev.* 1574 (1987); Jane Schacter, "Metademocracy: The Changing Structure of Legitimacy in Statutory Interpretation," 108 *Harv. L. Rev.* 593, 623–24 (1995) (hereafter Schacter).

32 501 U.S. 380 (1991).

33 The Constitution prohibited only *intentional* discrimination, but the statute prevented discriminatory results.

34 Some commentators might argue that the case is an example of enforcing "under-enforced" *constitutional* rights through statutory interpretation. See, generally, Lawrence Sager, "Fair Measure: The Legal Status of Underenforced Constitutional Norms," 91 *Harv. L. Rev.* 1212, 1213, 1217–20 (1978); William N. Eskridge Jr., *Dynamic Statutory Interpretation*, 286–89 (1994) (hereafter Eskridge, *Dynamic*). I prefer to view the decision as an example of the Court exercising lawmaking discretion to identify statutory rights in light of Republican values by drawing inspiration from the Constitution, frankly accepting the judge's creative interpretive role in determining statutory meaning.

35 The opinion (501 U.S. at 383) opens: "The preamble to the Voting Rights Act of 1965 establishes that the central purpose of the Act is '[t]o enforce the fifteenth amendment to the Constitution of the United States' "; and it begins its final paragraph (501 U.S. at 403) by affirming: "Congress enacted the Voting Rights Act of 1965 for the broad remedial purpose of 'rid[ding] the country of racial discrimination in voting' ".

36 See Cass Sunstein, "Beyond the Republican Revival," 97 *Yale L. J.* 1539, 1582 n. 232 (1988) (defending the rise in the federalism canon on this ground).

37 Michelman, "Republic," 1526.

38 Mashaw, 1686.

39 Epstein, "Modern Republicanism—Or the Flight from Substance," 97 *Yale L. J.* 1633, 1633 (1988).

40 Michelman, "Traces," 23.

41 Michelman, "Traces," 24.

42 Michelman, "Traces," 16. Not everyone finds abandoning democratic rhetoric refreshing. See Schacter, 607, 646–50. Schacter insists (647) that Republican

approaches are best understood as serving substantive democratic values and that "[d]emocracy represents perhaps our most potent vocabulary for expressing basic ideals about collective self-government, the conditions that make meaningful self-government possible, and, most importantly, the numerous and diverse values with which self-government is associated." See also Guido Calabresi, *A Common Law for the Age of Statutes*, 96–97 (1982) ("legal fabric . . . [is a] good approximation[] of one aspect of the popular will, of what a majority in some sense desires"). But see Morton Horwitz, "The Constitution of Change: Legal Fundamentality Without Fundamentalism," 107 *Harv. L. Rev.* 30, 57–65 (1993) (tracing the rise of democracy in recent years as a central legitimating concept).

43 Michelman, "Republic," 1537.

44 Michelman, "Traces," 76–77.

45 Robert Cover, "Nomos and Narrative," 97 *Harv. L. Rev.* 4, 15 (jurisgenerative), 40 (jurispathic) (1983) (hereafter Cover).

46 Cover, 40.

47 Dandridge v. Williams, 397 U.S. 471 (1970); San Antonio Independent School Dist. v. Rodriguez, 411 U.S. 1 (1973).

48 387 U.S. 118 (1967).

49 478 U.S. 186 (1986).

50 Pub. L. No. 649, para. 601, 104 Stat. 4978, 5067.

51 517 U.S. 620 (1996).

52 *Cong. Quart. Weekly Report*, 2597–99, Sept. 14, 1996.

53 Robin West, "Progressive and Conservative Constitutionalism," 88 *Mich. L. Rev.* 641, 650–51, 713–21 (1990).

54 If we had a consensus regarding substantive goals, approaches based on natural law would be more enthusiastically received. Eskridge, *Dynamic*, 182 (not a homogenous enough culture). A lack of consensus also helps to explain Eskridge's criticism of Ronald Dworkin's claim (in *Law's Empire*, 225 [1986]) that the judge can identify the right answer by working out "the best constructive interpretation of the community's legal practice." See Eskridge, *Dynamic*, 148 (we lack "an external standard of judgment"). Others (I think more accurately) characterize Dworkin's approach as "internal" to the judge's decision-making process, which avoids the objections applicable to natural law, but deprives the claim of any "value . . . for *the community*" (emphasis in original). Michelman, "Traces," 71.

55 See, generally, Philip Frickey, "Legislative Process and Products," 46 *J. Legal Educ.* 469, 473–75 (1996).

56 See Lewis v. United States, 118 S.Ct. 1135 (1998) (Scalia, J., concurring in the judgment) (the majority reads language as an "empty vessel" filled with "free-ranging [judicial] speculation"; Scalia reads the statute to refer to "traditional vocabulary and categories of the common law," which "produce[s] more predictable results than the majority's balancing test").

57 For example, speaking of a proximate cause requirement, Scalia says: "[I]t has always been the practice of common-law courts (and probably of all courts, under all legal systems) to require as a condition of recovery, unless the legislature specifically prescribes otherwise, that the injury have been proximately caused by the offending conduct." Holmes v. Securities Investor Protection Corp., 503 U.S. 258, 286 (1992) (Scalia, J., concurring in the judgment). See also Board of County Comm'rs. v. Umbehr, 518 U.S. 668, 695, 116 S.Ct. 2342, 2366 (1996) (Scalia, J., dissenting) ("As I have explained, I would separate the permissible from the impermissible on the basis of our Nation's traditions, which is what I believe sound constitutional adjudication requires").

58 David Shapiro, "Continuity and Change in Statutory Interpretation," 67 N.Y.U. L. Rev. 921, 941–50 (1992).

59 Antonin Scalia, A Matter of Interpretation, 28 (1997).

60 United States v. Fisher, 6 U.S. 358, 386 (1805).

61 See, generally, William N. Eskridge Jr. and Philip Frickey, "Quasi-Constitutional Law: Clear Statement Rules as Constitutional Lawmaking," 45 Vand. L. Rev. 593 (1992) (hereafter Eskridge and Frickey, "Quasi-Constitutional"); William N. Eskridge Jr., "Public Values in Statutory Interpretation," 137 U. Pa. L. Rev. 1007 (1989); John Nagle, "Waiving Sovereign Immunity in an Age of Clear Statement Rules," 1995 Wis. L. Rev. 771.

62 Poe v. Ullman, 367 U.S. 497, 542 (1961) (Harlan, J., dissenting).

63 See Landgraf v. USI Film Products, 511 U.S. 244, 261 (1994), where Justice Stevens noted that the canon against retroactive legislation remained strong but had weakened because of the change in the role of legislation: "The presumption against statutory retroactivity had special force in the era in which courts tended to view legislative interference with property and contract rights circumspectly. In this century, legislation has come to supply the dominant means of legal ordering, and circumspection has given way to greater deference to legislative judgments." Although Stevens went on to hold that prospectivity remained the appropriate default rule, his willingness to relax the traditional presumption prompted a concurring opinion from Justice Scalia, 511 U.S. at 287. Speaking as a strong traditionalist, Scalia stated: "I of course agree with the Court that there exists a judicial presumption, of great antiquity, that a legislative enactment affecting substantive rights does not apply retroactively absent clear statement to the contrary. The Court, however, is willing to let that clear statement be supplied, not by the text of the law in question, but by individual legislators who participated in the enactment of the law. . . . This effectively converts the 'clear statement' rule into a 'discernible legislative intent' rule. . . ."

64 Atascadero State Hosp. v. Scanlon, 473 U.S. 234, 242 (1985) ("Congress may abrogate the States' constitutionally secured immunity from suit in federal court only by making its intention unmistakably clear in the language of the statute").

The state's immunity in federal court, absent federal legislative override, is affirmed by the Eleventh Amendment to the Constitution: "The Judicial power of the United States shall not be construed to extend to any suit, in law or equity, commenced or prosecuted against one of the United States by Citizens of another State, or by Citizens or Subjects of any Foreign State." State immunity in federal court also extends to suits against a state by its own citizens. Hans v. Louisiana, 134 U.S. 1 (1890).

65 Pennhurst State School and Hospital v. Halderman, 451 U.S. 1, 17, 23 (1981) (federal grant-in-aid legislation is like a contract; if Congress wants to impose as a grant condition that there is a cause of action against the state, "it must do so unambiguously"; the statute in this case lacks the necessary "conditional language").

66 Gregory v. Ashcroft, 501 U.S. 452, 460–61, 464 (1991) (federal prohibition of mandatory retirement age did not apply to appointed state judges; the states' power to determine judicial qualifications was a "fundamental" state function, traditionally regulated by the states, and the Court "must be absolutely certain that Congress intended" such intrusion; the Court quoted from Atascadero, 473 U.S. at 242: the intrusion must be "unmistakably clear in the language of the statute").

67 Dellmuth v. Muth, 491 U.S. 223, 239–42 (1989) (Brennan, J., dissenting). See also Eskridge and Frickey, "Quasi-Constitutional," 621–23.

68 Atascadero State Hosp., 473 U.S. at 242. Dissenters reject the view that state sovereign immunity is grounded in "principles essential to the structure of our federal system." 473 U.S. at 247 (Brennan, J., dissenting).

69 Seminole Tribe of Florida v. Florida, 517 U.S. 44, 66 (1996), overruling Pennsylvania v. Union Gas Co., 491 U.S. 1 (1989).

70 517 U.S. at 100–185 (Souter, J., dissenting).

71 517 U.S. at 102 (Souter, J., dissenting).

72 517 U.S. at 69.

73 Hilton v. South Carolina Public Railways Comm'n., 502 U.S. 197, 205–6 (1991). The case involved a suit against a state-owned railroad for workers' compensation damages under the Federal Employers' Liability Act.

74 502 U.S. at 209–10.

75 Evans v. U.S., 504 U.S. 255 (1992).

76 City of Edmonds v. Oxford House, Inc., 514 U.S. 725, 728 (1995). The federal Fair Housing Act (FHA) prohibited discrimination in housing against persons with handicaps, but exempted "any reasonable local, State, or Federal restrictions regarding the *maximum number of occupants* permitted to occupy a dwelling" (emphasis added). The city's zoning code, governing areas zoned for single-family dwelling units, defined "family" as "persons [without regard to number] related by genetics, adoption, or marriage, or a group of five or fewer [unre-

lated] persons." The Court held that the city's zoning code provision was not exempt from the antidiscrimination provision of the FHA because it was a *land-use* restriction, not a *maximum occupancy* restriction.

77 504 U.S. at 290 (Thomas, J., dissenting).

78 514 U.S. at 744 (Thomas, J., dissenting).

79 Gregory v. Ashcroft, 501 U.S. 452 (1991).

80 Pound, "Common Law and Legislation," 21 *Harv. L. Rev.* 383, 387 (1908).

81 See, generally, Kahan, "Lenity and Federal Common Law Crimes," 1994 *Sup. Ct. Rev.* 345.

82 Romero, "Interpretive Directions in Statutes," 31 *Harv. J. on Legis.* 211, 216 (1994).

83 National Conference of Commissioners on Uniform State Laws, Uniform Statute and Rule Construction Act (1993), para. 18, and comments thereto.

84 See, e.g., Organized Crime Control Act of 1970, Pub.L. No. 91–452, para. 904(a), 84 Stat. 922, 947 ("shall be liberally construed to effectuate its remedial purposes").

85 Cites from the Scarborough case appear at 431 U.S. 563, 567, 569, 570, 572, 577 (1977).

86 The rule of lenity was also unavailing in Smith v. United States, 508 U.S. 223 (1993), yielding to policy considerations favoring a broad definition of the statute's coverage. The statute mandated sentence enhancement for someone who "use[s] . . . a firearm" while committing a crime of violence or drug trafficking. 508 U.S. at 227. The issue was whether the statute applied when the defendant bartered a firearm for cocaine. The Court emphasized that a gun used as an item of commerce still has destructive capacity, instantaneously convertible from currency to cannon. "We therefore see no reason why Congress would have intended courts and juries applying [the statute] to draw a fine metaphysical distinction between a gun's role in a drug offense as a weapon and its role as an item of barter; it creates a grave possibility of violence and death in either capacity." 508 U.S. at 240. Justice Scalia's dissent, 508 U.S. at 247 n. 4, responded that "[s]tretching language in order to write a more effective statute than Congress devised is not an exercise we should indulge in." See also Muscarello v. United States, 118 S.Ct. 1911 (1998) ("carry" a firearm applies to carrying one in the trunk of a car; the majority rejects the dissent's appeal to the rule of lenity).

87 431 U.S. at 578, 580.

88 United States v. R.L.C., 503 U.S. 291, 307 (1992) (Scalia, J., concurring in part and concurring in the judgment) ("it is not consistent with the rule of lenity to construe a textually ambiguous penal statute against a criminal defendant on the basis of legislative history").

89 504 U.S. 505 (1992).

90 The rule of lenity was also successfully invoked in Ratzlaf v. United States, 510 U.S. 135 (1994). The statute made it illegal to break up a transaction "for the

purpose of evading a financial institution's reporting requirement" (applicable to transactions of at least $10,000). A person "willfully violating" this provision was subject to criminal penalties. The Court held that the statute required knowledge by the person breaking up the transaction that his conduct was unlawful, based in part on the rule of lenity, and on the fact that the defendant's actions were not "so obviously 'evil' or inherently 'bad.'" 510 U.S. at 146. The dissent's disagreement was about how statutory policy interacted with values embodied in the lenity canon. It responded to the Court's view that the defendant's behavior was not "nefarious," with the observation that the defendant's actions were "not so plainly innocent." 510 U.S. at 154–55 (Blackmun, J., dissenting).

7 Ordinary Judging

1   See William N. Eskridge Jr., *Dynamic Statutory Interpretation* (1994) (hereafter Eskridge, *Dynamic*); T. Alexander Aleinikoff, "Updating Statutory Interpretation," 87 *Mich. L. Rev.* 20 (1988). See also Guido Calabresi, *A Common Law for the Age of Statutes* (1982).

2   Ronald Dworkin, *Law's Empire*, pp. 239–40 (1986).

3   See, generally, Gerald Gunther, *Learned Hand* (1994) (hereafter Gunther).

4   See William N. Eskridge Jr. and Philip Frickey, "Statutory Interpretation as Practical Reasoning," 42 *Stan. L. Rev.* 321 (1990) (hereafter Eskridge and Frickey, "Practical Reasoning"), discussing failure of "grand theory" and foundationalism.

5   H. L. A. Hart, "American Jurisprudence Through English Eyes: The Nightmare and the Noble Dream," in *Essays in Jurisprudence and Philosophy*, 126, 132–33 (1983).

6   Eskridge and Frickey, "The Making of the Legal Process," 107 *Harv. L. Rev.* 2031, 2032–33, 2036 (1994). See also Edward Rubin, "The New Legal Process, the Synthesis of Discourse, and the Microanalysis of Institutions," 109 *Harv. L. Rev.* 1393 (1996).

7   Eskridge, *Dynamic;* Eskridge, "Dynamic Statutory Interpretation," 135 *U. Pa. L. Rev.* 1479 (1987).

8   See, e.g., David Shapiro, "Continuity and Change in Statutory Interpretation," 67 *N.Y.U. L. Rev.* 921, 941–50 (1992) (hereafter Shapiro) (arguing for a judicial tilt toward continuity).

9   West Virginia University Hospitals, Inc. v. Casey, 499 U.S. 83, 100–01 (1991). The entire quotation is as follows: "Where a statutory term presented to us for the first time is ambiguous, we construe it to contain that permissible meaning which fits most logically and comfortably into the body of both previously and subsequently enacted law. We do so not because that precise accommodative

meaning is what the lawmakers must have had in mind (how could an earlier Congress know what a later Congress would enact?), but because it is our role to make sense rather than nonsense out of the corpus juris."

10 Frank Easterbrook, "Statutes' Domains," 50 *U. Chi. L. Rev.* 533, 544 (1983) (hereafter Easterbrook, "Domains").

11 I do not mean that political connection is a necessary condition to the judge's sense of institutional competence, a point that could be tested by comparative studies of statutory interpretation in other countries. I suspect that something about the job of ordinary judging would explain a practice of exercising judicial lawmaking discretion across legal cultures, regardless of the judge's sense of political connectedness.

The French experience would be especially instructive. Despite the unmistakable dogma that French courts cannot legitimately make law and the image of a judiciary drawn from the civil service, French judges seem to be at least as aggressive in making law as American judges. John Dawson, *The Oracles of the Law*, 401, 415 (1968) (hereafter Dawson). See also Mitchell de S.-O.-l'E. Lasser, "Judicial (Self-)Portraits: Judicial Discourse in the French Legal System," 104 *Yale L. J.* 1325 (1995); Mitchell de S.-O.-l'E. Lasser, " 'Lit. Theory' Put To the Test: A Comparative Literary Analysis of American Judicial Tests and French Judicial Discourse," 111 *Harv. L. Rev.* 689 (1998). See, generally, *Interpreting Statutes: A Comparative Study* (D. Neil MacCormick and Robert Summers, eds., 1991).

It is also possible that the apolitical image is misleading. Many judges serving on the French Council of State are appointed by the Council of Ministers and act as advisers to the government, and judges on the Constitutional Court are appointed by politicians from among politicians or those active in political life. Judicial specialization also may contribute to a sense that judges understand how statutes operate, with consequences for interpretation. See John Bell, "Principles and Methods of Judicial Selection in France," 61 *S. Cal. L. Rev.* 1757, 1761–63, 1771–72 (1988).

12 Herbert Jacob, "The Effect of Institutional Differences in the Recruitment Process: The Case of State Judges," 33 *Jl. of Public Law* 104, 110, 115 (1964) (judges sitting in 1955). See also Bradley Canon, "The Impact of Formal Selection Processes on the Characteristics of Judges—Reconsidered," 6 *Law & Soc. Rev.* 579, 583, 591 (1972) (for 1961–68, 19.3 percent of the judges had been state legislators and 51.5 percent prosecutors); Henry Glick and Craig Emmert, "Stability and Change: Characteristics of State Supreme Court Justices," 70 *Judicature* 107, 108, 111 (1986) (for 1980–81, 20.2 percent of the judges had been state legislators and 21.5 percent prosecutors). See also Henry Glick and Craig Emmert, "Selection Systems and Judicial Characteristics: The Recruitment of State Supreme Court Judges," 70 *Judicature* 228, 232–33 (1987).

13 Henry Glick, *Supreme Courts in State Politics*, 127 (1971) (all judges held "pub-

lic positions" before going on the court); Henry Glick and Kenneth Vines, *State Court Systems*, 49–50 (1973) (selection tied to the processes of state politics; judges had held political offices); Kathleen Barber, "Ohio Judicial Election— Nonpartisan Premises with Partisan Results," 32 *Ohio St. L. J.* 762, 766, 767–70 (1971) (judicial nomination through party activity).

14 Sheldon Goldman, "Reagan's Second Term Judicial Appointments: The Battle at Midway," 70 *Judicature* 324, 328 (1987) (data for Reagan, Carter, Ford, Nixon, and Johnson appointees). See also Henry Abraham, "Why Supreme Court Justices Get There: Qualifications & Rationalizations," 287, *in* Sheldon Goldman and Austin Sarat, *American Court Systems* (2d ed., 1989) (judges were in "public life," if not the legislature).

15 Henry Abraham, "Appointments to the Supreme Court," reprinted in Henry Glick, *Courts in American Politics*, 106 (1990).

16 Henry Glick, *Courts, Politics, and Justice*, 97–98 (1983).

17 Ronald Beiner, *Political Judgment*, 13–14 (1983) (hereafter Beiner).

18 Hannah Arendt, *Lectures on Kant's Political Philosophy*, 101 (1982), with an interpretive essay by Ronald Beiner (hereafter Arendt, *Lectures*). Unfortunately, Arendt died with the first page of a work on judgment in her typewriter; it was meant to complete a triology, the first two volumes of which dealt with Thinking and Willing. Michael Denneny, "The Privilege of Ourselves: Hannah Arendt on Judgment," in Hannah Arendt: *The Recovery of the Public World*, 245 (Melvyn Hill, ed., 1979) (hereafter Denneny).

19 Arendt, *Lectures*, 105.

20 Arendt, *Lectures*, 40, 119–20. See also Beiner, 12–19, and Denneny, 245–74, discussing Arendt's views about Kant's Critique of Judgment. See, generally, Hanna Pitkin, *Wittgenstein and Judgment*, 232–35 (1972) (comparing political and aesthetic judgment).

21 Beiner, 37.

22 Arendt, *Lectures*, 10, 15.

23 Beiner, 5. See also Arendt, *Lectures*, 10 ("taste" as a favorite eighteenth-century topic).

24 Gregory Alexander, "Time and Property in the American Republican Legal Culture," 66 *N.Y.U. L. Rev.* 273, 320–21 (1991); Henry May, *The Enlightenment in America*, 346 (1976); Jay Fliegelman, *Declaring Independence*, 74 (1993).

25 Fliegelman, *Declaring Independence*, 26, 74.

26 Stephen Conrad, "James Wilson's 'Assimilation of the Common-Law Mind,'" 84 *Nw. U. L. Rev.* 186, 187 (1989).

27 *The Works of James Wilson*, vol. 1, 377 (Robert McCloskey, ed., 1967).

28 Barnes v. Kline, 759 F.2d 21, 46–47, 61 (D.C. Cir. 1985) (Bork, J., dissenting), vacated for mootness, 479 U.S. 361 (1987).

29 Denneny, 263.

30 Denneny, 262.

31 See Dennis Curtis and Judith Resnik, "Images of Justice," 96 *Yale L. J.* 1727, 1757-58 (1987) (suggesting that blindfolded image of justice developed in the late sixteenth century to separate the judge from the sovereign).

32 Anthony Kronman, "Living in the Law," 54 *U. Chi. L. Rev.* 835, 852 (1987) (hereafter Kronman).

33 Arendt, *Lectures,* 43; also at 71, 73-74; Denneny, 252 (explaining Arendt's view that Kant's Critique of Judgment "grounded plurality as no other philosopher had, making the presence of others an *a priori* prerequisite for [judgment]").

34 Arendt, *Lectures,* 43.

35 Kronman, 853.

36 Denneny, 261.

37 Denneny, 265. See also Arendt, *Lectures,* 72 ("woo . . . agreement").

38 Beiner, 37.

39 Arendt, *Lectures,* 72, 105.

40 Beiner, 2.

41 See Beiner, 17-18, discussing Arendt's essay, "Truth and Politics," in *Between Past and Future,* 241.

42 Arendt, *Lectures,* 69-72; Beiner, 39, 49-51.

43 Dawson, 85-87.

44 G. Edward White, *The American Judicial Tradition,* 43-45 (1988). In England, official reports of judicial opinions began in the early nineteenth century and evolved into the current system of approved reports. However, there was never a legal requirement that judges write opinions. Until 1779 the law lords did not allow any reporting of their decisions; "authorized" reports began only in 1814. Dawson, 80-84, 89. See also Sir William Holdsworth, "Law Reporting in the Nineteenth and Twentieth Centuries," in *Anglo-American Legal History Series,* series 1, no. 5 (1941).

45 The reluctance to admit doubt is a strong feature in our judicial tradition. See Prakash Mehta, "An Essay on Hamlet: Emblems of Truth in Law and Literature," 83 *Geo. L. J.* 165, 185 (1994). The fear is that acknowledging doubt undermines public confidence in judging; see Louis Jaffe, *English and American Judges as Lawmakers,* 7-8, 14 (1969) (explaining and disagreeing with this point of view). Mehta argues that openly struggling with doubt would enhance judicial persuasiveness; 83 *Geo. L. Rev.,* 176-85. Expressions of judicial doubt are unusual enough to attract commentary in the *New York Times*. See Linda Greenhouse, "When a Justice Suffers from Indecision," July 14, 1996, 5 ("Late in the Supreme Court term that ended last month, in the course of an opinion addressing Government regulation of indecent programming on cable television, Justice Stephen G. Breyer did something unusual. He acknowledged publicly that he was not sure how to decide the case.")

46 Beiner, 40. See also Beiner, 11 (discussing Gadamer's view that Kant's position was nonpolitical and nonmoral).

47 See, generally, William N. Eskridge Jr. and Philip Frickey, "Statutory Interpretation as Practical Reasoning," 42 *Stan. L. Rev.* 321 (1990); Frank Michelman, "Traces of Self-Government," 100 *Harv. L. Rev.* 4 (1986); Richard Posner, "Legal Formalism, Legal Realism, and the Interpretation of Statutes and the Constitution," 37 *Case W. Res. L. Rev.* 179 (1986); Richard Posner, "Statutory Interpretation—In the Classroom and in the Courtroom," 50 *U. Chi. L. Rev.* 800 (1983); Thomas Grey, "Holmes and Legal Pragmatism," 41 *Stan. L. Rev.* 787 (1989); David Farber and Philip Frickey, "Practical Reason and the First Amendment," 34 *U.C.L.A. L. Rev.* 1615 (1987); Cass Sunstein, "Interpreting Statutes in the Regulatory State," 103 *Harv. L. Rev.* 405 (1989); Martha Minow and Elizabeth Spelman, "In Context," 63 *S. Cal. L. Rev.* 1597 (1990) (hereafter Minow and Spelman).

48 William James, *Pragmatism*, 27 (Kuklick, ed., 1981) (1907) (hereafter James) ("There is absolutely nothing new in the pragmatic method. . . . Aristotle used it methodically").

49 Beiner, 73.

50 Arendt, *Lectures*, 4 ("Judgment deals with particulars"), 76 ("Examples are the go-cart of judgments").

51 Arendt, *Lectures*, 4.

52 Beiner, 74–75.

53 James, 28, 32, 92, 98. See also Peirce's discussion of the "pragmatic maxim": "Consider what effects, that might conceivably have practical bearings, we conceive the object of our conception to have. Then, our conception of these effects is the whole of our conception of the object." Charles S. Peirce, *How to Make Our Ideas Clear*, para. 402, 62 (Vittorio Klostermann, 1968).

54 James, 109.

55 Theodore Sedgwick, *A Treatise on the Rules Which Govern the Interpretation and Construction of Statutory and Constitutional Law*, 192 (1857) (Pomeroy ed., 1874) (hereafter Sedgwick).

56 Francis Lieber, *Legal and Political Hermeneutics*, 89 (Charles C. Little & James Brown, 1839) (hereafter Lieber). Even James Kent at the beginning of the nineteenth century referred favorably to the "practical good sense" of a Mansfield or Burke over Bentham. "Letter from Chancellor Kent to Edward Livingston—Penal Code," 16 *American Jurist* 361, 370 (1837).

57 Roscoe Pound, "The Scope and Purpose of Sociological Jurisprudence, III," 25 *Harv. L. Rev.* 489, 516 (1912).

58 Eskridge and Frickey, *Practical Reasoning*, 323–24. Aristotle disagreed with Plato, for whom ideas were unconnected with action in light of experience. A perpetual mystery is why the Platonic philosopher returns from the sunlight (the realm of philosophy) to the cave (the shadow world of politics).

59 See Cass Sunstein, *Legal Reasoning and Political Conflict* (1996) (hereafter Sunstein, *Legal Reasoning*).

60 Sunstein, *Legal Reasoning,* 4–5.

61 Eskridge, *Dynamic—1994,* pp. 55–56, 200. See also Eskridge and Frickey, *Practical Reasoning,* 351.

62 Gunther, 33, 35–36.

63 Easterbrook, "Domains," 550–51 (judges who are capable of thinking themselves into the minds of departed legislators can be counted "on one hand"—an intended pun, I hope—so that judges end up discovering their own conceptions of the good). See also Public Citizen v. U.S. Dept. of Justice, 491 U.S. 440, 473 (1989) (Kennedy, J., concurring) ("spirits . . . tend to reflect less the views of the world whence they come than the views of those who seek their advice").

64 Gunther, 592.

65 Antonin Scalia, *A Matter of Interpretation,* 47 (1997). I criticize this argument in chapter 5.

66 Robin West, from a feminist perspective markedly different from Scalia's, suggests that judging is inadequate to the task of long-term reform. Robin West, "Progressive and Conservative Constitutionalism," 88 *Mich. L. Rev.* 641, 650–51, 713–21 (1990) (hereafter West).

67 Sometimes, the pragmatic case for textualism applies only to selected areas of law. For example, some statutes might require the kind of certainty that textualism can provide. Modern judges who are usually associated with considerable judicial discretion often become textualists when the right statute comes along. For example, in United California Bank v. United States, 439 U.S. 180, 211 (1978) (Stevens, J., dissenting), Justice Stevens stated: "In final analysis, this case requires us to consider how the law in a highly technical area can be administered most fairly. I firmly believe that the best way to achieve evenhanded administration of our tax laws is to adhere closely to the language used by Congress to define taxpayers' responsibilities. Occasionally there will be clear manifestations of a contrary intent that justify a nonliteral reading, but surely this is not such a case." See also Robert Rasmussen, "A Study of the Costs and Benefits of Textualism: The Supreme Court's Bankruptcy Cases," 71 *Wash. U.L. Q.* 535, 571–98 (1993) (hereafter Rasmussen) (making a pragmatic case for applying the strictly textualist approach to the bankruptcy code).

68 See Public Citizen v. United States Department of Justice, 491 U.S. 440, 468, 471 (1989) (Kennedy, J., concurring) ("The Framers of our Government knew that the most precious of liberties could remain secure only if they created a structure of government based on a permanent separation of power." See, e.g., *Federalist* 47–51 (James Madison): "It remains one of the most vital functions of this Court to police with care the separation of the governing powers. That is so even when, as is the case here, no immediate threat to liberty is apparent." "I believe the Court's loose invocation of the 'absurd result' canon of statutory construction creates too great a risk that the Court is exercising its own 'WILL instead of JUDGMENT,' with the consequence of 'substituti[ng] [its own] plea-

sure to that of the legislative body.'" *Federalist* 78, 469 (Clinton Rossiter, ed., 1961) (Alexander Hamilton).

69 Judge Friendly thought that competence, not legitimacy, was the major issue in explaining the judicial role, given the creative tradition of common law judges. Henry Friendly, "Reactions of a Lawyer—Newly Become Judge," 71 *Yale L. J.* 218, 226 (1961). Competence, however, was a serious concern. Friendly gave as an example the problem of what to tell juries about the tax-free nature of personal injury recoveries; at 227–28. It seemed unfair not to discount a tax-free recovery, but courts had a lot of trouble figuring out how best to discount the award—were awards inadequate (because of such things as attorneys' fees or likely improvements in health which prolonged life), or excessive (because of inadequate account being taken of unpaid taxes)? How can future tax rates be reasonably estimated? A legislative solution was therefore preferable to a judicial solution. But legislatures were busy with more important matters. He therefore suggested that a body of experts work out answers to these questions for legislative consideration, on the theory that they were sufficiently apolitical to garner widespread support. Friendly may have been too sanguine about the apolitical nature of the size of damage awards. Certainly, plaintiff's attorneys would not share that view. Hidden political minefields often destroy the hope of an apolitical legislative solution.

70 Barker v. Wilson [1980] 2 All E.R. 81 (Q.B.).

71 See, generally, William N. Eskridge Jr., "Gadamer/Statutory Interpretation," 90 *Colum. L. Rev.* 609 (1990); Eskridge, "Fetch Some Soupmeat," 16 *Cardozo L. Rev.* 2209 (1995).

72 In re Erickson, 815 F.2d 1090, 1092–93 (7th Cir. 1987) (Judge Easterbrook discussing the meaning of "chair").

73 See State v. Cain, 613 A.2d 804 (Conn. 1992) (the majority held that 911 calls were not "statements," but the dissent argued that the statute's text clearly applied and that its application was not unworkable, only expensive).

74 Easterbrook, "Domains," 544.

75 See Edward Rubin, "Legal Reasoning, Legal Process and the Judiciary as an Institution," 85 *Calif. L. Rev.* 265, 270 (1997).

76 See, generally, Cass Sunstein, *Legal Reasoning*, ch. 5, 121–35 (In Defense of Casuistry).

77 In re Erickson, 815 F.2d 1090 (7th Cir. 1987).

78 815 F.2d at 1094.

79 I do not mean that textualists never embrace reliance on a statute's purpose to determine statutory meaning. They would welcome doing so in the relatively trivial case of clearing up textual ambiguity: is a "monarch" a butterfly or a ruler?

80 Frank Easterbrook, "The Court and the Economic System," 98 *Harv. L. Rev.* 4, 14–15 (1984).

81 815 F.2d at 1092, 1095.

82 Antonin Scalia, *A Matter of Interpretation* 25 (1997).

83 William N. Eskridge Jr., "Spinning Legislative Supremacy," 78 *Geo. L. J.* 319, 330–37 (1989); David Farber, "Statutory Interpretation and Legislative Supremacy," 78 *Geo. L. J.* 281, 283–92 (1989).

84 Easterbrook, "Domains," 548–49.

85 See, e.g., Joseph Story, "Law, Legislation and Codes," in *Encyclopedia Americana*, appendix 7, 587 (Francis Lieber, ed., 1831) ("But is it possible to foresee, or to provide beforehand, for all . . . cases?"); Lieber, 121 ("Men who use words . . . cannot foresee all possible complex cases . . .").

86 State v. Dickinson, 263 N.E.2d 253 (Ohio App. 1970), affirmed, 275 N.E.2d 599 (Ohio 1971).

87 See Commonwealth v. Cass, 467 N.E.2d 1324 (Mass. 1984); State v. Horne, 319 S.E.2d 703 (S.C. 1984); State v. Knapp, 843 S.W.2d 345 (Mo. 1992); Hughes v. State, 868 P.2d 730 (Okla. 1994).

88 See, e.g., Werling v. Sandy, 476 N.E.2d 1053 (Ohio 1985) (wrongful death statute).

89 See Daniel Halperin and Eugene Steuerle, "Indexing the Tax System for Inflation," in *Uneasy Compromise: Problems of a Hybrid Income-Consumption Tax,* 387 (Aaron, Galper, and Pechman, eds., 1988).

90 Miles v. Apex Marine Corp., 498 U.S. 19, 27 (1990). This statement appeared in a case dealing with whether seamen were entitled to "loss of society" damages in common law wrongful death cases. The Court had previously allowed these damages to longshoremen. Sea-Land Services, Inc. v. Gaudet, 414 U.S. 573 (1974). The Court's explicit reasoning denying loss of society damages to seamen in Miles relied on a far-fetched argument about deference to legislative intent. See David Farber and Philip Frickey, "In the Shadow of the Legislature: The Common Law in the Age of the New Public Law," 89 *Mich. L. Rev.* 875, 903–4 (1991).

91 MacMillan v. Director, 445 A.2d 397 (N.J. 1982).

92 The parallel between the "life care" case (MacMillan) and the sixteenth-century Heydon's Case, discussed in chapter 1, is striking. Arguably, the statutory list overlooked the life care arrangement, and the statutory objective would be served by a judicial extension, just as Parliament had overlooked copyholds when it listed property interests that could not be used to avoid Henry VIII's seizure of church property.

93 Knetsch v. United States, 364 U.S. 361 (1960); Goldstein v. Commissioner, 364 F.2d 734 (2d Cir. 1966).

94 Congress eventually legislated at length to prevent certain interest deductions. The effective date of the provision appears after the section reference. Internal Revenue Code of 1986, secs. 163(d) (1972), 263A(f) (1987), 264(a)(3) (1963), 264(a)(4) (1986), and to discourage tax avoidance schemes where interest deductions were a factor, IRC, secs. 465 (1976), 469 (1987).

95 McBoyle v. United States, 283 U.S. 25, 26 (1931) (airplanes were well-known when the statute was passed).

96 United States v. Perryman, 100 U.S. 235 (1879).

97 See, e.g., Central States v. Lady Baltimore Foods, Inc., 960 F.2d 1339 (7th Cir. 1992) (Posner, J.) (correcting a statute that refers to the date on which nothing happened relevant to the statute's goals). See also Huidekoper's Lessee v. Douglass, 7 U.S. 1, 64–72 (1805) (Chief Justice Marshall) (correcting text which refers to two time periods, only one of which is possible).

98 United States National Bank of Oregon v. Independent Insurance Agents of America, Inc., 508 U.S. 439 (1993) (internal textual evidence that placement of quotation marks is a drafting error).

99 See United States v. Locke, 471 U.S. 84 (1985), involving a statute that required filing "prior to December 31," rather than "on or before December 31." Although no reason was apparent for cutting off the opportunity to file before the end of the year, which almost certainly resulted from a drafting error, the Court refused to correct the error (with three dissents). Judge Posner disagrees with the Court's decision. Richard Posner, *Law and Literature: A Misunderstood Relation,* 255–56 (1988).

100 Rasmussen, 572–73, 593–94.

101 Frederick Schauer, "Formalism," 97 *Yale L. J.* 509, 540–44 (1988).

102 Felix Frankfurter and Nathan Greene, *The Labor Injunction* (1930); Helen Thomas, *Felix Frankfurter,* 18, 80 (1960); Leonard Baker, *Brandeis and Frankfurter,* 138, 147, 205–6 (1984).

103 United States v. Hutcheson, 312 U.S. 219, 245 (1941) (Roberts, J., dissenting).

104 See Shapiro, 941–50; West, 650–51, 713–21.

105 James, 98; also at 32, 101.

106 West Virginia University Hospitals, Inc. v. Casey, 499 U.S. 83, 101 (1991).

107 499 U.S. at 101.

108 Watt v. Alaska, 451 U.S. 259, 280–81 (1981) (Stewart, J., dissenting).

109 The quotation is a paraphrase from Justice Scalia's opinion in West Virginia University Hospitals, Inc. v. Casey, 499 U.S. 83, 101 (1991) ("It is our role to make sense rather than nonsense out of the corpus juris").

110 Watt v. Alaska, 451 U.S. 259 (1981).

111 Sorenson v. Secretary of Treasury, 475 U.S. 851 (1986).

112 See, generally, Paul Kahn, "Gramm-Rudman and the Capacity of Congress to Control the Future," 13 *Hastings Const. L.Q.* 185 (1986); Anthony D'Amato, "Can Legislatures Constrain Judicial Interpretation of Statutes?" 75 *Va. L.Rev.* 561 (1989); Alan Romero, "Interpretive Directions in Statutes," 31 *Harv. J. on Legis.* 211 (1994).

113 Another situation where prior law might bind the creation of later law occurs when an earlier statute states that later law can only do something "expressly." Deciding what is an "express" provision in the later statute cannot be separated

from considering policy implications. For example, the federal Anti-Injunction Act states: "A court of the United States may not grant an injunction to stay proceedings in a State court except as expressly authorized by Act of Congress . . ." 28 U.S.C. para. 2283. In Vendo Co. v. Lektro-Vend Corp., 433 U.S. 623, 630, 631, 647, 651 (1977), a later antitrust statute known as the Clayton Act authorized injunction relief, stating: "[A]ny person . . . shall be entitled to sue for and have injunctive relief . . . , against threatened loss or damage by violation of the antitrust laws . . . when and under the same conditions and principles as injunction relief against threatened conduct that will cause loss or damage is granted by courts of equity." All of the judges agreed that a statute can authorize an injunction in federal court against state court proceedings without specifically mentioning either the Anti-Injunction Act or state court proceedings. They also agreed with the test stated by the three-judge plurality opinion—determining whether a later statute authorizes an injunction depends on whether an act of Congress can be given its intended scope only by a stay of state court proceedings. That was about all the judges could agree on. Their actual decision adopted a "policy coherence" approach. Three judges found no express authorization to enjoin state court proceedings in the Clayton Act, appealing to the "fundamental principle of a dual system of courts." They distinguished an earlier case permitting an injunction, which involved a federal *civil rights* statute, where the legislative history affirmed the importance of federal court availability to protect civil rights against unconstitutional state court action. Four judges stated that the Clayton Act included a power to enjoin state court proceedings so that "a man does not have to wait until he is ruined in his business before he has his remedy," referring to the antitrust law as "that basic charter of economic freedom."

114 506 U.S. 194 (1993).

115 Dictionary Act of 1871, Feb. 25, 1871, ch. 71, para. 2, 16 Stat. 431 (1871). In 1947, the act was codified and enacted into law as 1 U.S.C. para. 1, 61 Stat. 633 (1947).

116 Pub. L. No. 86-320, 73 Stat. 590 (1959), amending 28 U.S.C. para. 1915(a).

117 The majority assumed that the issue was whether the "context [of the later law] indicates otherwise." 506 at 199–200. The dissent stated the issue as whether the "presumption codified in 1 U.S.C. para. 1 . . . has . . . been overcome because the context 'indicates otherwise.'" 506 U.S. at 212-13 (Thomas, J., dissenting). The only qualification was that the Court would not adhere to an "absurd" interpretation of the later law, which would result from following the Dictionary Act definition. Justice Thomas's dissent was joined by Justices Blackmun, Stevens, and Kennedy.

118 Before 1978, the Supreme Court held that the Dictionary Act was permissive. First National Bank v. Missouri, 263 U.S. 640, 657 (1924) (whether singular includes plural); Monroe v. Pape, 365 U.S. 167, 191 (1961) (defining "person"), *overruled by,* Monell v. Dept. of Social Services, 436 U.S. 658 (1978).

Numerous pre-Rowland lower court decisions (dealing with whether singular includes plural and vice-versa) also denied that the Dictionary Act was mandatory. United States v. Iddeen, 854 F.2d 52, 54–55 (5th Cir. 1988); Metallics Recycling Co. v. Commissioner, 732 F.2d 523, 526 (6th Cir. 1984); Delpro Co. v. Brotherhood of Railway Carmen, 676 F.2d 960, 963–64 (3d Cir. 1982); Georgetown Univ. Hospital v. Sullivan, 934 F.2d 1280, 1284 (D.C. Cir. 1991); Toys Manufacturers of America, Inc. v. Consumer Product Safety Comm'n., 630 F.2d 70, 74 (2d Cir. 1980); Franklin Savings Assn. v. Director, 740 F. Supp. 1535, 1543 (D. Kan. 1990); Sampson v. Andrus, 483 F. Supp. 240, 243 (D.S.D. 1980).

119 In 1978 the Court in Monell held that the Dictionary Act was mandatory, but the decision made sense because the word "person," which the Court had to interpret in Monell, appeared in an 1871 statute, passed only a few months after adoption of the Dictionary Act. 436 U.S. 658, 688–89 (1978). Conventional approaches to statutory interpretation consider linguistic usage when a statute is adopted, and the Dictionary Act was strong evidence of 1871 usage.

Law review commentary justifies the result in Monell by the contemporary passage of both the Dictionary Act and the Civil Rights Act of 1871. See Harold Lewis and Theodore Blumoff, "Reshaping Section 1983's Asymmetry," 140 U. Pa. L. Rev. 755, 785 (1992) (within two months); Russell Glazer, "The Sherman Amendment: Congressional Rejection of Communal Liability for Civil Rights Violations," 39 U.C.L.A. L. Rev. 1371, 1407 (1992) (same session).

Justice William Brennan, who authored Monell, also has emphasized the contemporaneous passage of the Dictionary Act and the Civil Rights Act. See Will v. Michigan Dept. of State Police, 491 U.S. 58, 77–78 (1989) (Brennan, J., dissenting) (Dictionary Act adopted two months before Civil Rights Act of 1871). See also Rhode Island Affiliate, ACLU v. Rhode Island Lottery Comm'n., 553 F.Supp. 752, 767 (D.R.I. 1982) (Dictionary Act adopted "months before" para. 1983); Marrapese v. State of Rhode Island, 500 F. Supp. 1207, 1210 (D.R.I. 1980) (noting that the Supreme Court had referred to the Civil Rights Act of 1871 against the backdrop of contemporary legal thought and the recently enacted Dictionary Act). Compare Foster v. Walsh, 864 F.2d 416, 418 (6th Cir. 1988) (relies on 1860s' usage of the term "person" and cites the Dictionary Act for evidence of contemporary usage).

120 506 U.S. at 199–200. The party arguing that "person" did not include an association had relied explicitly on the legislative history of the 1959 act in its argument to the Court. Petitioner's Brief on the Merits, 11–16; Petitioner's Reply Brief on the Merits, 3–6; Petitioner's Supplemental Brief, 1–5. That history showed that the only reason for the 1959 change was to extend the statutory benefit of proceeding in forma pauperis to aliens, not just citizens; there was no intent to include associations. H.R. Rep. No. 650, 86th Cong., 1st Sess. 2 (1959); S. Rep. No. 947, 86th Cong., 1st Sess. 2 (1959). Moreover, three of the four lower court

opinions which had held that an association was *not* a "person" before the Rowland opinion relied on this legislative history. FDM Mfg. Co., Inc. v. Scottsdale Ins. Co., 855 F.2d 213, 214–215 (5th Cir. 1988); Move Organization v. U.S. Dept. of Justice, 555 F.Supp. 684, 692 (E.D. Pa. 1983); Honolulu Lumber Co. v. American Factors, Ltd., 265 F. Supp. 578, 580 (D. Hawaii 1966), affirmed on other grounds, 403 F.2d 49 (9th Cir. 1968).

121 506 U.S. at 199–200.

It is surprising, though textualist in spirit, that the Court relied on a 1942 dictionary for this textual definition of context, even though considerable support for its narrow textual interpretation of the word "context" existed in historical legal materials. See William Blackstone, *Commentaries on the Laws of England,* vol. 1, 59 (list of statutory interpretation criteria includes "the words, the context, the subject matter, the effects and consequence, or the spirit and reason of the law"). Many opinions, both older and more recent, echo Blackstone, referring to context separately from other criteria of statutory meaning. Older opinions refer to "subject-matter or the purposes and objects . . . , [and] the context," Dred Scott v. Sandford, 60 U.S. 393, 615 (1856) (Curtis, J., dissenting). Newer cases include U.S. Dept. of Energy v. Ohio, 503 U.S. 607, 622–23 (1992); Shell Oil Co. v. Iowa Dept. Of Revenue, 488 U.S. 19, 25–26 (1988); King v. St. Vincent's Hosp., 502 U.S. 215, 221–22 (1991); Conroy v. Aniskoff, 507 U.S. 511, 515 (1993). See also J. G. Sutherland, *Statutes and Statutory Construction,* sec. 47.02, vol. 2A, 138 (Norman Singer, 5th ed., 1992); Felix Frankfurther, "Some Reflections on the Reading of Statutes," 47 *Colum. L. Rev.* 527, 538 (1947).

122 506 U.S. at 203–5.

123 506 U.S. at 220 (Thomas, J., dissenting).

124 506 U.S. at 214 (Thomas, J., dissenting).

125 The Court was not completely unaware of these difficulties. It justified its reasoning by noting that, according to the Dictionary Act, "context" need only "indicate," not "require," that the "person" exclude an association. 506 U.S. at 200. In the majority's view, the more relaxed term ("indicates") allows the Court some leeway "in the awkward case where Congress provides no particular definition [in the later statute], but the definition in [the Dictionary Act] seems not to fit." But without a doubt the Court considered much more than textual context to determine what the later law "indicated."

126 See, generally, Julian Eule, "Temporal Limits on the Legislative Mandate: Entrenchment and Retroactivity," 1987 *Am. B. Found. Res. J.* 379.

127 The rivalry between competence and legitimacy as the preferred way of understanding judging extends well beyond the statutory interpretation issues we have addressed. It includes debates over whether judges should defer to legislative history, and whether courts should infer a cause of action from a statute that does not explicitly so provide. Appendices to this chapter discuss the contrast

between competence and legitimacy analysis of these issues: legislative history (appendix A) and inferring a cause of action (appendix B).

128 Lewis Carroll, *Through the Looking Glass*, 79 (Macmillan Co., 1966).

129 Albertson's Inc. v. Commissioner, 42 F.3d 537, 540 (9th Cir. 1994) (on rehearing).

Index of Cases

Index

William Popkin is the Walter W. Foskett Professor of Law at Indiana University. He is the author of *Materials on Legislation: Political Language and the Political Process,* 2d ed. (1997), *Fundamentals of Federal Income Tax Law,* 3d ed. (1998), and *The Deduction for Business Expenses and Losses* (1973).

Library of Congress Cataloging-in-Publication Data
Popkin, William D.
Statutes in court : the history and theory of statutory
interpretation / William D. Popkin.
p.   cm.
Includes index.
ISBN 0-8223-2328-1 (cloth : alk. paper)
1. Law—United States—Interpretation and construction—History.
2. Judicial discretion—United States—History.   3. Law—
Interpretation and construction.   4. Judicial discretion.
I. Title.
KF425.P67   1999
348.73'22—dc21   98-43552 CIP